"There is little doubt in my mind that this meticulous study of the inner life of Toronto's Jarvis Street Baptist Church, one of the most famous Baptist congregations in Canada, is of utterly vital importance in understanding the Canadian version of the Fundamentalist-Modernist controversy during the first three decades of the twentieth century. Dr. Wilson moves beyond the simplistic affirmation that this controversy was only about doctrine. Rather, as he ably shows from his minute study of the archives at Jarvis Street, this controversy also had roots in the larger socio-cultural changes that were transpiring on the Canadian landscape during this era. Highly recommended!"

—Michael A. G. Haykin, professor of church history,
The Southern Baptist Theological Seminary

"In a case-study of the fashionable Jarvis Street Baptist Church, Toronto, Paul Wilson demonstrates that members of its nineteenth-century business elite gradually discarded traditional spiritual priorities. The process culminated when in 1921 the church's minister, the imperious T. T. Shields, divided his church by publicly denouncing the laxity of his own deacons. Socio-cultural change, not just intellectual broadening, was responsible for secularization, a conclusion which undoubtedly applies to many other congregations across the evangelical world."

—David Bebbington, emeritus professor of history, University of Stirling

"This essential book for our times offers a compelling exploration of the complex interplay between faith and finance. Through meticulous research and engaging writing, Paul Wilson skillfully navigates the intricate world of inner-church politics and business, shedding light on the challenges faced by everyday Christians in their relationship with God and material wealth during pivotal moments in Canadian history. Wilson illustrates how Canada's economic growth influenced Christian communities, revealing how their choices shaped broader theological conversations in unexpected ways. With his signature depth of insight and clarity, Wilson invites readers to reflect on these important dynamics."

—James Tyler Robertson, associate professor of Christian history,
Tyndale University

"Using the business class at Jarvis Street Baptist Church as a case study, Paul R. Wilson presents an interesting look into the changes in (and challenges to) Baptist spirituality that occurred in Ontario around the turn of the twentieth century, the effects of which were both significant and long-lasting. This study is meticulously researched and compellingly argued. It is a must-read for those interested in Baptist history in Canada."

—Taylor Murray, instructor of Christian history, Tyndale University

"An exceedingly well-researched volume that sheds new light on the turn of the century changes that occurred in iconic Jarvis Street Baptist Church, Toronto. Paul Wilson argues that key businessmen in the church were influenced by powerful social and religious forces to reimagine Christian piety as well as social standing among the affluent business class in Toronto. Wilson also argues that such a trajectory was a secularizing one that eventually led to conflict with concerned fundamentalists at Jarvis Street."

—Gordon L. Heath, professor of Christian history, McMaster Divinity College

Baptists and Business

Monographs in Baptist History

VOLUME 30

SERIES EDITOR
Michael A. G. Haykin, The Southern Baptist Theological Seminary

EDITORIAL BOARD
Matthew Barrett, Midwestern Baptist Theological Seminary
Peter Beck, Charleston Southern University
Anthony L. Chute, California Baptist University
Jason G. Duesing, Midwestern Baptist Theological Seminary
Nathan A. Finn, North Greenville University
Crawford Gribben, Queen's University, Belfast
Gordon L. Heath, McMaster Divinity College
Barry Howson, Heritage Theological Seminary
Jason K. Lee, Cedarville University
Thomas J. Nettles, The Southern Baptist Theological Seminary, retired
James A. Patterson, Union University
James M. Renihan, Institute of Reformed Baptist Studies
Jeffrey P. Straub, Independent Scholar
Brian R. Talbot, Broughty Ferry Baptist Church, Scotland
Malcolm B. Yarnell III, Southwestern Baptist Theological Seminary

Ours is a day in which not only the gaze of western culture but also increasingly that of Evangelicals is riveted to the present. The past seems to be nowhere in view and hence it is disparagingly dismissed as being of little value for our rapidly changing world. Such historical amnesia is fatal for any culture, but particularly so for Christian communities whose identity is profoundly bound up with their history. The goal of this new series of monographs, Studies in Baptist History, seeks to provide one of these Christian communities, that of evangelical Baptists, with reasons and resources for remembering the past. The editors are deeply convinced that Baptist history contains rich resources of theological reflection, praxis and spirituality that can help Baptists, as well as other Christians, live more Christianly in the present. The monographs in this series will therefore aim at illuminating various aspects of the Baptist tradition and in the process provide Baptists with a usable past.

Baptists and Business

Central Canadian Baptists and the Secularization of the Businessman at Toronto's Jarvis Street Baptist Church, 1848–1921

Paul R. Wilson

Foreword by Taylor Murray

PICKWICK *Publications* · Eugene, Oregon

BAPTISTS AND BUSINESS
Central Canadian Baptists and the Secularization of the Businessman at Toronto's Jarvis Street Baptist Church, 1848–1921

Monographs in Baptist History 30

Copyright © 2025 Paul R. Wilson. All rights reserved. Except for brief quotations in critical publications or reviews, no part of this book may be reproduced in any manner without prior written permission from the publisher. Write: Permissions, Wipf and Stock Publishers, 199 W. 8th Ave., Suite 3, Eugene, OR 97401.

Pickwick Publications
An Imprint of Wipf and Stock Publishers
199 W. 8th Ave., Suite 3
Eugene, OR 97401

www.wipfandstock.com

PAPERBACK ISBN: 978-1-6667-8085-7
HARDCOVER ISBN: 978-1-6667-8086-4
EBOOK ISBN: 978-1-6667-8087-1

Cataloguing-in-Publication data:

Names: Wilson, Paul R., author. | Murray, Taylor, foreword.

Title: Baptists and business : Central Canadian Baptists and the secularization of the businessman at Toronto's Jarvis Street Baptist Church, 1848–1921 / by Paul R. Wilson : foreword by Taylor Murray.

Description: Eugene, OR: Pickwick Publications, 2025 | Series: Monographs in Baptist History 30 | Includes bibliographical references and index.

Identifiers: ISBN 978-1-6667-8085-7 (paperback) | ISBN 978-1-6667-8086-4 (hardcover) | ISBN 978-1-6667-8087-1 (ebook)

Subjects: LCSH: Baptists—Canada—History. | Christians—Canada—History. | Business—Religious aspects—Christianity. | Business people—Canada—History.

Classification: BX6251 W55 2025 (paperback) | BX6251 (ebook)

VERSION NUMBER 05/06/25

This book is lovingly dedicated to my wife and best friend, Yvonne Wilson. Her never-ending patience, unwavering support, and consistent belief in this project made its completion possible.

Contents

Foreword by Taylor Murray | xi
Preface | xiii

INTRODUCTION
Baptists and Business in Central Canada, 1848–1921: History and Historiography | 1

CHAPTER 1
Central Canadian Baptists and the World, 1848–1921 | 21

CHAPTER 2
Business in Theory and Practice: The Central Canadian Baptist View of Business, 1818–1921 | 52

CHAPTER 3
Business in the Church: The Beginning of Secularization, 1848–1880 | 82

CHAPTER 4
Serving God and Mammon: Secularization Through Sociocultural Integration | 121

CHAPTER 5
Maintaining Separation: The Myth and the Reality | 172

CHAPTER 6
Secularization and Schism: The Fight for Control of Jarvis Street | 202

CHAPTER 7
Conclusion | 245

Appendix 1: Selected Sample of Businessmen from Jarvis Street Baptist Church, 1818–1921 | 255

Appendix 2: Examples of Religious and Social Interconnections | 259

Bibliography | 261

Index | 275

Foreword

THE EARLY TWENTIETH-CENTURY SATIRIST Will Rogers once quipped that "a man only learns in two ways: one by reading, and the other by association with smarter people." In my case, Paul is one of those "smarter people" whose association I treasure dearly. With the publication of *Baptists and Business*, I'm pleased that not only do I get to learn by being in close proximity to Paul, but I also get to read his words.

When I was a graduate student, I got to know Paul by reading his work, especially on Baptist fundamentalism in Canada. His tone was sympathetic yet critical, his argumentation was convincing, and his research was both meticulous and comprehensive. Years later, when I actually met Paul in person, I discovered that he was as kind and generous a person as he was a talented historian. Throughout my academic life, he has been a mentor, collaborator, and valued friend.

Paul has always had a keen interest in the history of Baptists in Ontario. In this excellent work, he continues his research in this area by tracing a pivotal period in the denomination's history. He notes that the quest for respectability in Canadian society at the turn of the twentieth century had effectively changed priorities for many wealthy and business-minded Baptists. The spiritual values that had long governed Baptist life in the central region of Canada had been supplemented or even displaced by a new desire for material success.

Enter T. T. Shields, the fundamentalist pastor of Jarvis Street Baptist Church in Toronto. Jarvis Street was, at that point, one of the largest and wealthiest Baptist churches in the country. As would later become routine for Shields, he waged war on the so-called "worldly amusements" that he believed were eroding the spiritual life of his church and the larger Baptist community. The result was a significant congregational schism that saw the departure of many of the church's wealthiest congregants. This event was one of the earliest in Shields's ministry that would later earn him the sobriquet "the Battling Baptist" and, in some notable ways, set the stage for the later denominational schism experienced by the Baptist Convention of Ontario and Quebec in 1927.

The research that forms the basis for this study is of special note. Beginning in the early 1990s, Paul was among the first professional historians to plumb the depths of the rich archives at Jarvis Street, which had been closed to researchers for many years. Utilizing these resources and others, Paul's work is the most detailed exploration of this consequential church schism and the underlying factors to date.

Paul's evaluation and retelling of these events fill an important gap in the scholarly literature. By looking at the changing attitudes toward the material world—a tension "between God and mammon"—within the Baptist community in Ontario, especially as they manifested in this notable Toronto church, he documents an understudied and often overlooked period in the denomination's history, and he does so with an incisive and thoughtful analysis that is also highly readable. With *Baptists and Business*, Paul has made a valuable contribution to the field—one that will, no doubt, find its way into numerous bibliographies to come.

Taylor Murray

Seminary Faculty and Department of Distributed Learning
Tyndale University, Toronto, ON

Preface

THE EMINENT CANADIAN HISTORIAN, the late George Rawlyk, once noted that by the late nineteenth century some Canadian evangelicals, including some Baptists, had adopted "the gospel of narcissistic, therapeutic self-realization underpinning North American consumerism" and become part of "a respectable middle-class movement that explicitly downplayed emotionalism. Cultural and theological accommodation to the exigencies of an expanding and rapidly developing nation soon became the twentieth century norm."[1] This book examines and analyzes a series of sociocultural adjustments and religious accommodations by middle- and upper-middle class businessmen from Toronto's Jarvis Street Baptist Church. The findings here lend support, depth, and color to Rawlyk's assertions.

For over thirty years, I have had the honor and privilege of researching and writing about the Canadian Baptist experience. Many people have supported me in this endeavor. First and foremost, I want to thank Roger Hall, Professor Emeritus at the University of Western Ontario, whose thoughtful insights and wise advice made this book better in every respect. I am also deeply indebted to my colleagues and friends in the Canadian Baptist Historical Society. Taylor Murray wrote the Foreword for this book and generously offered his time and expertise in getting this manuscript ready for publication. Gord Heath provided encouragement and the opportunity to share some of my findings with the CBHS. Doug Adams, whose outstanding PhD dissertation about T. T. Shields followed my work on this project, willingly engaged in an ongoing conversation

---

1. Rawlyk, *Aspects of the Canadian Evangelical Experience*, xvii.

about the history of Jarvis Street and the many joys and challenges associated with researching Baptist history.

This book would never have happened without the support of the deacons at Jarvis Street Baptist Church, who gave me access to the unprocessed church archives and office space for many months. A legion of archivists also offered their time, guidance, and expertise. My sincere thanks to each and every one of these dedicated practitioners.

I am also indebted to Michael A. G. Azad Haykin, who kindly provided me with a pathway to publication. My sincere thanks to the editors at Wipf and Stock for their patience and persistence.

All of these people and many more helped to bring this book to light. My hope is that this work will provide insight into a little-known and seldom-understood aspect of Canadian Baptist history.

Introduction

Baptists and Business in Central Canada, 1848–1921
History and Historiography

Introduction

IN 1916, AT THE start of a war-driven economic upturn, an article in *The Canadian Baptist*, a major denominational organ in the country, asked a series of disturbing questions:

> Can it be truthfully said that religion in its various aspects is keeping pace with the general prosperity? Are there indications that in religious affairs men and women of the churches of various denominations are manifesting growing activity in the practical side of Christianity? Are we satisfied with the results in the sphere of Christian benevolence and missionary endeavour?[1]

For many central Canadian Baptists, the answer to these questions was a resounding "No!" From a variety of sources, laments about the negative effects of a business-dominated culture on Baptist faith and practice were common. In 1921, an editorial in *The Canadian Baptist* expressed the view that material prosperity was at least partly responsible for the decline of religious devotion among second-generation Baptists:

> Then we must remember that many Baptists of the first generation were brought into the church in the days when they were struggling up from poverty. The little church also was composed

---

1. "Prosperity and Religion," *Canadian Baptist* [hereafter *CB*], August 17, 1916.

of those who had little of this world's goods. Sometimes as the years go by our people acquire wealth. It does them no harm. On the contrary it seems to give them enlarged opportunities for usefulness; but we think that we have witnessed instances where their children have felt the evil effects of too much money. It is hard to maintain the simplicity of Christian family life amidst the surroundings, which so generally accompany wealth.[2]

Indeed, nowhere were the effects of increased wealth and worldliness more apparent than within the life of the Baptist businessman.[3] Increasingly, they faced direct and indirect challenges to their faith. The expanding demands of business threatened, in some cases, to displace religious activities altogether. In addition, the growing tendency to measure spirituality by material prosperity altered the place and power of religion in the lives of many Baptist businessmen. Still, many Baptists accepted the rise and dominance of business as a providential consequence of "Canadian Progress."[4] It was disagreement over the degree of acceptance, not acceptance itself, that produced conflict within the Baptist church.

Committed to the Calvinistic principles of industry, integrity, and stewardship, few central Canadian Baptists would countenance the rejection of capitalism. Instead, between 1848 to 1921, they wrestled with questions related to the results of capitalist enterprise. What were the Baptist businessman's stewardship responsibilities? What constituted separation from the world? What was worldliness? And how could Baptist businessmen be in the world but not of it? The search for answers to these questions became a primary concern for central Canadian Baptists.

Baptists in Canada: A Brief Statistical Survey

Census statistics reveal important information about Baptist struggles and successes between 1851 and 1921. The region most shaped by the

---

[2]. "Baptists of the Second Generation," *CB*, June 2, 1921.

[3]. In keeping with the realities that the majority of Baptist business people in this period were male and this study focuses on male subjects, the terms "businessman" and "businessmen" are used throughout this book.

[4]. This quotation is the title given by William Stewart, editor of *The Canadian Baptist* to W. A. Foster's famous address, "Canada First or Our New Nationality." It was published in *CB* on September 28, 1871. For a discussion of the impact of the Foster address, see Berger, *Sense of Power*, 62–63. For an early Baptist view of the rise of business and its consequences see "Mammon," *Toronto Christian Observer* [hereafter *TCO*], April 1851.

Baptist presence in Canada was the Maritimes. In particular, Nova Scotia and New Brunswick remained bastions of Baptist strength throughout this period. Nationally, the number of Baptists peaked in 1871 and 1881 when 6.8 percent of the population claimed Baptist affiliation. By 1921, the percentage had dropped to 4.8 percent. Ontario statistics showed a similar pattern. From 3.4 percent of the province's population in 1842, the number claiming Baptist affiliation jumped to 4.8 percent by 1851 and reached a high of 5.5 percent in 1881. Between 1881 and 1921, Baptist strength stayed near 5 percent, with a slight decline by 1921 to 4.8 percent.

In Toronto, the location of our study, Baptist growth lagged behind both national and provincial levels. In 1861, Baptists accounted for only 2.9 percent of the city's populace. When compared to the provincial figure of 4.4 percent, the numbers in Toronto were thought by some Baptists to be disappointing. In the decade between 1871 and 1881, the situation improved as the Baptists moved from 3.1 to 4.2 percent of Toronto's population. Despite this increase, the number of Baptists in Toronto in 1881 lagged behind the Ontario and Canadian figures, which stood at 5.5 percent and 6.8 percent, respectively. By 1901, Toronto had caught up with the rest of the province. Both claimed 5.3 percent of the population as Baptists. The national level was slightly higher at 5.9 percent. Toronto Baptists made up 5 percent of the city's population in 1921. This percentage slightly exceeded the 4.8 percent recorded for both Ontario and Canada.[5]

The Present Study: Secularization Argument and Microcosmic Approach

This book's argument is straightforward: In the case of a selected sample of twenty-five businessmen from Jarvis Street Baptist Church in the period between 1848 and 1921, business helped to secularize religion. In the predominantly agricultural and rural pre-capitalist society of Upper Canada before 1850, central Canadian Baptists were committed to an otherworldly perspective that made spiritual values their first priority. In the last half of the nineteenth century, industrialization, urbanization, and

---

5. The conclusions reached in this section are based on *Census of Canada* 1851–1921, and the tables found in Grant, *Profusion of Spires*, 224. See also Gauvreau, "Protestantism Transformed," 96; Airhart, "Ordering a New Nation," 102–4.

commercialization put pressure on Baptist businessmen to accommodate materialistic values that suited the new business-dominated culture. Many Baptist businessmen changed their priorities. They put respectability ahead of righteousness and mammon ahead of "the Master."[6]

The evidence presented here suggests that business was a powerful agent of secularization. Simply expressed, business encouraged commitment to a new materialistic social ethic at the expense of an older, more spiritual social ethic. Although Baptist businessmen continued to profess their belief in the doctrines of sanctification, stewardship, and separation, their acceptance of practices traditionally considered "worldly" by their coreligionists, provides evidence for increasing secularization.

The attacks of pastor T. T. Shields on worldliness after the First World War brought the issue of secularization among Jarvis Street's businessmen to the surface. As perhaps Canada's most outspoken and combative fundamentalist, Shields became the secularized businessman's most formidable adversary.[7] The battles between Shields and the church's businessmen revealed the presence of conflicting worldviews that resulted from the dramatic social and cultural changes that had reshaped religious belief and practice over the past three-quarters of a century.

Methodology

This study uses a modified qualitative version of the English parish study approach.[8] The intent is to closely examine changes in the religious beliefs and values of one social group, businessmen, in one particular church, Jarvis Street Baptist Church, Toronto (for a listing of the sample, see Appendix 1). As one of the country's largest and most influential Baptist churches between 1848 and 1921, and with many of its records still extant in raw form and largely unexplored, Jarvis Street Baptist Church is

---

6. This title, of course, refers to Jesus Christ.

7. Research and debate about the fundamentalist views held by T. T. Shields has been extensive. For some of the most important contributions, see Adams, "War of the Worlds"; "Fighting Fire with Fire," 53–106; "Great Contention," 119–56; Wilson, "Torn Asunder," 34–80; Dozois, "Dr. Thomas Todhunter Shields"; Ellis, "Gilboa to Ichabod," 109–26; Russell, "T. T. Shields," 263–80; Tarr, "Another Perspective," 209–24; Parent, "Christology of T. T. Shields."

8. English historians have long appreciated the value of the microcosmic approach in the study of religious history. See, for example, Dickens, *Lollards and Protestants in the Diocese of York*. For examples of Toronto Baptist church histories, most of which are not scholarly, see Goertz, *Century for the City*; Allen and Calder, *Trials and Triumphs*; Tomlinson and Fountain, *From Strength to Strength*.

well suited to the needs of the scholar interested in an original microcosmic study of business and its impact on religion. In addition, the church's relocation in 1875 to what Austin Seton Thompson has called "Toronto's Champs Elysees" made it likely that it would attract sufficient numbers of businessmen for analysis.[9] The choice of subjects began with the consultation of church and city directories, assessment and census rolls, and biographical sources to construct basic social profiles of possible sample members. Out of a list of seventy-five potential candidates, I have selected a sample of twenty-five by using an approach that resembled what sociologists sometimes call "quota sampling."

Candidates had to meet certain criteria. Church membership at any stage of the church's history was the first requirement. The only businessman included who did not meet this condition was clothing manufacturer, John Northway, owner of John Northway and Sons. He never bothered to take out formal membership at Jarvis Street[10] The emphasis in selection was on merchants, manufacturers, and what Michael Bliss has called "money men."[11] This latter category included businessmen who founded or invested heavily in banks, trust companies, stock brokerage firms and insurance companies. Still, a couple of noteworthy professionals that were heavily involved in business ventures and played a key role in the history of Jarvis Street have also been included. Although the primary focus of this study is the period from 1848 to 1921, some distinctive Baptist businessmen from the era when Baptists first came to Toronto have been selected to provide context and continuity.

Frankly, the major criterion for final selection was the availability of source material. Although few business and personal papers are extant for the businessmen examined here, it is possible to piece together their social and cultural views from church minutes, trade journals, Baptist and

9. Thompson, *Jarvis Street*, 132–62.

10. The reasons for Northway's lack of membership at Jarvis Street are somewhat unclear, but his gradual adoption of liberal theology and the social gospel are likely reasons. In 1877, Northway became a member of the Baptist Church in Tillsonburg, Ontario. By 1920, he attended Jarvis Street on Sunday mornings and the churches of other denominations on Sunday evenings. Northway's commitment to Baptist causes, especially higher education, and his self-identification as a Baptist never wavered. For these reasons, he has been exempted from the membership criterion and included in this study. For evidence that supports these views and a fuller understanding of Northway's changing religious views, see his Diaries in Northway Company Ltd. Fonds, Trent University Archives, Peterborough, Ontario, Boxes 1–3, 9. See also Wilson, *John Northway*, 47, 191–92, 199–206.

11. Bliss, *Northern Enterprise*, 255–82.

other religious periodicals, newspapers, government documents, and the records of business and charitable organizations. Whenever possible, Jarvis Street's businessmen have been allowed to speak for themselves.

Before addressing historiographical issues, a number of terms and concepts require definition and discussion. Drawing on the work of Bryan Wilson, Owen Chadwick, Jeffery Cox, and David Marshall, secularization refers here to a negative process through which religious beliefs, values, and practices are modified or removed so that they lose "social significance" and, consequently, their influence on an individual, group or institution.[12] Near the end of the study, I have also used the term secularism to indicate the growth of indifference and hostility to orthodox Baptist beliefs, values, and practices.[13]

The emphasis of the present study is on the increasing distance between Baptist theory and practice in the lives of Jarvis Street's businessmen. In contrast to David Marshall, who focuses on the role of intellectual change in the secularization process, this study argues that in the case of Jarvis Street, the evidence for secularization lay primarily in the reshaping or rejection of Baptist practice by the church's business element. An important underlying assumption is that without practice, beliefs and values become meaningless. Thus, while giving intellectual assent to doctrine is important, the ultimate test of a doctrine's significance resides in the actions of the professing believer.

The concept of sociocultural integration is defined as any move towards social and cultural conformity and away from religious distinctiveness or separation.[14] It refers specifically to the ways in which Jarvis Street's businessmen adjusted or eliminated countercultural facets of their religion to fit better within the mainstream of Canadian culture. This concept is also used to indicate the accommodation or acceptance

---

12. Wilson, *Religion in Secular Society*, xiv. The most complete discussion of secularization from an intellectual standpoint by a Canadian historian is found in Marshall, *Secularizing the Faith*, 15–24. See also Chadwick, *Secularization of the European Mind*, 14–18; Cox, *English Churches*, 10–16. For a more recent contribution to the ongoing conversation and debate about secularization from an American perspective and its impact on New York Baptists, see Johnson, *Power of Mammon*, xvii–xxi, 33–53, 136–45.

13. For further explanation of the differences between secularization and secularism, see Quebedeaux, *Worldly Evangelicals*, 19.

14. Sociologists often use the terms "social integration" and "cultural integration" to refer to functions of the socialization process by which members of a society come to share common values, beliefs, norms, and law. For convenience, these terms have been synthesized. For definitions and usage, see Teevan and Hewitt, *Basic Sociology*, 32–33, 54, 359. See also Clark, *Developing Canadian Community*, 115–82.

of beliefs and values that made Jarvis Street's businessmen like those around them.

Respectability is also an important concept. The term is used here to represent the desire for social status based on character, wealth, and position. For Jarvis Street's businessmen, the achievement of respectability often involved the abandonment of Baptist values like simplicity and moderation and the accommodation of the materialistic and hedonistic values, such as display and excess, associated with a new social ethic.[15]

While the first chapter deals with the important Baptist doctrine of separation in greater detail, here it is sufficient to note that for Baptists, separation meant the maintenance of moral purity and religious demarcation. John Webster Grant has claimed that "by 1867 church and world [in Ontario] were virtually identical in composition, and traditional means of discipline became increasingly difficult to enforce."[16] Ironically, this apparent fusion of sacred and secular worlds served to promote the doctrine of "entire separation" in Baptist circles.[17] Even as discipline relaxed, many Baptists continued to assume the presence of secular carnal forces that encouraged moral or ethical laxity, cultural conformity, and spiritual compromise. Separation included religious belief and practice within both the church and everyday life. Its intent was to produce spirituality through the preservation of individual moral purity and the Baptist identity.

The remainder of this introduction focuses on previous historical interpretations of the business religion relationship in Canada.

---

15. This definition of respectability has benefitted from Thompson, *Rise of Respectable Society*; Walvin, *Victorian Values*; Prentice, *School Promoters*, 66–87. For specific signs of respectability among Toronto's elite, see Careless, *Toronto to 1918*, 124, 128, 161–72.

16. Grant, *Profusion of Spires*, 167–68.

17. The historical development of this doctrine is complex. The doctrine of separation was based on certain New Testament passages (2 Cor 6:14–16; Rom 16:17–18; 1 Tim 6:3–5) that emphasized the believer's separation from impurity. In the fundamentalist-modernist controversies in both the United States and Canada (1910–1927), the issue of separation from doctrinal apostasy and moral laxity came to the fore. For a discussion of how fundamentalists applied separation to American culture, see Marsden, *Fundamentalism and American Culture*, 32, 36, 38–39, 124–31; *Understanding Fundamentalism and Evangelicalism*, 34, 68, 71, 73, 100, 106, 110, 184. For a brief examination of this doctrine in the Canadian Baptist context, see Wilson, "Central Canadian Baptists," 62–66. For a contemporary Canadian Baptist perspective, see "Separation from the World," *CB*, January 26, 1882. For a fundamentalist view of amusements see the famous sermon by Shields, "Christian Attitude Toward Amusements," as reprinted in Tarr, *Shields of Canada*, 208–18.

Following this discussion, chapters 1, 2, and the first section of chapter 3 examine the central Canadian Baptist worldview. Specifically, chapter 1 presents the Baptist position on problem of "the world"; chapter 2 discusses the Baptist view of business; and chapter 3 marks the transition point from the provision of contextual information to a microcosmic focus. After a brief discussion of church division, discipline, and disputes, this book provides a short history of Jarvis Street and the impact of business on the church. While the contextual background on central Canadian Baptists is lengthy, it is essential for understanding the changes that business brought to the religion of Jarvis Street's businessmen. Chapter 4 explores their attempt to combine service to God and "mammon." Chapter 5 examines the abandonment of separation by Jarvis Street's businessmen. Finally, chapter 6 shows how the fundamentalist cultural perspective held by T. T. Shields and his supporters, and the more liberal-modernist approaches to the culture taken by Jarvis Street's business element, resulted in congregational schism.

The Business-Religion Relationship in Canadian Historiography

Despite numerous studies that have significantly enhanced our understanding of Canadian religion and business in the nineteenth and early twentieth centuries, the nature of their relationship remains largely unexplored. Currently, religious historians like David Marshall, Phyllis Airhart, and Michael Gauvreau have been responsible for not only revising the interpretations put forward in liberal-nationalist and denominational histories of the past, but also stimulating interest in unexplored aspects of our religious history. Without exception, their work has enhanced our understanding and appreciation of religion as a powerful component in the Canadian experience. Similarly, business historians such as Michael Bliss and Douglas McCalla have undertaken both specific and general studies that have provided a general outline of economic policy, trends, and developments. Their studies of individual entrepreneurs, companies and financial institutions have given us an understanding of how business operated at the entrepreneurial and corporate levels.[18] These efforts have provided a solid basis for further analysis of important social and economic relationships.

18. See, for example, Bliss, *Canadian Millionaire*; *Northern Enterprise*; McCalla, *Upper Canadian Trade*.

Until recently, Canadian historians focused primarily on the connection between Protestantism and capitalism. Most, like D. C. Masters in his Toronto history of 1947 and Arthur Lower in *Colony to Nation* in 1946, assumed but did not prove that the Weber-Tawney model[19] supplied the answer to the riddle of the interaction between religion and economics in the Canadian context. In particular, Lower's portrayal of a "dynamic Calvinist-commercial with its devotion to acquisition and its haunting fear of animal 'robustness'" and Masters's claim that "there is a close connection between the Protestant ideals of individualism, energy and plain living and the process of capitalist accumulation" have remained staples in Canadian historical writing.[20] Sociologist John Porter, in *The Vertical Mosaic*, also sustained the Weberian argument concerning the connection between the worldly asceticism of Calvinism and Protestant acceptance of capitalism.[21] Curiously, any further in-depth study of the exchange between capitalism and Calvinism in the Canadian context has not been offered. Despite considerable testing of the Weber-Tawney thesis in other contexts, including Gordon Marshall's study of the relationship between Calvinism and capitalism among Scottish Presbyterians and Simon Schama's examination of seventeenth-century Dutch culture, Canadian historians have been content to leave the theory largely intact and untested at home.[22]

This study provides some insight on the impact of capitalism on the Calvinism of Jarvis Street's businessmen. At certain points throughout this study, evidence is presented that supports the contention that Calvinism continued to shape the Baptist view of business even though capitalism eventually modified its message and principles. In the experience of Jarvis Street's businessmen, there is evidence of an exchange in which Calvinism rationalized capitalism while capitalism redefined Calvinism.[23]

---

19. For the model in its original forms, see Weber, *Protestant Ethic*; Tawney, *Religion and the Rise of Capitalism*. For a somewhat dated summary of the ongoing debate over the Weber thesis, see Green, *Protestantism, Capitalism, and Social Science*.

20. Lower, *Colony to Nation*, 69–71; Masters, *Rise of Toronto*, 30–31.

21. Porter, *Vertical Mosaic*, 98–100, 287–90.

22. Marshall finds that Weber is "vindicated" in the Scottish Presbyterian experience. See Marshall, *Presbyteries and Profits*, 222–61. In contrast, Schama identifies weaknesses in Weber's thesis. See Schama, *Embarrassment of Riches*, 322–23, 335.

23. I have benefitted from Gary Scott Smith's analysis of the secularization of American Calvinism. See Smith, *Seeds of Secularization*.

To date, there have been only a few studies that confront the business-religion relationship in its Canadian Baptist context in any way. In his 1974 groundbreaking examination of social and religious factors in the fundamentalist-modernist schisms among Baptists in North America, in the period from 1895 to 1934, Canadian Baptist historian Walter Ellis argued that "stable, middle and upper class churchmen" were "moving away from church as the central reference point and were intent upon giving expression to a cosmopolitan pattern in keeping with their affluence and professional status."[24] In a subsequent article entitled, "Gilboa to Ichabod," Ellis noted the use of "Bay Street language" in the dedication sermon preached by Reverend J. L. Burrows, DD,[25] in the new Jarvis Street Baptist Church.[26] In his study of how social and religious factors contributed to the creation of schisms, Ellis implicated the business-religion relationship as a causal factor when he suggested that wealth, worldliness, and a growing social heterogeneity played a key role in the departure of the bulk of the business element from Jarvis Street Baptist Church in 1921.[27] His work underscores the need for a study that examines more explicitly the business-religion relationship in the Baptist context.

In an examination of Maritime Baptists, George Rawlyk has argued that "in the twentieth century much of what would be preached by the new prophets of evangelical consumerism and greed, would, in fact, be the antithesis of nineteenth century evangelicalism."[28] His argument, while stimulating, raises a number of critical questions. How did such a transformation happen? What forces prompted evangelicals to replace spiritual with material values? And specifically, what role did business play in this cultural transformation? The current revival of interest in the study of Canadian religion has only marginally improved our knowledge of the business-religion relationship among Baptists. While the work of George Rawlyk and Walter Ellis has drawn our attention to the rise of a materialistic social ethic and culture, the impact of these developments on evangelical religion in Canada has yet to be sufficiently explored.

---

24. Ellis, "Social and Religious Factors," 175–76.

25. Although "Reverend" is an adjective, not a title, and—to be technically correct—should be preceded by "the," many Baptists used the title form. I have adopted this usage throughout this study.

26. Ellis, "Gilboa to Ichabod," 109.

27. Ellis, "Gilboa to Ichabod," 122–23.

28. Rawlyk, *Champions of the Truth*, 37.

Beginning with Alan Wilson's *John Northway*, business historians began to acknowledge the important interplay between religion and business in the lives of most businessmen. While Wilson focused primarily on Northway's business life, he set out, in a cursory fashion, some of the tense exchanges between religion and business experienced by one Toronto Baptist businessman.[29]

In his 1972 University of Toronto PhD thesis, entitled, "A Living Profit: Studies in the Social History of Canadian Business, 1883–1911," and his subsequent book of the same title, Michael Bliss defined what has since become entrenched stereotypes of the business-religion relationship. Essentially, Bliss argued that religion had, at best, a minimal effect on a businessman's attitudes or business practices. What mattered most to the businessman was not adherence to his religious values but business success.[30] Even though this attitude had certainly become common by the 1880s and religious values were clearly eroding, Bliss fails to explain why businessmen had come to adopt this perspective. In his later biography of Joseph Flavelle, Bliss finds that religion played a key role in providing the ethical foundation for Flavelle's business endeavors.[31] As a business historian, Bliss may be forgiven for not examining religion's impact on business more thoroughly. His work underscores the need for historians to examine how the influence of religion on business practice declined between 1848 and 1921.

In a discussion about the wide-ranging effects of the social gospel on Canadian Protestants, and in particular Methodists, Richard Allen has suggested that this movement produced a "new businessman" who "appropriated the social service credo and gave expression to it" in his own "particular ways."[32] Although the present work only begins this conversation, this intriguing suggestion merits testing in the Baptist context. Allen admits that "the struggle was difficult" for Baptists who attempted to keep the social gospel alive in their churches.[33] How, then, did Baptist businessmen respond to the new gospel?

In what is perhaps the most complete attempt to examine the business-religion relationship, Allen Robertson, in his study entitled, "John Wesley's Nova Scotia Businessmen: Halifax Methodist Merchants,

29. Wilson, *John Northway*, 193–206.
30. Bliss, *Living Profit*, 10.
31. Bliss, *Canadian Millionaire*, 9–13, 119, 170–71, 504–6.
32. Allen, *Social Passion*, 146.
33. Allen, *Social Passion*, 15.

1815–1855," has shown how one group of evangelical businessmen reconciled their pursuit of capitalism with their religious values. Robertson has concluded that Halifax Methodist merchants struck a "balance" between "faith and secularism" that "permitted" them to "help mould the province's governmental and economic life in a vital, dynamic manner."[34] Robertson's study makes an important contribution to our understanding of the business-religion relationship. His analysis provides a useful backdrop for this microcosmic study of another group of businessmen with strong religious ties. The question of whether Jarvis Street's businessmen adopted a social accommodation strategy similar to that used by Halifax Methodist merchants is addressed in chapters four and five.

Only a few studies, then, have explored the ongoing exchange between religion and business in Canada from 1848 to 1921. The effects of the business-religion relationship generally remain an enigma in Canadian historiography.[35] This study seeks to help bridge the gap by examining the struggle of one group of Toronto Baptist businessmen to come to terms with a business-religion relationship that remained complex and dynamic.

Materialism, Consumer Culture, and Secularization in Canadian Historiography

Another avenue that Canadian historians have pursued is the relationship between Protestantism and emerging materialistic culture. Historians have used a variety of concepts, theories, and approaches in an attempt to explain the connections between the two and changes in individual and group behavior in both the religious and business contexts.

Thorstein Veblen's much debated and enduring thesis of 1899 concerning "conspicuous consumption," as practiced by what he calls the "leisure class," provides a stimulating starting point for discussion. For Veblen, reputability, comfort, waste, high-bred manners, the ability to consume "the right kind of goods" freely, and "in a seemly manner,"

---

34. See the Preface in Robertson, *John Wesley's Nova Scotia Businessmen*, xi. One should also read the Afterword, 169–73.

35. One should note that to various degrees, explorations of the business-religion relationship and the challenge of serving God or mammon, for Baptists and other Christians, have received attention from historians in other contexts. For Britain, see, e.g., Jeremy, *Capitalists and Christians*, 353–93. For the United States, see, e.g., Long, "Turning . . . Piety into Hard Cash," 236–61.

are the marks of "conspicuous consumption" necessary for one to claim membership in the leisure class.[36] While one may question certain assumptions underlying Veblen's thesis, his premise that an industrialized society elevates the value of leisure and consumption to new heights and increases class exclusiveness deserves to be taken seriously.

In his analysis of American culture, T. J. Jackson-Lears has argued that the rise of a "consumer culture" in the United States, between 1880 and 1930, "required more than a national apparatus of marketing and distribution; it also needed a favourable moral climate."[37] For Lears, "the crucial moral change" delivered in part by a transformation of religious values "was the beginning of a Protestant ethos of salvation through self-denial toward a therapeutic ethos stressing self-realization in this world."[38] Similarly, Rosalind Williams, in her study of mass consumption in late nineteenth century France, found that "the commercial revolution brought both the opportunity and need to reassess values."[39] The role of religion and business in the reassessment process does not, however, receive its due in Williams's analysis.

The burgeoning literature on the development and advancement of consumer culture in Canada provides some useful context for this study. Bettina Liverant's study of the emergence of consumer consciousness in English Canada, for example, "looks at some of the processes through which it [Canadian consumer society] was built up and diffused."[40] Employing an intellectual historical methodology to examine the development and diffusion of a key sociocultural and socioeconomic reality, Liverant argues that in English Canada "the rise of consumer society was not simply the result of economic changes in productivity and affluence; it involved and required changes in ways people think."[41] Furthermore, "there was no single factor or turning point in the mergence of consumer society" but "gradual changes in people's awareness of themselves and others as consumers."[42] Liverant acknowledges and partially examines religion as both a mitigating and contributing factor. Religious "social conservatives," she argues, resisted consumerism while

36. Veblen, *Theory of the Leisure Class*, 75. For the entire argument, see 68–101.
37. Jackson-Lears, "From Salvation to Self-Realization," 4.
38. Jackson-Lears, "From Salvation to Self-Realization," 4.
39. Williams, *Dream Worlds*, 4.
40. Liverant, *Buying Happiness*, 7.
41. Liverant, *Buying Happiness*, 3.
42. Liverant, *Buying Happiness*, 7.

religious "progressives" who embraced the "social gospel" saw increasing affluence and access to consumer goods as offering the "possibility" to achieve greater socioeconomic equality.[43]

Narrowing the focus to a Toronto-based case study, Joy Santink's analysis of Methodist Timothy Eaton's department store enhances one's understanding of how the new consumer culture began, grew, and functioned within particular segments of Canadian society[44] Santink also briefly examines the effects of Eaton's Methodist upbringing and faith on his approach to business matters. Particularly noteworthy were Eaton's belief that "God helps those who help themselves" and that his faith "would comfortably allow for the integration of the spiritual and the temporal sides of life."[45] He also held to the conviction that "hard times brought men nearer to God."[46] Other scholars, such as David Monod and Donica Belisle, have also chronicled and analyzed the emergence of consumerism and its impact on the Canadian economy and culture.[47] The work of these scholars has deepened our understanding of this complex sociocultural change.

This book argues that the presence of such a culture in Canada, for at least the period from 1890 to 1921, acted as a powerful force in the redefinition of Baptist beliefs and values. Chapter 4 examines the practice and promotion of consumerism by Jarvis Street's businessmen and provides an assessment of how their religion changed as a result.

In what is undoubtedly an extensive analysis of materialism and its impact on nineteenth century Protestantism in Ontario, William Westfall has concluded that despite religion's efforts "to temper the worst excesses of a capitalist political economy," it failed to slow the engine of "self-interest and greed" that "continued to propel the world along the tracts of capitalistic development."[48] Westfall chronicles a process. First, debate shifted from "what type of Christian one should be" to how much materialism was acceptable.[49] "Secularism," argues Westfall, "became the common and

---

43. For Liverant's examination of these two groups, see *Buying Happiness*, 17–30.
44. For Santink's discussion of changes in shops and shopping, see Santink, *Timothy Eaton*, 39–57.
45. Santink, *Timothy Eaton*, 24.
46. Santink, *Timothy Eaton*, 88–89.
47. See, for example, Monod, *Store Wars*; Belisle, *Purchasing Power*.
48. Westfall, *Two Worlds*, 207.
49. Westfall, *Two Worlds*, 80.

omnipresent enemy."⁵⁰ Next, religion, particularly in its ordered form, sought "to forge a powerful religious world that could counterbalance the growing materialism of the Victorian age."⁵¹ Accommodation was reached through the notion of "progress" which integrated elements of the secular and materialistic with those of the sacred and spiritual.⁵² Finally, Westfall maintains that by the late nineteenth century, the failure of religion to control materialism had become evident.⁵³ While Westfall is to be commended for providing us with a general understanding of how materialism eroded religious authority, studies that examine the effects of materialism on specific denominations, local congregations, and individuals are needed to evaluate and complete the picture.

One religious group that has been particularly studied for its response to materialistic pressures is the Methodists. Neil Semple has noted that Methodists actively refashioned their faith to accommodate the demands of a new material culture. Indeed, he argues that for Ontario Methodists in the late nineteenth century, "material advance was a sure harbinger of social and moral progress."⁵⁴ Like Westfall, Semple sees religion and materialism as allies in the late nineteenth century. Where they disagree is on the question of whether this alliance should be viewed negatively or positively. In contrast to Westfall, Semple clearly sees materialism welcomed by Methodists in the 1870s and 1880s.

Another insightful analysis of Methodist thought concerning materialism is Marguerite Van Die's study of Nathanael Burwash. Van Die confronts the tensions between religion and materialism directly. Her analysis of the role that "the increased affluence of the laity" played in the reshaping of Burwash's Methodism is particularly instructive.⁵⁵ Her claim that Burwash moved from criticism to acceptance of "the businessman's ethic" reinforces Semple's earlier conclusions.⁵⁶ Her focus on one individual's struggle illustrates the need for scholars to become more focused in their examination of the important exchanges between evangelicalism and capitalism.

50. Westfall, *Two Worlds*, 80.
51. Westfall, *Two Worlds*, 125.
52. Westfall discusses the idea of progress in both its moral and material sense. See Westfall, *Two Worlds*, 163–65.
53. Westfall, *Two Worlds*, 205–08.
54. Semple, "Impact of Urbanization," 328.
55. Van Die, *Evangelical Mind*, 12.
56. Van Die, *Evangelical Mind*, 68–78.

Certainly, the concept of secularization is not new, nor is the claim that commercial and industrial expansion took their toll on religion a novel claim. In 1992, David Marshall provided an extensive review of the historical literature on secularization.[57] Similarly, in 2006, Michael Gauvreau and Ollivier Herbert offered an extensive review and critique of secularization theory and scholarship in both the British and Canadian contexts.[58] Attention and debate about secularization within Canadian historical circles has lessened since then. Therefore, this introduction includes only an abbreviated examination of the most significant and relevant past Canadian studies.

In his *Church and Sect in Canada*, S. D. Clark maintained that material improvements "led to a deterioration among the population generally of evangelical religious values and to a strengthening of worldly attitudes and outlook."[59] "Secularism," Clark asserted, "constituted a direct threat to the position of the more evangelical churches in the community."[60] While questioning Clark's church-sect typology, succeeding historians have agreed that capitalism challenged evangelicalism even if they are divided on the question of whether the evangelical response and its subsequent results had a negative or positive impact on faith and practice.

Canadian intellectual historians following Clark have been engaged in a lively debate over how Canadian religious history should be interpreted. Some historians, like Richard Allen, Marguerite Van Die, Phyllis Airhart, and Michael Gauvreau, have suggested that evangelicals responded positively to the immense social and cultural changes that confronted them in the late nineteenth and twentieth centuries. Others, most notably Ramsay Cook, William Westfall, and David Marshall, have argued that despite their efforts to thwart the forces of change, evangelicals were the victims of a secularization process that eroded their values and beliefs. What follows is a brief analysis of the most recent contributions to this debate.

David Marshall, a proponent of the secularization thesis, has argued that previous liberal-nationalist interpretations of Canadian religious history failed to account for a decline in religious belief and certainty. Using positivist assumptions, Marshall contends that profound intellectual, social and cultural changes after 1850 produced a "crisis of belief"

---

57. For Marshall's review, see *Secularizing the Faith*, 3–24.
58. Gauvreau and Hubert, "Beyond Church History," 3–45.
59. Clark, *Church and Sect in Canada*, 339.
60. Clark, *Church and Sect in Canada*, 339.

for Canadian evangelicals.[61] While Marshall's evidence points to growing intellectual disillusionment and doubt among the clergy, he fails to go beyond the speculative identification of cultural and social factors that secularized Protestant religion generally. Marshall's examination of the secularization process is confined almost exclusively to the intellectual sphere. This narrow approach leaves many important aspects of secularization unexplored. In particular, the lay response to secularization within the Canadian sociocultural context should be examined to see if Marshall's thesis is credible. Otherwise, secularization will remain a remote concept that may or may not help explain the social and cultural experience of Canadian protestants after 1850.

In direct response to Marshall, Michael Gauvreau has argued that Canadian evangelicals actively resisted the onslaught of Darwinian theory and liberalism through a refashioning of their theology "that permitted a constructive dialogue with certain modern thought."[62] For Gauvreau, the evangelical solution, expressed through a new "historical theology," provided the bridge between religion and science.[63] Instead of viewing higher criticism and science as a threat, Gauvreau maintains that Canadian evangelicals responded positively to the challenges set before them by co-opting their opponents' methodology and refashioning their message to meet new cultural realities.

Again, while Gauvreau's interpretation provides an intellectual alternative to the secularization thesis, it fails to explain why Canadian evangelicalism declined within the culture generally. Gauvreau almost entirely ignores the impact of social and cultural change on religious conviction and practice. He wrongly assumes that a complete understanding of the shifting place of religion within Canadian society is possible by focusing exclusively on evangelical intellectuals and their ideas.

It is the contention here that both Marshall and Gauvreau are erroneous in assuming that the explanation for the profound religious changes that occurred in the Canadian context after 1850 abides solely within the purview of pulpit and lectern. While it cannot be denied that the clergy and intellectuals often took the lead in proposing new ideas and adopting new courses of social behavior, the true test of acceptance is found in the actions and attitudes of the laity. It is time to move to the pews

---

61. Marshall, *Secularizing the Faith*, 3–24.
62. Gauvreau, *Evangelical Century*, 6.
63. Gauvreau, *Evangelical Century*, 137–43.

and examine the intellectual and practical responses of the laity to the religious challenges they faced. While the untrained Baptist businessman might lack the knowledge to employ the sophisticated techniques used by theologians to arrive at a hermeneutical system, the Baptist emphasis on individual accountability ultimately held the layperson responsible for their understanding, acceptance, and application of truth. Canadian intellectual historians, like Marshall and Gauvreau, have often overlooked or trivialized attempts by the laity to wrestle with their faith.

This study argues that because the laity daily faced the responsibility of translating religious theory into practice, their thoughts and actions merit more consideration. For the Baptist businessman, faith was tested by the demands and decisions made behind the shop counter, on the floor of the stock exchange, or in his factory. In their personal lives, the pressures associated with prosperity and power increasingly put their beliefs to the test. In the final analysis, the practical choices and actions taken in these areas indicated both the nature and impetus of their faith. If and when Baptist doctrine and/or practice became secondary or irrelevant, the Baptist businessman's religion was secularized.

Other historians have also questioned the utility of the secularization thesis. Phyllis Airhart, in *Serving the Present Age*, has suggested that what has been interpreted as secularization in the early twentieth century might better be described by American religious historian Martin Marty's notion of "a migration of religiosity away from organized institutions to individuals themselves."[64] This novel but vague idea misconstrues secularization as a process limited to the institutional sphere. In fact, secularization also affected individual religious experience profoundly.

Attempts to locate and characterize the Protestant response to the new urban-industrial world have produced similar disagreements among scholars. Richard Allen, in *The Social Passion*, maintained that the social gospel was a positive and largely successful response to the external attacks of secular society. To Allen, religion achieved both renewal and relevance in the modern world through its discovery of a social conscience. In essence, Allen denies that Protestantism succumbed to secularization; indeed, it was revitalized.[65]

In contrast to Allen, Ramsay Cook, in *The Regenerators*, found that an eclectic group of liberal Protestant Victorian reformers unwittingly

---

64. Airhart, *Serving the Present Age*, 125, 187n12.
65. This argument is advanced in the conclusion of Allen, *Social Passion*, 352–56.

promoted secularization by their attempts "to salvage Christianity by transforming it into an essentially social religion."[66] Cook sees secularization as an internal and external process that gradually rendered religion irrelevant. John Webster Grant has argued that while religion's credibility clearly suffered from the effects of urban-industrial development, secularization also operated as an outside force in its reshaping.[67] In an analysis that includes "the central Canadian Baptist commercial elite," George Rawlyk counters that "internal decay" brought about by "American consumerism" produced a "far greater negative impact on the nineteenth century evangelical consensus than did the various manifestations of the so-called modern scholarship."[68] What emerges from these arguments is the need for a new synthesis that recognizes the importance of both external intellectual and internal sociocultural challenges in the secularization process.

This study proposes that internal decay and external attacks combined to secularize religion. Materialism, consumerism and worldliness grew along with the intellectual uncertainty and profound socioeconomic changes that confronted Canadian Protestants between 1848 and 1921. However, the evidence presented in this study supports Rawlyk's assertion that the effects of sociocultural change on religion were far more devastating than any intellectual challenge.

Unfortunately, as Rawlyk has observed, scholars interested in the relationship between Christianity and culture have been reluctant "to explore the often-fascinating connection between evangelical religion and evolving Canadian society."[69] It is understandable that historians have been hesitant; the task of analyzing such a relationship is both arduous and risky. To date, Canadian historians have provided us with a general outline but few specifics concerning the effects of material development on religion. This study seeks to increase our knowledge of the business-religion relationship and our understanding of how it functioned within the larger social context. Through its modified parish study approach, this analysis tests assumptions concerning the relationship between the rise of a business-dominated culture and religious decline.

Specifically, this book argues that between 1848 and 1921, business challenged and ultimately secularized the faith and practice of Jarvis

66. Cook, *Regenerators*, 4.
67. Grant, *Profusion of Spires*, 135, 196–97, 225–26, 229.
68. Rawlyk, "A. L. McCrimmon," 36.
69. Rawlyk, *Ravished by the Spirit*, 110.

Street's businessmen. In the often intense conflicts between material and spiritual values, materialism, and consumerism emerged triumphant. This victory, though never total, represented a powerful convergence of internal and external forces that combined to erode religious authority. Thus, while Jarvis Street's businessmen continued to participate in religious activities, both their religious attitudes, actions, and commitment showed definite signs of decline. Material prosperity and business success made an indisputable, if often subtle, contribution to religion's demise. Increasingly persuaded that mammon must become master, Jarvis Street's businessmen slowly modified their religion to suit the demands of a new materialistic social ethic and a business-dominated culture.

Chapter 1

Central Canadian Baptists and the World, 1848–1921

THE RELATIONSHIP BETWEEN DEVOUT Christians and the secular world has always been problematic. From its inception, Christianity required believers to live paradoxically: They were to be in the world but not of it.[1] Where should the line between worldliness and otherworldliness be drawn? Within the various streams of Protestantism, the search for an answer to this question resulted in a variety of lifestyles. Some Christians chose sociocultural isolation, others integration. In many ways, the Canadian Baptist experience represents another important—but to date largely unexplored—response to worldliness.

What Central Canadian Baptists Believed: A Brief Summary

Before any meaningful discussion of the central Canadian Baptist world view is possible a basic understanding of their doctrine, as proclaimed in the nineteenth and early twentieth centuries, is necessary. At the core of the central Canadian Baptist faith[2] lay six distinctive doctrinal

---

1. This well-known phrasing comes from John 17:14.
2. This is a convenient term to describe a doctrinal consensus amongst Regular Baptist churches in Central Canada.

beliefs. First, central Canadian Baptists believed in a regenerate church membership. In a paper read before the Ministerial Institute in 1880, Daniel A. McGregor, who became Principal of Toronto Baptist College in 1889, succinctly expressed the central Canadian Baptist position: "A Regular Baptist Church is a society of converted persons. Regeneration is not only a doctrinal belief, but an indispensable qualification for church fellowship."[3] McGregor defined regeneration as "personal salvation through faith in the Son of God" and "a personal quickening from a state of spiritual death to life in Christ."[4] He flatly rejected the Roman Catholic, Anglican, and Quaker notions of birthright membership: "A Regular Baptist Church is not composed of parents and their children, but of believers, and believers only. Christian parentage gives no title to and no fitness for its fellowship."[5]

In addition to their belief in personal regeneration as a prerequisite for church membership, central Canadian Baptists believed that the Bible was the supreme authority in all matters of faith and practice. For example, the *Declaration of Faith for the First Baptist Church, Brantford*, stated,

> We believe that the Holy Bible was written by men divinely inspired, and is a perfect treasure of heavenly instruction; that it has God for its author, salvation for its end, and truth without mixture for its matter; that it reveals the principles by which God will judge us; and therefore is, and shall remain till the end of the world, the true centre of Christian union, and the supreme standard by which all human conduct, creeds and opinions should be tried.[6]

A similar declaration was contained in the doctrinal statements of other central Canadian Baptist churches.[7]

Third, central Canadian Baptists believed in what Jarold Zeman has called the "absolute competence of the individual before God."[8] As E. W.

---

3. The paper, entitled "What Constitutes a Regular Baptist Church?," is in *Memoir of Daniel Arthur McGregor*. For this specific reference, see 153.

4. "What Constitutes a Regular Baptist Church?," 153–54.

5. "What Constitutes a Regular Baptist Church?," 153.

6. Shenston, *Jubilee Review of the First Baptist Church*, iv.

7. See, for example, "Articles of Faith" art. 1 (MS) in *Bond Street Baptist Church Minute Book, 1845–1855*, Jarvis Street Baptist Church Archives [hereafter cited as JSBCA]; *Declaration of Faith, Covenant and Rules of Order*, 3.

8. Zeman, "Changing Baptist Identity," 10.

Dadson, best known for his editorship of *The Canadian Baptist* during its transition to a privately run business venture in the early 1880s, noted, "Religion is an entirely personal matter; its obligations are to be voluntarily assumed; and nobody except the individual concerned has any right to accept, reject, or otherwise decide in regard to its ordinances."[9] Underlying Dadson's statement was a belief in the priesthood of all believers, the liberty of each person's conscience, and a rejection of hierarchical church authority and prescribed credal tests. In addition, Dadson pointed to the reality that membership in a Baptist church was voluntary. No one became a member by birth. Membership had to be requested, and was granted on profession of faith and after believers' baptism by immersion. Moreover, support for Baptists causes was entirely dependent on the voluntary financial goodwill of the membership.

Furthermore, central Canadian Baptists believed in the separation of church and state. In response to Bishop John Strachan's 1825 characterization of Baptists as "dissenters" who formed one of the "inferior sects" and occupied one of the "extravagant and dangerous" religious "extremes" in the Upper Province and his constant calls for church establishment, Baptists used the press and petitions vigorously to defend their anti-establishment position.[10] Articles that appeared in the *Montreal Register*, an important Baptist paper in the 1840s, condemned Strachan's "rank sectarianism" and his religious "bigotry" and argued that his "exclusiveness" would not "be half so grievous and odious, if his form of religion depended on voluntary support, and not on the bounty of the State."[11] In another act of protest, the Canada Baptist Union, then-based primarily in Montreal, sent a petition to the provincial legislative assembly in 1844. The petition clearly defined the Baptist position:

> The denomination of Christians called Baptists has ever been foremost in maintaining the principle that man, not being responsible to man for his belief, civil governments have no right to distinguish between religious sects by giving one a privilege or imposing on another a disability.[12]

9. Farmer, *E. W. Dadson*, 163.

10. Strachan, "Sermon on the Death," 8–9. For an overview and analysis of the Baptist position and attitudes, see Moir, *Church and State*, 11–12.

11. "Gleanings from the Late Charge of Bishop Strachan," *Montreal Register* [hereafter *MB*], March 23, 1842. For the Baptist view that church establishment had no legal foundation in Upper Canada, see "Are There Dissenters in Canada?" *MB*, April 20, 1842.

12. As cited in Renfree, *Heritage and Horizon*, 104. A copy of the petition is also found in Wells, *Life and Labors*, 148–49.

In addition to their protestations against a state religion, Baptists called for the application of the voluntary principle in public policy.

On the Clergy Reserves and university questions, Baptists like Robert Alexander Fyfe, the pastor of March Street Baptist Church, Toronto, led the fight for voluntarism in the early 1840s.[13] The Baptist press put its full weight behind the endeavors of the denomination's leaders. For example, in 1845, the *Montreal Register* demanded "that the Clergy Reserves may be sold as soon as possible and the proceeds of the sales appropriated to General Education on liberal principles."[14] As Donald Creighton has noted, Baptists succeeded in gaining the support of other denominations in their fight for the separation of church and state, and the voluntary principle "increasingly won approval from Methodists and the Free Church."[15]

By the early 1850s, voluntarist agitation had resulted in the realization of three Baptist goals. The formation of the University of Toronto in 1849 was, as Walter G. Pitman has noted, "the fulfilment of all the dreams of the Baptists."[16] The founding of a public education system based on what A. J. McLaughlin called "the democratic principle" in 1850, and the "secularization" of the Clergy Reserves in 1854 were also considered triumphs in public policy for the Baptist voluntary principle.[17]

Fifth, central Canadian Baptists believed in congregational polity. Authority and decision-making power in a Baptist Church lay ultimately with the membership. While deacons and elders (pastors) were elected by the congregation to serve as leaders, their decisions were subject to

---

13. For a discussion of the efforts of Robert A. Fyfe, see Gibson, *Robert Alexander Fyfe*, 130–65. One should also consult Wells, *Life and Labors*, 144–57, 171–90. For a general study of both issues, see Moir, *Church and State*, 27–128. The Constitutional Act of 1791 gave the Church of England (Anglican) special privileges including the setting aside of 1/7 of all future land grants "for the support and maintenance of a Protestant clergy." In fact, 1/7 of all land was provided for use by the Church of England. This favoritism became a cause of great controversy. Baptists and other "non-conformists" vehemently opposed this policy. The Clergy Reserves were eventually secularized in 1854. Similarly, Baptists objected to state-funded education that applied a religious test and/or promoted one religious view, namely Anglican, in the classroom. In the 1840s, Baptists were at the forefront of opposition to the creation and structure of King's College in Toronto and the push for "General Education on liberal principles." For more details, see Renfree, *Heritage and Horizon*, 103–8; *Montreal Register*, January 1845.

14. "Clergy Reserves," *MB*, January 16, 1845.

15. Creighton, *Story of Canada*, 120.

16. Pitman, *Baptists and Public Affairs*, 147.

17. McLaughlin is quoted in Renfree, *Heritage and Horizon*, 108.

congregational approval. Each congregation exercised control over its own affairs. As D. A. McGregor noted, "Individual churches are the highest executives of Christ on earth."[18]

Sixth, central Canadian Baptists stayed true to their non-sacramental roots. They practiced two "ordinances," believer's baptism and the Lord's Supper. Neither ordinance conferred salvation on the participant. Instead, they were outward expressions of personal saving faith. Article XIV of the *Declaration of Faith for First Baptist Church, Brantford*, set out the typical central Canadian Baptist view:

> We believe that Christian Baptism is the immersion in water of a believer; into the name of the Father, and Son, and Holy Ghost; to show forth, in a solemn and beautiful emblem, our faith in the crucified, buried and risen Saviour, with its effect, in our death to sin and resurrection to a new life; that is prerequisite to the privileges of a church relation, and to the Lord's Supper; in which the members of the church, by the sacred use of bread and wine, are to commemorate together the dying love of Christ, preceded always by solemn self-examination.[19]

While statements similar to this can be found in many early central Canadian Baptist declarations of faith,[20] some Baptists of English origin opposed the strict close communion stance of their more Calvinistic brethren. Controversy over whether the Lord's Supper should be open to all confessing Christians or only those who had followed the Lord in the waters of baptism remained a source of bitterness and resentment in Ontario well into the late nineteenth century. As Harry Renfree has observed, the open communion position eventually "became the norm—this despite the continuing inclusion of a close communion clause in many church constitutions."[21]

One final note concerning the central Canadian Baptist doctrinal position warrants discussion. The term "regular" indicated belief in the major tenets of Calvinism. As D. A. McGregor explained,

> The faith that characterizes a Regular Baptist Church, in reference to the way of salvation, may be briefly designated as Pauline

18. McGregor, "What Constitutes a Regular Baptist Church?," 164.
19. Shenston, *Jubilee Review*, xiii.
20. See, for example, Upham, *Baptist Position*.
21. Renfree, *Heritage and Horizon*, 203. For the history and perspectives of Canadian Baptists on the ordinance of Communion, see Heath et al., *Baptists in Canada*, 34–35, 41, 120–29.

or Calvinistic. By the election of grace, by the redemption of Christ, by the power of the Spirit, by belief of the truth, apart from any human merit, men are made new creatures in Christ Jesus, and preserved unto the day of His coming.[22]

Many central Canadian Baptist churches included Calvinistic statements in their Articles of Faith.[23]

Throughout the nineteenth and early twentieth centuries, these six doctrines and a Calvinistic perspective formed the basis of faith for many central Canadian Baptists. It was these beliefs that Baptists fought to protect both within their own constituency and in the public context. Numerous doctrinal controversies and the long road to Baptist union show that the maintenance of doctrinal unity and the establishment of Baptist institutions were goals that were not easily achieved. In both of these areas, the Baptist responses to an increasingly secular world had profound effects.

The Central Canadian Baptist View of the World

Historians are divided on the question of whether external intellectual attacks or internal decay caused by social and cultural change lay at the root of religion's decline between 1848 and 1921. Undoubtedly, both contributed.

Few intellectual historians would argue with George Rawlyk's contention that the rise of Darwinian thought in the 1860s and 1870s, higher criticism, the critical study of the methods and sources used by biblical authors, in the 1870s and 1880s, and comparative religion, the historical-scientific investigation of relation between the world's religions, at the turn of the century, "helped to reshape the contours of North American Protestantism."[24] For Baptists specifically, as Clark Pinnock has pointed out in his insightful article on modernism at McMaster University, "the tumultuous struggles between liberalism

---

22. McGregor, "What Constitutes a Regular Baptist Church?," 159.

23. See, for example, "Articles of Faith" art. 6 in *Bond Street Baptist Church Minute Book, 1845–1855*, JSBCA. "We believe in the free and Sovereign Election of God, and that those who are thus Chosen by Him, and really born of the Spirit, will be kept until the day of redemption."

24. Rawlyk, "A. L. McCrimmon," 36–39.

and fundamentalism in theology were to disturb Baptist life in North America for at least half a century" (1887–1927).²⁵

Rawlyk has identified four intellectual camps that emerged among the Baptists in the period 1880–1914. The fundamentalists demonstrated a "growing obsession with theological purity."²⁶ In direct opposition were the liberals, who sought to "make Christianity especially relevant to the new age" through their openness to scientific methodology and theological reinterpretation.²⁷ In the middle of the theological spectrum were two more moderate groups: "the conservative evangelicals," who maintained their evangelical beliefs and held little fear of modernity, and "the liberal evangelicals," who sought "to keep a foot in both camps" through the application of "an accommodationist spirit."²⁸ According to Rawlyk, it was this latter approach that won the loyalty of "the emerging central Canadian Baptist commercial elite."²⁹

These persuasive classifications are useful in distinguishing the different cultural perspectives that emerged among Baptists between 1880 and 1921. While the importance of external intellectual challenge should not be discounted in any analysis of religious decline, it is the contention here that the changes to individual religious practice brought about by the acceptance of materialism constituted a more insidious and powerful attack. Again, as Rawlyk has observed, "a convincing case may be put forward that the evangelical consensus suffered more from internal decay than external attacks."³⁰ And at "the core of this decay," argues Rawlyk, "was the cancer of consumerism."³¹

Rawlyk's analysis raises a number of important questions. Where is the evidence to support the assertion that internal decay was more responsible than external attack for religion's decline? What course did internal decay follow? How, specifically, did the acceptance of materialism affect religious commitment and practice? And finally, without prejudging the issue, what contribution, if any, did the central Canadian Baptist commercial elite make to the triumph of the material over the spiritual?

---

25. Pinnock, "Modernist Impulse," 193.
26. Rawlyk, "A. L. McCrimmon," 38.
27. Rawlyk, "A. L. McCrimmon," 38.
28. Rawlyk, "A. L. McCrimmon," 39.
29. Rawlyk, "A. L. McCrimmon," 39.
30. Rawlyk, "A. L. McCrimmon," 36–37.
31. Rawlyk, "A. L. McCrimmon," 37.

With the emergence in mid-nineteenth century Canada of an urban-industrial society and the growth of an increasingly materialistic culture, the relationship between Christianity and culture captured the interest and attention of most Canadian Baptists. Indeed, in the period between 1848 and 1921, Baptist concern about the rise of business and the worldliness that it encouraged steadily increased. Ironically, this intensification occurred in Ontario after 1867, when, as many historians conclude, it appeared that the churches had triumphed in their efforts to Christianize the province.[32] While most central Canadian Baptists in the period between 1848 and 1880 accepted what David Marshall and William Westfall have identified as "a new powerful social ethic... which regarded economic development and material progress, rather than religion, as the foundation for a stable social order," they split over the degree of acceptance.[33] Cultural conservatives, like businessman Thomas S. Shenston of Brantford and pastor Joshua Denovan of Toronto, worried about the moral effects of this ethic. In 1873, in a speech on hard work, Shenston expressed his worries about the dangers of avarice and selfishness: "But surely it is not the only object for which we are placed in this world to exert our energies in selfishly surrounding ourselves with ease and comfort regardless of the suffering and wants of those around us."[34]

By the late nineteenth century, the conservative Baptist obsession with moral purity translated into calls for moral reform that ranged from a return to a moderate lifestyle to church enforcement of a more stringent moral discipline. In 1889, for example, Joshua Denovan, pastor of Immanuel Baptist Church, Toronto, chastised his fellow pastor Ira Smith of Beverley Street Baptist Church for "taking a new departure, *a la* modern Wesleyanism in the form of a *Married Man's Social* and a Sunday *Flower Festival*."[35] Denovan lamented the fact that "the baptized church of Jesus Christ" could not "be content with apostolic truth and simplicity."[36] He further charged that Smith's lack of propriety was

---

32. See, for example, John Webster Grant's assertion that by 1867, the churches had accomplished their mission of Christianizing the province. Grant, *Profusion of Spires*, 166–69.

33. Marshall, *Secularizing the Faith*, 23; Westfall, *Two Worlds*, 109–11, 123–25.

34. Thomas S. Shenston, "Speech on Hard Work," 1873, in Thomas S. Shenston Papers, Additional Papers, Metropolitan Toronto Reference Library [hereafter MTRL], 5.

35. "From Mr. Denovan," *CB*, July 18, 1889.

36. "From Mr. Denovan," *CB*, July 18, 1889. Denovan's charges brought a stern response from Ira Smith. See "Reply to the Rev. J. Denovan," *CB*, July 25, 1889.

symptomatic of the religious competition produced by the new social ethic which had promoted moral compromise:

> During this present period of rapid religious developments, when everything ecclesiastical seems bent on cutting the moorings of venerable custom and drifting recklessly out on the open sea of novel enterprise, when celebrities like the Reverend Drs. Wildfire, Sandfountain and Dustwell, Smokespring and Huntcrowd are straining their wits to popularize their ministry; when the cookstove-ice cream-flower pot apostasies, alternating with periodic and special revivals, string bands and prima donas from Boston, and interspersed with lectures spiced with fun, profanity and immodesty are in full blast-in these circumstances can it be any great wonder that a gentleman of Mr. Smith's experience and natural aspirations should be tempted to try the attractive power of something extra scriptural?[37]

To Denovan, the answer was obvious. Baptists like Smith were on the road to "apostasy" through the acceptance of such "vicious innovations."[38]

Meanwhile, cultural liberals supported the new social ethic by working for its accommodation and promoting a definition of progress in which they attempted to serve material and spiritual values simultaneously. In some areas, accommodation between religion and business proved mutually beneficial. In other areas, religion suffered. Business often encouraged hypocrisy. Commenting on the relationship between religion and business in the life of banker William McMaster, William P. Cohoe, observed "I have been told by customers of the Bank of Commerce that [McMaster] could be found in his office reading the Bible, but it was said that many of his decisions did not partake in any large measure [of] the altruistic teachings of the New Testament."[39] Cultural liberals like McMaster accommodated the new social ethic by compromising their religious values and accepting the common maxim that "corporations have no souls."[40]

---

37. "Mr. Denovan's Rejoinder to Mr. Smith's Letter," *CB*, August 1, 1889.
38. "From Mr. Denovan," *CB*, July 18, 1889.
39. As cited in Johnston, *Toronto Years*, 20.
40. American M. B. Anderson, who became the President of the University of Rochester, used this maxim in one of his articles on capitalism that appeared in *The Canadian Baptist* in the 1870s. For the quote, see "New Feudalism," *CB*, December 14, 1876. For more on Anderson's view, see "Moral and Economical Values," *CB*, May 18, 1876; Marsden, *Fundamentalism and American Culture*, 13–14.

Even the most vociferous Baptist cultural protester in central Canada, however, would not question the overall merits of capitalism. As George Rawlyk has observed, "Few, if any, central Canadian Baptists in the 1880s would have, or more accurately, could have, accepted the validity of Marx's penetrating prophetic insight into the essential nature of bourgeois-industrial society."[41] Both cultural conservatives and liberals rejected Marx's view that "the bourgeois epoch" brought "everlasting uncertainty and agitation" and turned the "holy" into the "profane."[42]

Until 1914, Baptists of every cultural persuasion gave their allegiance to capitalism. Central Canadian Baptists combined elements of their Puritan and Calvinistic past to arrive at an economic ethic that supported hard work, private property, entrepreneurship, and material prosperity. A circular letter addressed to the members of the Haldimand Association, a group of Regular Baptist churches in central Ontario, in 1861 noted "We admit that pecuniary means are necessary to support the Gospel ministry."[43] An article that appeared in *The Canadian Baptist*, the primary denominational paper for Baptists in central Canada, in 1865, assumed that Baptists should pursue both "worldly prosperity and soul prosperity," which depended on three elements: capital, effort, and discretion.[44] "Capital," the article stated, "is as necessary to prosperity as life to health."[45] On the connection between prosperity and effort, the writer noted that "Prosperity is the result of effort, just as health is the result of exercise."[46] The final element in material and spiritual prosperity was discretion:

> No man can prosper in the world, unless he speculates wisely, and lay out his wealth in a manner that will insure a speedy and increased return; so those who possess the wisdom that is from above all will be wise in their generation, and emulate the conduct of the children of the world. They will endeavour to find out the secrets of success, these are soon learned.[47]

---

41. Rawlyk, "A. L. McCrimmon," 38.
42. Rawlyk, "A. L. McCrimmon," 37.
43. *Minutes of the Haldimand Association, 1861*, 7.
44. "Worldly Prosperity and Soul Prosperity," *CB*, October 26, 1865.
45. "Worldly Prosperity and Soul Prosperity," *CB*, October 26, 1865.
46. "Worldly Prosperity and Soul Prosperity," *CB*, October 26, 1865.
47. "Worldly Prosperity and Soul Prosperity," *CB*, October 26, 1865.

Here an implicit acceptance of free enterprise capitalism was evident. Many Baptists were convinced that the principles shared by capitalism and Christianity put material and spiritual prosperity well within their grasp.

Still, the acceptance of materialism by central Canadian Baptists came gradually and often guardedly. Before 1880, Baptists welcomed the arrival of material prosperity. Increased wealth provided them with the opportunity to communicate their message more effectively through the enhancement of missions at home and abroad.

By the late nineteenth century, the consensus of earlier years had given way to controversy. Liberal Baptists, especially those living in urban centers, believed that material prosperity could be made the servant of the spiritual world. In contrast, fundamentalists and some conservative Baptists, based primarily but not exclusively in rural communities, argued that gaining the world would result in the losing of souls. In characteristic Baptist fashion, the ongoing debate over what constituted proper sanctification, separation, and stewardship proved increasingly divisive.

The remainder of this chapter examines the central Canadian Baptist worldview. The focus is on doctrine. In particular, the objective is to provide a general overview of Baptist thought concerning personal holiness, individual lifestyle and personal responsibility.

Sanctification

> But of him are ye in Christ Jesus, who of God is made unto us wisdom, and righteousness, and sanctification, and redemption. (1 Cor 1:30)[48]

The emphasis on separation that emerged among central Canadian Baptists in the last half of the nineteenth century grew out of the evangelical-revivalist emphasis on sanctification, a process by which the believer was made holy. In theory, central Canadian Baptists rejected the notion of adherence to a creed and salvation by good works. Yet, by the late nineteenth century, some had become convinced that sanctification required the adoption of a Baptist creed and a new ethical legalism which equated spirituality with external conformity to a prescribed set of rules and

---

48. This biblical quotation and those used hereafter are taken from the King James Version of the Bible, that most commonly used in Baptist churches of the period.

regulations.[49] In 1899, Joshua Denovan, the pastor of Immanuel Baptist Church, complained that "there are to be soon multitudes who seem to know nothing about 'crucifying' the flesh with the affections and lusts- people as vain, worldly and selfish, as they well can be."[50] As a solution, he proposed "the adoption of a short and clear Scriptural Confession of Faith similar in form to the Anglican Thirty-Nine Articles, or some condensed compendium of Doctrinal Truth resembling the Shorter Catechism of the Church of Scotland."[51]

By the early decades of the twentieth century, fundamentalists had seized the opportunity provided by increasing intellectual uncertainty and secularism, to insist that the line between the spiritual and the material be made clear. In their attempts to distinguish between sacred and secular, conservative and fundamentalist Baptists developed tests to measure the depth of an individual's spirituality. Adherence to a strict morality and the practice of the old Calvinistic idea of stewardship served the purpose well. Thus, sanctification, separation, and stewardship dominated the Baptist debate about the Christian's relationship with the world.

The evangelical revivals of the late eighteenth and early nineteenth centuries in Upper Canada left an enduring legacy on its religious landscape. Revivalism found its greatest expression among Methodists. Baptists, following the Methodist lead, used revivalist methods to call for personal salvation and a deeper spirituality. While both denominations in Ontario held certain beliefs, values, and goals in common, they also competed with each other for converts and increasingly emphasized their theological differences. In particular, as revivalism was reshaped after 1840 to meet what Neil Semple has called "the perceived needs of urban-industrial society," Baptists felt compelled to contrast their approach to resolving the problem of the believer's relationship with the world to that of their Methodist rivals.[52] Specifically, Baptists challenged certain Methodist theological views of sanctification and separation, while they generally agreed on the practices of stewardship and strict morality.

49. Canadian Baptists retained Luther's view of salvation; one was justified by faith alone. See, for example, Shenston, *Jubilee Review*, vii. For a discussion of ethical legalism, see Wilson, "Legalism, Liberty or License," 1–8.

50. "What Is the Standard of our Faith and Practice?," *CB*, August 17, 1899. For an extensive analysis of Joshua Denovan's prototypical fundamentalist views, see Wilson, "Joshua Denovan."

51. For a negative response to Denovan's view, see "Creed For Canadian Baptists," *CB*, August 17, 1899.

52. Semple, "Quest for the Kingdom," 103.

As the largest evangelical denomination with strong ties to the holiness movement, a particular stream of revivalism that began among American Methodists in the 1830s and emphasized the entire sanctification of the believer, Canadian Methodists set the tone for the discussion of sanctification among the country's Protestants. John Wesley's definition of sanctification as a second work of grace, appropriated by faith and manifested through a Christian perfection proved as controversial in North America as it had in England.[53] As Marguerite Van Die has noted, American Methodist evangelists James Caughley and Phoebe Palmer brought the "trans-Atlantic holiness revival" to Ontario in the 1850s.[54] Like Wesley, holiness Methodists claimed that entire sanctification was possible after a believer had experienced "a second conversion" in which the individual surrendered completely to God.[55] By the late nineteenth century, some Methodists had taken Wesley's teaching concerning perfection to its logical conclusion. They claimed that sinlessness was possible for the believer and, as Van Die argues, they made Christian perfection "a point of controversy within international Methodism."[56] The idea that a believer could choose to experience moral perfection in this life set these Methodists at odds with many Canadian Baptists, who, true to their Calvinist tradition, taught that humanity's "total depravity" constituted an insurmountable obstacle to sinless perfection. Not surprisingly, this difference served as a flashpoint for interdenominational debate.

Throughout the nineteenth century, Canadian Baptists took every opportunity to attack the "holiness" view of sanctification. In its September 25, 1862 issue, for example, *The Canadian Baptist* ran an article that directly challenged the position taken by many Methodists:

> While the Christian is in this world he will be imperfect. The dogma that absolute perfection can be attained in this life is without sanction in the word of God, and without confirmation in human experience ... Men who claim to be perfectly holy ... are woefully blind and presumptuous.[57]

---

53. For Wesley's defense of his position, see Wesley, *Plain Account of Christian Perfection*. For a secondary appraisal of Wesley's view and its results, see Rack, *Reasonable Enthusiast*, 96–99, 395–401. For the Ontario context, see Grant, *Profusion of Spires*, 164–66.
54. Van Die, *Evangelical Mind*, 80.
55. Van Die, *Evangelical Mind*, 80.
56. Van Die, *Evangelical Mind*, 83.
57. "Perfection," *CB*, September 25, 1862.

Here, the Baptist literal biblical hermeneutic and a reliance on personal experience, which had its roots in Scottish common sense realism, were utilized to argue that the sinless perfection advocated by holiness Methodists was untenable.

In his theological lectures at Woodstock College, the cathedral of Canadian Baptist opinion, Reverend R. A. Fyfe also offered a Baptist definition of sanctification and then contrasted it with that put forward by the Methodists. Frequently, Fyfe asked his students: "Wherein does sanctification differ from justification?"[58] In response to his own question, Fyfe replied, "The latter is instantaneous the former progressive; the one is out of us, the other is in us; the one is wrought, the other is the maturing of the germ which the spirit plants in the heart."[59] Fyfe then went on to argue that the "conception of perfection" held by some Methodists was "misguided" because of its "imperfect conception of the law and hence a very imperfect conception of its requirements."[60] This line of argument led Fyfe to conclude, "God's plan indicates that sanctification will be gradual."[61] Fyfe's case for a sanctification by degrees and his criticism of the Methodists was echoed by others.

In numerous editorials and articles written for *The Canadian Baptist* before 1880, Baptists consistently criticized the Methodists and articulated a common view of sanctification. An 1870 editorial entitled simply "Sanctification" presented a succinct and, by then, standard definition of the concept:

> Sanctification may either mean to make holy, to be in a holy state, or to be entirely set apart for God's service. It is a separation from sin and a progress in holiness. Sanctification begins in regeneration. From this period the believer dies more and more unto sin, and lives more and more unto God. . . . Sanctification goes on progressively and will not be perfect till the believer sits down at the right hand of God.[62]

For Baptists, sanctification remained a lifelong process of spiritual growth. Complete moral perfection came through glorification only after a believer's death. The same author offered a pointed criticism of the

---

58. Fyfe, *Theological Lectures*, 1867–1871 (MS), JSBCA, 197.
59. Fyfe, *Theological Lectures*, 1867–1871 (MS), JSBCA, 197.
60. Fyfe, *Theological Lectures*, 1867–1871 (MS), JSBCA, 198.
61. Fyfe, *Theological Lectures*, 1867–1871 (MS), JSBCA, 198.
62. "Sanctification," *CB*, July 7, 1870.

holiness Methodist view when he stated, "I am aware that some deny progressive sanctification, but those who see nothing in their own heart [sic] but perfect holiness must be blind indeed."[63] To present the Baptist view of sanctification was to criticize the Methodist one.

To Baptists, the holiness Methodist doctrine lacked credibility for three reasons. As evidence for the reality of entire sanctification, holiness supporters offered only a few biblical passages. Baptists disagreed with Methodist interpretation, using a literal hermeneutic to argue that they had strayed from the true teaching of Scripture. Many Baptists found the holiness position both offensive and dangerous. It smacked of arrogance to suggest that anyone could attain Christ's sinlessness in this life. Belief in perfectionism bordered on heresy in its implied eradication of both the sinful nature (humanity's inherent evilness) and sinful behavior (acts that are contrary to the law of God as defined by the Scriptures).[64] Finally, the holiness Methodist position did not bear up under the scrutiny of reason and experience. In a classic, if unwitting, application of Baconian induction and Scottish moral intuitionism, most Baptists concluded that a perfectionistic doctrine of sanctification failed to account for everyday experience and personal intuition, which suggested that no person was or could become perfect.[65] Humanity's total depravity made it unreasonable to claim that perfection in this life was possible.

Throughout the last half of the nineteenth century, Baptists were strong apologists for progressive sanctification. According to this doctrine, it was possible for a believer, through successive steps of faith, to live an increasingly holy life. Perfect holiness, however, remained an unreachable goal. Baptists' understanding of progressive sanctification had a direct bearing on their view of the world. The Christian life was a battle against many evil forces that threatened to undo it. Progressive sanctification was evidence of the positive work of God in the life of the individual in the midst of a dark and depraved world.

Doctrinally, progressive sanctification lay at the heart of the Baptist outlook. Yet, the practical problems of the Christian's relationship with the world and a Christian's spiritual responsibilities required biblical

63. "Sanctification," *CB*, July 7, 1870.

64. See, for example, Fox, *Century of Service*, 87–88; Shenston, *Jubilee Review*, v.

65. This conclusion is partially based on Armour and Trott's assertion that Robert A. Fyfe, who taught moral philosophy at Woodstock College for seventeen years (1857–1874), was a follower of Scottish moral intuitionism. See Armour and Trott, *Faces of Reason*, 48.

solutions. In response to these problems central Canadian Baptists advocated separation and stewardship.

Separation

> Wherefore come out from among them, and be ye separate, saith the Lord, and touch not the unclean thing; and I will receive you. (2 Cor 6:17)

> Love not the world, neither the things that are in the world. If any man love the world, the love of the Father is not in him. (1 John 2:15)

While Baptists found the Methodists to be the most convenient external targets for censure on sanctification, their own internal struggle with the practical implications of the doctrine continued unabated in the late nineteenth and early twentieth centuries. Even as they rejoiced in their increasing prosperity, many Baptists became concerned about the simultaneous general growth of materialism and worldliness.

At both the individual and church levels, troublesome questions concerning the connection between sanctification and individual lifestyle stimulated debate and dissension. How did one define "the world"? How should one define separation from the world? Where was the line between Baptist morality and the world's morality? Was the demarcation between a Christian and the world absolute, or could Baptists practice different lifestyles and remain true to their faith?

Before 1880, these difficult moral questions split churches between cultural conservatives and liberals. Disputes and schisms over lifestyle issues, like the division over a secular business matter that troubled the Talbot Street Baptist Church, London, in the early 1850s or the schism at Bond Street Baptist Church, Toronto, in 1858 over the issue of preferential assignments indicate that a culturally initiated process of internal decay was well underway by the mid-nineteenth century.[66]

Questions about the connection between materialism and morality were further complicated by certain elements of Baptist belief and polity.

---

66. For the facts concerning the case at Talbot Street and an analysis of its "corrosive" effects, see Fox, *Century of Service*, 15–17. For the details of the Bond Street schism, see William Davies to James Davies, June 18, 1859, Papers of William Davies [hereafter WDP] (MS), Box 4044, File 2, University of Western Ontario, Regional Collection [hereafter cited as UWORC]. This letter also appears in Fox, *Letters of William Davies*, 49. One should also consult Langley Jr., *Correct Statement*.

Baptist theology accorded the individual liberty of conscience while Baptist polity stressed congregational autonomy. Theoretically, each Baptist had the right to interpret the Scriptures for himself/herself, and every congregation had control over its own affairs. In practice, however, Canadian Baptist leaders strove to achieve a strict moral conformity that would distinguish the Baptist believer from the unbelieving world. The challenge for Baptists was to maintain moral conformity without sacrificing individual liberty or congregational autonomy.

Separation from the world was a great practical challenge for Canadian Baptists from 1848 to 1921. But clearly defining "the world" also proved a difficult task. As an editorial in the May 1, 1879 issue of *The Canadian Baptist* noted, "Of course everything confessedly sinful in the world must be abandoned by the church member... But the perplexity begins when attention is turned from things positively and palpably sinful to other matters connected with the Christian's intercourse with the world in which there is room for difference of opinion."[67] Faced with the dilemma of defining the world so narrowly as to encourage withdrawal from it or so widely as to promote corruption by it, Baptists often returned to biblical definition. Another editorial in the February 23, 1882 issue of *The Canadian Baptist* stated, "And by the 'World' we do not mean simply the sphere of present existence, or the people by whom we are surrounded; but we mean the world which 'lieth in wickedness,' that world of which Satan is the god, and of which it is said that if any man love it, 'the love of the Father is not in him.'"[68] Such definitions did little to address the moral ambiguities surrounding specific pursuits, pleasures, and pastimes.

Worldliness weighed heavily on the minds of many other Canadian Protestants in the latter half of the nineteenth century. In 1873, for example, the *Doctrines and Discipline of the Wesleyan Methodist Church in Canada* instructed members of the united societies to do "no harm, by avoiding evil of every kind, especially that which is most generally practised."[69] In his counsel to fellow Christians, the famous Canadian Methodist evangelist Hugh T. Crossley dealt with the issue forcefully: "Keep off Satan's territory, and never be found where it would be a disgrace to die."[70] Still, as Neil Semple has argued, the "attractiveness of

---

67. "Church and the World," *CB*, February 23, 1882.
68. "Church and the World," *CB*, February 23, 1882.
69. *Doctrines and Discipline*, 76.
70. Crossley, *Practical Talks on Important Themes*, 299.

Methodism lay in its openness, not its exclusiveness. All were free to enter. Although it demanded separation from the corrupt world, it never became isolated from the society at large."[71]

Thus, while Methodists insisted on adherence to a strict moral code, they felt at liberty to pursue wealth and social status. As Marguerite Van Die, in her study of Nathanael Burwash, points out, "since virtue was accompanied by progress, there was little need to draw a sharp distinction between material and moral growth, and one could side with the progressive forces of the time [the 1860s] without hesitation."[72] Michael Bliss, in his analysis of Methodist pork baron Joseph Flavelle, has provided a detailed explanation of how the Methodist doctrine of sanctification was used as a rationalization for the accumulation of wealth.[73] Indeed, while a few more idealistic Methodists would continue to complain that "wealth promotes irreligion and worldliness" many condoned a new business ethic that encouraged individual material prosperity.[74]

On the surface, it appears that Baptists shared in the Methodist acceptance of the new worldly business ethic. Like their Methodist counterparts, many Baptists, between 1848 and 1880, welcomed material progress and prosperity. "We can afford to look back with some degree of complacency," noted an unidentified Baptist commentator on Canada's material progress in 1871, "for industry has produced abundant fruit, and we are reaping in joy a harvest sown in tears and trouble."[75] A few years later, a similar refrain included a note of praise for spiritual advancement: "I notice with pleasure the progress, spiritual and material," wrote a layperson to *The Canadian Baptist* in 1876, "our denomination is making in the provinces of Ontario and Quebec."[76]

Behind the applause for the arrival of economic advancement, many Canadian Baptists worried about the effects of material progress on their spiritual wellbeing. An article reprinted from the *Religious Herald* entitled "Dangers of Baptists" in the March 4, 1875 issue of *The Canadian Baptist* discussed the problem:

71. Semple, "Quest for the Kingdom," 102.

72. Van Die, *Evangelical Mind*, 76.

73. For Flavelle's comments on wealth, see Bliss, *Canadian Millionaire*, 84. For Bliss's discussion of the synthesis between sanctification and wealth and Flavelle's early view of worldliness, see 10–13.

74. This was E. H. Dewart's attitude. See Marshall, *Secularizing the Faith*, 3.

75. "Canadian Progress," *CB*, September 28, 1871.

76. "Surveying the Situation," *CB*, June 8, 1876.

> Prosperity is to communities, as to individuals, a slippery and dangerous elevation. So long as the churches of the early ages were poor, despised and persecuted, their progress was steady and their triumphs were glorious; but when they were taken into imperial favour, and became rich and popular, they lost their spirituality and grew formal, worldly and corrupt. They had a name which they lived and were dead. This degeneracy was the result of laws invariable in their tendency. Wealth, prosperity and success, which should inspire gratitude and call forth praise, too frequently engender pride, selfindulgence, worldliness, forgetfulness of God and moral corruption. The Baptist denomination is subject to these laws, and should most earnestly guard against their tendency, lest the triumphs secured by a century of self-denying toils and disinterested sacrifices should be lost.[77]

As this statement indicates, many Baptists supposed that material prosperity and progress would expose them to numerous worldly temptations. Separation from the world would enable the believer to resist these worldly attractions, some argued. But the old practical question remained: how did one separate from the world?

In 1882, many Canadian Baptists would have agreed with C. H. Wetherbe, then a pastor in Kinsey Falls, Quebec, who stressed the practical and sacrificial nature of separation in a sermon entitled, "Separation From The World":

> All these Divinely-given doctrinal truths and commands . . . show that the separation that exists between the true Christian and the world is something more than a mere profession; it is a life and practice which the very nature and genius of Christianity demands to be separate, is to be set apart-to be consecrated or sanctified. . . . As Christ denied himself, and bore His cross . . . we also ought to gladly deny ourselves of anything and everything which tends to impair our influence and usefulness and causes us to be a stumbling block unto others. . . . It is not conformity that we want; it is not being able to treat the world in its own way; but it is to stand apart and above, and to produce the impression of a holy and separated life.[78]

Here was a form of Christian asceticism to be practiced in the world. The Baptist paradox concerning the Christian's relationship with the world came to the forefront in their teaching about separation. Contact

77. "Dangers of Baptists," *CB*, March 4, 1875.
78. "Separation From the World," *CB*, January 26, 1882.

with the world without contamination by the world was the challenge. They were to avoid worldliness, which as pastor and later editor, E. W. Dadson noted, involved "customs, desires, aspirations, etc., which have nothing in common with the principles of Christ's gospel."[79] Living this paradox was a formidable, if not impossible, challenge. But many Baptists wholeheartedly believed that adherence to a strict moral code would preserve their separateness and spirituality while promoting their material prosperity.

For many Canadian Baptists before 1880, one's willingness to follow the strict morality set out in the Scriptures offered the best protection against contamination by the world and the best proof that one lived a separated life. Drawing heavily on Francis Wayland's *The Elements of Moral Science*, central Canadian Baptist intellectuals stressed the necessity for moral discipline in all human affairs.[80] As Robert Fyfe noted in his theological lectures, "Our standard of right and wrong will affect our theology."[81] If Baptist theology and testimony were to remain strong it was critical that Baptists have a clear understanding of their moral obligations.

In the classroom, at the family altar, from the pulpit, and through the pages of *The Canadian Baptist*, a definition of strict morality emerged as instruction was given on a wide range of subjects. For example, while not expressly forbidden, participation in "popular amusements" (gambling, dancing, card-playing, and theatre-going) was strongly discouraged. Baptists also stood firmly for temperance, the protection of the Lord's Day, and integrity in business and politics.[82] To be separate from the world meant practicing biblical moral dictates.

While the Baptist definition of morality found adherents in other denominations as well, their insistence that it be strictly followed reached a level that few others could match. On the topic of popular amusements, for example, the level of moral rhetoric reached new heights. "The grand

---

79. Farmer, *E. W. Dadson*, 128.

80. For Wayland's practical application of his moral theory, see Wayland, *Elements of Moral Science*, 137–365. Wayland's work was an enduring part of the curriculum for both men and women at the primary Baptist training school in Canada, the Canadian Literary Institute (1860–1881), later renamed Woodstock College (1881–1887), in Woodstock, Ontario. See, for example, *Catalogue of the Trustees*, 14–15; *Directory of the Studies*, 14–16.

81. Fyfe, *Theological Lectures*, 1867–1871 (MS), JSBCA, 6.

82. For a useful study of nineteenth century central Canadian regular Baptist views of the Lord's Day and their efforts to protect it, see Crocker, "Worthy Cause."

difficulty concerning the most of them," noted one Baptist writer in 1870, "is the devil controls them."[83] A circular letter to the Toronto Baptist Association in June 1878 warned, "Beware of any amusement that gives a distaste for home ... Beware of an amusement that leads to bad company ... Beware of amusements that may be a snare to others ... Beware of amusements that make large and improper demands on your time."[84] Following such guidelines would allow the Baptist believer to experience the "enjoyment" of "a purified soul."[85]

Despite such exhortations, after 1880, fundamentalists and some conservative evangelical Baptists became convinced that a cultural cancer of moral laxity and the intellectual cancer of liberalism were destroying Baptist faith and practice. To these Baptists, the symptoms were everywhere.

A debate in *The Canadian Baptist* over the use of a concert as a means for denominational fund-raising illustrates how divisions on a cultural ground were increasingly becoming apparent. This debate between a cultural conservative, Edmund Burke, and a cultural liberal, W. H. Nesbitt, brought to the surface many of the contentious issues.

In the December 3, 1908 issue, Edmund Burke,[86] the noted Toronto architect and member of Jarvis Street Baptist Church, criticized the actions of the Baptist Young Men's Union of Toronto for holding a "popular concert" in Massey Hall "in aid of City Missions."[87] Deeply disappointed, Burke expressed his horror "that a body of Christian young men" could "fall so far below the plane of enlightened Scriptural giving" which, in his view, "the Baptist churches of this country have aimed at and reached."[88] Had this circumstance arisen "forty or fifty years ago" he "could have put it aside with the thought that this was the way money was raised in those primitive days."[89] The whole affair "was to me, and I know many others a matter of shame and humiliation," Burke declared.[90] "Can it be that a new generation is growing up in ignorance

83. "Concerning Amusements," *CB*, August 25, 1870.
84. "Amusements or Recreations," *CB*, June 27, 1878.
85. "Amusements or Recreations," *CB*, June 27, 1878.
86. For an analysis of Edmund Burke's life and career, see Carr, *Toronto Architect Edmund Burke*.
87. "Matter of Shame," *CB*, December 3, 1908.
88. "Matter of Shame," *CB*, December 3, 1908.
89. "Matter of Shame," *CB*, December 3, 1908.
90. "Matter of Shame," *CB*, December 3, 1908.

of our position and teaching, and of the spiritual ground on which such work, to be pleasing to our Heavenly Father should be based?"[91] For Burke, the question was a rhetorical one. "If so," he continued, "it is high time that the religious press and the pulpit should begin a campaign of education regarding the true basis of Christian giving."[92]

A response from W. H. Nesbitt, Chairman of the Young Men's Union Concert Committee appeared in the December 24, 1908, issue of *The Canadian Baptist*. Nesbitt directly challenged Burke's historical assertions and claimed, "that forty or fifty years ago such a proposition [that of holding a concert in support of Missions] would indeed have been considered 'a matter of shame and humiliation,' but as time and civilization have advanced, men and women have, with but a few exceptions, become broader minded, and now view such matters in an entirely different light."[93] As part of his spirited defense of the concert as a means of fundraising, Nesbitt asked, "Where is the harm in giving the general public a good clean evening's entertainment, and using the funds so derived for the furtherance of the cause of Christ?"[94] Nesbitt went on to observe, "A certain majority of our citizens must have amusement and entertainment, and as long as no fault or objection can be found with the amusement itself, and the public receive full value for their money, what is the objection to giving the money to Christian causes?"[95]

In subsequent letters to *The Baptist*, as it was commonly called, Burke and fellow church member E. H. Roberts rebuked Nesbitt for his low view of giving. "There is no objection to good clean amusements and entertainments in their place," noted Burke, "and those patronizing such should receive full value for their money, but when tickets are sold on the plea that the proceeds are to help the Mission enterprise it puts the matter on a different plane entirely. Those people, especially the 'general public' to whom Mr. Nesbitt, has, perforce, to appeal, would not give fifty cents to the Mission, for Christ's sake, but for the sake of the entertainment or value received."[96] In a later letter endorsing Burke's objections, E. H. Roberts put forward further moral issues:

91. "Matter of Shame," *CB*, December 3, 1908.
92. "Matter of Shame," *CB*, December 3, 1908.
93. "Mr. Burke's Letter," *CB*, December 24, 1908.
94. "Mr. Burke's Letter," *CB*, December 24, 1908.
95. "Mr. Burke's Letter," *CB*, December 24, 1908.
96. "No Objections to Amusements, but-," *CB*, December 31, 1908.

> By asking anyone to buy with the idea of helping the Lord, whether it be a concert ticket or a supper ticket, or a garment or a piece of land, we lower his morals and stultify him if he accedes to our request. We lower the grace of giving to a piece of barter. We deny God's teaching that only a free-will offering is acceptable to Him. Let us have all Christian giving totally separated from buying and selling.[97]

The concern that young Baptists were cheapening their faith and compromising their morality by shifting their stewardship responsibility to the public is revealing. Certainly, the circumstance itself, and the controversy it engendered, demonstrate conflicting cultural perspectives and the steady erosion of the strict morality of the past.

Equally disturbing to fundamentalists was the evidence of a link between moral decay and modernism. The discovery by T. T. Shields, the fundamentalist pastor of Jarvis Street Baptist Church, that one of his deacons had joined a dancing club in Toronto contributed to a lasting church split in 1921. To Shields, increasing moral laxity and modernism were inextricably tied both to each other and to the majority of businessmen on his deacons' board who opposed him. In a later analysis of events, Shields declared:

> A Baptist Church deacon at a public dance was beyond doubt a symptom of serious illness, but had there been no complications, the patient might have made a rapid and complete recovery—but undoubtedly the McMaster [modernist] influence provided the complications.[98]

Metaphors aside, the fact that wealthy Baptist businessmen felt free to engage in such questionable practices as dancing spoke volumes about the toll that the new culture, with its materialistic social ethic, had exacted from the Baptist practice of separation.

Not surprisingly, much of the Baptist teaching concerning the practice of separation, between 1848 and 1921, was aimed directly at businessmen. They were expected to bring their high Baptist morality to the marketplace. To many Baptists, the response of businessmen to the spiritual challenges contained within the new social ethic was a litmus test of whether Baptist morality was holding firm. Some denominational leaders argued that if Baptist businessmen succumbed to worldliness, the

---

97. "Mr. Burke's Letter Endorsed," *CB*, January 14, 1909.
98. Shields, *Plot That Failed*, 238.

battle to maintain separation would be lost.[99] Consequently, the Baptist press sought to educate its readers on the principles of business ethics and fiscal responsibility. In 1852, for example, Toronto's own Baptist paper, the *Christian Observer*, offered instruction on poverty and debt:

> Poverty is a bitter draught, but may, and sometimes with advantage, be gulped down . . . But debt, however courteously it may be offered, is the cup of syren, and the wine, spiced and delicious though it may be, a subtle poison. The man out of debt, though with a flaw in his jerkin . . . is still the son of liberty . . . but the debtor . . . what is he, but a serf upon a holiday-a slave, to be reclaimed at any instant, by his owner, the creditor?[100]

Poverty, while distasteful, sometimes yielded spiritual fruit by developing Christian character. Debt was objectionable and onerous. Even if legal obligations to creditors were discharged through bankruptcy or compounding of debt, a Baptist businessman's moral responsibility to pay his debts in full remained. "Debts are always due until paid," proclaimed an article in the December 28, 1876, issue of *The Canadian Baptist*, "whether law compels or not."[101] In theory, the Baptist businessman must accept poverty over debt and follow a divine moral law in his debt repayment practices.

And what about the businessman who used credit? Was the use of credit a sin? It is clear that Baptist thought on this subject changed significantly in the last half of the nineteenth century. Before 1880, Baptist businessmen who used long-term credit were often suspected of wrongdoing. Furthermore, many Baptists believed that bankruptcy was a sin, and the name "bankrupt" was the social stigma applied to such sinners. In a speech on hard work written in 1873, Thomas S. Shenston, the prominent Baptist businessman from Brantford, articulated the typical Baptist view:

> Frugality is one of the most difficult things to practice in these days and yet very essential in order to obtain comparative wealth. . . . There is a glorious satisfaction in looking forward to a not very distant future when we could stand on a paid for carpet and not owing a $1 in the world. . . . Notwithstanding the road to comparative wealth is an economical road and those

---

99. See, for example, the arguments and analyses provided by E. W. Dadson in Farmer, *E. W. Dadson*, 128–29, 164–65, 203–5, 282–83.

100. "Poverty and Debt," *TCO*, October, 1852.

101. "Payment of Debts," *CB*, December 28, 1876.

> who travel it must disregard fashion and jeers, yet it is not without its solid comforts of which the embar[rassed] Bankrupts know nothing.... Is it not as plain as the road to market that by paying cash instead of purchasing on 6 months credit that you will save 5 and 6 per cent on each purchase?[102]

In Shenston's view, the practice of conservative Baptist values in both the personal and business life allowed one the opportunity "to cast in [his] lot with the 'few' in the 'narrow way' and shun the 'many' in 'the broad.'"[103]

By the late nineteenth century, attitudes had begun to soften. The earlier demand to avoid the use of credit gave way to tacit approval of its use as Baptists became more acclimatized to the realities of the business world. Church discipline relaxed, and Baptist thinking was adjusted: bankruptcy could be the result of uncontrollable circumstances instead of sin.[104] Calls for separation from the world were increasingly met by competing calls for its accommodation. On Sunday morning, August 11, 1907, pastor B. D. Thomas instructed his Jarvis Street Baptist Church congregation regarding the business religion-relationship:

> There is a prevalent conception that religion and business are widely separated spheres of activity—that they have little or nothing in common—that the more they are kept apart the better. Nothing could be more utterly out of harmony with right views of life and the teaching of God's Word. Business and religion, instead of being kept apart should be brought into co-relation. They were meant in eternal purpose to act and react upon each other helpfully. The spiritual is necessary to give motive and quality to the material activity, and the material activity is necessary to give expression to the spiritual life. We are not to abandon the material so as to secure the spiritual. This is to do

---

102. Thomas S. Shenston, "Speech on Hard Work," 1873, Thomas S. Shenston Papers, Additional Papers, (MS), MTRL. In the original manuscript, pages 1–20 is marked correctly. All other pages are either mismarked or without a page number. The page numbers used here follow the order in which they appear in the manuscript (28–29, 31–32).

103. Shenston, "Speech on Hard Work," 15.

104. These conclusions are the result of evidence found in the Bond Street and Jarvis Street Baptist Church Minute Books. For example, a brother [John] Tovell was censured by Bond Street Church for his bankruptcy despite "extenuating circumstances." One should see the *Minute Book, 1845–1855*, April 13, 1855, JSBCA. By contrast, in January 1897 on the occasion of the bankruptcy of McMaster and Company, James Short McMaster received a letter of support from Jarvis Street Baptist Church congregation. For the text of the letter see *Jarvis Street Baptist Church Minute Book, 1892–1910*, January 27, 1897, (MS), JSBCA.

> violence to all that is useful and valuable in life. To separate oneself from the world so as to secure a higher degree of holiness is moral cowardice of the most pronounced kind.[105]

This statement signified a remarkable change in central Canadian Baptist thought. By the early twentieth century liberal evangelical Baptists had rejected the notion that separation from the business world produced a deeper spirituality. They had embraced accommodation of the business world as the means of achieving great things for God.

By the late nineteenth century, evidence of a growing split among Canadian Baptists over the question of separation was mounting. For fundamentalists and some conservative evangelical Baptists industrialization, urbanization, the rise of business and commerce, and the growth of theological liberalism threatened to erode any clear demarcation between the world and the church. They feared that the arrival of modernity would, in practice, put an end to the Baptist concept of moral separation. In support of their case, they offered evidence of increasing worldliness, materialism, and spiritual lethargy.

In 1891, one editorial in *The Canadian Baptist* commented on the current state of Canadian Christianity:

> We were struck with a remark made by a well known Canadian writer in a secular journal, the other day, to the effect that there is too much of a kind of "otherworldly" selfishness among the members of our Christian churches. . . . The fact asserted or implied and deplored was that very many if not the great majority of professing Christians, when once their own salvation seems to be assured, are content to pass their lives in comfort and ease, with little of thought or care and less of self-denying effort, for the physical, social, and spiritual redemption of the lost masses around them. . . . It can hardly be denied that there is too much truth in the picture. Can it be that there is anything in the general tone of our preaching and exhortation, or in the atmosphere of our church life, to encourage such an attitude of mind and heart?[106]

---

105. "How to Make the Best of Both Worlds," *CB*, August 22, 1907. For biographical information about Thomas and some analysis of his ministry, see Haykin, *Jesus, Wondrous Saviour*, 74–89.

106. "Worldliness and Otherworldliness," *CB*, February 26, 1891.

The answer to this question seemed obvious. There was a crisis looming over the Baptist church, and culpability resided in complacency and worldliness.

Conservative Baptists blamed materialism for secularism and spiritual vacuum. In an editorial entitled "The Dominance of the Spiritual" that appeared in *The Canadian Baptist* on December 12, 1901, the writer commented on a profound change in Canadian values:

> For the dominance of the spiritual in all the great and little things of life we are praying, and to this end we are teaching. And while we pray and teach we mourn, because the spiritual seems to be thrust rudely aside constantly, in nearly every place by the material.[107]

The growing awareness that the material was displacing the spiritual called forth the strongest of Baptist diatribe; mammon was becoming master. In a circular letter to the churches of the Toronto Baptist Association in July 1882, Reverend Ira Smith, then a missionary pastor in Barrie, offered his view of the denomination's spiritual health:

> Just at this time, brethren, we have special reason to deplore the worldliness that is consuming the life of our churches. Christians forget their separation from the world and are becoming absorbed in the service of Mammon. . . . This will most probably account for the fewness of conversions in our congregations, the general apathy of the church and the want of harmony and brotherly love and confidence which so many are so bitterly deploring.[108]

Indeed, despite the warnings against materialism and worldliness, and intensified calls for a return to separation, the situation by the late nineteenth century appeared to be reaching a critical point for many Baptists. A new culture driven by economic and material concerns was replacing the religion-based culture of the past. Even as their religion was secularized through the internal attacks of a business-dominated culture, Baptist fundamentalists, conservatives, and even some liberal evangelicals embarked on a search for adequate responses.

The separation doctrine contained within the Baptist worldview failed to provide a long-term solution to the problem of the Christian's relationship with the world. As central Canada experienced the effects of rapid social and economic change, many Baptists, and businessmen

107. "Dominance of the Spiritual," *CB*, December 12, 1901.
108. "Spirituality of Our Churches," *CB*, July 27, 1882.

in particular, found separation to be increasingly impracticable. But hope for keeping spirituality ahead of materialism had not altogether vanished. The Baptist emphasis on stewardship remained a powerful obstacle to secularization.

Stewardship

> Moreover it is required in stewards, that a man be found faithful. (1 Cor 4:2)

> Then the merchant looked up from his mansion fair, Over the ocean, with troubled air, And thought of his treasures, in one short night, Whelmed in the deep by the tempest's might; And I knew by that pale brow's deepening gloom, He owned no treasures beyond the tomb![109]

The old Calvinist notion of stewardship seemed, for many Baptists, to hold out the best possibility for the reinstatement of spirituality as the first priority in the life of the individual believer. Thus, in the late nineteenth century, some Baptists rekindled their call to stewardship. An article taken from the Exchange and reprinted in *The Canadian Baptist* on May 18, 1876, defined a steward as "one who acts for another; who is bound to dispose of what has been entrusted to him for the advantage of his master, and in accordance with his master's wishes."[110] The article went on to point out what stewardship encompassed:

> Every gracious disposition, every calling in life, every relationship in society, every office in the Church, our time, our substance, our influence, these are all conferred on us as trusts, to be managed by us not for our own advantage and enjoyment merely, but for the welfare of society, and that God in all things may be glorified.[111]

In theory, stewardship obligated Baptists to surrender everything to the service of God. In practice, many Baptists found stewardship difficult. True stewardship required the believer to make unselfish and increasingly

---

109. These thoughts are those of Pamela Vining Yule, wife of Professor J. C. Yule of Woodstock College. The lines cited were contained in a poem entitled "Rich and Poor," which she wrote for *The Canadian Baptist*. See "Rich and Poor," *CB*, December 29, 1870.

110. "Stewards," *CB*, May 18, 1876.

111. "Stewards," *CB*, May 18, 1876.

countercultural choices. The Baptist businessman, for example, faced the difficult decision of re-investing profits in his business or giving them to his church. Both needed and deserved his financial support. The question of how to apportion his profits often proved troubling. In an attempt to address such concerns, leading Canadian Baptists advocated the acceptance of systematic giving. Through the use of contribution cards, subscriptions, and envelopes, Baptist leaders sought to convince the rank and file to give "a certain proportion" of their income, with "regularity" and "frequency."[112] Calls for systematic giving were proclaimed from the Bond Street Baptist Church pulpit in the 1860s.[113] By the late 1870s, many Baptist churches had followed Bond Street's lead and adopted a scheme of systematic beneficence.

Despite attempts by the Canadian Baptist leadership to educate its members as to the value of stewardship, the results remained unimpressive. A lack of funds in the mid-1870s prompted R. A. Fyfe, Principal of Woodstock College, to complain, "Our rich men have not yet begun to realize their obligations in regard to giving. Their contributions for general denominational work have been insignificant and paltry."[114] The gulf between the belief in and the practice of stewardship remained wide. Its existence provided more evidence for those Baptists who believed that only a renewed commitment to separation from the world would halt the destruction of their faith by hostile secular forces.

The acceptance of systematic giving was one in a long line of Baptist initiatives to encourage good stewardship. In the 1890s, the denomination turned to mass appeal methodology when it launched its own version of a "Forward Movement." Intended to put denominational finances on a solid footing, the movement enlisted the energies and endorsements of the denomination's most prominent businessmen and clergy. In pamphlets, pulpits, mass public gatherings, and press articles, the challenge to exercise financial stewardship went out to the faithful. The movement continued to be a popular means of raising revenue well into

112. Dyke, *Systematic Beneficence*, 4.

113. This was a favorite theme of Thomas Ford Caldicott, who was Pastor of the Bond Street Baptist Church from 1860 to 1869. He was one of the first Baptist leaders to challenge his co-religionists to adopt a scheme for "systematic beneficence" in October of 1863, when he spoke to the Baptist Missionary Convention of Canada West, in Hamilton. See Caldicott, *Systematic Beneficence*.

114. "What Are Our Rich Baptists Doing for Denominational Objects," *CB*, December 6, 1877.

the twentieth century. Its longevity was a testimony to the severity of the denomination's financial difficulties and its desire to find solutions.

Again, however, these efforts failed to stop the erosion of commitment to monetary stewardship. In a 1908 article written on behalf of the Layman's Missionary Movement for *The Canadian Baptist*, James Ryrie, a wealthy jeweller from Jarvis Street Baptist Church, made the frank admission that, "In the past too often it has been the fag ends of our energy and means only that have been devoted to this [the extension of the Lord's kingdom at home and abroad]—what has been left over after the demands of social, business and public life have been satisfied. But henceforth our object," Ryrie declared, "will be to place 'First Things First.'"[115] Despite Ryrie's efforts to engender enthusiasm for giving, wealthy Baptists increasingly succumbed to the temptation to shirk their religious fiscal responsibility. The concept of stewardship continued to erode. The Baptist worldview was in crisis.

Through the teaching of the church about stewardship, Baptists learned that their wealth, work, and life must serve and glorify God. Only through a life of stewardship could the Baptist believer demonstrate his sanctification and separation from this evil world. Unfortunately, many Baptists increasingly failed the stewardship test. The assaults of an emerging consumer culture resulted in the steady erosion of the Baptist commitment to stewardship.

Summary

In summary, the Canadian Baptist worldview remained fixed on three essential beliefs in the period between 1848 and 1921. Sanctification, as Baptists defined it, was to be an ongoing process by which the believer was transformed into the likeness of his master. An important aspect of sanctification was separation from the world. Separation required the Baptist believer to focus on maintaining his spiritual well-being and to reject any social, cultural, or political trend that prevented or interfered with that goal. On a more practical level, Baptists used the Calvinistic concern of stewardship and their own definition of strict morality as tests for separation and sanctification.

It has also been argued that the eternal attacks of an emerging business-dominated culture between 1848 and 1880 initiated a process of

---

115. "James Ryrie, Toronto," *CB*, January 23, 1904.

internal decay that split Baptists into two cultural camps. Cultural conservatives welcomed economic prosperity but warned that the materialism and worldliness that it encouraged would prove spiritually devastating if left unchecked. Cultural liberals felt confident that they could accommodate business and consumerism within their religious framework and claimed that they would make the material serve the spiritual. By the late nineteenth century, however, internal decay caused by the intrusions of materialistic culture had combined with external intellectual attacks to divide Baptists further into four rival groups, and to strip away the earlier confidence that a separation between Baptists and the wider Canadian culture could be maintained. In fact, the rise of theological liberalism in the 1880s and the modernist-fundamentalist conflicts of the 1920s added an external intellectual dimension to the potent and destructive clashes of differing cultural perspectives that had raged on among Baptists in central Canada for almost three-quarters of a century.

At the center of the controversy over the central Canadian Baptist worldview stood Baptist businessmen. Their vocation contained temptations and perils that made them especially vulnerable to moral compromise. Many Baptists realized that in order to address the problem of the Christian's relationship with the world sufficiently, their view of business had to be clearly defined. Few could anticipate the complexities that would make this undertaking so difficult.

Chapter 2

Business in Theory and Practice
The Central Canadian Baptist View of Business, 1818–1921

THROUGHOUT THE NINETEENTH AND into the early twentieth centuries, business was a key element in the central Canadian Baptist concern about worldliness. Many Baptists believed that by its very nature, business was a double-edged sword. On the one hand, it offered the daring and industrious entrepreneur the possibility of great wealth and better social standing. Business also provided an arena for the exercise of the Protestant work ethic, and the profits from business could be given to support Baptist causes. On the other hand, many Baptists expressed reservations about the rise of a business-dominated culture. The temptation to abandon God for mammon was a consistent theme in Baptist preaching and writing. The fear that businessmen would become covetous, dishonest, and worldly remained a constant worry. Thus, the business world received both praise and condemnation from Baptists. Recognizing its potential for both good and evil, many tirelessly exhorted Baptist businessmen to pass the tests of faith and practice that business life imposed. This chapter presents an overview of Baptist belief and practice in business between 1818 and 1921.

Although Baptists always considered merchandising to be an acceptable form of livelihood, the shift from an agrarian to an industrial-commercial economy in central Canada in the late nineteenth century challenged the power and place of religion in a businessman's daily life.

Baptist businessmen's unshakable commitment to material progress produced unprecedented prosperity that served as evidence of both religious and personal blessing. Yet, with success came problems. The ever-increasing demands of business life threatened to relegate religious devotion to the background.

The Contextual Background: English Baptists and Business in the Seventeenth and Eighteenth Centuries

The central Canadian Baptist view of business had its origin in the seventeenth-century beliefs and practices of early English Baptists. The emphasis among Baptist writers was decidedly negative and conservative. Perhaps the most noteworthy and influential literary work was John Bunyan's *The Life and Death of Mr. Badman*, published in 1680. With characteristic candor, Bunyan delivered his moral commentary on Badman's business sins through a dialogue between Wiseman and Attentive. The warnings were strong ones. In contrast to Badman, "all true Christians" must avoid "a making of the sheckle great" by defrauding creditors, fraudulent dealings with customers, and extortion of the poor.[1]

The business advice given to shopkeepers and traders by Puritan writers, like Bunyan, was direct and extensive. As Christopher Hill points out in his study of Bunyan and his church, "the perplexing advance of the capitalist economy" in seventeenth century England, encouraged discussion "of economic casuistry" in Baptist congregations.[2] The result of these discussions was a conservative economic perspective that stressed, among other things, the need for fair pricing, the elimination of idleness, and a marketplace characterized by equity.

In *The Life and Death of Mr. Badman*, Bunyan continually emphasized these themes. The merchant is instructed to avoid the temptations of selling his goods "as dear as he can," buying "as cheap as he can," and huckstering, buying up "the poor mans [sic] Victuals by whole-sale," and reselling it "to him again for unreasonable gains, by retale."[3] In addition to these instructions, merchants are warned against becoming cheats who are "*penny-wise and poundfoolish; that is he that loseth his good Sheep*

---

1. Bunyan, *Life and Death of Mr. Badman*, 97–116.
2. Hill, *Tinker and a Poor Man*, 234.
3. Bunyan, *Life and Death of Mr. Badman*, 109–11.

for a halfpennyworth of tarr; that loseth a soul for a little of the world."[4] Furthermore, a stern warning against attempts to "keep up . . . Trade and Repute . . . in the world . . . by the new engine of *Breaking*" is issued.[5] At the local church level, Baptists had been following Bunyan's admonitions since the revolution of the 1640s. Church leaders insisted that members of their congregations follow to the letter the biblical commands against fraud, lying, and cheating. Failure to do so brought swift and stern church discipline. At Bunyan's own Meeting in Bedford, England, on January 21, 1669, for example, Richard Deane was "cast out" of the congregation for "A loose and ungodly life, accompanied with defrauding in his calling, selling to severall persons deceivable goods, to the great dishonour of God, and scandall of our profession."[6]

English Baptists were equally strict when it came to borrowing money. At the Broadmead Church, Sarah Watkins was admonished in 1679 "for her scandalous, walking disorderly, not tending to her business, but making it a common practice to goe up and downe borrowing money from whomsoever she could, and not endeavouring to pay it again."[7] This type of disciplinary action was common among seventeenth-century Baptists. As Christopher Hill has noted, the Baptist demand for proper business ethics served the interests of sectarian survival through moral purity: "Correct economic behaviour was incumbent on believers; improper conduct reflected badly on the reputation of the church and therefore on God's cause."[8]

Yet, the conservative tone of seventeenth century Baptist writing and the ever-present prospect of stern discipline for a misstep did not deter a few Baptists from distinguishing themselves in their capitalist enterprises. The life of William Kiffin provides an outstanding example. In 1643, Kiffin entered the woollen cloth trade with Holland and within a few short years grew rich. His fortune was further enhanced when he supplied requisites for the English fleet in the war with the Dutch in 1652. In the early 1660s, Kiffin testified before a House of Commons

---

4. Bunyan, *Life and Death of Mr. Badman*, 106.

5. Breaking refers to the immoral practice of buying goods, selling them below cost to gain the confidence of customers and creditors, closing up shop and then negotiating a settlement with creditors that favors the businessman. Bunyan, *Life and Death of Mr. Badman*, 88–89. The issue of bankruptcy will be discussed in chapter 5.

6. *The Minutes of The First Independent Church [now Bunyan Meeting] at Bedford 1656–1766*, 55:63.

7. Cited in Goadby, *Bye-Paths in Baptist History*, 278.

8. Hill, *Tinker and a Poor Man*, 234.

committee and before the Privy Council in opposition to granting the Hamburg Company a monopoly over the woollen trade with Holland and Germany.[9] Michael Watts has claimed that while "it could be argued that the success of the Baptist merchant William Kiffin is a perfect illustration of the Weber thesis," it more likely that Kiffin "engaged in commercial ventures out of sheer necessity."[10] Whether calling or constraint motivated Kiffin is unclear. Perhaps it was a combination of both that drove this dissenter to pursue risky business ventures in a volatile and often hostile religious, political, and economic climate. Given the risks of the marketplace and the reprisals from civil and religious authorities that English Baptists often faced, it is not surprising that few were willing to rise to the challenge.

In the eighteenth century, the Baptist emphasis on industry and moral purity combined with urbanization and industrialization to propel some Baptists into the small bourgeois class. In a few urban centers, the sons of seventeenth-century Baptist artisans became small merchants and traders "of the middle rank."[11] Michael Watt has found that Particular Baptists were especially strong in Bristol, where they constituted over 4 percent of the population, and in the cloth-making towns of Bradford-on-Avon, Trowbridge and North Bradley, where they "occupied an important social position" and made up nearly 3 percent of the population.[12] Yet, as Alan Everitt has shown, the majority of Dissenters remained countryfolk, not townsfolk, before 1740.[13] In his study of English Baptists in the eighteenth century, Raymond Brown has observed that "Most churches were in rural areas" and "wealthy people were scarce among the Baptists so most members of these congregations saw little of England beyond their neighbouring villages and their local market town."[14] Isolation and insularity remained hallmarks of the English Baptist experience in the eighteenth century. Nevertheless, small pockets of these same Baptists used business to make their way up the social ladder.

9. The information on William Kiffin is taken from *Dictionary of National Biography*, 11:98–100; Ivimey, *History of the English Baptists*, 313–21; White, *English Baptists*, 129–30; Watts, *Dissenters*, 361–62.

10. Watts, *Dissenters*, 361–62. See also Wilson, "William Kiffin," 65–78; Johnson, "Peculiar Ventures," 61–70.

11. Cited in Porter, *English Society in the Eighteenth Century*, 195.

12. Watts, *Dissenters*, 282.

13. Everitt, "Nonconformity in Country Parishes," 186.

14. Brown, *English Baptists of the Eighteenth Century*, 10.

At this point, an important question warrants consideration: Did the Baptist view of business rest on religious convictions or was it shaped primarily by social and economic factors? According to Weber, the "ruthlessly radical . . . rejection of worldliness" by early continental Anabaptist leaders failed to result in the abandonment of private property or "practical worldly virtues."[15] In fact, Weber argued, in the period immediately following the Reformation, "the strict morality of the Baptists had turned in practice into the path prepared by the Calvinistic ethic."[16] For Weber, then, Calvinism was the determining factor in what early Baptists thought about business. In his testing of the Weber thesis within the seventeenth-century Scottish religious context, Gordon Marshall claims to have "identified several instances in which actors explicitly related their capitalist activities to Calvinist premises."[17] According to Marshall, such evidence suggests that "Weber, rather than the Marxists . . . correctly identified the relationship between the two worldviews, by attributing the development of the capitalist ethos to the nature of Calvinist teaching rather than vice versa."[18] In his study of eighteenth-century English society, Roy Porter maintains that most English dissenters used a combination of high moral scruples and strict discipline to promote upward social mobility and religious respectability.[19]

Challenging Weber's thesis, Michael Watts argues that the dissenting view of business and material success, between 1690 and 1730, was shaped more by social conditions than religious convictions. According to Watts, "the evidence of the Dissenting Registers suggests that a much higher proportion of Dissenters than of the population at large were engaged in commerce or manufacturers as merchants, tradesmen, or self-employed artisans, and the social and legal pressures of the eighteenth century helped to confine Dissenters to such occupations."[20] Furthermore, Watts contends, "When success came to Dissenting traders and craftsmen, it was not because they had been conditioned by their religion to make profits, but because they applied their mind and hands to the tasks which they and their Separatist forbears had always pursued."[21]

15. Weber, *Protestant Ethic*, 149.
16. Weber, *Protestant Ethic*, 149.
17. Marshall, *Presbyteries and Profits*, 261. For Marshall's evidence, see 221–62.
18. Marshall, *Presbyteries and Profits*, 261.
19. Porter, *English Society in the Eighteenth Century*, 195–99.
20. Watts, *Dissenters*, 360.
21. Watts, *Dissenters*, 362.

Success for Dissenters was also "assisted by the network of business connections and relationships that arose out of their denominational ties."[22]

Careful review and consideration of the available evidence for the English Baptist context leads one to the conclusion that both Weber and Watts are partially correct in their analyses of the causal relationship between religion, social conditions, and business. Weber was partly right in his assertion that Calvinism promoted capitalism. While their religion may not have socially "conditioned" English Baptists to make profits, the strict moral teaching associated with the literal biblical interpretation of Calvinism inculcated them in the moral and ascetic qualities necessary for business success. The disciplined lifestyle that grew out of their Calvinistic obsession with moral purity provided English Baptists with a sense of plan and purpose. This sense of purpose often gave the Baptist businessmen the will and drive to succeed in the most adverse circumstances.

While religion certainly shaped the English Baptist view of business, social, and economic factors also played important roles. As Watts has noted, there is no doubt that economic necessity encouraged some Baptists to enter business. Similarly, hostility and the fear of punishment for their nonconformity undoubtedly discouraged others from pursuing capitalistic enterprises. When English Baptists were provided with a tolerant social climate that permitted them access to the business world, they often prospered. The experience of William Kiffin shows that even when tolerance was low some Baptists could succeed. However, in general, when social tolerance was in short supply, Baptists seldom rose above the middle ranks of English society.

In local churches, eighteenth century English Baptists continued to exercise strict discipline over wayward members. Those found guilty of immoral business practices were strongly disciplined. At the Bedford Church in June 1702, for example, Richard Flint was ordered to withdraw from the congregation for "fraudulent dealing, of which there was proof, and dishonest and clandestine buying of goods of an apprentice to his master's damage."[23] At another church meeting held on December 30, 1756, Joseph Negus "was cast out of the Church for repeated acts of uncleanness, for lying, swearing, drunkenness and fraud etc."[24] These instances testify to the continuing vigilance of Baptist congregations.

22. Watts, *Dissenters*, 363.
23. Tibbutt, *Minutes of the First Independent Church*, 124.
24. Tibbutt, *Minutes of the First Independent Church*, 189.

Throughout the seventeenth and eighteenth centuries, English Baptists maintained a conservative view of business. While hard work, honesty, and making a profit were encouraged, Baptists were cautioned against greed, covetousness, and exploitation. The ever-present danger of worldliness encouraged Baptist churches to keep a watchful eye on the business practices of their parishioners and to exercise strict discipline when transgressions occurred.

The New World Experience: The Central Canadian Baptist View of Business and the Businessman

Baptists brought their old-world values to Upper Canada in the years following the War of 1812. The Scottish, Irish, and English Baptists who came often had different views of religion and morality. In his survey of the history of Bond Street Church in Toronto in 1876, one of its former pastors, Robert A. Fyfe, explained that the Baptist cause in Toronto was inhibited by "the want of homogeneity, among a considerable portion of her members."[25] The problem, according to Fyfe, was that "men of strong individuality, with set habits, made angular sometimes, by the peculiarities of some able ministers under whom they were trained in the old world" were "generally more anxious to lead than to follow."[26]

Still, despite their disagreements over certain religious "principles," that were "so strongly and sharply defined" that they stood "in the way of 'practice,'" Baptists from every part of the old world held on to an essentially Calvinistic and conservative view of business.[27] Like the Presbyterians, Scottish Baptists brought with them what W. Stanford Reid called "the Calvinistic-Presbyterian outlook on life."[28] This perspective gave Scottish Baptists "not only a sense of divine calling to work, but [also] a God-given responsibility to show initiative foresight and risk-taking."[29] While they might strongly disagree over the particulars, immigrant Baptists from England, Ireland, and Scotland shared common economic values and beliefs that had their roots in the seventeenth and eighteenth centuries.

---

25. Fyfe, *Forty Years Survey*, 13.
26. Fyfe, *Forty Years Survey*, 13.
27. Fyfe, *Forty Years Survey*, 13.
28. Reid, "Scottish Protestant Tradition," 120.
29. Reid, "Scottish Protestant Tradition," 120.

The remainder of this chapter examines areas of continuity and change in the central Canadian Baptist view of business. In theory, Baptists in Canada remained connected to the past through the concepts of stewardship, frugality, and industry. Nevertheless, the dramatic social, cultural and economic changes brought about by the arrival of industrialization and urbanization after 1850 led many Baptists to modify their view of business.

Throughout the nineteenth and early twentieth centuries, Baptists in central Canada retained an essentially conservative though dualistic view of business. Many held that business was a worthy calling. Baptists were encouraged to pursue business careers and taught to consecrate their business talent and practice stewardship of their time and profits. Others considered business a dangerous vocation that put the faith of even the most devout to the test. Baptist businessmen were constantly warned of the temptations of wealth and worldliness found in the secular business world. Through preaching and the printed page, Baptist businessmen were reminded of their spiritual priorities and encouraged to "stand fast in the faith" (1 Cor 16:13).

In an 1848 editorial, entitled, "Leading Men in the Churches" a writer for *The Evangelical Pioneer*, a Baptist weekly based in London, Ontario, noted the importance of the Baptist businessman:

> In all associations, voluntary or involuntary . . . we find men whose superior advantages or business tact fit them for exalted usefulness . . . if he [sic] possesses wealth, they are entitled to the full amount of power in every direction, which such possession ensures . . . and if he possesses a correct business talent, it must be consecrated to God, and employed in all suitable ways . . . to his glory. The church has a right to expect this-all this-for Christ expects it all; and woe to the man who withholds from the Lord more than is meet.[30]

Business talent was a God-given ability, and that calling must be used for the Master's greater glory. Over half a century later, W. W. Smith restated these beliefs in his address to the Northern Association entitled "The Consecration of Business Talent":

> Business talent is His then, and since no talent is given to remain idle, I am to use it for Him. Some men are possessed of this talent in a marvellous and pre-eminent degree. They were

---

30. "Leading Men in the Churches," *Evangelical Pioneer*, July 15, 1848.

> not designed for preachers, but they can push business. Is it not reasonable that we have as imperative a call as any preacher? That talent is the call; they are to gather up the silver and the gold for the King.[31]

This statement reflected Baptist thought concerning business generally and the responsibilities of each businessman. In accordance with traditional Calvinistic teaching, Smith argued that the ability to do business successfully was a blessed call of God. Businessmen were obliged to follow that call and serve the cause of Christ with their business talent.

It is also interesting that Smith equated the call to business as equal with the call to pastoral ministry. In their insightful and informative study of the professions in nineteenth century Ontario, R. D. Gidney and W. P. J. Millar have argued that the external pressures of religious pluralism and voluntarism were the primary causes of an erosion of "the social and cultural authority necessary" for the Protestant clergy to fulfil effectively the duties of "their sacred calling" and to keep up "the ideal of the professional gentlemen" which "seemed to be receding beyond their grasp."[32] While religious historians will undoubtedly debate the causal theory advanced by Gidney and Millar, their assertion that the clergy suffered a decline in respectability and status even as the church reached the height of its power in the late-nineteenth century appears accurate in the Baptist context. W. W. Smith's statement that the call to a businessman and the call to a preacher were spiritually equal represented an important change in Baptist thinking. In the early nineteenth century, young Baptists who answered the call to pastoral ministry were, in practice, accorded special status. While all were called, the "noble profession" of pastoral ministry exceeded all other calls in importance.[33] Smith's statement shows that by

---

31. "Consecration of Business Talent," *CB*, April 5, 1900.

32. Gidney and Millar, *Professional Gentlemen*, 282. As Gidney and Millar point out, urbanization and competition were also important factors in the decline of the clergy. For their entire argument concerning the changing relationship between clergy and laity see their chapter entitled, "Clergymen and the Ascendancy of the Laity," 268–82.

33. "Dr. Nott's Advice to Young Ministers," *Christian Messenger* [hereafter *CM*], September 25, 1855. I am using the term status to refer to the respect given those in the Baptist ministry. An article entitled "Our New Minister," which appeared in the July 19, 1860 issue of *Canadian Baptist*, for example, reminded the faithful that "There is but one man in every three or four hundred men who is fitted to become a really good and gifted minister, and that one man God has chosen and sent to be your minister." Respect did not always result in a pastor being paid a living wage. Baptists were constantly challenged to fulfill their obligation in this regard. See, for example, "Duty of Canadian Baptists," *CM*, December 28, 1854; "Honour to Whom Honour is Due," *CM*, July 12,

the end of the nineteenth century, many Baptists considered all vocations to be of equal spiritual value.

This is not to say that Baptist businessmen were immune to questions about their spiritual credibility. Smith put the matter plainly:

> The prevalent opinion today is that no business man can be successful as such and be honest. What a reflection upon our professedly Christian business men! If a merchant holds membership in one of our churches it is looked upon by the general public as a diplomatic act, as it gives him social position and mayhap increases his trade. He seldom gets credit for any sincerity of purpose on his part.[34]

Despite their problems with credibility, the calling to Baptist businessmen gained in status and respectability throughout the nineteenth century. Their endeavors were viewed as an important ingredient in the progress of the Baptist cause in central Canada. Business offered the church the potential benefits of material gain to fund its projects and new organizational methods to manage its affairs. But the business world was never considered the friend of religion by all or even by many Baptists. Even as material prosperity increased, their suspicions that business promoted spiritual decline grew stronger.

Baptist Fears: Wealth and Worldliness

At the heart of the central Canadian Baptist view of business lay the fear that the wealth generated by economic progress would promote materialism and worldliness among the denomination's businessmen. By the late nineteenth century, the traditional reservations of Baptist leaders had intensified. While many Baptists welcomed the economic prosperity that accompanied the rise of a business-dominated culture in the late nineteenth century, many voiced concerns about the negative spiritual impact of such prosperity.

Typical of the concerns expressed were those offered in a sermon preached to the Baptist congregation in Aylmer, Ontario, by Reverend James Cooper of Woodstock on Sunday, July 27, 1862. In his message,

---

1855. For a discussion of how a Baptist was called to the "Gospel Ministry," see Elgee, *Social Teachings of the Canadian Churches*, 63–64. For an early Baptist definition of the ministry, see Wells, *Life and Labors*, 262–63.

34. "Consecration of Business Talent," *CB*, April 5, 1900.

entitled "The Danger of Riches," Cooper noted, "it has become the experience of thousands that becoming rich, they fall into temptation and a snare, and into many foolish and hurtful lusts, which drown their soul in destruction and perdition."[35] Cooper blamed the absence of the old world class structure and new world free enterprise for excessive acquisitiveness in Canada West:

> It has often been remarked that there is a love of money and a keenness for property here, which, in the old countries are unknown. I have no doubt that this is quite true.... In the old countries the bulk of men have a weekly allowance with which to manage to get along, and that is about all they expect; the appetite for property is never aroused. Here it is not so; any man and every man may, in this fair province, begin to make money and rise. And then a great many persons seek a home on these shores for no other purpose than to make money. The Bible they bring with them says, "Seek first the Kingdom of God and his righteousness, and other things shall be added." Their practice reads it, "Seek first the world and its favours, and leave the affairs of the soul to a more convenient season."[36]

Some Baptists might question Cooper's idyllic view of the old countries, but few would challenge his central point that wealth was dangerous and that business provided many with the opportunity to acquire riches.

Warnings of this kind continued to be sounded throughout the nineteenth century. By the 1890s, concern had reached something like a fever pitch. On his retirement from the Presidency of the Baptist Convention of Ontario and Quebec in the Fall of 1892, Reverend B. D. Thomas observed,

> It is extremely difficult it would seem for the most saintly to see clearly through golden spectacles. Iniquity dressed in silks or clothed in broadcloth is not half as abhorrent in our eyes as when clothed in homespun or in fustian, and when it is ornamented with jewels and rendered effulgent with the splendour of a great name we often prostrate ourselves before it, as the Israelites did in the wilderness before the golden calf.[37]

The wealth that business brought often served as a cloak for dishonesty and promoted a new form of idolatry in materialism.

35. "Danger of Riches," *CB*, August 28, 1862.
36. "Danger of Riches," *CB*, August 28, 1862.
37. "Church and the Living Issues of the Hour," *CB*, November 3, 1892.

Nine years later, an editorial in *The Canadian Baptist*, entitled "Becoming Prosperous," discussed in more detail the growth and impact of personal wealth among Baptists:

> If any one who knows fairly well the Baptist churches in city, town and country, large and small throughout Quebec and Ontario, will sit down and call to mind the men in them who are becoming prosperous, he will probably be surprised to find how many of these there are. These prosperous men, in most cases started out with thrifty and industrious habits coupled with intelligent insight, and they had little besides these things. . . . We are fully aware that many who read this will not think that they belong to this class. . . . But if these men will think carefully over what they were worth fifteen years ago, and then compare that with what they are worth now, we are not afraid of many mistakes in proper classification. The number of men who can now be put in this list is now so large in our Baptist churches that we feel constrained, not to say forced, to express some ideas on the subject. . . . For the possession of wealth is a severe test. We are quite aware that many men will reply with a smile, that they are willing to submit to the test, and run the risk. But this is an old story and the only new thing about it is its application to the new and prosperous conditions of many Canadian Baptists. There is danger in wealth no one will deny. And this danger presses itself on our attention all the more forcibly because we have recently seen instances, where we might have expected better things that have proven how dangerous to character is the possession of wealth.[38]

This statement captured the essence of longstanding fears. Success in business gave some Baptists enormous fortunes. With riches came numerous temptations to abandon the pursuit of godly character. The editorial went on to note that wealth "hardens, it puffs up and makes vain, and it encourages such a subtle selfishness and self-assertion that no man who values what is really noble in life should regard this danger lightly."[39]

Still, despite the recognition that wealth and materialism threatened the very existence of religion, a few Baptists remained hopeful. In its editorial comment on the Baptist Union of Western Canada Convention in the February 13, 1913 issue of *The Canadian Baptist*, the writer expressed the hope that Baptists would keep their priorities straight:

38. "Becoming Prosperous," *CB*, October 3, 1901.
39. "Becoming Prosperous," *CB*, October 3, 1901.

> Frequently during the sessions there was complaint that the West was too much dominated by materialism. But we doubt if in this regard the West is very much worse than the East. There is an epidemic of materialism all over Canada just now. But not very much harm will result if there come honestly into the possession of God's own people large amounts of wealth that they will in turn devote to the furtherance of His Kingdom.[40]

The optimistic hope that greater wealth would translate into greater giving by the denomination's wealthy members did not, for the most part, transpire. Later this study will show that the trend among Baptist businessmen was away from giving and towards self-gratification; as wealth increased, stewardship declined.

Throughout the nineteenth and into the early twentieth centuries, many Baptists in central Canada retained a dualistic view of business. Viewed strictly in economic terms, business was a blessing. It provided opportunities for gainful employment, personal fulfilment, and social advancement. Yet, for many Baptists, business was responsible for spiritual decline. The constant emphasis on money-making and profit tested the faith of Baptist businessmen. The temptation to become selfish and self-reliant struck at the very heart of the Baptist belief in stewardship and trust in a sovereign God.

Along with the dangers of wealth, many Baptists believed that business also encouraged worldliness. In August 1853, an article that appeared in the early Baptist journal, the *Toronto Christian Observer*, recognized this problem of worldliness and offered the traditional conservative instruction and guidance:

> Business must be pursued honestly.... We must be governed in business by the great law of benevolence. We must not only be just to others... but also benevolent, seeking their good.... Here is a point where the Christian must ponder the injunction: "Be not conformed to this world." The laws of trade, the common maxims and the principles which govern business, are all selfish: "Look out for number one," is the conman law of the business world. But to seek the good of others equally with his own, must be the aim of the Christian in business as in everything else. He must be diligent in business while at the same time he must not become absorbed in business. He must preserve that difficult equilibrium enjoined by the apostle [Paul]: "Diligent in business, fervent in spirit, serving the Lord." The principal care of

---

40. "Materialism," *CB*, February 13, 1913.

the intercourse of the Christian with the world is in business. It is there that he is watched. It must be obvious, then, that if God is not glorified by the Christian in business, He will not be glorified by him at all; that if the great principles of the Gospel are excluded from business life, the world must be without a living exhibition of their superiority and power.[41]

This statement reveals the conservative Baptist assumption that the self-absorbed nature of business encouraged worldliness. The danger that worldly business values would replace sacred gospel principles remained a constant fear for culturally conservative Baptists who viewed the rise of a business-dominated culture with suspicion.

Warnings against worldliness continued through the late nineteenth century. Many Baptist leaders were quick to point out that the material prosperity which accompanied the rise of business had a spiritual downside. As E. W. Dadson noted in one of his many articles for *The Canadian Baptist*,

> There is no use talking around the matter. As the sin of worldliness is the great snare of all Christians, the present position of the Baptist denomination is not without danger in this direction.... This thing which God hates, has ever stood in the way of the progress of Christ's kingdom. The history of the Church is strewn with the wrecks which it has made; and without controversy the church or denomination which is borne on its current, if not done to death, is sadly crippled. Now that our denomination is riding prosperously, the note of warning which urges the path of safe sailing ought to be regarded as well sounded.[42]

Dadson expressed the official Baptist view concerning the problem of worldliness: Baptist leaders supported business endeavor but feared that the prosperity it produced would result in the acceptance of secular values and practices.

In the opening chapter of this study, the Baptist emphasis on separation from the world was discussed. The point that Christian businessmen must constantly be on their guard against becoming entangled in the affairs of this world remained at the core of Baptist teaching. Yet, by the early twentieth century, many Baptists had moved from a legalistic application of separation to what we shall see is a more integrated relationship

---

41. "Glorifying God in Business," *TCO*, August 1853.
42. Cited in Farmer, *E. W. Dadson*, 128.

with Canadian culture. While warnings concerning worldliness continued, *The Canadian Baptist* also encouraged social integration:

> It is certainly the will of God for His people to engage in the ordinary vocations of this world that they may earn their living and at the same time show forth to the world the saving and keeping power of Jesus Christ. Though it is the will of God for His people to engage in the business of this world, it can readily be seen that there are certain limitations as to the kind of business in which Christians may engage.[43]

This statement articulates a more integrated view of business. God wanted Baptists to be active in the business world without compromising their faith. The expectation that a Baptist businessman should practice moral separation and cultural integration simultaneously was a severe test. It was one that many would fail.

Wealth and worldliness lay at the heart of Baptist worries about business. While business gave Baptists more personal resources, it also challenged their perspective on the world. Baptist leaders were quick to appreciate the role of business as an agent of cultural integration. Their fear was that Baptist businessmen would abandon their spiritual values and embrace worldly ones. As it happened, their fears were well-founded.

"Getting All Our Honest Share": Business from the Central Canadian Baptist Businessman's Perspective

Throughout the nineteenth and early twentieth centuries, the reconciliation of business life with religious belief remained highly problematic for many central Canadian Baptist businessmen. The solutions offered by these businessmen through their personal advice, counsel, and modelling deserve careful consideration. Beginning in the mid-nineteenth century, two distinct philosophies of business developed within the Baptist community. Culturally conservative Baptist businessmen welcomed the arrival of capitalism but stayed committed to moral separation from the world. Cultural liberals embraced capitalism, professed belief in separation, but increasingly participated in cultural integration. These liberals altered traditional Baptist priorities. They placed social respectability above moral separation, material gain ahead of spiritual growth, and business success before personal stewardship. By the late nineteenth century, the response

---

43. "Christianity and Everyday Business," *CB*, July 20, 1922.

of Baptist businessmen to the rise of a business-dominated culture had become even more fragmented. The conservative and liberal philosophies of earlier years had given way to four philosophies that defined the business-religion relationship more diversely.

In the early nineteenth century, there were few Baptist businessmen in central Canada. Yet, the impressions and reflections that remain give some insight into their view of business. Clearly, many retained their old country values: frugality, industry, fairness, and charity. The example of Alexander Stewart, who emigrated from Scotland with his family and arrived in York in the autumn of 1818, is typical. For ten years, he taught school and engaged in an itinerant ministry. In March 1829, Stewart decided to open his own business as a land agent from his residence located at 76 Yonge Street. In the same year, he became the first "President" of the Baptist Church at York.[44]

Stewart worked hard in the land business, and like many other Baptist businessmen of the time, he faced numerous practical challenges to his faith. The issue of balancing Christian charity with the need to make a living was a constant source of challenge. In a letter to his assistant, William Taylor, Stewart's curt instructions reveal a sense of frustration: "We cannot live on wind working for strangers-charge them 3/ each for my trouble and postage. I work cheap but not grates [sic] except for friends."[45] In the same letter, Stewart agonized over what to do about overdue accounts: "But I must tell you Herbert Matthews has long been sick. I was at his house and I fear his recovery. He offers land, in Orilla at 1 1/2 dollars per acre but I find no purchaser. He owes £15.10 besides interest—am I to sue him or not?"[46] In a later letter to fellow Baptist John Sinclair of Lobo Township, Middlesex County, Stewart complained of mistreatment and failure on the part of his coreligionists to be fair in their business dealings with him: "I am very willing to serve my friends, but I must live and when they reap the benefit

---

44. This information on Alexander Stewart is based on Ivison and Rosser, *Baptists in Upper Canada Before 1820*, 21, 123, 126, 148–49; "Advertisement," *Colonial Advocate*, December 18, 1826; "Death Notice of Rev. Alexander Stewart," *Christian Guardian*, June 24, 1840; "Died," *Examiner*, June 24, 1840. For Stewart's own account of his early days see Alexander Stewart, "Register of Sermons Preached," (MS 210) Box 11, Louis Melzack Collection, Thomas Fisher Rare Book Library [hereafter TFRBL]. For a biography of Stewart, see Tomlinson, *From Scotland to Canada*.

45. Alexander Stewart to William Taylor, May 18, 1833, Alexander Stewart Papers, File 1, E. W. Banting Collection, MTRL.

46. Alexander Stewart to William Taylor, May 18, 1833, Alexander Stewart Papers, File 1, E. W. Banting Collection, MTRL.

it is right that they should pay me fair wages—while I do not charge above half what others charge."[47] Making a living was not easily reconciled with the demands of faith for fairness and charity.

Stewart was not the only Baptist businessman who struggled with such issues. John Eglinton Maxwell served as a Baptist pastor in York in the 1830s and later rented out his Toronto properties from his home in upstate New York. His reflections and actions reinforce the notion that some Baptists retained conservative business values in Upper Canada. In 1834, after reading Burn's *Jolly Beggars* to his landlord, Robert Cathcart, a prominent Baptist dry goods merchant in Toronto, Maxwell reaffirmed his belief in old world Baptist values: "Indolence and ignorance are the parents of poverty."[48] Later in his diary, Maxwell recorded his disgust with an incident in which two of his fellow Baptists were the victims of fraud:

> Feb 20/1835—Came home with John Cramp and Higgins. They had been employed by one Mr. Lewis who had contracted with the corporation to lay the foot paths with planks; he employed them to do a portion of the work and ordered them to nail the planks with 4 inch spikes; he cleared out to the states; when the work was examined by a committee from the corporation they ordered them to do the work with 5 inch spikes as that had been the terms of the contract by the corporation with Lewis. They had to comply with this mandate and thus lost all their labour. How painful to reflect on the dishonesty of some individuals and to observe the great misery others often suffer on their account.[49]

Maxwell's lament reveals a keen awareness of the dangers and abuses that existed in the business world.

His reflection on the dishonesty and misfortune of others, however, did not prevent Maxwell from confronting those with whom he did business. The available evidence suggests that Maxwell held a high moral view of business practice. He expected other businessmen to hold similar values, and when they engaged in dishonesty, he threatened them with severe consequences:

> A slight inspection of the accounts may convince you that you have charged me twice for the repairing done by Mr. John

---

47. Alexander Stewart to John Sinclair, January 12, 1836, File 3, E. W. Banting Collection, MTRL.
48. John Eglinton Maxwell, *Diary*, November 14, 1834, 34. MTRL.
49. John Eglinton Maxwell, *Diary*, February 20, 1835, 69. MTRL.

Edwards.... I hope you will see it best for your honour and standing both as a man of business and a Christian to settle the matter with me as quickly as possible. Unless this is immediately done you oblige me to make a thorough investigation of the whole business in Toronto. And if you are willing to submit to a thorough and public investigation of the whole business be assured I am. The demand I have, I have against you for errors in the last ac[count] is £4.16.7.5 the items were fully spread out in my letter to you of June 22nd. I trust that you will see it your duty to pay the above sum immediately to Messrs Cathcart and McMaster, merchants King Street as to Mr. Thomas Bell, 15 City Buildings.[50]

This letter written to William Osborne on October 12, 1842, reveals Maxwell's commitment to integrity. Evidently, his threat produced the desired results. In a letter to Thomas Bell, dated October 27, 1842, Maxwell noted that "Mr. Osborne has promised in three letters lately received to refund all the overcharges and double charges in his account, so soon as his health, which he says is very bad, will permit him to look over the account."[51] With this the matter was finally settled to Maxwell's satisfaction.

While Baptist businessmen were theoretically committed to a similar view of business integrity, they sometimes disagreed over what constituted a breach of that integrity. In the late 1850s, at Bond Street Baptist Church in Toronto, for example, provision merchant William Davies and dry goods merchant William McMaster took opposite sides in a dispute over preferential payments to creditors.

A Baptist from Bond Street named Francis T. Parson started a business in commission merchandising. William Davies initially invested cash in the venture. After about a year and some "shocking bad purchases," Davies became convinced that "Parson knew nothing of the practical part of the business" and with "ruin staring him in the face," he decided to end his partnership with Parson and withdraw his investment.[52] Parson agreed to pay Davies £250 immediately and the remaining balance of £600 in two instalments at six months and twelve months, respectively. Davies was guaranteed the interest-bearing rate of 10 percent. Before the second note came due Parson declared bankruptcy.[53]

50. John Eglinton Maxwell to William Osborne, October 12, 1842, Letterbook. MTRL.
51. John Eglinton Maxwell to Thomas Bell, October 27, 1842, Letterbook. MTRL.
52. William Davies to James Davies, June 18, 1859, WDP, Box 4044, File 2, UWORC.
53. William Davies to James Davies, June 18, 1859, WDP, Box 4044, File 2, UWORC.

Instead of paying Davies the remaining balance, Parson made preferential assignments to fellow Baptists William McMaster, the prominent wholesale dry goods merchant and Thomas Lailey, a wholesale clothier, both of whom held promissory notes but no other stake in the business.[54] Davies and his supporters protested, but the McMaster faction supported Parson and succeeded in imposing their will on the church.[55] As shoemaker William Langley Jr., a Davies supporter, later wrote, "Justice was mocked, fraud was whitewashed, and dishonesty encouraged."[56] The result of this conflict was the withdrawal of the Davies faction and the subsequent formation of Albert Street Baptist Tabernacle.

The Parson affair was important for many reasons. First, it signaled the development of differing business philosophies within Toronto's Baptist business community. Liberals like McMaster and Lailey were willing to adopt current commercial standards of morality at the expense of fairness to a fellow Baptist when the situation favored them. In contrast, conservative businessmen, like William Davies, were committed to a biblical morality that demanded just treatment in business matters regardless of the current worldly wisdom. They saw McMaster and his ilk as "commercial tricksters" who made the church of Christ their "refuge."[57]

Second, this incident showed the beginning of a more tolerant attitude towards bankruptcy. As Douglas Mccalla has noted, "It was common for nineteenth century observers to find the causes of business success or failure very much in the personal behaviour and characteristics of the businessman."[58] Baptists were certainly no exception in this regard. However, the refusal by the McMaster faction to discipline Parson ran counter to the traditional Baptist method of handling such cases. We shall return to this issue later. For now, it is sufficient to note that some Baptists had by the mid-nineteenth century begun to weigh circumstances more than character in their decisions about bankruptcy.

The gradual abandonment by some Liberal Baptist businessmen of certain traditional attitudes concerning fairness and bankruptcy did not mean that they suddenly changed their worldview. Old values died hard. Even the most liberal continued to profess a belief in industry,

---

54. William Davies to James Davies, June 18, 1859, WDP, Box 4044, File 2, UWORC.

55. For a complete account of the Parson affair from the perspective of the Davies faction see Langley Jr., *Correct Statement*.

56. Langley Jr., *Correct Statement*, 13.

57. Langley Jr., *Correct Statement*, 13.

58. McCalla, *Upper Canada Trade*, 151.

frugality, and fairness. In a speech on hard work given in 1873, Thomas S. Shenston, a Baptist businessman living in Brantford, offered his advice concerning "the road to comparative wealth" to a fictional young man he named "Jim."[59] Shenston's advice to the working-class apprentice included all of the conservative values which lay at the heart of the Baptist business ethos. First, he extolled the virtue of hard work: "If you are now where I hope and expect you are-that is an industrious, painstaking, obliging & tidy youth, putting forth your best exertions to master your trade-you are already a good way on the road to its [the acquisition of comparative wealth] realization."[60]

Next, Shenston stressed the need for a moral lifestyle. Shenston listed eleven practices that he adopted during his apprenticeship that put him on the road to comparative wealth:

> 1st I never read any but good books.
>
> 2nd I always lived within my income, which was only $45 the first year and $65 the last. 3rd I never spent $1 on tobacco or any other trash.
>
> 4th I never drank a drop of spirituous liquors.
>
> 5th I never took God's name in vain.
>
> 6th When well, I was never absent from the house of God on the Sabbath day.
>
> 7th I never was inside a saloon, tavern, circus or show.
>
> 8th I earned at "overwork" $25, being paid 12 1/2 cents an hour after 9 o'clock.
>
> 9th I never joined a band.
>
> 10th I never joined a fire company.
>
> 11th I never went out of town to play a "return match."[61]

For Shenston, it was "as plain as the road to market that young men should ac[cept] all these eleven things as part of the price to comparative wealth."[62]

---

59. For a biographical sketch of Thomas Shenston, see *Dictionary of Canadian Biography*, 12:967–68.
60. Shenston, "Speech on Hard Work," 8.
61. Shenston, "Speech on Hard Work," 21.
62. Shenston, "Speech on Hard Work," 21.

Third, Shenston argued that character was far more important than social status or wealth:

> Many foolishly imagine the only difference between the employers and the employees to be that the former have money and the latter have not. This is a very great mistake. Money is certainly most valuable, but I am strongly of the opinion that its value is generally very much overestimated. A young man at the age of twenty years with a good character and a good trade is richer than one with no trade and a bad character.[63]

Success lay in having a character above reproach. Shenston maintained that his own climb up the social ladder, from apprentice, to business partner, and ultimately to business owner, had nothing to do with luck and everything to do with hard work, planning, and good character:

> Do not think that you can be a smoking, spitting, cursing, swearing spendthrift till you are thirty years of age and then suddenly turn over a new leaf and think that will at once secure the confidence of all around you.... My unlucky friend confidence does not grow up in a night like a mushroom, but is of very slow growth. You must not expect to plant the stone of confidence today and eat the peach of results tomorrow.[64]

The confidence of others was earned through the careful cultivation of sterling character. According to Shenston, there was nothing sinister about the capitalist economic system or one's place in the social hierarchy:

> A very erroneous impression is entertained by the unlucky class, that those, who think they are lucky, desire to keep them down. Thirty years of experience in business, has convinced me to the contrary. Everybody that is deserving of confidence, and a great many that are not, can get as much credit and more than they ought to have.[65]

Thus, Shenston revealed his belief in the essential fairness of Canada's capitalist economic system. He was confident that men of worthy character would experience success.

On the question of using credit, Shenston advised caution. In his view, cash was always preferable. Although Shenston admitted that "frugality is one of the most difficult things to practice in these days"

63. Shenston, "Speech on Hard Work," 23.
64. Shenston, "Speech on Hard Work," 25.
65. Shenston, "Speech on Hard Work," 27 [mismarked 26].

he retained the traditional Baptist view that it was "essential in order to obtain comparative wealth."⁶⁶ Paying cash might put one out of step with the prevailing culture, but it protected against bankruptcy: "Notwithstanding the road to comparative wealth is an economical road and those who travel it must disregard fashion and jeers, yet it is not without its solid comforts of which the embarrassed bankrupts know nothing!"⁶⁷ Shenston then asked an important rhetorical question: "Is it not as plain as the road to market, that by paying cash instead of purchasing on 6 months credit that you will save 5 and 6 percent on each purchase?"⁶⁸ The answer for him, at least, was obvious.

Shenston also used his speech to advance his own political beliefs. With the recent Liberal victory of 1873 still in the minds of his audience, Shenston used fellow Baptist and Liberal Alexander Mackenzie and Liberal Edward Blake as his models of business success in Canada. He cautioned young Jim, however, to be realistic: "If God has not given the talents of an Alexander McKenzie [sic] or an Edmund Blake [sic], do not aim to reach their altitude . . . but content yourself with improving as best you can the abilities you have, which no doubt are equal to that of the great mass of mankind."⁶⁹ Shenston shared the Liberal view that success in business was the result of persistent self-effort and constant self-improvement.

Despite Shenston's Liberal political views, his advice stood well within the boundaries of traditional conservative Baptist thought concerning business. His advice was intended to encourage young men to adopt the values and methods that had proved successful in his own business life. The philosophy of industry, frugalness, and fairness espoused by Shenston drew heavily on past experience, Baptist teaching, and current models.

66. Shenston, "Speech on Hard Work," 28.
67. Shenston, "Speech on Hard Work," 31.
68. Shenston, "Speech on Hard Work," 33 [mismarked 31].
69. Shenston, "Speech on Hard Work," 8. Edmund Blake is probably Edward Blake, an evangelical Anglican who became the Liberal Premier of Ontario in 1871. In 1873, he was a minister without portfolio in the Mackenzie government. Alexander Mackenzie was Prime Minister from 1873 to 1878. Although his family was Presbyterian, Mackenzie became a Baptist. He joined a Baptist church outside Sarnia, and while in Ottawa, he attended First Baptist Church. He became a member of Jarvis Street Baptist Church, Toronto in 1879. For details of Mackenzie's religious experience and convictions, see Thomson, *Alexander Mackenzie*, 9–10, 26, 179, 211, 261, 299, 345. For a record of the Mackenzie family becoming members of Jarvis Street, see *Jarvis Street Baptist Church Minute Book, 1866–1881* (MS) January 15, January 24, February 2, 1879. JSBCA.

Another important exponent of the late nineteenth century Baptist view of business was William Kirkpatrick McNaught. His career closely followed the path espoused by Shenston. In 1867, McNaught worked in Toronto with fellow Baptist, William Hewitt Sr., who had a hardware store located at 111 Yonge Street. The following year McNaught became an apprentice to Robert Wilkes, under whom he learned the wholesale jewellery, cutlery, and plated ware business. By 1877, McNaught was a junior partner in the firm of Zimmerman, McNaught & Company. In 1879, the ambitious McNaught founded *The Trader and Canadian Jeweller*, a trade paper that became the organ of the Canadian jewellery trade. In 1884, he purchased a half interest in the watch case factory of R. J. Quigley. A year later, "The American Watch Case Company" was formed.[70]

In the pages of *The Trader*, McNaught articulated his philosophy of business. Like Shenston, McNaught offered his readers an essentially conservative view. His advice covered a wide range of issues. On the subject of business integrity McNaught had much to say. In typical Baptist fashion he argued for honesty, cooperation, industry, fairness, and perseverance. He also opposed the growing practice of using long-term credit. Perhaps the best summary of McNaught's values is found in a poem entitled "A Psalm for the Trade," which appeared in the February 1885 issue of *The Trader*:

> Tell us not in doleful numbers,
> Trade is done forevermore,
> That supply, demand outnumbers,
> And the drummer's days are o'er.
> Trade is real-trade is active,
> Better times again we'll see;
> To remain stagnation's captive,
> Is against all history.
> Time is long-bills maturing,
> Must be paid without delay;
> Such the only way insuring
> Better trade at early day.

---

70. The biographical information in this paragraph is based on Fraser, *History of Ontario*, 563–65; *Toronto Board of Trade*, 190; *Canadian Manufacturer*, May 1, 1891; Morgan, *Canadian Men and Women of the Time*, 788; Wallace, *Macmillan Dictionary of Canadian Biography*, 484.

> Shun this reckless competition,
> Look beyond the moment's gain,
> Learn that honest coalition,
> Is far better in the main.
> Stop this scheme of future dating,
> Ere it has become too late;
> Act at once and cease all prating
> Leave consignments to their fate.
> Lives of others all remind us,
> If our dealing's just and fair,
> That a better time will find us,
> Getting all our honest share.[71]

McNaught's optimistic conviction, that the trade cycle would eventually right itself, was a view shared by other entrepreneurs. Through organizations like the Canadian Manufacturers Association, McNaught worked hard to secure legislation that would protect business interests.[72] In the editorial columns of *The Trader* he regularly declared his view on the important business issues of the day. On the delicate subject of insolvency legislation, McNaught proclaimed: "What we want is an Insolvent Act at once, simple, expeditious and cheap, three qualities which are wholly lacking in the present Act."[73] In 1880, during a respite from the severe and prolonged depression following the Panic of 1873, McNaught offered his business readers an optimistic view of the economic turnaround and a strong word of warning:

> Without doubt, it can now be safely said that the long looked for "good times" have come again. . . . Inspite of what "old croakers" say, there is not the slightest doubt but that we are now fairly round the corner and on the highway to prosperity. . . . The fact the times are now good will not, we trust, lead to over speculation, one of the greatest evils to befall any business community; rather let them husband their resources and prepare for the period of depression which in a few years must follow

---

71. "Psalm for the Trade," *Trader and Canadian Jeweller*, February 1885.

72. For information on McNaught's involvement see Clark, *Canadian Manufacturers Association*, 14, 16–17, 37–39, 64n3, 86n18. McNaught was President of the CMA in 1891–1892.

73. *Trader*, December 1879. The underline is in the original version of this statement.

over trading. A great many traders in good times, when trade is brisk, and they are making money, are apt to put on too much style and spend more money on themselves than their circumstances will warrant; in commen parlance "they feel their oats," another very fruitful source of commercial disaster, which can easily be avoided if they would only exercise caution.... The careful man is generally the successful one.[74]

In this statement, McNaught stayed true to Baptist values; cautious conservatism remained the Baptist formula for business success. His advice to absconding debtors in 1882 was equally conservative and frank: "An honest man, although an insolvent, while he may not like to have to ask the leniency of his creditors, he has or ought to have the courage to meet his debtors face to face and state his case and ask his sympathy and assistance."[75] Like his other statements, this one contained a high moral tone that held the individual businessman wholly responsible for his commercial failures.

The conservative advice and values of both Shenston and McNaught reflected the Baptist belief that one must practice good stewardship in every area of life. Their undeniable support for the capitalist system grew out of a belief that honest, patient, individual entrepreneurship would be rewarded with profits and prosperity in this life. This shift in focus from otherworldliness to worldly success through business represented a fundamental alteration in Baptist thought.

By the early twentieth century, the range of thought concerning business among Baptists showed signs of fragmentation. Fundamentalists, like T. T. Shields, the pastor of Jarvis Street Baptist Church in Toronto, became convinced that many Baptist businessmen had compromised their faith. According to Shields, by 1920, many Baptist businessmen had abandoned "entire separation" from the world and accepted a "respectable worldliness" that allowed them to disregard their stewardship and to participate freely in worldly amusements like dancing, card-playing, and theatre-going.[76] Occasionally, a prominent Baptist businessmen offered advice and evidence that supported the fundamentalist view. In a 1908 article written on behalf of the Laymen's Missionary Movement, for example, James Ryrie, a wealthy jeweller from Jarvis Street Baptist Church, admitted that, "In the past too often it has been the fag ends of our energy and means

74. *Trader*, November 1880.
75. "Absconding Debtors," *Trader*, August 1882.
76. Shields, *Plot That Failed*, 126, 204, 210.

only that have been devoted to this [the extension of the Lord's kingdom at home and abroad]-what has been left over after the demands of social, business and public life have been satisfied."[77]

In the Spring of 1919, J. N. Shenstone, the son of Thomas Shenston, Treasurer of the Massey-Harris Manufacturing Company and a member of Walmer Road Baptist Church, echoed Ryrie's analysis in an address entitled "Stewardship In Business."[78] In what amounted to an admission that many Baptist businessmen had forgotten their stewardship obligations, Shenstone used the first part of Deut 8:18, "Thou shalt remember Jehovah, thy God, for it is He who giveth thee power to get wealth," to remind his fellow Baptists that "The power to work in steel, to buy and sell, to command men, is of God."[79] Furthermore, Shenstone noted that "Stewardship in business means God's will respecting our time and our wealth."[80] Statements such as these gave credence to fundamentalist claims that stewardship among the denomination's businessmen was waning.

Businessmen also provided fundamentalists with evidence of moral compromise in the area of worldly amusements. According to T. T. Shields, in an address to the Toronto Baptist Ministerial Association in November of 1920, Samuel John Moore, the Sunday School Superintendent of Dovercourt Road Baptist Church, Toronto, Director of the Bank of Nova Scotia and President of Pacific Burt Company and F. N. Burt Company, "expressed the view that the addiction of professing Christian people to . . . [worldly] amusements was greatly retarding, if not wholly paralysing, the efforts of the churches."[81] Even more disturbing to Shields was Moore's contention that "that he could not think of even half a dozen of the 'leading' Baptist laymen who would share his view as to what the Christian attitude toward these worldly amusements should be."[82] Moore's statements confirmed what fundamentalist moral reformers like Shields had long suspected; business had promoted moral compromise among the faithful.

77. "James Ryrie, Toronto," *CB*, January 23, 1904.

78. The difference in the spelling of the last name, Shenston(e), coincides with the spelling used by the principals.

79. "Stewardship in Business," *CB*, March 6, 1919.

80. "Stewardship in Business," *CB*, March 6, 1919.

81. Shields, *Plot That Failed*, 210. I am basing Moore's view on Shield's summary of the address.

82. Shields, *Plot That Failed*, 210.

At Jarvis Street Baptist Church, Shields followed the lead of American fundamentalists like John Roach Straton, pastor of Calvary Baptist Church in New York City, and on February 13, 1921, he preached his famous sermon on amusements in which he denounced those Christians who had become "lovers of pleasure more than lovers of God."[83] In the conclusion to his message Shields challenged any of his deacons "who thinks more of an evening at the theatre, of the diversion of a game of cards, or of the pleasure of the dance, than of the interests of a soul for whom Christ died" to make the choice to "resign either his pleasure or his office."[84]

Many of the deacons at Jarvis Street were businessmen. This sermon was an important event in crystallizing their opposition to Shields and a major post on the long road to what would become the Jarvis Street schism of 1921. Beyond its significance for Jarvis Street, this sermon illustrates that some fundamentalists had, by the post-war period, become convinced that Baptist businessmen had failed to pass the tests of faith issued by the secular business world. To fundamentalists, the Baptist businessman's desire for sociocultural integration often led to the abandonment of stewardship and separation.

While fundamentalists represented the extreme in their view of business, the majority of Baptists remained committed to their evangelical roots. Baptist evangelicals encouraged businessmen to maintain a balance between sociocultural integration and moral separation. In other words, evangelicals believed that businessmen could pursue their vocations in the world without taking on the moral standards of the world.

The views expressed in 1907 by R. D. Warren, Manager of the Standard Publishing Company (which published *The Canadian Baptist*) and President of the Baptist Convention of Ontario and Quebec, typify the evangelical line of reasoning. Warren instructed young men to "choose your business vocation in life not with a view to dollars and cents only, but rather with a view to your special adaptabilities, and to the opportunities which this or that calling or profession will afford you for the development of the best that is in you."[85] True to the evangelical willingness to accommodate the new materialistic social ethic within their religious framework, he also advised young Baptists to "Enter upon your business or professional life with the fixed purpose of making your business a success financially

---

83. Shields, *Plot That Failed*, 217. Shields prints the entire text of the sermon.
84. Shields, *Plot That Failed*, 228.
85. "New Year's Message," *CB*, January 3, 1907.

... in order that you may be able, in the highest measure possible, to help in the prosecution of Christian work."[86]

In addition to these instructions, Warren offered his view of the ideal lifestyle:

> Of course as business men there are certain fixed principles that must always have our attention. Personal and home wants must be attended to. Reasonable heed must be given to the social demands which business relations may involve. But our business life should be so balanced that the Lord's work should ever receive its full share of money, time and energy.[87]

For evangelicals like Warren, a balanced lifestyle that allowed business to flourish, home life to thrive, and the Lord's work to move ahead was the ideal that every Baptist should seek. While in theory the evangelical view of business kept all things in their proper perspective and place, the achievement of a balance between integration and separation would prove elusive for many Baptist businessmen.

While Warren's views represented the general evangelical perspective concerning business, not all evangelical Baptists agreed on the degree of cultural accommodation that they should practice. As George Rawlyk has pointed out, in the period between 1880 and 1914, Baptist evangelicals were divided into conservative and liberal camps.[88] While they worked together harmoniously during this period, they held increasingly divergent theological and cultural views.

Conservative evangelicals allowed the businessman to pursue sociocultural integration, but they placed strict moral limits on the extent of such integration. These evangelicals stood firm in their commitment to a traditional biblical basis for Baptist teaching on business ethics, amusements, and stewardship. Conservative evangelicals continued to look to the Scriptures and their church for moral guidance.

Liberal evangelicals took a more tolerant approach that left decisions concerning theology and culture to the individual. Under this ideology, each businessman was given more freedom in deciding how far to go with integration and what constituted moral business practice. Liberals allowed business to reshape their religion to a far greater extent than their conservative brethren. Financial and administrative

---

86. "New Year's Message," *CB*, January 3, 1907.
87. "New Year's Message," *CB*, January 3, 1907.
88. Rawlyk, "A. L. McCrimmon," 38–39.

methods learned in the business world were brought by liberals into the church context. At the personal level, liberals were often willing to compromise their business ethics for the sake of material success, and they often showed a willingness to engage in activities and lifestyles that more conservative Baptists found objectionable. As Rawlyk has noted, it was to this group that many "of the emerging central Canadian Baptist commercial elite belonged."[89]

At the opposite extreme to the fundamentalists were what might be called the liberal-modernists. These Baptists made it their objective to encourage the free flow of ideas and eliminate the remaining religious barriers to sociocultural integration. In the theological realm, such liberals questioned creationism and biblical infallibility. They also demanded that Baptist theology and practice be made relevant to current social and economic realities. For some Baptist businessmen, the liberal-modernist position offered a means of rationalizing their unrelenting pursuit of self-reliance and worldly respectability. For others, like Toronto clothing manufacturer John Northway, owner of John Northway and Son Limited, the acceptance of liberal-modernist theology required the Baptist businessman to pursue the noble objectives of social and economic justice. For Northway this meant the encouragement of co-operation between workers and management and a more equitable approach to profit distribution through profit-sharing.[90] Liberal-modernists were at the forefront of encouraging Baptist integration within the Canadian cultural mainstream.

In the years following the First World War, Baptists became increasingly polarized in their views of businessmen. As the theological and cultural battle lines between fundamentalists and modernists became more fixed, Baptist businessmen were under increasing pressure to declare their allegiance to sociocultural integration or separation. The tolerance of a Baptist evangelical consensus that allowed conservative evangelicals and liberal evangelicals to live in harmony between 1880 and 1914 disappeared when the businessman's lifestyle became an important element in the fundamentalist-modernist controversies of the 1920s. Many Baptist businessmen were caught in the crossfire of opposing theological and cultural views, convictions that both desired the support of the businessman.

89. Rawlyk, "A. L. McCrimmon," 39.

90. For details concerning Northway's progressive outlook and his profit-sharing plan see Wilson, *John Northway*, 173–87.

In the final analysis, central Canadian Baptists found business involvement highly problematic. While they supported and encouraged the arrival of capitalism, fundamentalist and some conservative evangelical Baptists propagated the view that the wealth and worldliness associated with business contributed to a decline in religious commitment in the late nineteenth and early twentieth centuries. By the end of the First World War, these Baptists were resolved to hold Baptist businessmen accountable for their choice of lifestyle. Purity of faith and practice, they argued, must be dominant. As self-appointed guardians of the faith, these Baptists kept a watchful eye on the denomination's businessmen.

The view of business as adopted by culturally liberal Baptists, which included many prominent businessmen, tried to harmonize the interests of religion and business. In a masterstroke of rationalization, liberal Baptists advanced the view that material success served a spiritual purpose, namely, the earthly expansion of the Kingdom of God. Without the material prosperity that business provided, the church would lack the resources needed to fulfil its mission. Thus, business was an honorable and essential calling in which the material benefits to be gained far outweighed any spiritual risks to be endured.

As we shall see in the next four chapters, the impact of secular business on church life and personal relationships within one specific congregation, that of Jarvis Street Baptist Church was dramatic. As business came to dominate Canadian culture in the last half of the nineteenth century, the church had to confront the conflicts between members that secular business produced. It also had to deal with the growing belief that the sacred religious world had much to learn from the secular business world. That abandonment of separation and stewardship for sociocultural integration and materialism by the church's businessmen also proved troublesome. In Jarvis Street, business helped to secularize religion and the effects were felt within the church context and beyond.

Chapter 3

Business in the Church
The Beginning of Secularization,
1848–1880

WHEN DID THE SECULARIZATION process begin for the Baptist businessman? This is a difficult question. Secularization affected every individual differently. Still, the secularizing effects of business on religion are clearly evident at certain points in the Canadian Baptist experience. Without question, the introduction of business methods to church administration and the church disruptions caused by secular business disputes profoundly altered the content and conduct of Baptist life.

In the particular case of Jarvis Street Baptist Church, the impact of business on both the individual businessman and church life, between 1848 and 1880, was dramatic. Disputes among members over secular business matters grew more frequent and disruptive as increasing numbers of businessmen joined the congregation. Church leaders and members often served as arbitrators in complex secular business matters that, on at least two occasions, resulted in major schisms. Unprepared and unqualified to settle disagreements over secular business matters, Baptist leaders both within and outside Jarvis Street called for the church to withdraw from this task in the 1860s. By the late nineteenth century, the responsibility for settling a secular business dispute with a fellow Baptist no longer lay with the congregation but with the individuals involved.

One purpose of this chapter is to demonstrate that the businessmen and pastors of Jarvis Street redefined the boundaries between sacred and secular and slowly implemented the removal of the congregation from its role as arbitrator in disagreements over secular business deals. By 1880, instead of bringing a dispute to the public forum of an open church meeting, members were expected to settle their differences over secular business personally and privately. This shift of responsibility from congregation to individual represented a retreat on the part of what would become one of Canada's premier Baptist churches. No longer would this Baptist congregation intervene in business matters that adversely affected the personal relationships of its members. At Jarvis Street, the contemporary secular axiom that "business is business and religion is religion" was becoming reality.[1]

In the area of church administration, the impact of business was also significant. As businessmen assumed positions of church leadership at Jarvis Street, they introduced a more businesslike approach to the management of the church's fiscal affairs. Increasingly, from the mid-nineteenth century, the church was dominated by members of the central Canadian Baptist business elite who demanded careful administration, a strong organizational structure, highly qualified pastors, and church programs that could rival the best that other denominations had to offer.

This chapter covers four important topics: An explication of Baptist theory concerning church divisions, discipline, and disputes; a brief history of Jarvis Street Baptist Church; a consideration of specific business disputes within the Jarvis Street congregation; and an overview of the introduction of business methods at Jarvis Street. Exploration of these subjects will reveal how secularization of the Baptist businessman began.

Division, Discipline, and Disputes in the Canadian Baptist Context

While the issues of division in the church, discipline, and private disputes among members have remained a constant concern throughout Christian church history, the attention given to these issues by nineteenth century Canadian Baptists was particularly intense. Theoretically, Baptists believed that each of these issues was to be addressed within the local church. Using biblical instructions—such as those given in the

---

1. For a contemporary discussion of this axiom, see "Doing It on Business Principles," *CB*, August 1, 1878. For later views see the sermons by B. D. Thomas, "How to Make the Best of Both Worlds," *CB*, August 22, 1907; T. T. Shields, "Christian Business Men," *CB*, January 25, 1914, T. T. Shields Papers, JSBCA.

Pauline epistles to the early church—as their guide and standard, many Canadian Baptist churches exercised a high degree of control over the moral practices of their members.[2]

In the early and mid-nineteenth century, strict conformity to the moral dictates of the church was both expected and encouraged. As the country became more urbanized, industrialized, and commercialized, many Baptist churches found their definitions of "proper" morality inadequate to meet the new complex moral challenges and questions that were the by-products of profound social and economic change. In particular, the problem of how to respond to the ethical challenges raised by a business-dominated culture troubled many Baptist congregations. By the late nineteenth century, some Baptist churches had followed the Methodists and Presbyterians in redefining their moral role in business matters by placing increasing responsibility for moral choices on the individual. Like other Protestant denominations, Baptists relaxed their discipline for business-related offenses. Moreover, Baptist churches relied more heavily on the secular court system to settle cases that had previously been within their prerogative.

The fear of schism or a permanent church split was constant for Canadian Baptists in the nineteenth century. Warnings to be on guard against internal strife and discord were common. An article taken from the *Examiner* on "Division in Churches" for example, appeared in the January 2, 1873, issue of *The Canadian Baptist*. The article declared that "notwithstanding the many inspired exhortations to be of the same mind, to the exercise of brotherly love, patience, forbearance, long-suffering, and forgiveness, the instances are common and numerous where churches are divided and weakened by their divisions."[3] Many Ontario Baptists knew from their own bitter experience that this statement was true.

By mid-century internal turmoil and division over doctrinal and personal issues had clearly visited many Baptist churches in the province. In 1822, at the first Regular Baptist church in Oxford Township, for example, disagreement over access to the Lord's Supper and the decision by several leading members, including Darius Cross and James Harris, to accept Arminian or "Free Will" doctrine resulted in a schism and the subsequent formation of a Free Communion Baptist church in the town of Oxford (Woodstock).[4] The Regular Baptist church in Oxford

2. See, for example, Eph 5:1–21; 1 Cor 6:1–8; Gal 6:1–10; 1 Thes 4:1–12.
3. "Division In Churches," *CB*, January 2, 1873.
4. Ivison and Rosser, *Baptists in Upper and Lower Canada*, 116.

Township was also troubled by disputes over a handkerchief, a piece of cloth, and a bargain over some rope.[5] In what became Talbot Street Baptist Church, London, quarrels over the administration of the Lord's Supper, the suitability of the pastor, and the scriptural validity of the office of church clerk, caused internal division in the late 1840s and 1850s.[6] Toronto Baptists particularly experienced the ravages of internal strife and schism, as we shall see.

The reasons for disunity were numerous. Among them were personal business rivalries and the desire for prominence and notoriety. In addition, Baptist immigrants brought with them strong and often conflicting convictions about church doctrine and polity. As Canadian-born Robert Alexander Fyfe, an early pastor of March Street and later Bond Street Baptist Chapel in Toronto, observed:

> Without reflecting on the character of a single individual, it cannot have escaped the notice of the observant that in a new country, where immigrants from all points of the compass are thrown together, even good men of the "same faith" are often very illy adapted to work together. . . . Each one would think, when the work was not done as he had been accustomed to see it done, that there must be something very wrong, and his conscience could not sanction wrong.[7]

Clearly, before 1850, in the formative years of the Baptist church in Canada, ethnic and cultural differences and personal rivalry produced conflict.

Canadian Baptists also took the maintenance of church discipline and faith among church members seriously. The list of offenses for which members could be "excluded" was long.[8] Drunkenness, sexual

---

5. This information is based on a summary of the church minutes found in Hotson, *Pioneer Baptist Work in Oxford County*, 17.

6. Information concerning these divisions is found in Fox, *Century of Service*, 13–15, 19–21.

7. Fyfe, *Forty Years Survey*, 13.

8. Exclusion was the Baptist equivalent to excommunication. It meant that an individual lost their membership, the fellowship of other Baptists, and was not allowed to attend the church or to partake of the Lord's Supper. One practical problem related to exclusion was the Baptist belief in congregational autonomy. While one congregation might exclude an individual there was no way to stop another Baptist congregation from granting that individual membership. Exclusion was not a permanent state and could be revoked upon the confession and repentance of the offending party. For a discussion of exclusion and its effects on Baptists, see Elgee, *Social Teachings of the Christian Churches*, 84–86.

immorality, stealing, criticizing one's brother, and business improprieties such as fraud, embezzlement, or the failure to pay one's debts were among the more common reasons for discipline. Although, as historian William Sherwood Fox pointed out, "in conformity with true Christian charity, the door for genuine repentance was held open," failure to follow the articles of faith and practice almost always resulted in the offender's removal from membership.[9] On December 18, 1840, the First Baptist Church in Brantford, for example, "excluded" one of its members "for neglect of duty, and a capital crime."[10] For that same year, the total number of exclusions was five out of a membership that stood at eighty-two by year's end.[11] In 1819, at the first Baptist church organized in Oxford Township, Nancy Brink was excluded for joining a Methodist class.[12] In a Baptist congregation, discipline was strictly maintained.

Finally, until the late nineteenth century, it was assumed in central Canadian Baptist circles that private disputes among members would be settled in public church meetings. In part, this method of dispute resolution reflected the conditions present in frontier society. For Baptists in Ontario, the harshness of pioneer life encouraged an austere, disciplined, and communal approach to religion that as John Webster Grant has noted, "made for tightly knit communities" but "must also have contributed an element of instability."[13] Thus, when two members disagreed about a personal or business matter, the case was brought to the church for discussion and resolution. In accordance with Baptist polity, the matter would be put to a vote of the congregation, whose decision was considered binding on the parties involved.[14]

Whatever the conflict, members were encouraged to seek a speedy settlement within their individual church. A literal interpretation of certain New Testament passages led Canadian Baptists to forbid their brethren to take another Baptist to court.[15] As we shall see, however, as business

9. Fox, *Century of Service*, 8. Fred Landon made a similar point in his *Western Ontario and the American Frontier*, 105–6.

10. Shenston, *Jubilee Review*, 14.

11. Shenston, *Jubilee Review*, 14.

12. Landon, *Western Ontario*, 105.

13. Grant, *Profusion of Spires*, 58. For the connection between frontier conditions and religion, see Elgee, *Social Teachings of the Christian Churches*, 82–86.

14. For evidence that this polity was followed, see Hotson, *Pioneer Baptist Work*, 11; Landon, *Western Frontier*, 106.

15. The most important passage was 1 Cor 6:1–8. "Dare any of you, having a matter against another, go to law before the unjust, and not before the saints? Do ye not know

disputes grew more complex and intense, this principle was frequently disregarded. One Baptist businessman might take another to court if he lost confidence in the church's ability to render a just judgement.

Theoretically, then, Canadian Baptists had both a theological basis and a practical framework for handling divisions, discipline, and disputes in the church. But the potential for trouble arising out of ethnic diversity, personal rivalry, and differing Baptist backgrounds loomed large for Baptist immigrants to Upper Canada. These challenges were largely unrecognized by pioneer Baptists as they struggled to establish themselves in a new and often hostile land. Once the overriding concern for survival had passed, however, and a greater number of Baptists achieved material prosperity, Baptist theology and its disciplinary structure were severely tested. This can be further exemplified by the experience of Jarvis Street Baptist Church.

Jarvis Street Baptist Church: A Brief History to 1875

"The mother church, now worshipping in its beautiful home on Jarvis Street, originated October 16, 1829, when appears the first written record."[16] This statement by E. O. White, in his 1901 *Baptist Calendar*, helped to standardize a false chronology of Baptist church origins in Toronto which has only recently been revised.[17] It is the intention here to set out accurately the background and development of the Baptist faith in Toronto.

Exactly when Baptist activity in Toronto began is difficult to establish with certainty. It is clear, as John Webster Grant has observed, that "the Baptists, who had a later start, never rivalled the Methodists in numbers"

---

that the saints shall judge the world? and if the world shall be judged by you, are ye unworthy to judge the smallest matters? Know ye not that we shall angels? how much more things that pertain to this life? If then you have judgments of things pertaining to this life, set them to judge who are least esteemed in the church. I speak to your shame. Is it so, that there is not a wise man among you? no, not one that shall be able to judge between his brethren? But brother goeth to law with brother, and that before unbelievers. Now therefore there is utterly a fault among you, because ye go to law one with another. Why do ye not rather suffer yourselves to be defrauded? Nay, ye do wrong, and defraud, and that your brethren" (KJV).

16. White, *Perpetual Baptist Calendar*, 62.

17. Fountain and Tomlinson, *From Strength to Strength*, 9. See also Haykin and Paul, *Set for the Defense of the Gospel*.

in the Upper Province.[18] In York, the Baptist effort was begun in earnest with the arrival of Alexander Stewart in 1818. A native of Perthshire, Scotland, Stewart experienced personal rebirth or salvation after hearing a Baptist evangelist in the Scottish town of Moulin. After preaching near Perth, Scotland, for a short time, Stewart came to Canada with his family and immediately set about the task of establishing a Baptist church in his adopted country.[19] In recalling the events of 1818, John Menzies, a Baptist who later became a member of the Disciples of Christ, noted,

> Brother Stewart from Perth and family came out then and we came up with them to York [now Toronto] and when we spent a few days there we found out that a few disciples that were like sheep that had no "shephard" [sic]. We formed the first Baptist Church that ever was in that place, where we continued about a year and a half, during which time several came to the place and joined the church.[20]

Here, then, was the beginning of the Baptist Church at York. The church struggled to survive, facing stiff competition from other religious sects who sought to gain a foothold in York at Baptist expense. "Shortly before we left Toronto," Menzies stated, "a few of the members embraced new sentiments, and altho, [sic] they were baptized and were several years with the churches in the Old Country, they withdrew from the church and maintained that they did not believe the Gospel till then and were not baptized."[21] Desertion to rival religious sects was only one of many problems encountered by York Baptists. When, in the spring of 1820, Menzies and Stewart carried their message to "the woods," York Baptists were again left leaderless.[22]

Internal strife also took its toll. A disagreement between Menzies and Stewart over "some worldly matters"[23] resulted in "the separation of

---

18. Grant, *Profusion of Spires*, 224.

19. For a biography of Stewart and a more detailed account of early Baptist activity in York (Toronto), see Tomlinson, *From Scotland to Canada*.

20. John Menzies to Elder Archibald Cameron, January 12, 1841. John Menzies Biographical File, CBA.

21. John Menzies to Elder Archibald Cameron, January 12, 1841. John Menzies Biographical File, CBA.

22. John Menzies to Elder Archibald Cameron, January 12, 1841. John Menzies Biographical File, CBA.

23. There are no specifics concerning what caused the disagreement. Stewart and Menzies may have held different views of a business matter or another lifestyle issue.

the church."[24] According to Menzies, "the most part" of the disgruntled members "joined those very men, that they parted with in Toronto for, what they called Berean sentiments."[25]

Following his disagreement with Menzies in 1820, Alexander Stewart continued his missionary endeavors, and he taught school in Toronto Township. Ill health forced him to return to York in 1826, where he commenced business as a land agent and gave the tiny Baptist congregation assertive leadership. Stewart's efforts to attract hearers included advertising in the *Colonial Advocate*: "A. Stewart . . . preaches every Lord's day (and will continue to do so regularly) at 11 o'clock forenoon, and at 6 o'clock PM in Mr. Patfield's School House."[26] Stewart's preaching activities became frequent and widespread. By 1828, Stewart's Sunday schedule included four services: one in Gaelic and three in English. Stewart also propagated his message by publishing his sermons.[27] In July 1827, William Lyon Mackenzie's printing house published Stewart's *Two Essays; The First On The Gospel; The Second, On The Kingdom Of Christ; And A Sermon On Baptism*. Orders for this pamphlet were received from Baptist

---

24. John Menzies to Elder Archibald Cameron, January 12, 1841. John Menzies Biographical File, CBA. The term "separation" is used here to refer to a church split or schism.

25. John Menzies to Elder Archibald Cameron, January 12, 1841. John Menzies Biographical File, CBA. The presence of "Berean" ideas in York is interesting. A Presbyterian minister named John Barclay founded the Bereans, also called Barclayites or Barclayans, at Edinburgh in 1773. Barclay taught a modified Calvinism, denied the existence of natural theology, stressed the supremacy of the Scriptures and the Holy Spirit's illumination of them as the keys to salvation by faith. While Canadian Baptists would have agreed with some of Barclay's ideas, his assertion that creation provided no proof for the existence of God stood in sharp contrast to their position that creation clearly testified to God's existence. Barclay also put forward biblical interpretations that clashes with the traditional Baptist view. He argued, for example, that the speaker in all first-person Psalms was Christ. Berean assemblies were founded in a number of Scottish and English cities in the late eighteenth century. After Barclay's death in 1798, most of the Berean congregations disappeared or joined the Congregationalists. For information on the Bereans, see *Dictionary of Scottish Church History and Theology*, 61–62; Escott, *History of Scottish Congregationalism*, 37–42; Bullock and Drummond, *Church in Victorian Scotland*, 1:45; 2:35; *Dictionary of National Biography*, 1:1086–87. For the Baptist position on natural theology see Fyfe, *Theological Lectures*, 4, 79; Farmer, *E. W. Dadson*, 136. For Barclay's view of the Psalms, see Barclay, *Preface to the Psalms*, 21.

26. *Colonial Advocate*, December 1, 1826.

27. Alexander Stewart, "Register of Sermons Preached," August 31, 1828. (MS) 210, Box 11, Louis Melzack Collection, TPRBL.

businessmen like James Lesslie, who distributed copies to the stores of Edward Lesslie and Sons in York, Dundas, and Kingston.[28]

In 1828, Baptists at York ordained Alexander Stewart as their first pastor. Among the Baptists, the process of ordination involved the calling of an ordination or examining council by the home church of the candidate. Invitations were sent to Baptist churches in the surrounding area. Each church selected delegates to sit on the ordination council. On a prearranged date, the candidate's doctrinal views and "fitness for ministry" were examined by the council and a decision made by vote of the council concerning the candidate's suitability for the gospel ministry. Ordination proceedings usually concluded with a worship service in which the new pastor was publicly set aside, by the laying on of hands, for the work to which God had called him.[29] Following Stewart's ordination, the *Colonial Advocate* reported the event:

> York Baptist Church—This religious society has been formed for some time, but has not, until now, obtained a settled pastor. Elder Alexander Stewart, was as we understand, ordained to the pastoral charge on the Sabbath before last.[30]

The installation of Stewart as pastor represented an important first step in establishing a permanent Baptist presence in the town. Still, Baptist success was far from assured.

Despite Stewart's tireless endeavors, the church's struggle for sound establishment continued. As Edith Firth has observed, "the Baptist congregation in York before 1834 was never large and because of its internal problems it had less impact on the community as a whole than other churches."[31] The church met in the home of Alexander Stewart at 76 Yonge Street until it rented the Old Masonic Hall in Market Lane.[32] In

---

28. Alexander Stewart, "Returns for Subscribers for Essays on the Gospel and Kingdom of Christ," May 25, 1827, York, (MS) 210, Box 11, Louis Melzack Collection. TFRBL. James Lesslie was a close friend and political ally of William Lyon Mackenzie.

29. Baptists define ordination as the appointment, commissioning or setting aside of a person for the gospel ministry. For an explanation of ordination and a discussion of the ordination process, see Mikolaski, "Canadian Baptist Ordination Standards and Procedures," 10–22.

30. "York Baptist Church," *Colonial Advocate*, May 29, 1828.

31. Firth, *Town of York*, lx.

32. These locations are given by John Carter, a longtime member of the church in "Reminiscences of the Baptists of Toronto," *CB*, April 22, 1886. Henry Scadding notes that Stewart used the Masonic Hall for a school. Fellow Baptist Thomas Ford Caldicott, who became pastor of the church in 1860, also taught school in the same Hall. For details, see Scadding, *Toronto of Old*, 65.

1832, a small chapel was erected on March (now Lombard) Street. At the first church meeting for which written minutes survive, held October 16, 1829, Joseph Wenham, manager of the York Branch of the Bank of Upper Canada, was appointed church clerk. Finances were a constant concern of York's Baptists. One response was to adopt the established church practice of pew rents. Ministerial support came by subscription, where members pledged to give a specified amount of money, usually in each quarter, to pay the pastor's salary.[33]

Institutional development did not preclude internal strife over religious principles and practice. Disagreements about Calvinism surfaced in the early 1830s. Certain comments by James Lesslie in March 1832, hint of the trouble that was brewing:

> Mr. Fraser preached the sermon to Young Men in the evening on "Behold now is the day of salvation"—an animated & impressive discourse altho[ugh] savouring of the peculiar tenets of the Arminians.[34]

Lesslie's statement suggests that when it came to Calvinism, the sensibilities of theologically literate Baptists ran high.

Throughout the nineteenth century, deviations from the traditional Baptist belief in the five points of Calvinism were a constant source of concern and controversy. In 1855, for example, the *Christian Messenger* carried an article concerning "Hyper-Calvinists in the town of Dundas" who had been "excluded" from the Regular Baptist Church for the "great deal of trouble and unseemly contention" they had instigated while they were still part of the congregation.[35] Regular Baptists rejected the "antimission" position of the Hyper-Calvinists.[36] They took the doctrine of

---

33. The information given here is taken from *Minutes of the Baptist Church at York, 1829–1811* (MS), JSBCA; Firth, *Town of York*, lx, 98; *Directory of the Jarvis St. Baptist Church, August 1897*, Appendix. "Short History of the Jarvis Street Baptist Church," 50.

34. James Lesslie, *Diary*, March 25, 1832 (MS), Dundas Historical Society Museum. Lesslie's reference to Arminianism was probably a reaction against the teaching of the Freewill Baptists. They taught that Christ died for humankind not just the elect and that predestination was compatible with man's freewill to choose or reject salvation. This doctrinal position had its roots in the works of Jacobus Arminius (1560–1609), the famous Dutch Reformed theologian. For more detail on Arminius and Arminianism, see Bangs, *Arminius*. For the doctrinal position of central Canadian Freewill Baptists, see *Treatise of Faith of the Freewill Baptists*. This treatise was accepted by Freewill Baptists in central Canada in 1834.

35. "Hyper-Calvinists in Dundas," *CM*, June 14, 1855.

36. "Hyper-Calvinists in Dundas," *CM*, June 14, 1855.

limited atonement to its logical conclusion and characterized evangelistic endeavors as "needless."[37]

Later in the century, the decline of Calvinism was one reason for Charles Haddon Spurgeon, the famous English Baptist preacher, to charge, in August 1887, that "A new religion . . . being destitute of moral honesty, palms itself off as the old faith with slight improvements, and on this plea usurps pulpits that were erected for gospel preaching."[38] In March 1887, Spurgeon had declared, "We care far more for the central evangelical truths than we do for Calvinism as a system; but we believe that Calvinism has in it a conservative force which helps to hold men to vital truth."[39] While Spurgeon was willing to abandon the intolerance and rigidity that often accompanied the Calvinist theological system he was not willing to give up its doctrines. Spurgeon admitted that the "downgrade controversy," as it came to be called, was primarily "not a debate upon the question of Calvinism or Arminianism, but of the truth of God versus the inventions of men."[40] The result of such "doctrinal falsehood" Spurgeon argued, was "a natural decline of spiritual life."[41] While the tenets of Calvinism were overshadowed in the downgrade controversy by concern over the rise of modernism, they were at issue. As Tim Curnow *et al* pointed out in their study of Spurgeon, "it was not so much that the doctrines of grace as articulated by reformed theology were being explicitly denied, as they were not being definitely preached; it was not that they were being openly attacked, but rather they were being quietly ignored."[42]

Canadian Baptists kept a watchful eye on the downgrade controversy.[43] Many shared Spurgeon's concern over the growth of unortho-

37. "Hyper-Calvinists in Dundas," *CM*, June 14, 1855.

38. *The Canadian Baptist* carried Spurgeon's views soon after they appeared in the *Sword and Trowel*. For this statement, see "Another Word Concerning the Down-Grade," *Sword and Trowel*, August 25, 1887.

39. This statement appeared in the March 1887 issue of the *Sword and Trowel* and is used as cited in Curnow et al., *Marvelous Ministry*, 121.

40. *Sword and Trowel*, March 1887. For discussions of the downgrade controversy, see Curnow et al., *Marvelous Ministry*, 111–31; Kruppa, *Charles Haddon Spurgeon*, 404–44.

41. "Another Word Concerning the Down-Grade," *CB*, August 25, 1887.

42. Curnow et al., *Marvelous Ministry*, 111–12.

43. For examples of articles by Spurgeon that appeared in *Canadian Baptist*, see "Another Word Concerning the Down-Grade," *CB*, August 25, 1887; "Our Reply to Sundry Critics and Inquires," *CB*, September 22, 1887; "Case Proved," *CB*, November 24, 1887; "Fragment Upon the Downgrade Controversy," *CB*, December 8, 1887; "Restoration of Truth and Revival," *CB*, December 22, 1887.

doxy and uncertainty that accompanied the decline of Calvinism. One editorial in *The Canadian Baptist* expressed sympathy for Spurgeon's message and criticism of his methods: "While we sympathize in most part with the doctrinal views of Mr. Spurgeon, and regret as thoroughly as he does the tendency of this age towards the new in theology, we cannot help but believing that there would have been a better way of acting than the one he has chosen."[44] This criticism of method was for Spurgeon's withdrawal from Baptist Union in late October 1887. Support for Spurgeon's message included a commitment by many Canadian Baptists to traditional Calvinistic doctrine.

Another factor that led to dissention in the Baptist church at York was personal rivalry. The influx of younger, more able preachers and leaders introduced a destructive competitive spirit into the church. Thomas Ford Caldicott, who would later pastor Bond Street Church from 1860 to 1869, joined the church in this period.[45] A native of Northamptonshire, England, Caldicott was trained as a shoemaker. His love of study and preaching, however, gained him an opportunity to open a day-school in Leicester. He emigrated to Canada in 1827, and became a tutor for the 79th Highland Regiment. He subsequently became regimental schoolmaster with the rank of sergeant. Caldicott joined March Street Church in May 1831. While in Toronto, he opened Caldicott's Classical and Commercial Academy on Market Street and by 1833 he ran a small book and stationery store at 187 King Street East.[46]

Young John Carter, who became a deacon of the church in the late nineteenth century, was deeply impressed with Caldicott's oratorical skill. "He had a splendid, deeptoned musical voice," Carter later recalled, "and he deliberately and distinctly pronounced every word he uttered. So great were his services as a preacher in demand, not only in March Street Church, but also in the country, that he was strongly urged by many friends to give

---

44. "Mr. Spurgeon and the Baptist Union," *CB*, November 24, 1887.

45. Although pastor is a noun, it was often used by nineteenth century Canadian Baptists as a verb to describe the act of shepherding the flock of God. I have adopted that usage here and elsewhere in this chapter.

46. For the biographical information contained in this paragraph, see *Dictionary of Canadian Biography*, 9:112–13; *McMaster University Monthly*, January 1895, 145–54; Cathcart, *Baptist Encyclopedia*, 174; "Standard Bearer Fallen," *CB*, July 15, 1869; "Late Dr. Caldicott," *CB*, July 22, 1869; "Reminiscences of the Baptists of Toronto," *CB*, April 22, April 29, May 6, May 13, 1886; "Late Dr. Caldicott," *Globe*, July 10, 1869; *Minutes, 1829–1832*, May 22, 1831, September 11, 1831, JSBCA. For the last three years of Caldicott's Toronto pastorate, see *Minute Book, 1866–1881*, JSBCA.

himself wholly to the work of the ministry."[47] Caldicott eventually followed this advice and was ordained in 1834. He served as pastor for twenty-five years in Baptist churches in New England and New York before returning in 1860 to pastor his home church in Toronto.

A second gifted speaker who joined the church in the early 1830s was John Eglinton Maxwell. Maxwell emigrated from Scotland with his own ideas of Baptist polity and practice. He married Johanna Carfrae, daughter of Thomas Carfrae Jr., an influential and wealthy general merchant, and quickly gained approval to preach.[48] In his diary, Maxwell expressed his dissatisfaction with the quality of preaching: "Lord's Day, November 2, 1834—heard Mr Stewart's lecture from John XVII. his remarks were a little confused and incorrect."[49] By late November personal rivalry had led to charges of impropriety. Maxwell noted, "A meeting had been held in Mr Stewarts on Thursday at 2 PM when Mr Caldicotts affairs were freely canvassed. Many things were laid to his charge; he defended himself at some length and gave full satisfaction to all. He is now fully restored to the confidence of the church."[50] Although Caldicott once again set about the task of preaching, rivalries between the preachers persisted.

In December, increasing dissension and ill-feeling forced church leaders to try to settle the matter of a preaching schedule. Maxwell proposed that three preachers be used in rotation at various places "around Toronto." He also suggested "that a plan should be drawn out, of the place where, and the time when each individual should preach for six months beforehand." Stewart opposed Maxwell's proposal. He feared that "should the people know who was to preach . . . they might be induced to come at one time, when a preacher was to engage whom they favoured, and might forbear coming when one came whom they disliked." Stewart also contended that Maxwell's plan "was calculated to call forth unhappy feelings" among the leaders, "one finding himself in the shade while he saw the people running after another." Maxwell retorted that "it was the duty of every Christian to go and hear a man by whom they were edified, instead of one under whose ministry the precious time was wasted." Timothy Parsons, another preaching Elder, argued that "with respect to the

---

47. "Reminiscences of the Baptists of Toronto," *CB*, April 22, 1886.

48. This was undoubtedly a highly profitable match for Maxwell. For details on the Carfrae family and its rise to prominence, see Armstrong, *City in the Making*, 164–91; "Carfrae Family," 45–54, 161–81.

49. Maxwell, *Diary*, November 2, 1834, MTRL.

50. Maxwell, *Diary*, November 31, 1834, MTRL.

country it was of little consequence who preached ... but with respect to Toronto it was different; that here they had their likes and dislikes."[51] This debate over preaching deepened the hard feelings already evident among the leadership. Dissension led to division. In 1836, the Baptist church in Toronto experienced schism. Although the exact reasons for the division are unclear, it is likely that the personal animosity between Stewart and Maxwell played an important role in this event.

Toronto Baptists then entered another period of uncertainty. One group, under John Maxwell, returned to the Masonic Hall for their church services. A second small group remained with Stewart at the March Street chapel. Tensions continued to trouble this group, and after charges of indiscretion were brought against Stewart, he retired from the ministry and the church disbanded, renting the March Street Chapel to other religious groups.[52] Maxwell's flock continued to meet until he accepted a call to a Baptist church in Clyde, New York, in July 1838. Despite the attempts of Reverend Samuel Tapscott, Reverend Newton Bosworth, and an appeal for a missionary pastor to the Colonial Baptist Missionary Society, which resulted in the short pastorate of W. H. Coombs, the Baptist cause in Toronto continued to flounder until the mid-1840s. The lack of consistent visionary leadership and the persistence of internal tensions over polity and personality left the church with a membership of only thirteen in 1840.[53] But by the end of 1846, the number had grown to seventy-seven.[54] In its formative years from 1818 to 1840, the Toronto Baptist church experienced hard times that were products of frontier life and the differing backgrounds of its immigrant membership.

Nevertheless, with the installation of James Campbell from Scotland as pastor in 1842, the March Street Baptist Church began to grow. Still, after Campbell resigned in 1844, it was the ministry of the church's first Canadian born pastor, Robert Alexander Fyfe, that established the church on a firm footing (see Figure 1). Born October 20, 1816, to a Presbyterian father and a Baptist mother, on a farm in the parish of Ste. Philippe, near the village of Laprairie about fifteen miles south-east of Montreal, Fyfe was baptized by Reverend John Gilmour in April 1835. Convinced that the call of God to the gospel ministry rested upon him

---

51. All of the quotations in this paragraph are taken from Maxwell, *Diary*, December 19, 1834, MTRL.

52. "Reminiscences," *CB*, April 22, 1886.

53. "Reminiscences," *CB*, April 29, 1886.

54. *Minute Book, 1845–1855*, April 2, 1846, JSBCA.

and eager to complete his elementary and high school education, Fyfe enrolled at the Hamilton Literary and Theological Institution, later Madison University, which was located in New York State half-way between Buffalo and Albany, for the fall of 1835. By the summer 1836, Fyfe was physically exhausted and financially strapped. He returned home to Laprairie, desirous of regaining his health and replenishing his finances. When his health and financial situations did not improve as quickly as he had hoped, Fyfe enrolled as one of two students in the new Baptist Academy in Montreal in the fall of 1836. In the summer of 1837, he enrolled in the Manual Labor High School in Worcester, Massachusetts, where he studied and taught school for three years. Eventually, with the material assistance of the Ottawa Valley's prominent Baptist timber merchant, Stephen Tucker, Fyfe gained the opportunity for a proper theological education. In 1839, he entered the Newton Theological Seminary in Boston, arguably the best Baptist theological institution on the continent, and "having finished the regular course" he received his certificate on Graduation Day, August 24, 1842.[55]

Fyfe's call to March Street in September 1844 signaled a new beginning. When the votes of the members were counted, thirty-four supported the call while only six opposed. Of great concern to Fyfe, however, was the large number of abstentions. The church roll included sixty-four names.[56] Still, Fyfe set about the task of drawing a divided church together. He cultivated friendships with the deacons and businessmen in his congregation. He solicited the aid of dry goods merchants, Robert Cathcart and William McMaster, in securing property and devising plans for a new church building. By the late 1840s, Baptists like Fyfe were moving to embrace the values and aspirations of the emerging middle class. March Street, with its "miserable houses" and "vicious and miserable kind of people," did not provide a suitable setting for Toronto Baptists to realize their desire for respectability.[57] "Getting the church away from March Street and its surroundings was, humanly speaking," Fyfe later noted, "the first step towards permanent prosperity."[58] Fyfe's choice of

55. The information in this paragraph is found in Wells, *Life and Labors*, 18–170; Gibson, *Robert Alexander Fyfe*, 34–54; *Dictionary of Canadian Biography*, 10:295–96; Yuille, "Robert A. Fyfe (1816–1878), 12:243–67, Dent, *Canadian Portrait*, 104–7; McMaster University Monthly, June 1893, 1–8.

56. *Minute Book, 1845–1855*, Early Roll, September 4, 1845 and September 18, 1845.

57. Fyfe, *Forty Years Survey*, 12.

58. Fyfe, *Forty Years Survey*, 18. For further development of the argument about the desire of Fyfe and the March Street Baptists for respectability, see Wilson, "Caring for Their Community," 232–33.

words to describe this era in the church's history leaves no doubt about the growing desire among Baptists to place the sacred within the secular world through their own "epics in stone."[59]

In fact, despite a membership of less than a hundred, Fyfe succeeded in leading the church through a relocation and building program. In August 1847, a site was secured on the West side of Bond Street. Three weeks before the new neo-classical church building opened its doors for worship on June 25, 1848, Fyfe resigned. As Fyfe's biographers, J. E. Wells and Theo Gibson, have pointed out, internal pressure to make the church a strict communion fellowship was the major factor in Fyfe's decision to leave Toronto.[60] Even as the Toronto correspondent for the *Montreal Register* rejoiced that "the whole work has been completed with much harmony, by the zeal and energy of the people"[61] the *Globe* lamented Fyfe's departure:

> The departure of Mr Fyfe from Toronto has been deeply regretted by a numerous circle of friends of other persuasions, as well as those to whom he ministered. Mr. Fyfe was a most valuable member of the society in this city. To many religious and benevolent institutions he gave the benefit of his great zeal and activity, both at public meetings and in the transaction of their business. A warm friend of civil and religious liberty, he took a deep interest in the recent struggle for the ascendancy of liberal opinions in the province. In the question of opening up King's College, he took a more than ordinary share. His pen was ever ready in promoting the liberal cause which was essentially promoted by his exertions during his stay in Toronto, and it will not be easy to fill up the blank which his departure has made.[62]

As this tribute indicates, Fyfe took the March Street Baptists into the political and religious arenas of the day. Fyfe was the first Baptist pastor at March Street to encourage his congregation to participate actively in public affairs. In his efforts to bring about educational and political reform, Fyfe was a model for others to follow.

Fyfe's successor, James Pyper of Pontiac, Michigan, sought to build on Fyfe's foundation. In cooperation with A. T. McCord, Toronto's Chamberlain, the title given to the city treasurer at that time, Pyper founded

59. For an analysis of the changes in church architecture and their significance in nineteenth century Ontario Protestant culture, see Westfall, *Two Worlds*, 126–58.
60. Wells, *Life and Labors*, 203–5; Gibson, *Robert Alexander Fyfe*, 166–80.
61. "Opening of the Baptist Chapel, Toronto," *MR*, July 6, 1848.
62. This statement is quoted in Wells, *Life and Labors*, 216.

and edited the *Toronto Christian Observer*. In the three years of its existence (1849–1852), Pyper used the *Observer* to express Baptist opposition to church establishment, materialism, and slavery.[63] In addition to covering important social and political issues, the paper also communicated Baptist doctrine and principles with evangelistic fervor. Under Pyper, Bond Street Chapel experienced rapid growth. "I found it sixty strong," he noted, "and left it composed of about two hundred and sixty."[64] In 1853, the chapel was enlarged to accommodate more people (see Figure 2). Thus, the seeds sown by Fyfe bore fruit under Pyper.

Yet, even in the midst of this unprecedented numerical growth, controversy surfaced. Pyper's decision to allow Alexander Campbell, founder of the Campbellites, also known as the Disciples of Christ, to speak at Bond Street Church in the summer of 1855 drew severe criticism from fellow Baptists. Objections included the charge that "Campbell's unscriptural views of baptism" led logically to "the dangerous dogma of Baptisimal regeneration."[65] Campbell's call for an end to theological "hair-splitting" and "divisions" were deemed "insulting to our intelligence" by one Baptist "Layman."[66] In an earlier letter to *The Christian Messenger* under the headline "WHAT NEXT!—ALEXANDER CAMPBELL IN DR. PYPER'S PULPIT, PREACHING TO THE BOND STREET CHURCH," one Toronto layman asked in outrage, "Why should Baptist Churches throw open their doors to receive a man who shall hold in contempt the labour of our Christian Missionaries and tell us that our prayers are a farce; and our contributions a waste of money?"[67] In a letter of his own, Pyper defended his decision by suggesting that while Campbell held

---

63. See, for example, "Infidelity: Its Antidote," *TCQ*, March 1851; "Safe Slave," *TCQ*, March 1851; "Dangers of Fashionable Life," *TCQ*, August 1851; "Why the Rich Should Be Liberal," *TCQ*, March 1852; "Month That Is Past," *TCQ*, October 1852; "Clergy Reserve Question," *TCQ*, October 1852. Because of its own richness, the Black Baptist story has not been discussed in detail here. It certainly deserves more attention from Canadian Baptist historians. Many of the Blacks who came to Upper Canada were Baptists. In the southwest of the province, Canadian Baptists aided Black slaves in their escape from slavery through the underground railroad. For a brief notation about the founding of the Amherstburg Association and its early work, see Heath et al., *Baptists in Canada*, 41. Twelve former slaves under Elder Washington Christian, a native of Virginia, formed the First Baptist Church in York in 1826.

64. Letter from Pyper to *CM*, November 29, 1855.

65. "Layman's Protest Against Campbellism," *CM*, September 6, 1855.

66. "Layman's Protest Against Campbellism," *CM*, September 6, 1855.

67. "What Next?—Alexander Campbell In Dr. Pyper's Pulpit, Preaching to the Bond Street Church," *CM*, August 16, 1855.

views that contradicted Baptist doctrine, his ideas fell within the parameters of evangelical orthodoxy.[68] The controversy over Campbell served to confirm Pyper's earlier decision to resign. Tired and in ill health, he returned to Pontiac in the fall of 1855.

On October 14, 1855, Robert Fyfe returned to Bond Street as pastor. In this second tenure, from 1855 to 1860, Fyfe mediated squabbles over the use of musical instruments in worship and business disputes between members. Despite such difficulties, Fyfe's ministry also had its successes. His articles and addresses articulated Canadian Baptist distinctives and history from a liberal, progressive viewpoint and called for a more unified effort in reaching "the lost" and helping "the saved." Under Fyfe, Bond Street Church launched a mission to "west Toronto." Fyfe also provided the impetus for Ontario Baptists to found the Canadian Literary Institute in Woodstock, to meet the needs of Baptists for higher education. Fyfe's passion for the development of Baptist higher education led to his selection as the Institute's first principal and professor of theology in July 1860.[69]

The resignation of Fyfe that year saddened the members of Bond Street Baptist Church. Still, the arrival of former Toronto resident Thomas Ford Caldicott in 1860 was cause for great rejoicing. Caldicott served his congregation well. In a move designed to secure the church financially and make it more businesslike, Caldicott initiated and implemented "systematic beneficence." This system of giving involved the use of "cards of beneficence" on which a member pledged to give a set amount towards the elimination of the church building debt. A "weekly offering system" was also instituted.[70] These innovations, borrowed from the business world, "more than doubled" the church's revenues in the nine-year period of Caldicott's ministry.[71]

Caldicott also played the role of peacemaker in disputes between members and used his calm demeanor and quiet diplomacy to move church members away from confrontation and towards co-operation. As a pulpiteer, Caldicott's skills suited his situation: "his discourses were

---

68. "Alexander Campbell In Toronto," *CM*, August 23, 1855.

69. For the information in this paragraph and more detail on Fyfe's efforts in this period, see Gibson, *Robert Alexander Fyfe*, 215–80.

70. For more details, see Caldicott, *Systematic Beneficence*, 1–38.

71. This observation was made in an obituary in "Late Dr. Caldicott," *CB*, July 22, 1869. Church records for 1860 are not extant. In 1869, the church had $84.83 after all of its liabilities had been paid.

preeminently scriptural, methodical, and practical; and if not delivered with the fire and fluency of earlier years, they derived peculiar impressiveness from a commanding presence, a deep rich voice, and a calm deliberation."[72] But on July 9, 1869, Caldicott died suddenly from a massive heart attack.

With Caldicott's death, the position of pastor devolved to William Boyd Stewart. Initially an assistant to Caldicott, Stewart had been promoted to co-pastor before an official call was extended to him. The "very precarious" health of Caldicott prompted this unusual circumstance.[73] Indeed, by the time Stewart arrived at Bond Street from First Baptist Church in Brantford in July 1869, Caldicott had died. Stewart's first duty as pastor was to preach the funeral sermon of his predecessor.

Stewart's ministry was short but productive.[74] The Bond Street Church started another city mission in the east end of the city. It purchased land for the erection of a church building for its mission work on Parliament Street.[75] In the summer of 1871, the Baptist Church at Yorkville was organized. Bond Street sent twenty-six of its members to help establish this church.[76] By February 1872, thirty-one other members left to assist in the formation of the Parliament Street Baptist Church.[77] Each of these efforts reflected a strong commitment to local mission work. To Stewart belongs much of the credit for supporting these extensions of the Baptist cause in Toronto.

A chronic respiratory ailment forced Stewart to resign in May 1872. The choice of J. H. Castle as pastor in 1873, and the subsequent erection of a new church building on the Northeast corner of Jarvis and Gerrard Streets in 1875, received a mixed response from Toronto Baptists. According to William Davies, the wealthy meat packer from Alexander Street Baptist Church, Toronto, both the call extended to Castle and the construction of Jarvis Street Baptist Church was part of a "hateful" display or "spirit of centralization & aggrandizement" by

---

72. *McMaster University Monthly*, January 1895, 149.

73. *Minute Book, 1866–1881*, May 17, 1869, JSBCA.

74. For biographical information on Stewart see William Boyd Stewart, Biographical File, CBA. One should also consult *Jubilee Commemoration*.

75. *Minute Book, 1866–1881*, August 31, September 19, September 21, 1870, JSBCA.

76. *Minute Book, 1866–1881*, July 3, September 20, 1871, JSBCA.

77. *Minute Book, 1866–1881*, February 19, 1872, JSBCA.

Susan and William McMaster.[78] In a letter to a friend, Davies offered his interpretation of events:

> There has been built in this city recently a large Baptist Chapel, gothic, brown stone, spire pointing upward if not heavenward, marble baptistry &c &c cost $100,000 & odd, & the organ $7000 besides, & I believe it is all paid for, but it has been built regardless of the needs of the city. This congregation was in a part of the city which was thickly populated but they had an old fashioned building. One of the members, an MLC [Member of the Legislative Council], say a Senator, very wealthy, married an American [Susan Moulton McMaster], natural result they soon had an American minister [J. H. Castle], then this new building also American, then the Lady & the minister lay their heads together & get a professional singer a sort of *prima dona* & she is paid $300.00 per year and many were very much hurt about it. It has been sanctioned by a majority & and the result will be I expect that some of their best people will leave.[79]

Davies's analysis reveals a growing concern and resentment about the ostentation of fellow Baptists like the McMasters. Davies found their use of wealth for public display and the achievement of greater respectability highly objectionable.

Without question, the new building's exterior construction and interior appointments were well suited to its new home among the fashionable mansions of Jarvis Street. The Gothic structure of Queenston stone cost $103,000 to erect (see Figure 3).[80] William McMaster gave $60,000 to the project.[81] Trimmed in Ohio stone and set off by columns of New Brunswick granite around its doorways, the new structure boasted a tower, spire, and vane that rose 165 feet above the street below. The sanctuary contained a baptistry of polished copper curbed with "the best Italian marble," a pulpit desk of polished brass and pews made of walnut and chestnut covered in damask. The organ, with its 2240 pipes and more than 50 stops, cost $8,000 and was arguably the finest church instrument in Toronto.[82]

78. William Davies to a Friend, June 15, 1876. Box 4044, File 3, "Correspondence of William Davies," UWORC.

79. William Davies to a Friend, June 15, 1876. Box 4044, File 3, "Correspondence of William Davies," UWORC.

80. Ellis, "Gilboa to Ichabod," 109.

81. White, *Perpetual Baptist Calendar*, 64.

82. I have used the description of the new church building found in the account given in the "Jarvis Street Baptist Church," *Globe*, December 3, 1875.

In contrast to Davies's opinion, numerous articles in the city and denominational press celebrated the move to Jarvis Street. The *Globe* noted that the opening of the "magnificent church edifice" was "crowded to its utmost capacity, not only by members of the Baptist denomination, but by persons representing every Protestant church in the city."[83] A writer to the Methodist *Christian Guardian* noted, "The zeal and enterprise which has been exhibited in our city (during the last few years) in church building is truly marvellous. . . . The First Baptist Church, on Jarvis Street, just opened, is almost a cathedral, and a model in its completeness for Christian work."[84] *The Canadian Baptist* heralded the dedication of the new church building as an event that "marked a new era in the history of the denomination, not only in this city [Toronto], but throughout the Province."[85] In fact, as Baptist historian Walter Ellis has noted, "The church building was a concrete symbol of the rising status and power of evangelicals in Canada."[86]

The move to Jarvis Street epitomized the rise of Toronto's Baptist business elite. The new church stood as testimony to the material success achieved by a generation of immigrant dissenters. It also represented a move by Baptists to the cultural mainstream. After 1875, Baptists possessed an edifice that proclaimed them part of the social and religious establishment. D. C. Masters claimed that as William McMaster escorted a distinguished English visitor past Jarvis Street Baptist Church, he pointed out its fine architecture. His English guest commented, "The impertinence of these dissenters!"[87] Fictional or factual, the anecdote is telling. For Canadian Baptists, Jarvis Street Baptist Church was a powerful and enduring expression of devotion to a new materialistic social ethic that professed service to a religious ethos that was gradually losing its hold.

---

83. "Jarvis Street Baptist Church," *Globe*, December 3, 1875.

84. "Progress of Church Architecture in Toronto," *Christian Guardian*, December 22, 1875.

85. "Jarvis St. Dedication," *CB*, December 9, 1875.

86. Ellis, "Gilboa to Ichabod," 109.

87. Masters, "Canadian Bankers of the Last Century," 395.

"The Corruption Within": Business Disputes, Internal Decay, and the First Signs of Secularization

For Baptists at Jarvis Street, the rise of a business-dominated culture in the mid and late nineteenth century directly challenged church authority over the behavior of its members. This section examines three business disputes and analyzes the responses of businessmen, clergy, and the wider laity. It argues that business disputes between members reflected a negative trend. The church's control over the actions of its businessmen decreased as the complexities of business eroded the moral authority of the church and forced it to abandon its role as arbitrator.

Business disputes between members disrupted the life and ministry of Bond Street Baptist Church by the late 1850s. Working under the established practice that both personal and public conduct were subject to church scrutiny and discipline, church leaders, as two-time pastor Robert Fyfe pointed out, "generally brought" business disputes "before the whole church."[88] A major source of conflict was preferential assignment. This practice included a promise by the debtor to pay one creditor or group of creditors ahead of all others. This binding contract, often concluded without the knowledge of non-preferred creditors, resulted in their exclusion from any settlement of an insolvent estate. In the case of Watts v. Howell *et al.*, for example, Robert Shackell, upon finding that his debts exceeded his ability to pay, made an assignment on February 7, 1860, for the benefit of his creditors. In his assignment, Shackell specified that, after the sale of his property, all executions in "the hands of the sherriff or any bailiff of any division court in the county [of Brant]" should be paid "first."[89] He then stipulated that the fourteen creditors named in a schedule attached to the assignment be paid.[90] Finally, if any proceeds remained, the creditors not named in the schedule would receive what they were owed.[91]

Dissatisfied with this arrangement, Charles Watts, one of the creditors named in the schedule, took the matter to court, claiming that the assignment was preferential and that it contravened chapter 26, section 18 of the Consolidated Acts of Upper Canada. Both the County Court of Middlesex and on appeal, the Court of Queen's Bench found that,

---

88. Fyfe, *Suggestions to Canadian Baptist Churches*, 39.
89. Robinson, *Reports of Cases Decided in Court of Queen's Bench*, 21:255.
90. Robinson, *Reports of Cases Decided in Court of Queen's Bench*, 21:256.
91. Robinson, *Reports of Cases Decided in Court of Queen's Bench*, 21:256.

although there was no intent "to give a preference to any class of creditors," the wording of the assignment gave certain creditors preference.[92]

By the late 1850s, this practice had become a major concern for the provincial government and legislation was drafted to deal with preferences. Following the passage of legislation prohibiting such assignments, the Court or Assizes for the Counties of York and Peel meeting in Toronto in the Fall of 1858 was flooded with "nearly three hundred civil cases-many of them undefended issue on promissory notes."[93] Such notes were often involved in preferential assignments.

Within Bond Street Baptist Church, a series of incidents brought the issue of preferential assignments to the fore. In the case of John Tovell, partner in a tailoring and men's mercery establishment located at 50 King Street West, who declared bankruptcy in the winter of 1855, the church exercised the sternest discipline.[94] Tovell, who was set up in business primarily through the generosity of fellow church member David Paterson, a prominent Toronto hardware merchant, stood accused of a variety of offenses. Citing "certain rumours bearing upon the moral character of brother Tovell" that affected "his good standing in this church," the church appointed a committee on February 25, 1855, "to investigate his case and report."[95]

Members of the committee were drawn from both the congregation and the diaconate.[96] They included lawyer David Buchan, City Chamber-

---

92. Robinson, *Reports of Cases Decided in Court of Queen's Bench*, 21:259.

93. The first act to deal with the problem of preferential assignments was an "Act for Abolishing Arrest in Certain Cases and for Better Prevention and More Effectual Punishments of Fraud," *Statutes of Canada*, 1858, 22 Vic. 6, c. 96. For the situation in Assizes, see "Toronto Assizes," *Globe*, October 12, 1858.

94. In 1850, John Tovell was an agent for J. [Joseph] Stovel who owned a tailoring business on King Street. In 1851, he became a teacher in a local common school. By 1854, he was a partner in the tailoring and men's wear firm of Tovell & Haig, which rented a store located at 50 King Street West. For information on John Tovell, see Middleton, *Municipality of Toronto*, 1:539; *Rowsell's City of Toronto*, 129; City of Toronto Assessment Rolls, 1854, Ward of St. George's, No. 42, City of Toronto Archives [hereafter CTA]; City of Toronto Assessment Rolls, 1855, ward of St. George's, No. 47, CTA. See also the advertisements in the "Tailoring and Mens' Mercery Establishment," *Examiner*, February 15, 1854; "Omar Pasha Flying Cape," *Globe*, January 1, 1855; "Grenville Robe," *Globe*, January 19, 1855.

95. Minute Book, 1844-1855, February 25, 1855, JSBCA.

96. The diaconate was the name given to the board of deacons. They were elected by the congregation to serve as spiritual leaders and manage the business affairs of the church. For a detailed description of their duties, see, for example, *Declaration of Faith, Covenant and Rules of Order*, 11-12.

lain Alexander T. McCord, clothing wholesaler Thomas Lailey, druggist James F. Lyon and printer John Carter. In its report submitted on April 3, the committee charged that "Tovell commenced business not only without any adequate capital, but with a debt of nearly £400 hanging on his head" and that he was "a party to giving a preference to one creditor to the prejudice of all the rest."[97] On April 10, Tovell read a defense before the church in which he claimed that he had been "tricked" into a preferential assignment by a large firm in the city.[98] Unconvinced by Tovell's defense, the church moved to expel him:

> Moved by Brother Dadson, seconded by Brother John Ross. That the Church records its deep regret, that brother Tovell should so far have overlooked his duty as a professed follower of Christ, as to have been a party to acts admitted and proven by the investigation just closed. That our responsibility to Christ as our King and Lord and our duty to each other compel us to adopt a measure which will at once vindicate the honour of Christ's cause, and be most likely under the blessing of God to promote the eternal welfare of Brother Tovell himself. That therefore he be and is clearly excluded from the fellowship of the church until he affords credible evidence that he has repented of the evil he has done; and the Church Clerk is hereby directed to erase the name of John Tovell from the church books.[99]

This act of discipline appears to have achieved the desired result given a subsequent amendment which read,

> That in the opinion of this church, brother Tovell has erred in breaking his obligation with Brother Paterson who so kindly put him in a position to commence business; and that in respecting the claims of only one of his creditors in making the late assignment he did an act which renders him deeply censurable in the eyes of this church. In view however of the extenuating circumstances connected with these acts, and the confession of repentance he has now submitted, Resolved: That he be publically admonished by a letter from the pastor and the deacons after having been submitted to the Church for its approval.[100]

---

97. This report is quoted in Langley, *Correct Statement of the Proceedings*, 10.
98. This report is quoted in Langley, *Correct Statement of the Proceedings*, 10.
99. *Minute Book, 1844–1855*, April 13, 1855, JSBCA.
100. *Minute Book, 1844–1855*, April 13, 1855, JSBCA.

Unfortunately for Tovell, the original motion passed while the amendment was defeated. This decision should have settled the matter. However, acrimony over how the church handled Tovell's case persisted. On April 26, "The pastor presented the petition of Brother James Ryrie [Sr.] [a carpenter] and thirty eight others praying that the case of Mr. Tovell be resubmitted to a full meeting of the church."[101] Countering this motion, David Paterson and his allies argued that it was "inexpedient to reopen" the case.[102] The Paterson faction triumphed. Although most Tovell sympathizers stayed in the church, the factionalism and ill-feeling created by his case unsettled the membership and strained relationships.

The Tovell case was a key factor in Pyper's decision to resign in early June 1855. Although he cited "ill health" as the reason for his departure, the stress associated with handling this dispute provided the proverbial "last straw" in Pyper's ministry and led to his search for a more tranquil charge. On August 2, 1855, *Christian Messenger* reported,

> We are informed that Dr. Pyper is about to return to Michigan, and resume the pastoral oversight of the church in Pontiac; so that our informant was in error in stating, that Dr. P. was about to cease from all ministerial pastoral labour, until such time as his health was recruited. Pontiac is a much less laborious field than Toronto, and one upon which brother Pyper will be likely to regain the health and strength he has lost, in consequence of the continued attacks of the ague, superintended by his unfortunate contiguity to the large marsh on the shore of the lake-which has in great measure unfitted him for the discharge of the onerous duties connected with pastorate of the Bond Street Church, Toronto.[103]

The "onerous duties" cited by *The Messenger* most assuredly included the Tovell affair. They also included internal conflicts between leaders with different objectives. In January 1856, William Davies, a member of Bond Street engaged as a provision dealer, observed,

> There is a rather strong feeling in our church against 1 of the deacons & there have been some very hard things said of him. Last Thursday at a Ch[urch] Meet[in]g the oldest member of the church attacked him most virulently & ended up by calling on him to resign his office & let a better take his place. Though

---

101. *Minute Book, 1844–1855*, April 26, 1855, JSBCA.
102. *Minute Book, 1844–1855*, April 26, 1855, JSBCA.
103. "Rev. Dr. Pyper and the Bond Street Church, Toronto," *CM*, August 2, 1855.

> I think a good deal that he said was true I could not uphold him in attacking him in that manner. He (the deacon) is one of the most wealthy merchants in the city. He is said to be worth £250,000, but he is very obstinate & self will'd & likes to lead the minister by the nose & they accuse him of persecuting and driving away Dr. Pyper.[104]

Based on the figure given and those holding the office of deacon at the time, it is highly probable that William McMaster is the deacon mentioned here. Unfortunately, there is no evidence to corroborate Davies's accusation concerning McMaster's role in Pyper's departure. Still, his statement reveals that tumult plagued the church in this period. In a broader sense, the growing demands associated with ministry in the heart of Toronto also took a heavy toll on pastors.

The internal difficulties experienced by Bond Street Baptist Chapel reflected, in part, external changes in the economic, social, and cultural contexts. As Toronto became more urbanized, industrialized, and commercialized, new pressures and demands challenged both pastors and people. Unchecked, the drive, initiative, and competitiveness that served Baptist businessmen well in the secular business world, brought divisiveness and dissention to the church.

Had the Tovell incident been an isolated one, its impact on religious practice and church polity might have been minimal. However, in 1857, Bond Street Baptist Chapel was again disrupted by another business matter. Again, the case involved preferential assignments. Francis T. Parson, a commission merchant, entered into a partnership with William Davies. Davies, who was led to believe that Parson was "in good circumstances," put up a substantial amount of capital (£850) while Parson agreed to manage a store selling foodstuffs.[105] After Parson made "some shocking bad purchases" Davies, who saw "ruin staring him in the face" demanded a dissolution.[106] It was agreed, much to Davies's dislike, that he should be paid £250 immediately and the remainder (£600) in two notes at six months and twelve months at the interest-bearing rate of ten per cent. The first note was paid, but before the second came

---

104. William Davies to James Davies, January 13, 1856. WDP, Box 4044, File 1, UWORC.

105. William Davies to James Davies, June 18, 1859. WDP, Box 4044, File 3, UWORC.

106. William Davies to James Davies, June 18, 1859. WDP, Box 4044, File 3, UWORC.

due, Parson declared bankruptcy.[107] Davies discovered that he had no capital in the business and that he had "carried on business from the first on dis[ounts] obtained on notes made for his accommodation by . . . [William] McMaster & [Thomas] Lailey."[108] Parson then assigned all of his remaining assets over to McMaster and Lailey to cover their promissory notes for £750, leaving Davies with nothing.[109]

Feeling defrauded by his Baptist brother, Davies charged Parson with impropriety and deception at the next regular church meeting on May 25, 1858. A committee was appointed to investigate the case: deacon Stephen Dadson, a haberdasher, deacon James F. Lyon, druggist, James Girvin, baker and confectioner, and deacon Benjamin Clark, a carpenter, and presented a report which exonerated Parson. After the report was read, howls of protest and charges of "whitewashing" filled the air of the next church meeting held on June 29.[110] Supporters of Parson, who included pastor Robert A. Fyfe, deacons William McMaster, James F. Lyon, and Stephen Dadson came to his defense and supported the report. This display of collusion galvanized those who supported William Davies in his call for the discipline of Parson. In an attempt to save face, the committee withdrew the report. Fyfe then drafted a resolution which stated that the committee "after a careful and prayerful examination" could "find no evidence to sustain the charge" by Davies that Parson had deceived him.[111] After a heated discussion, the resolution passed. Subsequently, shoemaker William Langley Jr., a supporter of Davies, introduced a resolution that recorded the Church's "unqualified disapproval of preferential assignments."[112] Citing the Tovell case, Langley noted the "glaring inconsistency of those who were now found defending this case."[113] In response, an amendment to the Langley reso-

---

107. William Davies to James Davies, June 18, 1859. WDP, Box 4044, File 3, UWORC.

108. William Davies to James Davies, June 18, 1859. WDP, Box 4044, File 3, UWORC.

109. William Davies to James Davies, June 18, 1859. WDP, Box 4044, File 3, UWORC.

110. Langley, *Correct Statement of the Proceedings*, 19.

111. Langley, *Correct Statement of the Proceedings*, 10.

112. Langley, *Correct Statement of the Proceedings*, 10.

113. Langley, *Correct Statement of the Proceedings*, 10.

lution was handed by McMaster to Fyfe, who passed it on to Dadson, who gave it to Lyon to present.[114] It stated,

> Whereas brother Parson, in preferring brethren Lailey and McMaster, in the peculiar circumstances, only acted according to well-known principles of equity which prevail among all honourable businessmen, we, as a church, dismiss all further consideration of the case.[115]

The assertion that Parson had followed an ethical course was dubious at best. Even as the Parson case was deliberated efforts to pass provincial legislation, which made preferences of the kind given to McMaster and Lailey illegal, were underway. Certainly when coupled with the articles carried by the Toronto press concerning the evils of preferential assignments the "Act for Abolishing Arrest in Certain Cases and for Better Prevention and More Effectual Punishment of Fraud" passed on August 16, 1858, was a potential source of embarrassment to the Parson-McMaster faction.[116] In his charge to the "Grand Jury" before the Toronto Assizes on October 11, 1858, Judge J. H. Hagarty noted, for example, that the new legislation included, "some stringent provisions against those preferences of particular creditors by persons in difficulty which have been so long permitted to disgrace and demoralize our commercial system."[117] These claims challenge the June 29 amendment put forward in the Parson case. While the faction supporting Parson sincerely may have believed that he "acted according to the well-known principles of equity which prevail among all honourable businessmen," it is more likely that the amendment was an attempt to rationalize their behavior.[118] McMaster and his allies must have been aware of the hardship that Parson's use of preferential assignment brought to William Davies who had lost hard cash. Whether the motive was personal rivalry or revenge for some earlier wrong, the Parson case brought out the worst in many of Bond Street's Baptist businessmen.

Not surprisingly, the passage of the amendment hardened the division between the Parson-McMaster faction and Davies's supporters.

---

114. Langley, *Correct Statement of the Proceedings*, 12.

115. Langley, *Correct Statement of the Proceedings*, 12.

116. Prior to 1858, it was not fraudulent for one to assign property to whomever one preferred. This act made such preferences illegal. *Statutes of Canada*, 1858, 22 Vic. 6, c. 96.

117. "Toronto Assizes," *Globe*, October 12, 1858.

118. Langley, *Correct Statement of the Proceedings*, 12.

Convinced that support for Parson was immoral and that the leadership of Bond Street Church was corrupt, Davies and a small group of supporters withdrew and formed their own Baptist church on Albert Street.

With victory secure, the Parson-McMaster faction moved to punish their opponents. William Langley Jr., for example, was excluded from the church for his expressed opposition to the support given Parson. In an effort to exonerate himself, he wrote a pamphlet entitled, *A Correct Statement of the Proceedings in Bond Street Baptist Church Whereby a Member was Tyrannically Expelled for Telling the Truth!*[119]

A year later, the reprisals continued against those who had withdrawn from Bond Street Baptist Church to found the Albert Street Baptist Tabernacle. William Davies noted with some delight that "we are going on I think prosperously in our little church . . . My wife's sister," Davies reported, "has come forward to profess her faith in Christ and next Sabbath she is baptized at the Bath House in this city, the Bond Street Folks having refused us the use of their Baptistry."[120] Davies also noted that "Dr. Fyfe has passed a law that no letters shall be granted to any who wish to leave Bond Street to join us."[121] Davies summarized his feelings about the attitudes and actions of his adversaries at Bond Street when he stated, "I do not care because I feel that nothing they can do can injure us, but we can injure ourselves like individuals who have more to fear from the corruptions within than from the temptations without."[122]

Davies's view reflected a growing concern with internal decay. How were Baptists going to stop the growth of avarice, arrogance, and the erosion of their strict moral standards? To Davies and many other Baptists, the business disputes in Bond Street Baptist Church indicated that the evils of the business world were no longer remote external temptations; they resided within the church. Individual Baptists were succumbing to selfish and carnal desires for material success. That the achievement of material success might involve moral compromise seemed to matter less at Bond Street as time went on.

Even some of those opposed to Davies came to recognize the insidious threat to Baptist belief and practice posed by such internal

---

119. For a photocopy of this document, see the File on Bond Street Baptist Church, Toronto, at CBA.

120. William Davis to James Davis, June 18, 1859. WDP, Box 4044, File 2, WORC. For a description of the Albert Street Baptist Tabernacle see *Globe*, March 13, 1860.

121. William Davis to James Davis, June 18, 1859. WDP, Box 4044, File 2, WORC.

122. William Davis to James Davis, June 18, 1859. WDP, Box 4044, File 2, WORC.

disagreements over business matters. In an 1866 pamphlet entitled *Suggestions to Canadian Baptist Churches, Pastors, and Deacons*, the former pastor of Bond Street, Robert A. Fyfe, included a remarkable section on "Settling Business Difficulties." Reversing his earlier position, Fyfe recommended that "business difficulties" should be settled, "if at all possible, out of the church meeting."[123] Fyfe offered two reasons for supporting private settlement. First, he argued that "the church was designed for the mutual spiritual benefit of its members, and not to settle intricate business difficulties."[124] Basing his conclusion on 1 Cor 6:1–7,[125] Fyfe maintained "that the early churches met for spiritual edification, and not to spend hours in debating conflicting interests."[126] In addition, Fyfe noted that "rarely has a dispute about . . . a supposed overreach in business, been settled in an open church meeting without creating sores in the body. It has been supposed that every matter *must* be brought before the church. This is a grave mistake."[127] By redefining the role of the church in business-related matters, Fyfe drew a clearer line of demarcation between sacred and secular, and he legitimized the Baptist business elites' pursuit of respectability. As Daniel Goodwin has noted, "If Baptists were to play a role in the new order, the emerging business elite would have to be free from local church discipline in matters relating to commerce. This price for respectability was one that leaders such as Fyfe were willing to pay."[128] Thus, based on his experience at Bond Street and his growing conviction that respectability was essential for Baptists, Fyfe conceded that the church was ill-suited and unequipped to act as arbiter in business disputes.

Fyfe proposed an alternative: individual deacons should take the initiative in resolving business conflicts. "We therefore lay it down as a rule," Fyfe stated, "that those deacons who settle out of the church meeting the greatest number of disputes or difficulties, render the most important service to the church which appoints them."[129] Fyfe went on to suggest that a wise church "will thank the deacons for saving them

---

123. Fyfe, *Suggestions to Canadian Baptist Churches*, 39.
124. Fyfe, *Suggestions to Canadian Baptist Churches*, 39.
125. This biblical passage is quoted earlier in this chapter (see note 14).
126. Fyfe, *Suggestions to Canadian Baptist Churches*, 40.
127. Fyfe, *Suggestions to Canadian Baptist Churches*, 39.
128. Goodwin, "Footprints of Zion's King," 202.
129. Fyfe, *Suggestions to Canadian Baptist Churches*, 40.

from trouble, if not from the danger of division."[130] Again, Fyfe drew upon the troubles of the past. The schism at Bond Street over the Parson case pushed Fyfe to find a resolution.

Fyfe was critical of the use of church councils for the settlement of business disputes. He argued that the practice of referring a business matter that the church "cannot settle" to "an 'advisory council'" was ineffective.[131] "The contestants remain of the same opinion," Fyfe contended, "and take the advice of the council if it suits them."[132] Although he found the advisory council wanting, Fyfe noted that "the only 'councils' which are of any value are those which are 'councils of arbitration,' bodies to which the parties calling them, agree to submit the case, and abide by their decision."[133] For a biblical model, Fyfe cited the actions of the Jerusalem Council and argued that it "more nearly resembled the kind of which we now speak," that is, the arbitration council.[134] "It would save much time and trouble," Fyfe instructed his readers, "if the brethren who feel disposed to call councils, would first agree to abide by the decision of the brethren whom they invite to hear their case."[135] Decisions made by councils needed to binding if disputes were to be settled. Instead, as the Parson case at Bond Street demonstrated, many Baptist churches called councils that did nothing more than exacerbate already serious disputes.

For Bond Street Baptist Church, Fyfe's "suggestions" could not have been timelier. In 1866, the church was, for a third time, disrupted and divided by a business dispute. Bond Street's records are silent about this incident. Nevertheless, the records of Alexander Street Baptist Church contain sufficient information for the historian to piece together the course of events. Evidently, P. R. Randall of Bond Street Baptist Church entered into a business partnership with fellow church member Henry E. Parson of Parson Brothers, Coal Oil merchants, of 51 Front Street East. According to Richard Coleman, a salesman with Parson

---

130. Fyfe, *Suggestions to Canadian Baptist Churches*, 40.
131. Fyfe, *Suggestions to Canadian Baptist Churches*, 40.
132. Fyfe, *Suggestions to Canadian Baptist Churches*, 41.
133. Fyfe, *Suggestions to Canadian Baptist Churches*, 41.
134. Fyfe, *Suggestions to Canadian Baptist Churches*, 41. The issue in dispute before the Jerusalem Council was whether Gentile Christians had to be circumcised. The matter was put before a council of apostles and elders for judgement. For the biblical account, see Acts 15:1–41.
135. Fyfe, *Suggestions to Canadian Baptist Churches*, 41.

Brothers, a "difficulty occurred" between Randall and Parson.[136] The church's handling of the case created hard feelings and some members, like Coleman, withdrew. Bond Street then excluded or dropped from the membership roll the names of those who had withdrawn. On October 19, 1866, Richard Coleman explained his reasons for leaving and chronicled his own history and circumstances in a letter to the Bond Street Church Clerk, John Carter:

> In October of 1861 I moved to this city and deposited my letter of dismission with the Bond St. Church with who [sic] I Remained in full fellowship until the difficulty occurred between brethren H. E. Parson and P. R. Randall when believing from the knowledge I possessed of the facts that injustice had been done to the former by the latter who was I believed verily guilty of a great crime. I felt that my usefulness was thereby impaired and that I could no longer enjoy fellowship with them in the degree that heretofore existed. I therefore withdrew from them but in order to retain my standing in the denomination I asked for letters of dismissal having hopes that another church would be organized or failing this to rejoin the church in Hamilton. Subsequently I learned that my name was dropped from the Church Book having been notified by the clerk to that effect.[137]

The experience of Richard Coleman was certainly not unique. Although the exact number of defectors is impossible to ascertain with certainty, the *Jarvis Street Minute Book, 1866-1881* shows that numerous requests for dismissal to Alexander Street came throughout the fall of 1866 and the succeeding year.[138] In an effort to resolve outstanding problems with regard to the transfer of church membership from Bond Street to Alexander Street, a joint committee of pastors and deacons from the two churches met on December 6, 1867, in Dr. T. F. Caldicott's study. The minutes of the meeting summarized the agreement:

> The unanimous feeling of the meeting as expressed by the various delegates was that all parties who have been excluded from Bond St. Church or whose names have been dropped for irregularity should make due acknowledgement to the satisfaction of Bond St. Church for their improper and irregular

---

136. Richard Coleman to John Carter, October 19, 1866. Alexander Street Baptist Church Records, 1866–1904, Box 1, General Correspondence File 1866–1904, CBA.

137. Richard Coleman to John Carter, October 19, 1866. Alexander Street Baptist Church Records, 1866–1904, Box 1, General Correspondence File 1866–1904, CBA.

138. *Minute Book, 1866–1881*, October 2, 1866, May 9, 1866, JSBCA.

conduct and . . . in this manner [be] reconciled to the latter church. The way would be open for such parties to unite with Alexander St. Church.[139]

With this agreement the way was cleared for those who had left Bond Street over the Parson-Randall affair to find a new church home. Although business disputes would continue to cause difficulty in the church, the leadership of Bond Street gradually shied away from handling these disputes in public church meetings. Instead, church leaders began to bypass the congregation, set aside acrimony, and meet privately to arrive at an amicable settlement.

At Bond Street Church there was a transitional phase in the late 1860s and 1870s when business disputes were referred to a deacon's committee for settlement. On June 22, 1877, for example, church minutes simply note that, "the Committee appointed on 23rd March 1877 to enquire into and report on the matter in dispute between brethren [H. A.] Schomberg and [Robert] Lawson, brought in a lengthy and exhaustive report, exonerating brother Lawson from Wilful [sic] intention to any way wrong brother Schomberg. Committee discharged with thanks."[140] Unfortunately, the committee report is not extant, and consequently, the details of this case must remain a mystery. This is the last recorded incident of a business dispute. After 1880, the church minutes are silent on such disagreements.

Thus, by the late nineteenth century, the practice of Bond Street Baptist Church had changed significantly. From bringing every business dispute between members before the church for deliberation, the church shifted the responsibility of settlement to a deacon's committee and finally to the individuals involved. Disagreements over business matters posed a serious threat to church unity and survival. For church leaders, it became both expedient and necessary to re-emphasize the spiritual role of the church in the life of the individual believer while it gradually withdrew from the settlement of business disputes. In short, as business came to dominate the culture and the lives of its church members, Baptist

---

139. "Minutes of a Joint Committee on Excluded or Dropped Members," December 6, 1867. Alexander Street Baptist Church Records, 1866–1904, Box 1, General Correspondence File, 1866–1904. CBA.

140. *Minute Book, 1866–1881*, June 22, 1877, JSBCA. *Might's Toronto City Directory for 1877*, 297, lists Robert Lawson as a grocer located at 484 Yonge Street. H. A. Schomberg is listed as a furniture dealer located at 655 Yonge Street. See *Might's Toronto City Directory for 1877*, 358.

churches were forced to relinquish their role as arbiters. In surrendering this role, the church gave way to business interests and individual morality. This was an important step towards secularization.

Business Methods in the Church

Coinciding with the disruptions caused by business disputes was the introduction and acceptance of business methods in urban Baptist churches. In particular, increasing attention was paid to administrative structure and finances. In both of these areas, new methods patterned after those used in business were implemented. At Jarvis Street, these changes tied the church ever more closely to the Toronto Baptist business elite. A church run on business principles stood a good chance of attracting the majority of the city's prominent Baptist businessmen. Knowing this, Jarvis Street actively became more businesslike in the management of its affairs.

In theory, power in a Baptist church rested in the hands of the congregation. The October 28, 1880, issue of *The Christian Helper* carried a paper read at the Ministerial Institute in Jarvis Street by D. A. McGregor, who was then pastoring in Stratford, Ontario. The paper was entitled simply, "What Constitutes a Regular Baptist Church?" One of the key distinguishing marks of a *regular Baptist church*, McGregor *suggested, was "its form of government"* which he called "congregational independency."[141] This concept explained a principle later Baptists would identify as individual church "autonomy," and ensured that the center of effective decision-making rested with the congregation.[142] On the crucial matter of pastoral and diaconal leadership, for example, McGregor noted that "the church has the power to elect persons to, or depose them from, these official positions, but it has no power to change the offices themselves."[143] In other areas, such as dispute settlement, major financial decisions, and policy changes, church members had their say by a show of hands or a secret ballot. A Baptist church, then, was theoretically a republican democracy ruled by congregational vote.

---

141. McGregor, *Memoir of Daniel Arthur McGregor*, 164.

142. The principle of local church "autonomy" was first articulated in the early twentieth century by the American Southern Baptist theologian, E. Y. Mullins. See Mullins, *Baptist Beliefs*, 64.

143. McGregor, *Memoir of Daniel Arthur McGregor*, 163.

In the nineteenth century Canadian Baptist context, a growing acceptance of business principles and methods undermined congregational rule by concentrating power in the hands of a few. An article appeared in the *Examiner* on February 19, 1891, which claimed to "know [of] a large number of Baptist churches in which the 'Board of Deacons' is really the governing body."[144] In response, an editorial that appeared in *The Canadian Baptist* on February 26, 1891, remarked, "We do not know whether this tendency exists to a dangerous extent amongst our Canadian churches, but there is reason to fear that the rule of 'the Board' is not altogether unknown amongst us."[145] While admitting that "such a system of government is not Baptistic, but Presbyterian, and 'that it is well to be on our guard against this tendency'" the editorialist failed to see the link between centralization in the church and the importation of business methods.[146] If, as in the case of Jarvis Street, a large number of deacons were businessmen, the temptation to act like business directors while serving as deacons was strong.

As we have already seen, William Davies thought that Jarvis Street was ruled "by a spirit of centralization and aggrandizement."[147] Still, despite its condemnation of centralization, this editorial advocated "the necessity of doing church business on business principles and by business methods. In all our church work, and all our work for the Master," the editorial concluded, "let things be done 'decently,' that is, in a becoming manner, and 'in order,' that is, by a proper system."[148] By favoring changes that made the church more businesslike, Baptists admitted that important lessons were to be learned from the secular business world.

An earlier article taken from the *Examiner* and reprinted in *The Canadian Baptist* set out to challenge the notion "that business principles ought not to have any bearing on religion."[149] In answer to the question, "But why should the Lord's business not be done in a business way?" the writer argued that the church had "a double function."[150] While "religious work" was its primary concern, the author contended

144. Quoted in "Church Business," *CB*, February 26, 1891.
145. Quoted in "Church Business," *CB*, February 26, 1891.
146. Quoted in "Church Business," *CB*, February 26, 1891.
147. William Davies to a Friend, June 15, 1876. Box 4044, File 3, "Correspondence of William Davies," UWORC.
148. *CB*, February 26, 1891.
149. "Doing It on Business Principles," *CB*, August 1, 1878.
150. "Doing It on Business Principles," *CB*, August 1, 1878.

that "as society is now constituted, this work can be successfully prosecuted only by the aid of considerable sums of money.... The church is therefore of necessity," the author concluded, "not only a religious body but a business body."[151] The author criticized "Christians" who thought that "sound business principles" were "valuable for anything else, but worthless in church affairs."[152]

At Jarvis Street, between 1848 and 1880, the gradual acceptance of business methods became most evident in the areas of church government and finance. The regular recording of minutes, the use of rules of order, and a growing desire to systematize church endeavors reflected the dominance of the business elite on the deacon's Board. Given that the overwhelming majority of the deacons were businessmen, it is also not surprising that the collection and disbursement of finances became the Board's major focus.

The different schemes for raising money adopted by the church show an increasing sophistication. Initially, a system of pew rents was used.[153] By the 1840s, subscriptions were solicited from the membership for the support of the pastor. These pledges could be paid annually, semi-annually, or quarterly.[154] In the 1860s, largely as a result of the efforts of Thomas Ford Caldicott and his preaching on the subject of "systematic beneficence," a "weekly offering system" was adopted. This method of raising revenue was designed to create both a steady and increased cash flow. As Robert Lawson, treasurer of Bond Street Baptist Church, explained in a letter to *The Canadian Baptist* on December 1, 1870, "the mode of operation" was "simple."[155] Pledge cards were distributed to the members. On these, they pledged their support. Upon the return of the cards to a deacon or the treasurer, the member was given another card, a package of fifty-two envelopes, and an assigned number. On the second card, the subscriber promised to continue his donations "until the officers of the Church are notified to the contrary in writing."[156] Lawson claimed

---

151. "Doing It on Business Principles," *CB*, August 1, 1878.

152. "Doing It on Business Principles," *CB*, August 1, 1878.

153. For a diagram of how the pews were assigned, see *Directory of the Jarvis Street Baptist Church, 1897*, Appendix, "Short History," 51.

154. *Finances in Sterling of the March Street Baptist Church, 1840–1846*, "Annual Subscribers to the Support of Rev. W. H. Coombs and the Expenses of His Preaching in the Baptist Chapel in March Street, Opened July 5, 1840" (MS), JSBCA.

155. "Weekly Offering System," *CB*, December 1, 1870.

156. "Weekly Offering System," *CB*, December 1, 1870.

that under the new system, church revenues had increased "by nearly $4,000."[157] To critics who claimed that "it could not be made to work in villages or thinly settled places," Lawson responded that as long as it was "properly carried out," there could be "no question of its success."[158] Efforts to improve church finances through new sales methods such as this show how business exerted its influence on the conduct of church affairs. In fact, the church became increasingly dependent on business for new ideas and methods that enabled it to compete better for converts. Thus, in subtle ways, business helped to secularize religion by tying it more closely to the secular world and by deemphasizing the traditional Baptist reliance on "faith" that God would meet all needs.

Business played an important role in Baptist church life in the nineteenth century. From an almost exclusive reliance on their own ability to settle business disputes and discipline members internally in accordance with the Scriptures, Baptists at Jarvis Street and elsewhere had largely relinquished this role by the end of the nineteenth century. A reliance on secular business methods simultaneously eroded their dependence on a faith that stressed supernatural intervention over business methodology. At the institutional level, then, business secularized religion by changing its focus from the divine to the human, from the sacred to the secular. With his church committed to using business principles, the individual Baptist businessman at Jarvis Street could not help but be encouraged to fix his sights more firmly on his own personal material success.

---

157. "Weekly Offering System," *CB*, December 1, 1870.
158. "Weekly Offering System," *CB*, December 1, 1870.

Figure 1. Reverend Robert Alexander Fyfe was Pastor of March Street, 1844-1848, and Bond Street, 1855-1860, Baptist Chapels (JSBCA).

Figure 2. Bond Street Baptist Church Chapel built in the neo-classical style in 1848, housed the congregation until 1875. Lithograph by Woodward Grant and Co., 1875 (JSBCA).

Figure 3. This postcard of Jarvis Street Baptist Church, ca. 1900, illustrated that Baptists were capable of erecting Gothic cathedrals. The church was constructed in 1875 (Public Domain).

Chapter 4

Serving God and Mammon

Secularization Through Sociocultural Integration

> No man can serve two masters: for either he will hate the one, and love the other; or else he will hold to the one, and despise the other. Ye cannot serve God and mammon. (Matt 6:24)

BY THE LATE NINETEENTH century, many Canadian Baptist businessmen were convinced that it was possible to serve the interests of religion and business simultaneously. Moreover, where business and religion could be harmonized within the context of the church, they sought to solidify the relationship. When the demands of business conflicted with religious belief or practice, however, accommodation or acceptance of new cultural realities became the normative response. For many, concerns about the affairs of this world equaled and then exceeded their spiritual concerns. Thus, religious commitment was secularized through sociocultural integration.[1]

The effects of secularization were abundantly evident within the cadre of Toronto's business elite in Jarvis Street Baptist Church. They were among the first Baptists to confront the challenges of an increasingly

---

1. The term "secularized" is used here to refer to a lessening of religious commitment through the abandonment of both belief and practice. For further elaboration, see Marshall, *Secularizing the Faith*, 7. See also the lengthy discussion of secularization by sociologist Steve Bruce in *House Divided*, 7–29.

dominant business culture with its materialistic social ethic. Though individual responses varied in degree, the moral impact of integration on many Baptist businessmen was unmistakably negative.

This chapter examines the process by which certain Baptist businessmen altered their religious beliefs and practices to reflect the new materialistic social ethic. Publicly, Scripture's injunction about the impossibility of serving God and mammon was affirmed; privately, the Canadian Baptist business elite rationalized the relationship that was, in fact, the reality.

"Not Slothful in Business, Serving the Lord": Rationalizing the Business-Religion Relationship

Throughout the latter half of the nineteenth century, Canadian Baptists found themselves constantly adjusting their views on the troublesome relationship between business and religion. As secular demands on businessmen's time, energy, and money increased, so did the pressure to make business matters their priority. By the turn of the century, the prevailing viewpoint changed as many Baptists became convinced that it was possible simultaneously to serve both God and mammon. In the mid-nineteenth century, there was no equivocation about the position that religion should occupy in the life of the businessman. "The church is first in her demands," stated an article entitled "Religion and Business" that appeared in the November 20, 1862, issue of *The Canadian Baptist*, "and we cannot neglect her claims without the effect being disastrous both to her and to ourselves also."[2] The serious threat posed by business was clearly spelled out, "Man was not made to live by bread alone, and while it is true that diligence in business has the authority of a Divine injunction, yet fervency of spirit needs to be conjoined with it, lest devotion to temporal things engross our mind and eclipse our faith."[3] The need to maintain proper priorities was constantly emphasized. As one article on prosperity noted, "Spiritual wealth is the principal thing, though it may not amount to much at first, yet it is a thing that increases; the talents if profitably laid out, gain others."[4] Warnings to those who would blur the lines between God and mammon were stern:

---

2. "Religion and Business," *CB*, November 20, 1862.
3. "Religion and Business," *CB*, November 20, 1862.
4. "Worldly Prosperity and Soul Prosperity," *CB*, October 26, 1865.

> In short, the minimum Christian knows that he cannot serve God and Mammon—he would if he could—but he will come just as near to doing so as he can, and yet not lose his soul. He stands so close to the dividing line between the people of God and the people of the world, that it is hard to say on which side of it he actually is found. . . . Beware lest you find at last that in trying to get to heaven with as little religion as possible, you have missed it altogether—lest without gaining the whole world, you lose your own soul.[5]

According to core Baptist belief, therefore, serving God and mammon clearly was thought impossible. Those who dared try risked the loss of salvation—their eternal security.

By the early twentieth century, Baptists had altered their view of the business-religion relationship. The change, evident in the attitude of B. D. Thomas, pastor of Jarvis Street from 1882 until 1903, typified the experience of many Baptists. Two months after his arrival in Toronto, Thomas expressed confidence that his new Canadian congregation had their priorities straight:

> I have visited over two hundred homes. In most, I found evidence of the most ample comfort; and in not a few the luxurious elegance which betokens wealth. I was immediately impressed with the fact that life is less anxious and intense here than in the large cities of the States. Money making is not a passion so supreme and all commanding. Not in a single instance in my intercourse with the people at their homes has the 'almighty dollar' nor, business in any form been introduced.[6]

This positive appraisal of the attitudes present in his Toronto congregation proved incorrect. By 1899, Thomas had come to the conclusion that, despite material progress, Christianity in Canada was in crisis. In one sermon entitled "Let the Redeemed of the Lord Say So," he offered a rather severe critical analysis of the changes in religious perspective:

> If we honestly compare the Christianity of the present day, especially in our larger centres, with what went under the name even thirty or forty years ago, we shall; I think, come to the conclusion that with all our advancement we have lost something out of our religious lives that we could ill afford to lose. The simplicity,

---

5. "Minimum Christian," *CB*, July 6, 1865.
6. "My Pastorate in Toronto," *CB*, October 1, 1882.

the unconventionality, the outspokenness of Christianity, call it what you please, is fast becoming a lost art.[7]

Thomas's concern about religion's decline also led him to criticize the growth of materialism and worldliness. In 1902, he used Heb 13:5 as the basis for the following observations:

> It is doubtful whether there is another passage in the whole of God's word so timely. We are living in an age of money-making. The opportunities for the accumulation of large wealth were never greater. The popular mind has become infatuated with the alluring possibility. The contentment of other days has given place to a feverish unrest and the laudable ambition to acquire moderate competence, to an over-mastering passion for abundance. This feverish grasping after money, or for ought else that the world has to offer is the most demoralizing and baneful aspect of the times.[8]

Avarice and materialism threatened both religion and society in general. Thomas's penetrating cultural analysis undoubtedly unsettled the large contingent of businessmen occupying the church's pews at the time. Yet, a few years later, in 1907, he articulated an accommodating view of the business-religion relationship:

> There is a prevalent conception that religion and business are widely separated spheres of activity—that they have little or nothing in common—that the more they are kept apart the better. Nothing could be more utterly out of harmony with the right views of life and the teaching of God's Word. Business and religion, instead of being kept apart should be brought into co-relation. They were meant in the eternal purpose to act and react upon each other helpfully.[9]

Thomas's assertion that the interests of business and religion were complementary and could be pursued simultaneously can be interpreted as an apology for serving God and mammon: "If a man is diligent in business with a proper regard to his higher relations and obligations it is as surely indicative of his Christian character as 'being fervent in spirit.' The two worlds in which we are by the very necessities of our complex

---

7. "Let the Redeemed of the Lord Say So," *CB*, November 16, 1899.
8. B. D. Thomas, "Garden of the Redeemed," in *Canadian Baptist Pulpit*, 1.
9. "How to Make the Best of Both Worlds," *CB*, August 22, 1907.

life brought into relation are not antagonistic to each other."[10] Thus, for Thomas, "the old theory that in order to secure heaven you must deny yourself all the good and sweet of earth has no foundation in fact."[11] Religion and business evidently could and should live together amicably. Thomas's change of heart represented a widespread abandonment of an earlier Baptist asceticism that was suspicious of the worldliness of business and advocated self-denial over self-aggrandizement. Whatever temptations business contained Thomas now stood convinced that the true Christian was able to "make the best of both worlds."[12]

Other Baptists shared Thomas's opinion that business and religion could be easily conjoined. "The man with a character which is the outcome of a regenerated life," declared an editorial in the September 27, 1906, issue of *The Canadian Baptist*, "will not find it difficult to conduct his business affairs in an honourable fashion or to maintain a good reputation with all those with whom business affairs necessarily bring him into contact."[13] While Baptists generally accepted the truth of this statement, practical pressures on Baptist businessmen increased in the quarter century after 1880. Many were caught between the need to satisfy the demands of their church and the exigencies of more liberal business morals. Church leaders encouraged businessmen to pursue success but not at the expense of their religious obligations. Despite the confident assertions that conflicts could and should be overcome, many Baptist businessmen struggled with stewardship, business ethics, and avarice. Although they seldom articulated these struggles, many gradually accepted the "ways of the world"; convinced that they must move with the times, they began to embrace worldly beliefs and values.

"Christ Sitting Over Against the Treasury": The Decline of Monetary Stewardship

Jesus unseen, who yet all hearts can see, Still sits and overlooks the treasury; Cast in your offerings, as his cause invites, Ye rich,

---

10. "How to Make the Best of Both Worlds," *CB*, August 22, 1907.
11. "How to Make the Best of Both Worlds," *CB*, August 22, 1907.
12. "How to Make the Best of Both Worlds," *CB*, August 22, 1907. This quote is part of the sermon title.
13. "Not Slothful in Business, Serving the Lord," *CB*, September 27, 1906.

your talents; and ye poor, your mites; Render to God the things that are his due; He gave his Son-who gave himself for you.[14]

For where your treasure is, there will your heart be also. (Matt 6:21)

At times, some Baptists confidently expressed the belief that their denomination's businessmen were accommodating business and religion successfully. As an editorial entitled "Not Slothful in Business, Serving the Lord," noted in 1906, "Indeed, it is one of the glories of our churches that so many of our devoted and active Christian workers have distinguished themselves in business life and have, by honourable means, built up for themselves fortunes that they are in turn devoting to the advancement of the cause of Christ."[15] Yet, in 1877, Robert Fyfe, former pastor of Bond Street, complained that "our rich men have not yet begun to realize their obligations in regard to giving."[16] Whatever analysis was offered, monetary stewardship remained an important testing ground for the Baptist faith. With respect to Baptist businessmen, the question remains: Did wealthy Baptist businessmen in the years between Fyfe's analysis and that given in the editorial adopt and maintain a high level of stewardship? The evidence available for wealthy businessmen from Jarvis Street indicates that they had not.

Within Jarvis Street Baptist Church, certain signs pointed to a decline in giving among the church's businessmen. In August 1878, for example, the deacons of Jarvis Street called deacon William Hewitt Sr., a well-known Toronto hardware merchant, to account for "not having for some years contributed to the weekly offering fund."[17] When the case was brought before the church for its consideration that evening Hewitt, "appeared unwilling to state his reasons for declining to bear his share of the church expenses."[18] A subsequent report offered by a Committee of three deacons on November 22, 1878, recommended that no further action be taken.[19] The reasons for the decline in Hewitt's

---

14. *CB*, October 26, 1865. This is the only verse of a poem entitled "Christ Sitting Over Against the Treasury."

15. "Not Slothful in Business, Serving the Lord," *CB*, September 27, 1906.

16. "What Are Our Rich Baptists Doing For Denominational Objects?," *CB*, December 6, 1877.

17. *Minute Book, 1866–1881*, August 30, 1878. JSBCA.

18. *Minute Book, 1866–1881*, August 30, 1878. JSBCA.

19. *Minute Book, 1866–1881*, November 22, 1878. JSBCA.

financial stewardship are not entirely clear. A church record entitled *Finances in Sterling of the Bond Street Baptist Church,* July 1840 to September 1846, shows that he gave regularly and systematically to the church.[20] Evidently, Hewitt abandoned this practice later in life. Unfortunately, the giving records needed to examine the Hewitts' long-term giving pattern are not extant. They may have been lost in the church fire that destroyed the building in March 1938.

Business reverse might explain Hewitt's change of heart and habit. In the winter of 1879, he assigned to his creditors and afterwards compromised on liabilities of $50,000. When Hewitt failed to meet the third payment in his settlement, the creditors moved to dispose of the remaining assets. Hewitt had overextended himself purchasing real estate.[21] It is probable that he was a victim of the economic downturn that began in the last two quarters of 1873 and largely lasted until 1879.[22] Ben Forster has noted that "there was no railway panic or banking crisis in September 1873 as occurred in the United States. But the economy became congested, and in 1874, prices began to drop, with business activities slowing in the third and fourth quarters. Merchants were left with huge inventories."[23] Despite some challenges, Hewitt apparently survived the early months of the economic slump. In November 1873, an agent for R. G. Dun & Company reported "their usual am[oun]t of bus[iness] have made some bad debts but are holding their own if not improving their situation."[24] By December of 1874, Dun's agent noted Hewitt's intent "to enlarge his premises."[25] Perhaps this was one of the decisions that led Hewitt down the road to insolvency.

20. *Finances in Sterling, 1840–1846,* JSBCA. Entries for 1844 and 1845 show that William Hewitt contributed 7 pounds, 6 shillings on a quarterly basis to support the church.

21. For the information on Hewitt's bankruptcy, see *Trader,* August 1880.

22. The Dun and Bradstreet *Reference Books* for January 1873 through January 1879 rated William Hewitt & Company's pecuniary strength at E-$25,000–50,000. Its general credit rating was 2 (good). Ratings were suspended late in 1879. See, for example, *Reference Book,* July 1873, 495; *Reference Book,* September 1879, n.p.; *Reference Book,* January 1880, 445.

23. Forster, *Conjunction of Interests,* 86. For an analysis of the economic downturn in the 1870s, see Forster, *Conjunction of Interests,* 86–109. For an explanation of business cycles, see Pomfret, *Economic Development of Canada,* 179–88.

24. R. G. Dun and Company Records, MG 28 III 106, vol. 26, York 1843–1877, National Archives of Canada [hereafter NA], 246.

25. R. G. Dun and Company Records, MG 28 III 106, vol. 26, York 1843–1877, NA, 246.

Although the exact reason for Hewitt's failure to tithe remains a mystery, his evasiveness when questioned about his longstanding laxity was rightly considered cause for concern. At Jarvis Street, which prided itself on setting a model for other Baptist churches to follow in financial matters, the failure by a deacon to attend to his responsibility in regard to monetary stewardship was a very serious embarrassment. Whatever the state of Hewitt's business affairs, the deacons of Jarvis Street obviously felt that Hewitt's attitudes and actions put the reputation and witness of the congregation at risk. According to contemporary Baptist reasoning, Hewitt's lack of giving had the potential to undermine the credibility of the gospel message that members of Jarvis Street were responsible to share with their community. For a deacon to profess love and loyalty to Christ and then not give of his material substance to support the cause of Christ was hypocrisy. Without the proper practice of Christian stewardship by the congregation's leaders, evangelization, or the proclamation of the gospel, by its individual members would be ineffective.

A more insidious attack on the principle and practice of stewardship is found in the attitude of William Kirkpatrick McNaught (see Figure 4). As editor of *The Trader and Canadian Jeweller*, McNaught offered advice to his fellow businessmen concerning their obligations to charity. As a member of Jarvis Street Baptist Church and president of the American Watch Case Company, McNaught gained the attention and respect of Toronto's Baptist business community. In an 1883 editorial entitled "Why Merchants Fail," McNaught laid part of the blame on "free handed charity." "In regard to charitable subscriptions," declared McNaught, "he [the merchant] should remember that 'persons should always be just before they are generous.'"[26] To make the point even more dramatically, McNaught shared this piece of sarcastic poetry with his readers:

> Plank down, plank down your shekels;
> Don't say you can't afford;
> You'd better let your creditors wait,
> Than try to cheat the Lord.[27]

The implication for Baptist businessmen was clear. For them, the religious expectation that one give to the church before repaying creditors was ridiculous. Business debts must always have priority over gifts to

---

26. "Why Merchants Fail," *Trader*, June 1883.
27. "Why Merchants Fail," *Trader*, June 1883.

charity. Baptists, like Thomas Ford Caldicott, a former pastor of Bond Street, in his much-quoted sermon on Systematic Beneficence, had traditionally taught that the "first fruits" and not the leftovers of a man's means must be given to God.[28] Thus, while McNaught encouraged the merchant to do all for charity that "his means would allow,"[29] he altered Baptist giving principles and practices to suit the priorities of a business-dominated culture.

Other signs of waning stewardship are found in the bequests of Jarvis Street's prominent businessmen. In May 1881, Arthur Robinson McMaster made provision in his will for regular giving to the church's ministry to be continued: "I desire my wife out of her income to keep up my usual weekly offering to the Jarvis Street Church whereof I am a member and in the prosperity of which I feel so deep an interest."[30] William McMaster acted similarly. Church records reveal that weekly contributions in the amount of $208 came from his estate after his death in 1887.[31] He also left the bulk of his estate, some $900,000, to establish McMaster University.[32] Denominational endowments and local church bequests were not unusual for McMaster's generation.

In contrast, the succeeding generation of Baptist businessmen often left little to their church or any other charity. William Kirkpatrick McNaught, who died in Toronto on February 2, 1919, left his entire estate of $212,754.69 to his family. Nothing was donated to charity.[33] Harry Ryrie, a wealthy jeweller who died suddenly in 1917, bequeathed nothing to his church and only $8,000 to other charities. His estate was valued at $706,970.50. Only two Baptist causes, the home and foreign

---

28. Caldicott, *Systematic Beneficence*, 14.

29. "Why Merchants Fail," *Trader*, June 1883.

30. Archives of Ontario [hereafter AO], Record Group 22 [hereafter RG 22], Surrogate Court Records, County of York, Estate Files, No. 3459, Will of Arthur Robinson McMaster, May 7, 1881. This date, and the others cited in this section, refers to when the Will was filed in Surrogate Court and not to the date of death.

31. *Jarvis Street Baptist Church Treasurers Book, 1887-1914*, June 7, 1887 (MS), JSBCA.

32. The total amount of William McMaster's estate was $1,154,178.03. For his will see AO, RG 22, Surrogate Court Records, County of York, No. 6586. For records of how the assets of the estate were managed by its trustees see CBA, *McMaster Estate Minute Books*, February 19, 1891 to December 4, 1895, December 4, 1895 to December 28, 1899, January 26, 1900–April 14, 1905, May 10, 1905–December 17, 1920.

33. AO, RG 22, Surrogate Court Records, County of York, No. 39982, Will of William Kirkpatrick McNaught, February 20, 1920.

mission boards, received donations in the amount of $1,000 each.[34] To Harry Ryrie, city park benches were more important than any religious charitable cause. He willed $10,000 to the City of Toronto for "the purchase of one hundred park benches" costing $100 each, their design subject to the approval of his trustees.[35] "My desire is that fifty of these benches be placed in and about Island Park and the Lake Shore Frontage at Toronto Island where I have lived many summers and have realized the need of benches. I desire the remainder of the benches to be scattered throughout other Parks in the City of Toronto."[36] The bulk of Ryrie's estate went to family members. This evidence is proof of an important change of attitude. While in the late nineteenth century, bequests to religious endeavors were commonplace in the wills of Baptist businessmen, family and personal priorities had largely displaced these endowments by the early twentieth century.

The declining support of Jarvis Street's businessmen created financial hardship for the church. As early as the late 1890s signs were beginning to surface. In 1876, a year after the Jarvis Street Church was opened, small credit balances are recorded in all of its accounts.[37] By April 1, 1896, the church was carrying a floating debt of $5,360.80.[38] A year later the debt stood at $6,260.08.[39] Church members were constantly reminded of their financial obligations, and church directories usually included a section entitled "What is Expected," in which members received a list of their duties:

> It is expected that members will, as far as their ability will allow, bear a just proportion of the necessary expenses of the church, and also contribute to the various benevolent objects; this can always be done through the weekly offering system and through the stated collections, which are referred to in another part of this book, and which will be fully explained by the treasurers to all desiring information. Note-Members who, from adverse

---

34. AO, RG 22, Surrogate Court Records, County of York, No. 34353, Will of Harry Ryrie, February 25, 1914.

35. AO, RG 22, Surrogate Court Records, County of York, No. 34353, Will of Harry Ryrie, February 25, 1914.

36. AO, RG 22, Surrogate Court Records, County of York, No. 34353, Will of Harry Ryrie, February 25, 1914.

37. *Directory of the Jarvis Street Baptist Church, Toronto, 1876–1877*, 10.

38. *Directory of the Jarvis Street Baptist Church, Toronto, August 1897*, 14.

39. *Directory of the Jarvis Street Baptist Church, Toronto, August 1897*, 14.

circumstances or any sufficient cause cannot contribute, will always receive the most tender consideration.⁴⁰

Unfortunately, such reminders did little to stimulate more giving. At a church meeting held on April 22, 1898, deacon D. E. Thomson announced with some consternation that "it had been necessary to arrange for an overdraft at the bank."⁴¹ On September 24, 1900, a letter from deacon J. C. Scott, the church treasurer, was read to the deacons "calling attention to the fact that the Communion Fund was sagging behind and that unless the contributions increased he would be unable to pay the monthly am[oun]t which had been voted to our members in need."⁴² On October 30, 1907, the Finance Committee noted that the church was behind $3,200 in its contributions. On November 8, 1907, the Finance Committee "discussed ways and means of increasing the revenues of the Church."⁴³ It was decided that a "canvass" of "twenty members" should be conducted with a view to "induce them to increase their offerings so as they would aggregate $3,000 annually."⁴⁴

The canvass produced such positive results that the committee set out to solicit the financial support of a further twenty members.⁴⁵ At the October 14, 1908, meeting of the Finance Committee, "Brother Gunn presented a report showing a slight improvement in Weekly Offering payments for the half year, but a falling off in plate collections."⁴⁶ By January 26, 1909, the floating debt stood at $4,500.⁴⁷

Despite efforts to increase offerings, a floating debt remained a permanent fixture in the church's financial picture. It appears that the canvass, while successful on the surface, only encouraged members to

40. *Directory of the Jarvis Street Baptist Church, Toronto, August 1897*, 19.

41. *Jarvis Street Baptist Church Minute Book, 1892-1910*, April 22, 1898 (MS), JSBCA.

42. *Jarvis Street Baptist Church Minute Book, 1900-1903*, September 24, 1900 (MS), JSBCA.

43. *Jarvis Street Baptist Church Minute Book, 1907-1921*, November 8, 1907 (MS), JSBCA.

44. *Jarvis Street Baptist Church Minute Book, 1907-1921*, November 8, 1907 (MS), JSBCA.

45. *Jarvis Street Baptist Church Minute Book, 1907-1921*, November 22, 1907 (MS), JSBCA.

46. *Jarvis Street Baptist Church Minute Book, 1907-1921*, October 14, 1908 (MS), JSBCA.

47. *Jarvis Street Baptist Church Minute Book, 1907-1921*, January 26, 1909 (MS), JSBCA.

change their contribution method. Instead of putting an anonymous loose offering in the collection plate, wealthy members increasingly opted to use a numbered offering envelope that clearly identified the contributor to the church treasurer.[48] However, the desired increase in revenues did not accompany the change in methodology. The financial gain for the church was minimal.

By 1914, T. T. Shields, who had become pastor in 1910, had grown weary of the debt and the persistent state of financial crisis. Later, he recalled his response to Jarvis Street's financial situation:

> In the early part of 1914 I decided that it was time to act; I therefore told the deacons that until I became pastor of Jarvis Street, I had never presided at the Annual Meeting of any church at which I was pastor, where a deficit had been reported, and that I had done so for the last time at Jarvis Street. I pointed out that it was utterly unnecessary. Jarvis Street people had plenty of money to meet their obligations when they were due; that it was not honouring to the church nor to the Lord to treat its business affairs so carelessly.
>
> Furthermore, I told them that the man who, more than anybody else, was held responsible for the state of a church, in public estimation, was the pastor; and I did not propose to bear the responsibility any longer. At the same time I pointed out the need for extension in several directions, with the result that the deficit of six thousand dollars, which by sheer carelessness had been allowed to accumulate, was met, and the sum of sixty thousand dollars was subscribed for a new building.[49]

Shields's handling of the church's financial situation is illuminating. His motivation was both personal and corporate. For Shields, the integrity of both pastor and church were put at risk by the "slipshod"[50] manner in which church business was conducted. As a fundamentalist, Shields reacted against what he perceived to be an erosion of established Baptist practice. For him, the elimination of the floating debt represented an attempt to recapture the high moral principles of Ontario's vanishing evangelical moral consensus. His actions sent a clear message to his congregation that a more liberal attitude towards church finances was

---

48. For a record of the giving in this period and more details on how the envelope system worked, see *Jarvis Street Baptist Church Tithing Ledger, 1906–1911* (MS), JSBCA.

49. Shields, *Plot That Failed*, 35–36.

50. Shields, *Plot That Failed*, 35. Shields's term for how church finances were handled.

unacceptable. Nevertheless, his radical conservatism and autocratic approach was undoubtedly resented by some businessmen at Jarvis Street. Some of the same deacons that Shields chided for their financial laxity in 1914 would turn on him in 1919. The result of the ensuing power struggle would be a schism by 1921.[51]

The problem of declining stewardship was not restricted to Jarvis Street Baptist Church. In the 1890s, some Canadian Baptists certainly expressed concern about the lack of financial support. An editorial in the April 20, 1899, issue of *The Canadian Baptist* analyzed "the situation":

> The convention year will be closed within a fortnight. We have entered upon a period of increased prosperity. The earth has yielded her increase. Business has revived. There is more abundant employment for all who desire it. In many departments of labour, wages have been raised. Notwithstanding all this, our Boards are facing the close of the year with concern, lest the deficits which have been embarrassing their work for the past few years should be enlarged rather than wiped out. There can be no question, this is not as it ought to be. The treasury of the Lord should share in the tide of prosperity which is flooding over the land. To fail to increase our contributions for the Lord's work when there is increased income is the poorest way to show our appreciation of the divine goodness through which alone all blessing comes.[52]

Denominational coffers, then, were also feeling the pinch from the decline of monetary stewardship.

In response to the severe financial need, efforts like the Forward Movement and the Laymen's Missionary Movement sought to engender enthusiasm for stewardship among the faithful. The Forward Movement, which began for Canadian Baptists in the late 1890s, was both an interdenominational and denominational effort to encourage a higher level of commitment to spreading the gospel message and living a sanctified life.[53] The Laymen's Missionary Movement was also both an interdenom-

---

51. This schism will be analyzed in chapter 6. For contrasting interpretations of Shields and information on the 1921 schism, one should consult Tarr, *Shields of Canada*, 72-84; Russell, "Thomas Todhunter Shields," 263-80; Ellis, "Social and Religious Factors," 52-179.

52. "Situation," *CB*, April 20, 1899.

53. A number of papers, pamphlets, and articles were written by the denomination's prominent businessmen concerning the Forward Movement and published by the denomination. Monetary stewardship was a primary emphasis in much of the

inational and denominational effort which had as its aim the "evangelization of the whole world" in thirty years.[54]

Usually headed by the denomination's most respected Toronto businessmen, these campaigns for stewardship renewal and revival targeted the Baptist laity. Prominent businessmen from Jarvis Street played a leading role in these endeavors. In his role as Chairman of the Baptist Home Missions Board for twenty-one years, member of the Forward Movement Committee of the Toronto (Baptist) Association and the Baptist Laymen's Missionary Movement Committee, jeweller James Ryrie, became a recognized spokesman for stewardship causes. Under headlines in *The Canadian Baptist* like "Let George Do It," "Concerning Criminally Careless Christians," and "James Ryrie, Toronto,"[55] Ryrie promoted his cause and challenged fellow Baptist businessmen to fulfil their stewardship obligations.

Quartus B. Henderson, who joined Jarvis Street in 1901, and became president of the printing firm of Davis & Henderson Limited, authored a pamphlet entitled *The Dollar in Business and Religion* in support of the Forward Movement. In it, Henderson argued that a variety of causes were at the root of the denomination's financial crisis. First, ignorance about the shrinking value of the dollar hurt stewardship. "The dollar of today and the dollar of five or six years ago are two entirely different things," Henderson declared, "and the only time when we value the dollar on its old basis is when it comes to giving to

---

literature. See, for example, Baptist Forward Movement, *General Scheme*; *Financial Objective*; *Spiritual Aims of the Baptist Forward Movement*; *Now Concerning the Collection*; "What Is the Forward Movement?," *Forward Movement News*, January 7, 1920; "Our Twentieth Century Forward Movement," *CB*, August 4, 1898; "Forward Movement," *CB*, June 29, 1899; "Forward Movement Tidings and Teachings," *CB*, December 11, 1919. For an analysis of the Forward Movement among Baptists, see Goertz, "Missed Opportunity," 304–42.

54. For information on the Laymen's Missionary Movement, see "Call to Baptist Laymen," *CB*, January 2, 1908. James Ryrie's name appears below this article along with the names of the other members of the Laymen's Committee. "Laymen's Missionary Movement," *CB*, January 23, 1908. The quote used is taken from "$4,000 Offering," *CB*, March 5, 1908. "Baptist Laymen's Missionary Movement Convention," *CB*, May 21, 1908; "Laymen's Movement in Toronto," *CB*, November 25, 1909; "Layman to Laymen," *CB*, September 18, 1913. This is a letter written by James Ryrie concerning the Baptist Laymen's conference that was held in Toronto, from September 30 to October 1, 1913.

55. "Let George Do It," *CB*, February 20, 1919; "Concerning Criminally Careless Christians," *CB*, July 16, 1914; "James Ryrie, Toronto," *CB*, January 23, 1908.

the Lord's work."⁵⁶ Henderson went on to challenge the contention that church expenditures had increased too rapidly:

> In one of the leading churches of our denomination the expenditure for the year ending in 1918 was less than 4 per cent greater than the expenditure six years ago. Can you tell me of any business institution or organization in the country where the operating cost has not increased from 50 per cent to 75 per cent? Why is it that our giving to the church is still on the old basis, and everything else on the new?⁵⁷

One of Henderson's "leading churches" may well have been Jarvis Street. Indeed, his point concerning the rise of church expenses had the ring of truth for the members of his own congregation. To those Baptists who maintained that the war had impoverished them, Henderson retorted, "that the first year of peace has proven to be one of the most prosperous in our history."⁵⁸ He went on to show that in order to raise $450,000, which was 100 percent more than the $225,000 named by the Forward Committee, each Baptist in Ontario and Quebec (some 60,000 members) would need to contribute $7.50.⁵⁹ "It would not surprise me at all," wrote Henderson, "that the church members of the denomination spend more than this amount on amusements."⁶⁰ To those who dared to suggest that they had tired of giving, Henderson responded, "Dare you stop to think what would happen if the Creator got tired of giving?"⁶¹ He concluded with a challenge:

> My fellow Canadian Baptists, we ought all to give more than we have been giving. We are not too poor to give. We dare not say that we are tired of giving, and we most certainly have cause to give. Let us see that our gifts are worthy of disciples of the Great Giver who gave His all that we might be free.⁶²

This stirring appeal was typical of those used in the Baptist Forward Movement. In the wider context, the efforts of James Ryrie and Quartus B. Henderson illustrated the desire of some prominent Baptist businessmen

---

56. Henderson, *Dollar in Business and Religion*, 1.
57. Henderson, *Dollar in Business and Religion*, 2.
58. Henderson, *Dollar in Business and Religion*, 3.
59. Henderson, *Dollar in Business and Religion*, 4.
60. Henderson, *Dollar in Business and Religion*, 4.
61. Henderson, *Dollar in Business and Religion*, 5.
62. Henderson, *Dollar in Business and Religion*, 6.

to dissociate themselves from the decline in giving and establish themselves as standard bearers in the fight to restore financial priorities. While one must be careful not to overstate the case, there is little doubt that the Baptist businessman's commitment to stewardship declined in the late nineteenth century. Although failures in stewardship are observable at many points in church history, the changes in attitude and action exhibited by Jarvis Street's businessmen in the late nineteenth century are clear evidence of secularization. Despite efforts to increase stewardship at both the local and denominational levels, Baptist businessmen increasingly put business, family, and personal obligations first.

The Decline of Business Ethics

As Baptist businessmen pursued sociocultural integration in the last half of the nineteenth century, their ethical standards also changed. They modified their views of business morality in keeping with the prevailing culture. The church's refusal to involve itself in settling business disputes, its encouragement of an alliance between religion and business, and its increasingly liberal attitude in matters related to business practice combined to free businessmen from the threat of church discipline. Armed with the knowledge that the church would not act, some Baptist businessmen became involved in business situations that a generation earlier would have brought immediate condemnation.

One area in which ethics declined particularly was that of business-labor relations. In his examination of the Baptist perspective on labor, George Rawlyk has suggested that

> Canadian Baptists were once widely regarded as being the "champions of the oppressed." Their evangelicalism was a fascinating blend of experiential religion and profound social concern. And this blend would characterize-until at least the third decade of the twentieth century—a wide spectrum of the Baptist belief stretching from liberalism on the one extreme to fundamentalism on the other, a spectrum to be found in all regions of Canada.[63]

There is ample evidence in the central Canadian context to support Rawlyk's suggestion that many Baptists empathized with the working class and downtrodden. McMaster Professor J. L. Gilmour put the

---

63. Rawlyk, "Champions of the Oppressed?," 105.

matter plainly: "The Baptists have sympathy with all the proper aspirations that are meant to find expression on Labour Day, and they hope, that we may all learn to look not only on our own good but on that of our brethren."[64] Baptists, perhaps more than any other Protestant denomination, recognized the linkages between the labor movement and Christianity. As Richard Allen has noted this was particularly true for those Canadian Baptists who embraced the social gospel.[65] Even fundamentalists who criticized the theological underpinnings of the social gospel would have agreed with E. W. Dadson that "the best Baptists are found just as often among washerwomen and soil-delvers as among those who attend fashionable lectures."[66]

Nevertheless, this is not to suggest that Baptists were immune to class conflict. As historians Walter Ellis and Mary Bulmer Hill have shown, class antagonisms played an important role in the fundamentalist-modernist schisms among Canadian Baptists between 1895 and 1934.[67] Even within Jarvis Street, considered by many Baptists to be a "high-class" church, the social constitution of the congregation was diverse. For example, in his examination of Jarvis Street's social profile in 1913, Ellis showed that among the congregation's four major occupational groups (professions-entrepreneurs, managerial-sales, white collar, blue collar-labor), blue collar-labor constituted the largest group with 35.78 percent.[68] This high percentage in what was perceived to be a wealthy business and professional urban Baptist congregation points to the reality of the labor presence and the potential for class conflict.

Still, important questions remain unanswered. What was the response of Toronto's Baptist business community to the worker's plight? Did Toronto's Baptist employers treat their workers any differently than employers from the city's other denominations? Is there any observable change in the attitudes and actions of Baptist businessmen towards their workers over time?

Unfortunately, the evidence needed to provide definitive answers to these questions from the experience of businessmen from Jarvis Street Baptist Church in the period between 1880 and 1921 is lacking. The best

64. "Baptists and Labour," *CB*, September 1, 1921.
65. Allen, *Social Passion*, 68–69, 106–7, 138–39.
66. Farmer, *E. W. Dadson*, 201.
67. See Ellis, "Social and Religious Factors," 32–178, 211–34; Hill, "From Sect to Denomination," 1–153.
68. Ellis, "Social and Religious Factors," 169.

available evidence suggests that Baptist businessmen treated their employees in a manner similar to their counterparts in other Protestant denominations. As well, it is clear that the response of Jarvis Street's businessmen to the worker's grievances followed no uniform pattern.

On the positive side, certain Baptist employers made genuine efforts to promote their employee's well-being. The clothing retailer, wholesaler and manufacturer, John Northway, of John Northway & Son Limited, for example, typified the Baptists whom Rawlyk and Allen describe (see Figure 5). As Alan Wilson observed, Northway "was a simple Christian entrepreneur, who drew his compassion from his deep religious convictions."[69] To his workers, that compassion consisted of pioneering efforts to establish welfare and pension plans among them. Beginning in 1913, Northway set aside monies in a "Special Wages Fund" for the relief of employees who had suffered hardship.[70] In a January 1914 entry in his diary Northway encapsulated the current Social Gospel ethic, "'The Fatherhood of God is meaningless without the brotherhood of man.'"[71] By 1915, Northway had hired Albert Hurd as social service coordinator for John Northway & Son Limited. As Wilson has noted, "His decision to engage a man to examine the social and economic needs of his employees preceded the outbursts of general labour unrest that followed the War, and made him a pioneer in this aspect of the field of employee relations in medium-sized industry in Canada."[72]

Despite his benevolent attitude, John Northway experienced the occasional difficulty in his relationship with labor. In early February 1903, for example, a cutters' strike affected John Northway & Son Limited and another clothing manufacturer with Baptist connections, Lailey, Watson & Bond, demonstrating that even the most sympathetic Baptist businessmen sometimes found themselves at odds with their workers.[73] In this case, the central issues were a reduction in the work week from 55 to 49 hours and certain restrictions on the hiring of apprentices. Lailey, Watson & Bond resisted initial calls for arbitration, claiming that "there was nothing to arbitrate."[74] Within a few days, that stance gave way to

69. Wilson, *John Northway*, 174.
70. Wilson, *John Northway*, 176.
71. Wilson, *John Northway*, 174.
72. Wilson, *John Northway*, 176–77.
73. "Garment Workers," *Toiler*, February 6, 1903.
74. "Nothing to Arbitrate," *Toronto Daily Star*, February 4, 1903; "Strikers Vigilant," *Toronto Daily Star*, February 5, 1903.

compromise as other employers gave in to union demands.[75] A final agreement to end the strike did not come easily.[76]

Another paternalistic and progressive thinker in business-labor relations was the Baptist meat packer William Davies, "one of the few Canadian businessmen of the 1880s that shared his profits with his employees." This action provided "a powerful incentive to stay with Davies."[77] In addition, through voluntary wage increases in good times and minimal layoffs in bad times, the company displayed a genuine concern for its workforce.[78]

Not all Baptist businessmen were as generous or progressive as Northway and Davies. Indeed, by the late nineteenth century, some members of the new generation of Baptist businessmen accepted mistreatment or exploitation as a means to maximize profits. At Firstbrook Brothers' box-making factory (see Figure 6), for example, anti-union sentiments, the employment of boys under the legal age limit, and numerous accidents revealed attitudes and actions that by Baptist ethical standards might be thought immoral. Yet, in his testimony before the Royal Commission on the Relations of Labour and Capital, Joseph Firstbrook, whose brothers John and William were the principal owners of the firm and members of Jarvis Street, steadfastly denied all suggestions that management was in any way negligent, exploitive, anti-union, or anti-worker. At one point, Firstbrook was questioned about the frequency of accidents:

> Q. Would it surprise you if one of your old hands should make affidavit that accidents take place about twice a month?
>
> A. I should simply say the man was a liar. I can prove it. I should not be surprised if they should say accidents occur daily, or something of that sort. I have heard some of our former employees saying they occurred every day, and so on. I should be surprised to hear anybody tell me that we have an average of two accidents a month, or an accident in two months, and I think when you consider the fact that we have a great many

---

75. "To Settle a Strike," *Toronto Daily Star*, February 7, 1903.

76. I have not been able to find any reference as to when the cutters' strike actually ended. After some signs of compromise by the employers, negotiations took a turn for the worse in mid-February. The pressers were called out in sympathy. "Pressers Called Out," *Toronto Daily Star*, February 14, 1903.

77. Bliss, *Canadian Millionaire*, 36, 118.

78. Bliss, *Canadian Millionaire*, 118.

more machines than any other wood-working establishment in Toronto, you must make some allowance for that.⁷⁹

The confrontational and defensive tone taken by Firstbrook belies his claims of innocence. His distrust of workers is revealed in his charge that they are habitual liars. In addition, Firstbrook blamed accidental injuries and deaths on worker carelessness and claimed that the Knights of Labor did nothing but cause trouble. "The men are better off than they were in the places they came from" Firstbrook declared, "and our business is in more satisfactory form. We have no Knights of Labour now. We had so much trouble with them that if I were guaranteed the same amount of trouble for the next two years I would close down the shutters and go and work for somebody else."⁸⁰ While the Firstbrook brothers were in no way responsible for a wildcat strike by Knights of Labor members in May 1887, it is also apparent that company management strongly opposed any move to make their company a union shop.⁸¹

To the charge of employing child labor, Firstbrook also pleaded innocent. In response to questions about the firm's employment of boys, Firstbrook claimed, "we have three boys between twelve and fourteen; the others are older."⁸² Asked if these younger boys were employed in the dangerous task of carrying lumber from the saws, Firstbook responded, "No; they are working on the nailing machines."⁸³ Yet despite Firstbrook's claim that underaged boys were not employed in his factory, the case of McIntosh versus Firstbrook Box Company first heard in Divisional Court of the High Court of Justice on April 25 to 26, 1904, clearly showed that the company made no effort beyond the word of the child to ascertain the age of the boys that it employed. The company also did not provide sufficient warning as to the dangers of the work environment.

In response to worker agitation for better industrial standards and working conditions in the late 1870s, the Ontario government moved to address the problem of child labor and employer negligence. In 1887, a revision of The Ontario Factories' Act of 1884 made it illegal for boys under twelve years of age and girls under fourteen years of age to be hired in any factory. A further amendment of The Factories' Act in 1889 made

79. Canada, *Report of the Royal Commission*.
80. Canada, *Report of the Royal Commission*, 4.
81. "Trouble at Firstbrook Bros.," *Globe*, May 11, 1887.
82. Canada, *Report of the Royal Commission*.
83. Canada, *Report of the Royal Commission*.

it illegal for boys under fourteen years to be hired in a box factory like Firstbrook's. Compensation legislation designed to ensure worker safety and guard against employer negligence also became significant in the case of McIntosh v. Firstbrook Box Company.[84]

In this case, a boy of ten lied about his age, claimed that he was fourteen and was hired for the nondangerous tasks of stacking and gluing boxes. On his second day on the job, he took a circuitous and dangerous route back to his job and inadvertently placed his left hand on a buzz-planer, which severed one finger and part of another on his left hand. He and his mother subsequently sued for damages, alleging that the Firstbrook Box Company had violated the Factories' Act and been negligent in not warning of the dangers present.[85]

Although the court found for the defendants, reservations about the company's behavior were apparent throughout the appeal process. At the appeal heard June 29, 1905, for example, Judge J. A. Garrow noted:

> There was some evidence that the master here had not discharged his whole duty to a new boy of even the assumed age, for, while he was not at work at a dangerous machine, there were such machines in the room where he was employed, and he was not warned about approaching them, or to use only the safe way in going to or coming from his work.[86]

The implication here is that the foreman who hired the boy, and by extension the Firstbrook Box Company, paid little attention to worker safety. Furthermore, Judge Featherstone Osler noted, "It is not without some doubt and hesitation that I concur in affirming the judgement . . . there is plausibility in the suggestion that the defendants have not

---

84. For an overview of provincial and federal legislation designed to protect factory workers, see Drummond, *Progress Without Planning*, 234–35. For the legal background, see Risk, "Nuisance of Litigation," 418–91. For the sections of the Factories' Act prohibiting child labour, see *Revised Statutes of Ontario 1887* [hereafter *RSQ*], "Act for the Protection of Persons Employed in Factories," [also may be cited as "Ontario Factories' Act," 47 Vic. c. 39, March 25, 1884) c. 20s, s. 2., s.s. 5., s. 6., s.s. 1; *Statutes of the Province of Ontario* "Act to Amend the Ontario Factories' Act," 52 Vic. c. 43, March 23, 1889. Schedule A, which lists those factories subject to the Act is revised to include "Box Factories," for the first time. For some of the relevant legislation on negligence, see, for example, *Statutes of the Province of Ontario* "Workmen's Compensation for Injuries Act," 55 Vic. c. 30, April 14, 1892; *RSO 1897* "Act to Secure Compensation to Workmen in Certain Cases," c. 160.

85. The information in this paragraph is taken from Smith, *Ontario Law Reports* (1904), 8:419–39.

86. Smith, *Ontario Law Reports* (1904), 10:527.

shown that they scrutinized with sufficient care the boy's statement of his age."[87] Thus, while Firstbrook was not found guilty of negligence or violation of the Factories' Act, its actions in this case showed little concern for the safety of its young workers and an absence of any preventative measures to ensure against hiring underaged employees. By Baptist standards, the Firstbrooks failed to fulfil their moral obligation to young McIntosh and his mother.

In the latter part of the nineteenth century, there was a growing willingness on the part of some Baptist businessmen from Jarvis Street to engage in what many Canadian Baptists would have considered immoral and questionable business practices. On April 26, 1878, for example, a committee of deacons reported that J. F. McDonald "was guilty of embezzlement of the funds of the Northern Railway Company."[88] Not surprisingly, a motion was passed to exclude McDonald from the church.

In a more complicated court case, William Kirkpatrick McNaught was sued by W. E. Stavert of the Bank of Montreal for failing to repay a promissory note for $17,030.[89] As the prosecution examined McNaught, certain questions concerning the propriety of two of his actions were raised. McNaught served as a director of the Sovereign Bank from late fall 1904 until it was absorbed by twelve other Canadian banks in 1908. It appears that during his tenure, he was a party to a questionable stock purchase and a scheme designed to suppress potentially damaging publicity concerning the state of the bank's affairs after a reorganization at the Sovereign in June 1907.[90]

In his examination concerning the purchase of stock (worth $58,000 in January 1907) A. W. Anglin, the counsel for the plaintiffs, attacked McNaught's business integrity.[91] At one point in the proceedings McNaught was clearly on the defensive:

---

87. Smith, *Ontario Law Reports* (1904), 10:528.

88. *Minute Book, 1866–1881*, April 26, 1878. JSBCA.

89. AO, RG 22, Unprocessed Chancery Court Records, County of York, City Suits and Country Causes, Stavert v. McNaught, 11 Statement of Claim, Filed October 6, 1908, Box 175, Case 1399.

90. The Sovereign Bank was organized between 1900 and 1902 by Duncan M. Stewart. The principal investors included the German Dresdner Bank and J. P. Morgan and Company of New York. For more detail on the Bank and its absorption, see "Sovereign Bank Absorbed; Its Obligations Guaranteed," *Globe*, January 18, 1908.

91. Stavert v. McNaught, "Examination of W. K. McNaught," March 12, 1909, Box 175, Case 1399.

> Q. Do you have other stock that is not in your name?
>
> A. Yes.
>
> Q. How much?
>
> A. $58,000 bought by Mr. Stewart [of the Sovereign Bank] ... It was put in my name originally by Mr. Stewart without my knowledge.
>
> Q. All of it?
>
> A. No. The first 100 shares.
>
> Q. When did you assume liability?
>
> A. Well the stock I refer to was stock bought by the late general manager himself without our knowledge or having anything to do with it, for the purpose of keeping up the price of the bank's stock and after it came to the knowledge of the directors, or after it came to the knowledge of the people in New York they insisted on the directors taking it over or they wouldn't make any advances to the bank, and it was in this way it came about. That is the reason I say I don't acknowledge I ever owned the stock.[92]

Further testimony reveals that McNaught then signed an agreement to take over a portion of the stock. Still, more pressure was applied by the New York investors, including J. P. Morgan, for McNaught and the other directors to assume full liability.[93] Prosecution lawyer A. W. Anglin queried McNaught's response to this pressure:

> Q. What did you do?
>
> A. I think it was transferred into our names, some of it, and then they wanted it taken out of our names and put in somebody else's names to make it look better.
>
> Q. And that was done?
>
> A. I think that was done. I think that is the way it stood at the time of this transaction.
>
> Q. What about the stock? Did you pay any money?
>
> A. No.

---

92. Stavert v. McNaught, "Examination of W. K. McNaught," March 12, 1909, Box 175, Case 1399.

93. Stavert v. McNaught, "Examination of W. K. McNaught," March 12, 1909, Box 175, Case 1399.

Q. What did you do?

A. Nothing.

Q. Did you become in any way on the face of things responsible for any moneys directly or indirectly in that connection?

A. I can't just say now what position I was in regard to that. The thing was mixed up and I hadn't thought of it for a long time. My recollection is I did guarantee the stock which was taken over by my son [C. B. McNaught].[94]

In further questioning about McNaught's business interests, Anglin introduced the fact that he had borrowed $80,000 to $90,000 on the basis of his bank stocks in the depression of mid-summer 1907.[95] For Anglin, this action was indicative of McNaught's dishonesty. Assuming that McNaught had allowed Stewart to transfer all of the $58,000 worth to him, his total holdings would have amounted to no more than a maximum of $78,000. Still, McNaught claimed under oath that he was entitled to borrow the cash that he did because equity was always in his favor.

Anglin's examination exposed questionable business practices by Baptist moral standards. McNaught's willingness to go to almost any length to boost the Sovereign Bank's sagging public image compromised his integrity. His lack of attention related to the transfer of stock into his name left the impression of negligence, and his overvaluation of his stock for borrowing purposes smacked of dishonesty. These actions certainly put his previous reputation among fellow Baptists as "a most capable business man [sic] having a good record for aggressiveness and integrity" at risk.[96]

Further evidence of McNaught's abandonment of what Baptists might call "proper" business ethics can be found in later testimony, which revealed his involvement in efforts to squelch and suppress potentially harmful publicity. After the Sovereign Bank's reorganization in 1907, concern about the actions of a disgruntled former employee named Graham Brown gained the attention of the new Board of Directors. Of particular concern was Brown's threat to distribute a circular calling for an investigation into the Bank's affairs. Fearing a run on the

---

94. Stavert v. McNaught, "Examination of W. K. McNaught," March 12, 1909, Box 175, Case 1399.

95. Stavert v. McNaught, "Examination of W. K. McNaught," March 12, 1909, Box 175, Case 1399.

96. *CB*, December 14, 1905.

Bank, McNaught testified that a series of meetings were held to determine a course of action. Present at most or all of the meetings were Aemillus Jarvis, President, F. G. Jemmett, General Manager, Robert Cassels, Assistant Manager, and lawyer W. J. Boland. At a meeting held in McNaught's house, it was decided that he should meet privately with ex-employee Brown to hear his grievances.[97]

In his face-to-face meeting with McNaught, Brown demanded a letter of recommendation, $2,000 cash in additional retiring allowance, and a "buy-back" of the 131 shares of bank stock that he had purchased at the request of D. M. Stewart to help keep the bank's stock value high. These stocks had a market value of $17,000. McNaught then went to meet his associates at the Royal Canadian Yacht Club. According to McNaught's testimony, Jarvis recommended that the directors, who ran the bank before the reorganization of 1907, buy the stock. McNaught claimed to respond, "I said so far as I was concerned personally that I wouldn't spend a five cent piece in buying up any more stock in that way and you can count me out."[98] Boland argued that although it was illegal, it should be done for the bank and the shareholders. Cassels agreed. When Anglin asked, "Did Jarvis assent to what you had said and give authority to buy the stock of the bank?" McNaught answered, "Yes, absolutely, but I don't remember the words that he used."[99] Convinced that he was authorized to settle the matter, McNaught met with Brown the next morning at the National Club and presented him with the letter, $2,000 and the stock. "I told [Brown]," McNaught testified, "we agreed to take that stock off his hands as he wanted, and to my astonishment he said I must have that $17,000 before two o'clock or the circular goes out."[100]

Caught by surprise, McNaught scrambled to meet Brown's demand for cash. McNaught had Boland make a note for the amount. which he then endorsed. The actual procedure followed by McNaught and Boland came out in court:

---

97. Stavert v. McNaught, "Examination of W. K. McNaught," March 12, 1909, Box 175, Case 1399. The facts in this paragraph are taken from McNaught's testimony.

98. Stavert v. McNaught, "Examination of W. K. McNaught," March 12, 1909, Box 175, Case 1399.

99. Stavert v. McNaught, "Examination of W. K. McNaught," March 12, 1909, Box 175, Case 1399.

100. Stavert v. McNaught, "Examination of W. K. McNaught," March 12, 1909, Box 175, Case 1399.

> Yes, he [Boland] drew a cheque for the amount and then he said to me, now, I am going to give my own cheque to Montgomery,[101] but I will take my cheque over to John Guinane[102] at the shoe store and I will trade cheques and we will pay with Guinane's cheque for this stock, and I had given him [Boland] the letter. Mr. Jemmett had given the letter upstairs ... so Boland had everything.[103]

This statement reveals McNaught's complicity in a series of unethical practices. Even though McNaught gave all of the documents to Boland, who actually completed the transaction with Brown, McNaught was a party to the cover-up that paying Brown with Guinane's cheque was intended to accomplish. If the deal with Brown was above reproach why did Boland, with McNaught's knowledge and complicity, go to such lengths to keep the payout a secret? The payment of "hush money" to Brown was by Baptist standards dishonest. But McNaught's deceit went even further. Even though he testified that "this was the end of it as far as I was concerned," McNaught participated in a more general cover up of the entire transaction.[104]

At an August 5, 1907, meeting of the Board of Directors, the method of payment for Brown's stock was not disclosed. McNaught, Jarvis, and Jemmett had secretly agreed that any disclosure should be delayed. In fact, by McNaught's own admission, disclosure did not take place until after January 18, 1908, when Jarvis announced that the Sovereign Bank had "gone out of business" and would be absorbed by other leading banks.[105] Under Anglin's strong and persistent questioning, McNaught steadfastly maintained his innocence. Although McNaught was not found guilty of impropriety, his desire to maintain a sterling public image led him to acquiesce in Brown's blackmail, participate in a money laundering scheme

---

101. Montgomery may have been Robert J. Montgomery who was manager of the Canadian Bank of Commerce branch located at 796–798 Yonge Street in Toronto until 1905. He would have known Jarvis, Jemmett, and others previously associated with the Commerce. See, for example, *Canadian Bank of Commerce Charter and Annual Reports 1867–1907*, Annual Report for 1905, 1:633.

102. John Guinane's shoe store was located at 15 King Street West.

103. Stavert v. McNaught, "Examination of W. K. McNaught," March 12, 1909. Box 175, Case 1399.

104. Stavert v. McNaught, "Examination of W. K. McNaught," March 12, 1909. Box 175, Case 1399.

105. For the entire statement, see "Sovereign Bank Absorbed," *Globe*, January 18, 1908.

to prevent the Brown stock deal from becoming public knowledge and refuse to disclose the deal to the Sovereign Bank's directors. These actions displayed a moral laxity that Baptists claimed to shun.

Another indication that business ethics were slipping was the growing tendency among Baptist businessmen to seek redress for disputes and grievances in the secular courts. In June 1859, William Davies recorded one of the earliest cases involving a fellow Baptist named Parsons who had defrauded him: "I have sued him & got judgement for my am[oun]t and costs, but when the sheriff goes to levy he says these goods are not mine they are my brothers."[106] Both Davies's court action and Parsons's reaction are revealing. The fact that Davies, after seeking a solution in the church, would then take the matter to court violated the early Baptist principle that such offenses and disputes between members should be settled within the fold. Davies's suit sent a clear message that past Baptist church practices were ineffective or unsatisfactory. Parsons's response demonstrates the disparity between what some Baptists claimed to believe and how they actually behaved.

Unprocessed Chancery Court records for the period 1868 to 1921 indicate that disagreements between Baptists over personal and business matters were occasionally brought before the High Court of Justice. In 1893, for example, in a case concerning the will of James Davies, one of the will's executors, John Firstbrook (the boxmaker from Jarvis Street), found himself at odds with William Davies (the pork-packer from Alexander Street) over "the true construction of the said will and the right of the parties thereunder."[107] In another instance in 1904, John and William Firstbrook sued their brother Joseph Firstbrook, proprietor of the Havana Cigar Company, for failure to pay a promissory note for $35,600 and an overdrawn amount of $4890.52.[108] Baptists were gradually moving away from their commitment not to sue a Baptist brother.

Increasingly, Baptist businessmen found themselves in Chancery charged with a variety of ethical offenses. In September 1884, William K. McNaught defended himself against the charge of "fraudulent misrepresentation" in a land deal that he had concluded with a Toronto

---

106. William Davies to James Davies, June 18, 1859. WDP. Box 4044, File 2, UWORC.

107. AO, RG 22, Unprocessed Chancery Court Records, County of York, City Suits and Country Causes, Firstbrook v. Davies, Box 191, Case 923.

108. AO, RG 22, Unprocessed Chancery Court Records, County of York, City Suits and Country Causes, Firstbrook v. Firstbrook, Box 81, Case 811.

widow, Jane Riddell.[109] Although McNaught was found innocent, the case revealed business methods that were confusing, if not misleading. The case involved the sale of lands owned by the Temperance Colonization Society. This colonization company was formed in the early 1880s for the purpose of establishing what Douglas Hill has called "an island of abstention" in the area that is now the city of Saskatoon.[110] The company owned 213,760 acres of land.[111] McNaught never owned any of the Temperance Colonization Society's lands. He only held the right of selection on land. Jane Riddell thought that McNaught was engaged in buying land for her. A serious misunderstanding occurred when McNaught advised Riddell to buy stock instead of land. When she followed this course and her stock was called (repurchased at a predetermined price by the company), she sued McNaught for fraud.

Testimony at the trial shows that McNaught failed to meet his moral obligation to Jane Riddell by ensuring that she understood the nature of the stock transaction. McNaught made a healthy profit of $750 from the transaction. He invested only $250 in company stock and sold his shares for $1,000. Meanwhile, Jane Riddell, who testified that this "was my first business transaction of that kind," was left to flounder on her own and probably incurred a substantial loss on her investment of $1300. McNaught, who strongly advised Riddell to buy the stock as an investment for her son, offered no advice on when to sell.[112]

While McNaught had no legal obligation to help her, his knowledge of her circumstances and Christian conscience should have prompted him to show more concern for her well-being. Perhaps gender had something to do with McNaught's failure to act. It certainly was an issue at the trial when McNaught was asked:

---

109. AO, RG 22, Unprocessed Chancery Court Records, County of York, City Suits and Country Causes, Riddell v. McNaught, "Writ of Summons," Filed May 22, 1884, Box 115, Case 311.

110. Hill, *Opening of the Canadian West*, 178.

111. This figure is taken from Lalonde, "Colonization Companies," 101–14. One colonization company not covered by Lalonde is the Settlers' Colonization Company. It was organized by a group of Baptist businessmen and clergy in 1882. Its first president was Thomas Lailey, a Toronto clothing wholesaler. For the prospectus and other information, see "Baptist Colonization Society," *CB*, April 6, 1882; "Settlers' Colonization Company," *CB*, April 20, 1882; "Colonization Society," *CB*, May 11, 1882.

112. Riddell v. McNaught. The information in this paragraph is found in "Statement of Claim," Filed June 14, 1884; "Examination of W. K. McNaught," September 9, 1884, Box 115, Case 311.

> Q. You could easily perceive that Mrs. Riddell wasn't a business woman [sic] couldn't you?
>
> A. I don't know that I ever had much to do with business women [sic].
>
> Q. Was she acquainted with business?
>
> A. There are very few women that are acquainted with business: she came to me and talked to me the same as any lady would: I didn't take her for a fool. I thought she was a woman of good strong common sense.[113]

McNaught's claim is difficult to assess. Clearly, he held many of the stereotyped views of women common at the time. To McNaught, the business world rightly belonged exclusively to men. A woman ventured into this domain at her peril. McNaught's inaction reflected these assumptions and beliefs. In this case, his attitudes were challenged in court, and though he was absolved of wrongdoing, his lack of compassion or concern for Jane Riddell and his willingness to take advantage of her were contrary to his Baptist moral values.

Another reason for court action against Baptist businessmen was failure to pay debts. In a case begun on November 30, 1880, John Burnett Craigie sued William A. Firstbrook, who was then a member of Immanuel Street Baptist Church, for failure to pay a mortgage on land and premises in Somerville Township, Victoria County.[114] The court found for the plaintiff. Firstbrook was required to pay $1087.61 to the plaintiff for the outstanding debt.[115] In a similar case begun on June 9, 1881, James Benny, Thomas Peck, and James H. Peck sued the trustees for the insolvent estate of former Jarvis Street deacon and hardware merchant, William Hewitt Sr., for default of payment on a number of mortgages in Toronto. Again, the plaintiffs won judgment for payment of $18,902.73 and delivery of the mortgaged premises.[116]

---

113. Ridell v. McNaught, "Examination of W. K. McNaught," September 9, 1884, Box 115, Case 311.

114. Craigie v. Firstbrook, "Bill of Complaint," Filed November 30, 1880. Box 90, Case 625.

115. Craigie v. Firstbrook. In this case a "Fie Fa" was issued on March 28, 1888. This document gave the Sheriff the right to seize property equal to the value of the debt.

116. AO, RG 22, Unprocessed Chancery Court Records, County of York, City Suits and Country Causes, Benny v. Hewitt, "Bill of Complaint," Filed June 9, 1881, Box 94, Case 306. The judgement in this case was given December 6, 1881.

These actions evidence a change in Baptist moral standards within the business context. Careful attention to the payment of debts was a basic Baptist tenet. As we have already seen, the failure of some Baptists to fulfil their financial obligations in business was carried over into the church. Thus, by the early 1890s running the church's affairs on a deficit had become an established practice at Jarvis Street.

Baptist business ethics declined markedly in the period between 1880 and 1921. Defaulting on debts, disregarding the safety and welfare of others, exploiting workers for personal gain, and adopting dishonest business practices were the most apparent signs that many Baptist businessmen succumbed to the temptation to compromise their ethical standards for the sake of business success. With the rise of industrial capitalism in the late nineteenth century, the pressures for sociocultural compromise exerted on individual Baptist businessmen were intense. While some Baptists resisted such pressures others accepted them as part of the price of "progress."

"The Danger of the Age": "Conspicuous Consumption" and the Acceptance of Avarice

In its opening issue for 1888, *The Canadian Baptist* ran an article from the British *Congregational Magazine*, entitled, "The Danger of the Age." At one point in his analysis, the author observed:

> In material things our people are moving, as if in an hour out of the limitations and moderation of the past, into all the resources and wealth of the most luxurious nations. The temptation to get money and to spend it, to view it as the means to all good and the end of all desire, is becoming stronger and seemingly more irresistible, continually.[117]

If materialism and avarice now dominated English culture, could their influence on Canadian culture be far behind?

There was ample evidence in the actions of Toronto's Baptist businessmen between 1848 and 1921 to suggest that some Canadian Baptists were quick to follow the English example. For Baptists, the process of rationalizing avarice spanned two generations. It began in the mid-nineteenth century with the acceptance of new cultural realities, such as industrial capitalism, and the gradual abandonment of

---

117. "Danger of the Age," *CB*, January 5, 1888.

Christian business ethics. Later, Baptist businessmen sought to sanctify greed through generosity. With the support of church leadership, philanthropy became a rationalization for the uncontrolled pursuit of wealth and worldly goods. By the late nineteenth century, the earlier injunction to "Get that you may Give" had become, for many, a quaint anachronism.[118] By 1921, many Baptist businessmen had followed the 1907 "homily" of A. R. Doble of the Bank of Montreal, to "Make Unto Yourselves Friends of the Mammon of Unrighteousness."[119]

Perhaps the most outstanding example of the move from moderation to excess is found in the activities of dry goods merchant William McMaster (see Figure 7).[120] Shrewd, aggressive, and with a keen business acumen, McMaster possessed an acquisitive drive that few of his co-religionists could match. Although few personal or business financial records remain, the records of R. G. Dun and Company show how quickly McMaster's fortune grew. In 1850, McMaster and Company earned $10,000.[121] By 1858, the most conservative estimates of Dun's agents put the value of the business at "$200,000 upwards" per annum.[122] In 1862, one agent estimated the value to be in the $500,000 to $750,000 per annum range and declared McMaster and Company "the best business in the Upper Province."[123]

In 1866, William McMaster turned his dry goods business over to his nephews, Arthur Robinson and James Short McMaster, to pursue banking and other commercial interests that brought him a second

---

118. This injunction was the headline for an article taken from the Congregationalist. See "Get That You May Give," *CB*, October 26, 1876.

119. Doble, "On the Cultivation of One's Banker," 37–39.

120. For more biographical information on McMaster, see *Dictionary of Canadian Biography*, 11:574–78; Johnston, *Toronto Years*, 18–44, 54–55, 59, 69, 214, 230, 232, 246–49. "Memoir of Susan Moulton McMaster," Biographical File for Susan Moulton McMaster, CBA; Biographical File for William McMaster, CBA; D. E. Thomson, "William McMaster," *McMaster University Monthly*, 1891–1892, 97–103; D. C. Masters, "Canadian Bankers of the Last Century, I: William McMaster," *Canadian Banker* (1942), 389–96; Cathcart, *Baptist Encyclopedia*, 773; Dent, *Canadian Portrait Gallery*, 3:72–73; Rose, *Cyclopedia of Canadian Biography*, 464–65; *Canadian Biographical Dictionary and Portrait Gallery*, 166–71.

121. NA, R. G. Dun and Company Records, MG 28 III 106, vol. 26, Toronto 1843–1877, 200.

122. NA, R. G. Dun and Company Records, MG 28 III 106, vol. 26, Toronto 1843–1877, 200.

123. NA, R. G. Dun and Company Records, MG 28 III 106, vol. 26, Toronto 1843–1877, 276.

fortune. At the probate of his will in 1887, McMaster's estate was valued at $1,154,178.03.[124]

As Charles M. Johnston has noted, for "Baptist and non-Baptist alike, McMaster was regarded as an inspiration to all those seeking material success on a grand scale."[125] Doctor B. D. Thomas, pastor of Jarvis Street, said in his memorial address that McMaster displayed a puritanical character and drive that served him well in a fiercely competitive business world. "Starting at the lowest rung of the ladder," Thomas observed, "he pressed upward until he was numbered among the princes of a mighty city." His secret to success lay in the "sometimes rugged and precipitous highway of painstaking, persistent, honest industry." Yet despite McMaster's material success, Thomas noted that "he was not without defects in the general nature of his character. . . . In the heated contests of business and politics he struck against weaker natures with a force which hurt them and antagonized them." Still, Thomas excused McMaster's shortcomings: "William McMaster was not only great but good. He had a large and generous nature. Beneath what often appeared a rigorous exterior there throbbed a generous heart." Although Thomas claimed that "McMaster graduated late as a philanthropist," he also rationalized away any suggestion of avarice by noting that "he came out with honours which God permitted him to carry down to ripe old age." At the conclusion of his message, Thomas addressed the large number of businessmen present in the congregation about trying to serve God and mammon:

> Ye men of business who stood by the departed in the battle and the strife, who walked with him in the high places of honour and affluence, who have gathered, as he did, the fruitage of an industrious and energetic life, have you "laid up for yourselves treasures in Heaven?" I fear that some of you are getting the world losing your souls.[126]

Thomas's words called attention to the spiritual dangers inherent in business life. The acceptance and promotion of material success that McMaster typified exposed Baptist businessmen to even greater temptations for religious compromise.

124. AO, RG 22, Surrogate Court Records, County of York, Will of William McMaster, Filed for Probate, October 25, 1887. No. 6586.

125. Johnston, *Toronto Years*, 21.

126. This quotation and the five preceding it in this paragraph are taken from "Funeral Address of B. D. Thomas Given in Jarvis Street Baptist Church," *CB*, October 6, 1887.

As Johnston has suggested, McMaster's influence was not confined to Baptist circles. The Methodist blacksmith T. S. Limscott, in his book *The Path of Wealth or Light From My Forge*, used McMaster as an example of one who embodied the Protestant ethic. "A native of Ireland," stated Limscott, "he left his own country for Canada, a poor young man, and by earnest attention to business became a millionaire."[127] This success was justified by the fact that McMaster "was a princely giver to Christian and benevolent institutions."[128] Although the praise heaped on McMaster often bordered on hagiography, his undeniable success ensured his enduring reputation as a model Canadian entrepreneur.

Other Baptist businessmen emulated McMaster. Businessmen like clothing retailer and wholesaler Thomas Lailey, whom one of Dun's agents called "a protege of W[illia]m McMaster," implemented the dry goods merchant's business philosophy and methodology and depended on McMaster to "stand at his back."[129] The same was true of chemical manufacturer and wholesaler William Elliot. Like McMaster and Lailey, Elliot moved from retailing to wholesaling. He also diversified his business interests and joined a group of capitalists that included McMaster in establishing the Canadian Bank of Commerce and the Confederation Life Association (known today as the Confederation Life Insurance Company). Elliot shared McMaster's commitment to amassing a large personal fortune, guaranteeing future wealth by passing on the business to family members and rationalizing material gain by giving both time and resources to church and denomination.[130]

Gaining large personal fortunes was not enough; some Baptist businessmen revealed an unquenchable desire for material goods. In the words of philosopher-economist Thorstein Veblen in his pioneering theoretical analysis of "the leisure class," Jarvis Street's businessmen

---

127. Limscott, *The Path of Wealth or Light From My Forge*, 148.

128. Limscott, *The Path of Wealth or Light From My Forge*, 148.

129. NA, R. G. Dun and Company Records, MG 28 III 106, Volume 26, Toronto 1843–1877, 182.

130. For a brief description of the life and career of William Elliot see, Philip Creighton's article in *The Dictionary of Canadian Bibliography*, 12:296. For raw data on Elliot's early endeavors in the pharmaceutical trade see, Lyman Pharmaceutical Company Records, William Lyman and Company, *Journal G*, No. 2, 1852–1853; Lymans, Clare and Company, *Journal A*, No. 1, 1860–1861; Lymans, Clare and Company, *Ledger A*, Volume 9, 1860–1861; Lymans, Clare and Company, *Journal C*, No. 10, 1864–1865. These records are available at the McGill University Archives, Private (MS), Business and Economics V.

increasingly adopted the practice of "conspicuous consumption."[131] Luxuries became necessities as Baptist businessmen moved from meeting their needs to satisfying their wants.

The most outstanding examples of this change in attitude are reflected in their houses. From humble lodgings, that included living with his employer, Robert Cathcart, William McMaster steadily improved his living situation as his wealth increased. By the mid-1840s, he occupied a small residence on Church Street and, in the early 1850s, purchased a townhouse on Grenville Street.[132] By the late 1850s, William McMaster was engaged in building a mansion. As one of Dun's agents noted on March 26, 1859, "William McMaster is wealthy. He is building a large house at a cost of $25,000. Owns valuable Real Estate."[133] The extravagant amount spent by McMaster to build his palatial Italianate Villa (see Figure 8) on thirty acres of land on Avenue Road Hill set a new standard.

The message that McMaster had achieved both wealth and respectability was clearly evident in the residence itself and in the surrounding grounds. "Rathnally,"[134] as the McMaster estate was called, became the venue for many important and lavish social gatherings. A banquet held in honor of George Brown upon his retirement from political life, left an indelible impression:

> The McMasters made an awful splurge last night. They had invited a very large party of leading Reformers for 7 1/2 o'clock but whether for dinner or what no one knew. The Mowats, Blakes, John Wilsons, Adam Wilsons, McMurrich, Dallases, Mackenzies + a lot of others were to be there-but only gentlemen came + several of them were amissing. It turned out to be Tea + supper we were invited to. The supper was a magnificent affair-a grand sit-in-to-the-table affair in Mrs Webb's grandest style. The folding doors between the two large rooms had been thrown open+ the table run down the whole length. Of course it had been set out all ready, and it was not easy to shorten it-so there are two hundred feet of table + one hundred feet of people to fill it! The gaps were fearful + there were fine men servant to wait on us!

---

131. Veblen, *Theory of the Leisure Class*, 68–101.

132. *Brown's Toronto City Directory and Home District Directory, 1846–47*, 47; Hall, *Per Ardua*, 14.

133. NA, R. G. Dun and company Records, MG 28 III 106, Volume 26, Toronto 1843–1877, 200.

134. Some sources spell the name "Rathnelly."

The house is a magnificent one + it is really a pity the old fellow does not know better how to use it.[135]

While the McMasters' entertainments sometimes failed, what Veblen called their "wasteful" consumption continued unabated.[136] In addition to holding celebrations in his home, McMaster also entertained business elites elsewhere. As George Brown noted, "McMaster gives a grand spread at the [National] Club tomorrow night. to some of the English Directors of the GRRW [Grand Trunk Railway], who are here now."[137] On December 23, 1869, Egerton Ryerson, the renowned Methodist leader and Chief Superintendent of Education in Ontario, wrote to his daughter, "I go today to Luncheon at one to the Hon. Mr. McMaster's, to meet Mr. Alderman Dakin & other gentlemen."[138] In June 1872, Ryerson again recounted to his daughter, "I was at McMaster's yesterday at Luncheon to meet Sir Thomas Dakin etc. It was a very splendid affair in all respects. The principal gentlemen of the city were there."[139] These gatherings of prominent people provide ample evidence of McMaster's integration with Toronto's social elite.

Further evidence that McMaster was embracing the values of the wealthy is found in his construction of a second mansion on the north side of Bloor Street just east of Yonge in 1877 (see Figure 9). This Victorian-style city mansion afforded McMaster better access to Toronto's commercial and cultural center. The grounds included a low ornamental fence with gates that closed off the drive that meandered through landscaped lawns to the porte-cochere. The house featured a wide sweeping staircase that focused attention on a stained-glass window containing a tree, deer crest, and motto "Per Ardua."[140] Thus, guests were immediately struck by the symbols of McMaster's success. Once inside the mansion, guests were shown to the library on the left or the elegant French drawing-room on the right. Exquisite marble fireplaces, frosted glass paneled doors embossed with the McMaster monogram and inlaid walnut table and bookcases were only a few of the many interior features that caught

135. George Brown to Anne Brown, February 23, 1868, George Brown Papers [hereafter cited as GBP], MG 24, B 40, vol. 8, 1670. A microfilm copy is in AO.

136. For a definition of this term and its application to the religious context, see Veblen, *Theory of the Leisure Class*, 115–21.

137. George Brown to Anne Brown, June 15, 1871, GBP, MG 24, B 40, vol. 8, 1839.

138. Sissons, *My Dearest Sophie*, 177.

139. Sissons, *My Dearest Sophie*, 226.

140. "Through Adversity."

the eye of visitors. A well-appointed dining room was the scene of many social gatherings. In short, the splendor of this second residence stood as a monument to the wealth and power of Toronto's leading late nineteenth century Baptist merchant prince.[141]

Following his uncle's example, in 1868, Arthur Robinson McMaster purchased a portion of William McMaster's real-estate holdings on the northeast corner of Jarvis and Wellesley Streets.[142] In keeping with other grand estates along Jarvis Street at this time, Arthur Robinson McMaster erected a splendid twenty-five-room mansion on the four-acre property (see Figure 10).[143] By 1870, the estate contained six brick outbuildings and was assessed at $22,600.[144] After Arthur McMaster's premature death in 1881, the house was sold to Eliza Massey, wife of Hart Massey, President of the Massey Manufacturing Company, for the considerable sum of $32,500.[145]

The building projects of William and Arthur Robinson McMaster reveal a growing appetite for material goods and a desire to display their newly acquired wealth in a conspicuous manner befitting their status. The abandonment of moderation and the acceptance of excess set a precedent that the succeeding generation of Baptist businessmen would seek to emulate and surpass. The McMaster mansions also symbolized the sociocultural integration of some Baptist businessmen and their departure from the simple and separated lifestyle of the past. By the late nineteenth century, devotion to mammon had brought the most prominent among Jarvis Street's businessmen great wealth, and while their religious commitment remained strong, self-actualization through service to mammon had become the priority for many. For McMaster's generation, the combination of service to God and mammon through philanthropic endeavors doubtless eased fears that mammon might displace God as the central focus of life and provided a convenient rationalization for the unfettered pursuit of wealth and the acceptance of consumerism. The growing commitment to mammon and its attendant materialism served as a primary stimulus in the secularization process.

---

141. For a greater appreciation of the architectural features described in this paragraph, see AO, J. C. B., and E. C. Horwood Collection [hereafter HC], C11-623-1-14, Langley, Langley, and Burke. One should also consult Hall, *Per Ardua*, 10, 19–21.

142. Thompson, *Jarvis Street*, 146.

143. Thompson, *Jarvis Street*, 150–53.

144. City of Toronto Assessment Rolls, 1870, Ward of St. David's, No 1194, CTA.

145. Thompson, *Jarvis Street*, 151–52.

This process that began in the late nineteenth century with the growing acceptance of materialism only expanded in the next generation of Baptist businessmen. While some Baptist businessmen, like John Northway, steadfastly resisted the temptation to build luxurious houses, others, like the Ryrie brothers, succumbed. Commenting on the partnership deal he struck with the Ryries in 1905, William Massey Birks of Henry Birks and Sons observed that it "gave them large personal income, resulting in their launching out in fine country and city homes."[146] James Ryrie (see Figure 11) took his share of the proceeds and promptly fulfilled his desire for more opulent living quarters. In 1905, he hired his good friend, fellow church member and noted architect, Edmund Burke, to build an understatedly elegant ten-room house in Rosedale at 56 South Drive.[147] A year later, Burke supervised the construction of James Ryrie's mammoth eighteen-room country estate home near Fair Lake Park in Oakville. Amenities on the estate included orchards and a tennis court (see Figures 12 and 13).[148]

By 1913, James Ryrie had again called on Burke's services for the construction of his wife's estate at 1 Chestnut Park Road (see Figures 14–16).[149] This stunning three-storey mansion contained twenty-nine rooms including servants' quarters and six bathrooms. A year after construction of this residence, James decided to indulge his love of music. He commissioned Burke to convert one of the third-storey storage rooms into an organ chamber for an automatic player Aeolian Organ. The American musicologist Orpha Ochse has explained the social significance of the organ James Ryrie purchased:

> For some twenty years, until about 1930, the installation of residence organs furnished the elegant music rooms of the wealthy with status symbols and helped to line the pockets of the organ builders. The Aeolian Company specialized in this field, but one could also choose from a wide selection of other builders, among them Skinner, Möller, Austin, and Kimball. Aeolian had been making automatic player mechanisms for both reed organs and pianos, and the adaption of a similar device to the organ was largely responsible for the popularity of

---

146. NA, William Massey Birks, "Notes on the History of the Company," Henry Birks and Sons Company Records, MG 28 III 55, Volume 1, File 39.

147. For architectural details of this residence, see, AO, HC, C11-949, Burke, Horwood, and White.

148. AO, HC, C11-949, 1629, 2667, Burke, Horwood, and White.

149. AO, HC, C11-949, 1630, 1632, 1631, Burke, Horwood, and White.

residence organs. Few who were blessed with the money to buy such organs were able to play them.[150]

It is not clear whether James Ryrie could play the organ. What is certain is that his indulgence in this act of "conspicuous consumption" was costly. The roof line of the mansion had to be altered to accommodate the organ pipes located at the top of the main staircase (see Figure 17).[151]

Like his brother, Harry Ryrie had a desire to display his wealth in the building of elegant houses. In 1899, he upgraded his home located at 164 Isabella Street. The renovations included the addition of an "Oriel Window" to the exterior and a remodelling of the dining room, bathroom, and kitchen.[152] Between 1903 and 1906 his cottage on Toronto Island was built. It had twelve rooms including six bedrooms and two baths.[153] In 1911, Harry used some of his profits from the deal with Birks to build a lavish residence on his newly acquired farm in Clarkson, Ontario.[154] An article that appeared in the *Star Weekly* shortly after his death in September 1917 captured the essence of Harry Ryrie's approach to building and furnishing his residences:

> Probably no house in Toronto was furnished with more exquisite taste, combined with less ostentation, than Mr. Ryrie's. When he had made up his mind to build a new house, he and his wife made it their hobby, literally for years, to collect rugs, tapestries and the like. There was for them no putting the matter into the hands of some upholsterer with carte blanche to furnish the house throughout. Everything bore the impress of their own individuality and personality.[155]

This statement reveals Harry Ryrie's desire to exercise direct control over all matters pertaining to his personal residences. The understated exterior appearance of his residence on Isabella Street helped to hide a passion for real estate, fine homes, and furnishings. The residences owned and built by Harry Ryrie conveyed in both subtle and direct ways a commitment to materialistic values and an adoption of consumerism.

150. Ochse, *History of the Organ*, 330–31.
151. The organ was installed in April 1914. Details of the renovations necessary for its installation are in AO, HC, C11-949, Burke, Horwood, and White.
152. AO, HC, C11-949, 822-2, Burke, Horwood, and White.
153. AO, HC, C11-949, 871, Burke, Horwood, and White.
154. AO, HC, C11-949, 1079, Burke, Horwood, and White.
155. "Harry Ryrie Was One Of Nature's Gentlemen," *Toronto Star Weekly*, September 22, 1917.

The building exploits of the Ryries were representative of wealthy Baptist businessmen. Their establishment of residences in neighborhoods such as Rosedale shows that Jarvis Street's businessmen followed the move north and west by Toronto's business elite in the late nineteenth century. The construction of cottages and extravagant summer homes also became common practice for many Jarvis Street businessmen.

In the early twentieth century, the practice of hosting and attending parties continued, but other activities indicative of a desire for a life of leisure and adventure became increasingly evident in the lifestyles of Jarvis Street's wealthiest businessmen. In addition to retreating to their country homes or cottages, the Ryrie brothers sought to satisfy their desire for travel and their love of sport. James Ryrie took numerous excursions to exotic destinations. Combining his interest in missions with his desire to see the world he made a trip to visit Baptist missionaries in India in 1902. In June 1910, *The Canadian Baptist* reported: "Mr. and Mrs. Jas. Ryrie and Mr. and Mrs. John Firstbrook have returned home after an extended visit to many of the mission fields in the far East, including stations in Ceylon, India, China, Japan, Manchuria and the Hawaiian Islands."[156] Pleasure trips also became a common facet of James Ryrie's lifestyle. On March 7, 1912, the social columns of the *Globe* included the following notice: "Mr. James Ryrie and family and Mr. S. J. Moore and family have sailed for Naples, where they intend motoring through the continent and England. they will be away about three months."[157] By contrast, Harry Ryrie preferred sport to travel. Playing golf at the Lambton Golf and Country Club became one of his favorite leisure activities.[158]

Another prominent Baptist businessman who showed an unrivalled passion for sport was William Kirkpatrick McNaught. McNaught became a nationally renowned lacrosse figure. His contributions to the sport included writing a book entitled *Lacrosse And How To Play It*.[159] McNaught also served as secretary and president of the National Amateur Lacrosse Association.[160] These activities signify a growing appetite for leisure on the part of some wealthy businessmen from Jarvis Street.

156. "Welcome Home," *CB*, June 30, 1910.

157. "Woman at Work and at Play," *Globe*, March 7, 1912.

158. On the day of his death, Harry Ryrie played golf at this club. "Harry Ryrie Dies Suddenly," *Globe*, September 17, 1917.

159. Copies of *Lacrosse and How to Play It* are available at the University of Western Ontario, Special Collection and the National Archives.

160. "Col. McNaught Passes Away," *Globe*, February 3, 1919.

In addition to participating in conspicuous consumption and leisure, the leading businessmen from Jarvis Street were among the most active promoters of the new consumer culture. Stuart Ewen, in his study of the impact of advertising's role in the development of American consumer culture in the early twentieth century, has argued that through advertising "consumption took on a clearly cultural tone."[161] According to Ewen, American businessmen in the early twentieth century tried to change the notion of "class" into "mass" thereby creating "an individual who could locate his needs and frustrations in term of the consumption of goods rather than the quality and content of his life (work)."[162]

In Toronto, Baptist businessmen appear to have supported a similar transformation. Those businessmen from Jarvis Street engaged in the jewellery trade, for example, worked hard to convince the public that certain luxuries had become necessities. Following the example set by Timothy Eaton, the Ryries published their first catalogue early in 1886. With his usual enthusiasm, W. K. McNaught lauded the event in the columns of *The Trader*:

> We have just been presented with a new and valuable work by James Ryrie, of Toronto, otherwise known as "Ryrie, the Jeweler," entitled "Ryrie's Christmas Annual." The work is divided into seven chapters, and is of absorbing interest to anyone wishing to get full value for their money. Chapter I, Tells what to buy for a Gentlemen; Chapter II, How to make a Lady happy; Chapter III, Shows how to give a child pleasure; Chapter IV, Don't forget the baby; Chapter V, How to Add to the Comfort and Elegance of Home; Chapter VI, Treats of Things in General. As brevity is the soul of wit, as also the measure of literary talent, this little work must rank high in the Canadian Literary world. It is almost needless to add that although the author disinterestedly points out that Ryrie's is the best place to buy jewelry of all kinds, his advice is none the less to the point.[163]

This early effort to promote Ryrie jewellery contained something for everyone and was designed to appeal to the masses. As the Ryries's business became more sophisticated and specialized, catalogues targeted at the wealthy mail order customer emphasized certain products and employed a marketing strategy that promoted goods on the basis of superior

---

161. Ewen, *Captains of Consciousness*, 42.
162. Ewen, *Captains of Consciousness*, 43.
163. "Rising Canadian Author," *Trader*, January 1886.

quality, price, and service.¹⁶⁴ The opening letter in the 1913 catalogue offered a typical Ryrie sales pitch:

> While we give the most careful attention to the smallest order entrusted to us, we have this year given most prominence in our catalogue to fine Jewelry, especially Diamonds and Sterling Silverware.
>
> No house in the world is in a better position than ours to sell fine goods at prices closest to the actual cost of production.
>
> Our Diamonds are of the highest quality; are bought direct from the cutters for "prompt cash," and enter Canada "duty free."
>
> With the exception of special novel mountings, from the art centres of Europe, we design and mount all our precious stones.
>
> Almost all the Sterling Silver is from our own factory also.
>
> With these advantages and a thoroughly organized Mail Order Department, we can assure you prompt and satisfactory service, always with the understanding that if, for any reason, or no reason, you wish to return your purchase, your money will immediately and cheerfully be refunded.¹⁶⁵

This letter was carefully crafted to attract buyers. The guarantee of satisfaction and the promise of a refund "for any reason" were refinements of Timothy Eaton's highly successful marketing slogan that promised "money refunded if goods are not satisfactory."¹⁶⁶ The Ryries also advertised in Baptist publications and the *Globe*.¹⁶⁷ Perhaps the greatest testimony to the success of the Ryries as promoters of consumerism came at a 1919 Canadian Jewellers Convention when the president remarked:

---

164. In his history of Henry Birks and Sons, A. Robert George estimated that in the 1890s both Birks and Ryries were spending $50,000 a year on catalogues. See George, *House of Birks*, 27.

165. This letter was written by Harry Ryrie, SecretaryTreasurer of Ryrie Brothers Limited. NA, Henry Birks and Sons Limited Company Records, MG 28 III 55, vol. 7A, catalogue for the Ryrie Brothers Limited, Toronto, 1913. This catalogue contained 123 pages. Much of the catalogue was in color. Other catalogues for 1915 and 1929 are extant in the Birks Records.

166. Santink, *Timothy Eaton*, 121–38. See also the picture of the 1897–1898 Fall and Winter Catalogue in Santink, *Timothy Eaton*, following page 148.

167. See, for example, the back cover on the *Baptist Year Book, 1883*; "Story of the Diamond, Chapter 25," *Globe*, February 19, 1919. This was the last in a series of advertisements that ran in the *Globe* in January and February 1919.

"Thank God for the Birks and the Ryries. They put the jewellery business on the map!"[168] (see Figure 18).

While the Ryries certainly did their best to encourage consumerism, the efforts of William Kirkpatrick McNaught surpassed all others. In the pages of *The Trade*, McNaught promoted his own products and provided advice for other businessmen on how to better market their goods. In the March 1886 issue of *The Trader*, for example, McNaught sought his potential buyers, the jewellery retailers, when he declared, "The 'Perfection' Watch Case, put upon the market last month by the American Watch Case Co., has proved to be the biggest success of any Case the company ever made. The demand is unprecedented, and everybody pronounces it the best cheap watch case they ever handled for the money."[169] In addition to pushing his own product lines, McNaught offered advice to those in the jewellery business on how to advertise effectively. In an article entitled "Does It Pay to Advertise?," McNaught offered his readers practical, conservative advice:

> 1st Advertising to pay at all, requires to be truthful . . . 2nd Don't advertise anything you are not prepared to carry out . . . 3rd If advertising is worth doing at all, it is worth doing well . . . (a) His matter should be original and attractive . . . (b) He should take plenty of space . . . (c) Be careful as to the kind of type that is used in your advertisements. advertisers should always get a proof copy of their advertisements, so as to make certain that theirs will show up as different from any others in the paper. (d) Change your matter with every issue of the paper . . . (e) Last, but not least, advertise in a good live paper that has a good circulation amongst the very people you want to reach.[170]

Here was a prominent Baptist businessman from Jarvis Street offering advice to others on how to use the media tools available for the promotion of consumerism. By the late nineteenth century, the businessmen of Jarvis Street could clearly be counted among the most active and innovative supporters of the new consumer culture.

A growing love of leisure and the practice and promotion of conspicuous consumption were key elements in the secularization process. Many of Jarvis Street's businessmen accepted the new materialistic social ethics part of their sociocultural integration with mainstream Canadian

---

168. This quote is taken from George, *House of Birk*, 27.
169. *Trader*, March 1886.
170. "Does It Pay to Advertise?," *Trader*, July 1883.

culture. By the late nineteenth century, Baptist businessmen exhibited a love for wealth, success, and consumption that rivalled anything found elsewhere in Canada. While many Baptists continued to profess the rejection of mammon, the increasingly extravagant lifestyles of Jarvis Street's businessmen challenged those assertions. For some Baptists, this growing gulf between belief and practice indicated a spiritual crisis of unprecedented proportions. Still, many remained convinced that material gain and spiritual growth could be harmonized. Determined to realize material success, they embraced a consumer culture that promoted enjoyment and excess, undermining religious commitment.

The push for sociocultural integration that characterized the attitudes and actions of culturally liberal Baptist businessmen from Jarvis Street in the late nineteenth century had a profound impact on the Baptist faith. As moral authority shifted from institutions to individuals, many Baptist businessmen became lax in their commitment to stewardship and Christian business ethics. Declining morality and rising materialism constituted an assault on religious beliefs and values that few Baptist businessmen could resist. When faced with the choice of serving God or mammon, Baptist businessmen tried initially to serve both, but eventually made material concerns their first priority. Religion was increasingly marginalized and secularized.

Though the businessmen from Jarvis Street would continue to profess belief in separation from the world, it was becoming evident that their lifestyles showed little difference from the secular world. The distance between myth and really widened as they pursued sociocultural integration at the expense of their separatist religious values. Instead of having a lifestyle informed by the Christian values of modesty and moderation, Baptist businessmen accepted the materialistic values associated with a new consumer-oriented business-dominated culture. The challenge of trying to maintain separation in the face of growing worldliness and secularism would become the ultimate testing ground for the Baptist businessman's faith.

Figure 4. Colonel William Kirkpatrick McNaught of the 109th Regiment of Volunteer Militia, a jewellery manufacturer and wholesaler, typified the culturally liberal businessman. His willingness to compromise his business ethics and his editorials in *The Trader* made him a notable figure (Greene, *Who's Who and Why 1917-18*).

Figure 5. John Northway, pictured here in 1915, was perhaps the most theologically liberal of Jarvis Street's businessmen (Northway Company Ltd., Fonds 70-003, Box 62, Trent University Archives).

Figure 6. This somewhat exaggerated rendering Firstbrook Brothers Box Factory, illustrates that Baptists left their mark on Toronto's industrial landscape. Firstbrook Bros. Factory, King Street Toronto, [photograph], ca. 1897 (Unidentified photographs collected by the firm of Burke, Horwood, and White, C 11-949 L 2057, Archives of Ontario).

Figure 7. William McMaster provided a model of success and respectability that other Baptist businessmen emulated. William McMaster, [photograph], n.d. (Unidentified photographs collected by the firm of Burke, Horwood, and White, C 11-949 S 197, Archives of Ontario).

Figure 8. "Rathnally." William McMaster's country estate as it appeared in 1897. The Italianate Mansion, built in the late 1850s set a new standard for opulence among Baptists (MTRL, T33394).

Figure 9. William McMaster's Bloor Street Mansion, 1957. Built in 1875, to provide McMaster with quarters closer to his business concerns (MTRL, T 34148).

Figure 10. Arthur Robinson McMaster's Jarvis Street Mansion. This mansion constructed in the late 1860s showed that William McMaster's model was not lost on his nephew (CTA, Fonds 1244, Item 3070).

Figure 11. James Ryrie, a wealthy jeweller from Jarvis Street, would become an unofficial leader of the dissidents in the schism of 1921 (Greene, *Who's Who and Why 1919-20*).

Figure 12. James Ryrie's Fair Lake Park Estate, Oakville, 1915. This "summer home" built in 1906, represented an acceptance of "conspicuous consumption." James Ryrie—Fair Lake Park Mansion Exterior, Oakville, 1915 (Unidentified photographs collected by the firm of Burke, Horwood, and White, C 11-949 AO 1629, Archives of Ontario).

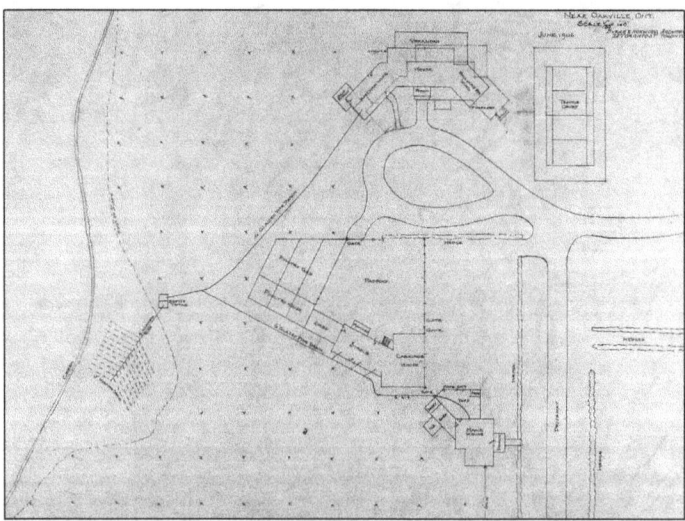

Figure 13. Block Plan of James Ryrie's Fair Lake Park Estate, Oakville. Amenities included a tennis court and orchards. James Ryrie Block Plan Edgemere Oakville, [drawing], n.d. (Unidentified photographs collected by the firm of Burke, Horwood, and White, C 11-949 AO 2667, Archives of Ontario).

Figure 14. Erected in 1913, according to his wife's specifications, this mansion was the "crowning jewel" in James Ryrie's building spree. James Ryrie's Chestnut Park Mansion Exterior, Burke, Horwood, and White, [photograph], 1915 (Unidentified photographs collected by the firm of Burke, Horwood, and White, C 11-949 AO 1630, Archives of Ontario).

Figure 15. This picture of the front entrance hall shows the understated elegance that characterized the Ryries' decorating style. James Ryrie— Front Hall Chestnut Park Mansion, [photograph], 1915 (Unidentified photographs collected by the firm of Burke, Horwood, and White, C 11-949 AO 1632, Archives of Ontario).

Figure 16. Ornaments and mementos from the Ryries' trips abroad are noteworthy in this picture of their library. James Ryrie's Library—Chestnut Park, Burke, Horwood, White, [photograph], 1915 (Unidentified photographs collected by the firm of Burke, Horwood, and White, C 11-949 AO 1631, Archives of Ontario).

Figure 17. Located at the top of the third-floor staircase, the roofline had to be altered to accommodate these organ pipes. Undoubtedly, sound filled the mansion when the Aeolian Organ was played.

James Ryrie Chestnut Park Organ Pipes Drawing, [drawing], n.d. (Unidentified photographs collected by the firm of Burke, Horwood, and White, C 11-949 AO 2682, Archives of Ontario).

Figure 18. A picture that became a postcard showing Ryrie Bros., Yonge and Adelaide Streets, ca. 1910 (CTA, Fonds 1568, Item 0339).

Chapter 5

Maintaining Separation
The Myth and the Reality

The Church and the World walked far apart On the changing shores of time;

The World was singing a giddy song, And the Church a hymn sublime.

"Come give me your hand," cried the merry World, "And walk with me this way";

But the good Church hid her snowy hand,

And solemnly answered "Nay, I will not give you my hand at all,

And I will not walk with you;

Your way is the way of endless death, Your words are all untrue."

"Nay walk with me but a little space," Said the World, with a kindly air; "The road I walk is a pleasant road, And the sun is always there;

Your path is thorny and rough and rude, And mine is broad and plain;

My road is paved with flowers and gems, And yours with tears and pain . . ."

Half shyly the Church approached the World, And gave him her hand of snow;

Maintaining Separation

The old world grasped and walked along, Saying in accents low:

"Your dress is too simple to suit my taste; I will give you pearls to wear,

Rich velvet and silk for your graceful form, And diamonds to deck your hair."

The Church looked down on her plain white robes,

And then at the dazzling World,

And blushed as she saw his handsome lips, With a smile contemptuous curled.

"I will change my dress for a costlier one" Said the Church with a smile of grace; Then her pure white garments duffed away, And the World gave in their place

Beautiful satins and shining silks, And roses and gems and pearls . . .

"Your house is too plain," said the proud old World,

"I'll build you one like mine;

Carpets of Brussels and curtains of lace, And furniture ever so fine."

So he built her a costly and beautiful house Splendid it was to behold;

Her son and her beautiful daughters dwelt there,

Gleaming in purple and gold;

And fairs and shows in the halls were held,

And the World and his children were there,

And laughter and music and feasts were heard In the place that was meant for prayer.

She had cushioned pews for the rich and great To sit in their pomp and pride,

While the poor folks, clad in their shabby suits,

Sat meekly down outside . . .

The Church looked back with a sigh and longed To gather her children in.

But some were off in the midnight ball, And some were off at play,

> And some were drinking in gay saloons;
>
> So she quietly went her way . . .
>
> The sons of the World and the sons of the Church
>
> Walked closely hands and heart,
>
> And only the master that knoweth all Could tell the two apart.[1]

This poem by Matilda C. Edwards expresses the dismay of one Canadian Baptist over the loss of separation between the church and the world. By the late nineteenth century, many Baptists were coming to see what historian John Webster Grant later observed, that the "church and the world were virtually identical in composition."[2] This reality disturbed fundamentalists. By the early decades of the twentieth century, their prevailing sense of an emerging cultural crisis put them on alert.[3] Restoration of the moral and theological certitude associated with a fading "evangelical consensus" became their objectives.[4]

After 1880, Canadian Baptists became increasingly fragmented in how they related to the materialistic culture that increasingly surrounded them. While many liberals and conservatives pursued and encouraged sociocultural integration, fundamentalists resisted all attempts to place Baptists within the cultural mainstream. Disagreement over both the definition and application of "separation from the world" grew steadily

---

1. "Church and the World," *CB*, May 15, 1879.

2. Grant, *Profusion of Spires*, 167.

3. For an analysis of fundamentalism and the cultural crisis in the United States in what George Marsden has called "The Crucial Years: 1917–1925," see Marsden, *Fundamentalism and American Culture*, 141–95. Mark Parent, for example, has argued that the First World War instilled a new militancy in T. T. Shields. For the complete argument, see Parent, "T. T. Shields and the First World War," 42–57. For a discussion of Shields's move from a positive to a negative view of the culture, see Parent, "Christology of T. T. Shields," 232–72.

4. Canadian religious historians generally agree that an evangelical consensus on certain core doctrines and values was forged by Protestants from many denominations in mid-nineteenth century Ontario. This consensus dominated the province's Protestant culture until the doctrinal controversies and social changes of the late nineteenth century brought about its decline. For examples of how the term "evangelical consensus" is used, see Airhart, *Serving the Present Age*, 3–11. For specific information on the contents of this consensus, see Van Die, *Nathanael Burwash*, 9–10; Marshall, *Secularizing the Faith*, 25–48; Grant, *Profusion of Spires*, 104–11.

as liberals and conservatives struggled with its countercultural implications. While many Canadian Baptists continued to profess separation, its practice declined markedly, especially after the turn of the century. Among the denomination's most prominent businessmen, acceptance of materialism and more liberal moral values effectively eliminated actions that marked them out as Baptists.

Secularization compelled some to redefine the church, emphasizing its social and cultural functions at the expense of its traditional moral and spiritual roles. At Jarvis Street Baptist Church, redefinition met resistance in the person of T. T. Shields. As the theological battle lines were drawn between 1910 and 1920, Shields grew more sensitive to opposition at Jarvis Street. He particularly resented efforts by some of his leading businessmen parishioners to compromise with theological liberals and accommodate worldly morality. By 1919, antithetical cultural perspectives had compromised the moral consensus that had unified the church in the late nineteenth century.

This chapter examines the move away from separation toward sociocultural integration by Jarvis Street's businessmen in the late nineteenth century. Bankruptcy, the nature of amusement, and the role of church music show how businessmen rejected the norms that characterized separation in business, in their personal lives, and at church.

"Owe No Man Anything": Bankruptcy and Baptists

Perhaps no issue troubled Canadian Baptists more in the last half of the nineteenth century than insolvency. Concern about declining moral standards and an accompanying softening of church discipline for bankruptcy disturbed many conservative Baptists. For them, any action that absolved the debtor from his financial obligations was thought to encourage dishonesty and violate the Pauline command "owe no man anything" (Rom 13:8). In contrast, more liberal Baptists supported insolvency laws that were, in their view, fair to both debtor and creditor.

Canadian Baptists inherited a long tradition of strict discipline for bankruptcy. As Michael Watts noted in his study of early English dissenters, "bankrupts were usually excommunicated from the gathered churches."[5] While "in some cases . . . the rule against bankruptcy was exercised with compassion," generally, the treatment of bankrupts was

---

5. Watts, *Dissenters*, 335.

"particularly harsh."⁶ The underlying assumption was that bankruptcy was usually the result of sinful acts. By the early nineteenth century, British Baptists had only slightly moderated their views. In an 1821 article for the *Baptist Magazine* pastor Micah Thomas stated the typical Baptist position:

> Be it premised and understood, that all failures in trade and commerce are not intended to be associated with the iniquity in question. Many exceptions in the enormous aggregate will be readily conceded; and every feeling heart is prepared to shed the tear of compassion and sympathy over the disasters of the really unfortunate. But when surveyed in their huge amount, it is highly probable that not one instance out of ten, or perhaps twenty, in cases of bankruptcy, can be entirely exonerated from blame and criminality. In a great many instances, they are a complete mass of nefarious transactions, and embody all the guilt and atrocity of absolute swindling.⁷

While admitting that uncontrollable events could cause business failure, Thomas and other Baptists believed that sin, not circumstance, caused the vast majority of bankruptcies.

Many British Baptists brought this uncompromising view with them to Canada. Writing about his own experience in 1859, the provision dealer William Davies complained, "The Law is alter'd now, a man cannot be imprison'd for debt now. I wish he could, I believe it would fetch the money then."⁸ Davies's attitude reflected the hardline legalistic approach favored by conservative Baptists. In their denominational paper, Baptists were taught that "the law of love makes the path of duty not so hard to find, if we are only willing seekers of it. It requires that every kind of obligation be fulfilled, fully met without any evasion."⁹ An earlier piece put the matter plainly:

> Men may sophisticate as they please. They can never make it right, and all the bankrupt laws in the universe cannot make it right for them not to pay their debts. There is a sin in this neglect as clear and as deserving of church discipline as in stealing or false swearing. He who violates his promise to pay, or withholds his payment of a debt, when it is within his power to meet his

---

6. Watts, *Dissenters*, 335–36.
7. "Bankruptcy," *Baptist Magazine*, 1822.
8. William Davies to James Davies, June 18, 1859. WOP, Box 4044, File 2, UWORC.
9. "Owe No Man Anything," *CB*, October 1, 1868.

engagement, ought to be made to feel that in the sight of all honest men he is a swindler. Religion may be a very comfortable cloak, under which to hide; but if religion does not make a man deal justly, it is not worth having.[10]

In the mid-nineteenth century, Canadian Baptists stood opposed to any measure that excused bankruptcy and absolved a debtor from his debts.

Changes to Canada's insolvency laws, in part, put pressure on Baptists to secularize their belief and practice. Legislation passed by the Legislative Assembly in the early 1840s sought "to soften the rigor of the Laws, in that part of this Province called Upper Canada, affecting the relation between Debtor and Creditor, as far as a due regard to the interests of commerce will permit."[11] Among important changes that favored the debtor were an end to arrests for actions not subject to bail or arrest in a foreign country, for "any suit where the cause of action shall not amount to ten pounds" and execution "for any sum."[12] In August 1858, "An Act for Abolishing Arrest in Civil Actions in Certain Cases and for the Better Prevention and More Effectual Punishment of Fraud," abolished arrest for ordinary debts and made preferential assignments illegal in Canada West.[13] The end to preferences eliminated the immoral practice of favoring one creditor over another.

With Confederation came renewed efforts to formulate federal bankruptcy legislation. An Insolvency Act was passed in 1869.[14] This legislation was the first attempt by the federal government to address the issue of bankruptcy. The Act emphasized the rights of the creditor in any bankruptcy proceeding. On April 8, 1875, a revised version of the Act of 1869 received Royal Assent. It defined terms and specified obligations of creditor and debtor, protecting the rights and interests of both. In addition, the expedition of bankruptcy was quickened by specific rules

---

10. "Christian Duty of Paying Debts," *CB*, April 5, 1866.

11. *Provincial Statutes of Canada*, 1842, "Act to Abolish Imprisonment in Execution for Debt, and for Other Purposes Therein Mentioned," 7 Vic. c. 31. Preamble.

12. *Provincial Statutes of Canada*, 1842, "Act to Abolish Imprisonment in Execution for Debt, and for Other Purposes Therein Mentioned," 7 Vic. c. 31. Preamble.

13. *Provincial Statutes of Canada*, 1858, "Act for Abolishing Arrest in Civil Actions in Certain Cases and for the Better Prevention and More Effectual Punishment of Fraud," 22 Vic. c. 96.1s. *Provincial Statutes of Canada*. 1869, "Act Respecting Insolvency," 32–33 Vic. c. 16.

14. *Provincial Statutes of Canada*, 1869, "Act Respecting Insolvency," 32–33 Vic. c. 16.

governing procedure.[15] In 1880, however, the Insolvency Act of 1875 was repealed.[16] This left only legislation dealing with winding-up operations in force. Successive federal governments were either unsuccessful or unwilling to confront the bankruptcy issue.[17] The resulting legislative vacuum left both creditor and debtor open to abuse. The situation was finally resolved in 1919, with the passage of bankruptcy legislation that met many of the longstanding demands of the business community.[18]

Through the Toronto Board of Trade, Baptist businessmen from Jarvis Street expressed their opinions on bankruptcy and advocated stronger legislation. Before 1880 their sympathy lay with creditors. At an April 12, 1869, meeting of the Toronto Board of Trade, dry goods merchant Arthur Robinson McMaster, who chaired the Insolvency Committee, presented a report that recommended that no insolvent estate be assigned without permission of the creditors, that creditors be given the power to appoint a custodian to take possession of the insolvent's estate, and that an inspector be appointed to manage the estate along with the official assignee.[19] Subsequently, "An Act respecting Insolvency," included these proposals.[20] At a council meeting held May 7, 1872, chemical wholesaler and manufacturer William Elliot seconded the motion to send a memorial to parliament, which stated, "This Board view with alarm the repeal of the Insolvent Act of 1869 without some provision whereby all creditors will have equal rights and claims in & to an estate taken possession of by the Sherriff."[21] The protection of a creditor's interests was the primary concern of Baptist businessmen.

---

15. *Provincial Statutes of Canada*, 1875, "Act Respecting Insolvency," 38 Vic. c. 16.

16. *Provincial Statutes of Canada*, 1880, "Act to Repeal the Acts Respecting Insolvency Now in Force in Canada," 43 Vic. c. 1.

17. For an analysis of government reluctance to pass adequate bankruptcy legislation and the response of the Toronto business community to the situation, see Stanford, *To Serve the Community*, 26, 43, 62, 150.

18. *Provincial Statutes of Canada*, 1919, "Act Respecting Bankruptcy," 9–10 Geo. 5, c. 36. One should also see the subsequent amendment, 1920, "Act to Amend the Bankruptcy Act," 10–11 Geo. 5, c. 34.

19. NA, MG 28 III 56, vol. 2, *Toronto Board of Trade Council Minute Book, 30 April 1850–24 January 1871*, April 12, 1869, 414. The report of the Insolvency Committee is also reprinted in the "Board of Trade. The Insolvency Act," *Globe*, April 13, 1869.

20. *Provincial Statutes of Canada*, 1869, "Act Respecting Insolvency," 32–33 Vic. c. 16.

21. NA, MG 28 III 56, vol. 3, *Toronto Board of Trade Minute Book, 21 January 1871–21 January 1887*, May 1, 1872, 33.

After the repeal of bankruptcy legislation in 1880, Jarvis Street businessmen pressed for new legislation and began to consider the effects on debtors as well as creditors. A January 1884 petition of the House of Commons, signed by "A. R. McMaster and Bro.," stated, "That justice alike to creditors and debtors requires that means be provided for the equitable distribution of the assets of debtors."[22] Concern for the just treatment of interests outside of the business community also received attention. At a November 6, 1893, meeting of the Board Council dry goods merchant James Short McMaster expressed concern that the proposed Insolvency Act ignored farmers.[23] Publicly, Baptist businessmen from Jarvis Street shared in the outrage of Toronto's business community over the "iniquitous condition of affairs" that government reluctance to pass bankruptcy legislation had created.[24] Privately, their attitudes and actions differed.

By the late nineteenth century, many Baptists had altered their view of the causes, obligations, and consequences of bankruptcy. For Canadian Baptists generally, the practice of automatically censuring an insolvent debtor grew increasingly unacceptable. In an article written for the April 29, 1886, issue of *The Canadian Baptist*, Joshua Denovan, pastor of Immanuel Street Baptist Church, articulated the changing trend:

> Few acquainted with business will dispute that, within the last thirty years, Bankruptcy from being a rare and exceptional event has become common and frequent; few will dispute that its prevalence has lowered the once high British standard of social and commercial morality; no thoughtful religious man will question that it has dishonoured and weakened the Christian church in herself, and banefully affected her influence upon the unconverted world. It is but a few years since [that]

22. NA, MG 28 III 56, vol. 3, *Toronto Board of Trade Minute Book, 21 January 1871–21 January 1887*, January 1884, 357. There is no record in the Journals of the House of Commons that this petition was submitted. It is clear that consideration of a debtor's rights and interests came slowly for the Toronto Board of Trade. Early in 1884 the Board changed its position and pushed for legislation that subjected a debtor to the undue hardship of ongoing liability. In its January 3, 1884, issue the *Globe*, in an article entitled "Bankruptcy Legislation," criticized the new proposal for its harshness. In its conclusion the article stated, "Punish with utmost rigor fraud, collusion and trickery. But when an honest debtor has honestly given up everything to his creditors, let him in justice as well as mercy be relieved from liabilities and obligations which if they still burden him must render his future utterly hopeless."

23. NA, MG 2s III 56, vol. 4, *Toronto Board of Trade Council Minute Book, 25 January 1887–31 January 1894*, November 6, 1893, 520.

24. NA, MG 2s III 56, vol. 4, *Toronto Board of Trade Council Minute Book, 25 January 1887–31 January 1894*, November 6, 1893, 520.

> the bankruptcy of the member of a Christian church was regarded as a matter sufficiently serious to demand a committee of enquiry, while now nothing short of a very strong public condemnation (if even that) will secure the appointment of such a committee. In this direction our morals are certainly loosening, our ecclesiastical standard of righteousness lowering more rapidly than some of us like to admit. "There's something rotten in the state of Denmark."[25]

Denovan's analysis expressed concerns shared by many of his brethren. The sense of moral decline and the resulting loss of spiritual separateness often evoked a strong response. One Baptist's response made the editorial columns of *The Canadian Baptist* in the summer of 1901: "An ardent, impulsive brother complains that the church has become so thoroughly secularized that, for the sake of his own peace and comfort, he must repudiate and withdraw from it."[26] The editor retorted:

> Stand by your church brother. Judge not before the time. Better, a thousand times better, to help resuscitate the church than to hasten its enfeeblement by an unheroic withdrawal from its greatest need.[27]

Despite such encouragement, desertions by disillusioned Baptists did occur. As Convention President Albert Azro Ayer, a Montreal dairy and produce merchant, noted at the Baptist Convention of Ontario and Quebec in 1913,

> Records show that Baptists in these two Provinces have increased threefold in the past forty years. What does this prove? These figures really show that we have not held our own families and that our losses have only been made up by our gains from outside. The inference is that the world and its attractions, have drawn many of our children and Sunday School scholars away.[28]

While some Baptists embarked on a search for ways to counteract the secularizing effects of worldliness and hold their own, others decided to keep Baptists in the cultural mainstream by accepting the "ways of the world."

25. "Credit and Bankruptcy," *CB*, April 29, 1886.
26. "Editorial," *CB*, July 4, 1901.
27. "Editorial," *CB*, July 4, 1901.
28. "President's Address: The Church and the World," *CB*, October 16, 1913.

Maintaining Separation

Within Jarvis Street Baptist Church, prominent businessmen spearheaded the drive to modify the church's stand on bankruptcy. Although discipline for failure to pay debts continued into the 1880s, the church grew lax in its treatment of bankruptcy. Leniency first became apparent in the 1850s. In 1858, the bankruptcy of produce merchant Francis T. Parson disrupted the church as supporters of William Davies, who had invested hard cash in Parson's business and upon assignment received nothing, opposed a faction led by William McMaster, who backed preferential assignments. Parson went undisciplined; Davies and his supporters left the church. By contrast, in 1855, John Tovell, a men's clothier, had been excluded after his bankruptcy in circumstances strikingly similar to those of Parson. Yet John McIntosh, an ironmonger bankrupted in the early 1850s, was allowed to retain his membership in Bond Street Church.[29] The inconsistent treatment of those involved in bankruptcy by a deacon's board dominated by wealthy and powerful businessmen points to both personal rivalry and increasingly permissive attitudes as causes for the church's alteration of traditional Baptist practice. The fear of personal financial failure may also have prompted some businessmen to encourage this relaxation. Whatever the primary cause was for their change in attitude, many businessmen at Jarvis Street abandoned the notion that bankruptcy always deserved church discipline.

By the late nineteenth century, the church no longer disciplined bankrupts, even when negligence or greed were the suspected causes of a businessman's failure. When deacon and hardware merchant William Hewitt overextended himself through the purchase of real estate, declared bankruptcy in 1879, and then defaulted on the third payment to his creditors, the church did nothing.[30] Purposeful ignorance and "looking the other way" had replaced stern discipline. The traditional Baptist practice of holding a brother or sister accountable for their actions was clearly waning.

Even more startling were the extraordinary actions taken by the church to remove the earlier sinful stigma of bankruptcy from those businessmen caught in circumstances beyond their control. On January 22, 1896, the church took the unprecedented step of issuing a letter of sympathy to insolvent hatter and furrier, deacon Joseph Lugsdin:

---

29. For details of the Parson and Tovell cases, see Langley, *Correct Statement of the Proceedings in Bond Street Baptist Church*, 4–23; William Davies to James Davies, June 18, 1859. WOP, Box 4044, File 2, UWORC.

30. *Trader*, July 1880.

> Resolved. That the church has been grieved to hear that deacon Joseph Lugsdin has been compelled through embarrassment caused by the severe business competition which now prevails to make an assignment for the benefit of his creditors. We sympathize deeply with him in this trouble and desire to express our continued confidence in his integrity and Christian character.... Our recognition of the truth of the view which he expresses as to the danger to which a person in his position is exposed of having aspersions thrown upon his character which however groundless may injuriously affect the church in which he holds an important official position constrains us to accept his resignation, but we do so with the hope that when this danger has passed away he will again feel at liberty to give us the benefit of his services as a deacon.[31]

The tenderness of these words stood in marked contrast to the terse language used to expel those involved in bankruptcy in earlier years. Like Lugsdin, James Short McMaster received a letter of support after his dry goods business, McMaster and Company, went bankrupt in January 1897 (see Figure 19). Again, the church membership expressed "their deep sympathy with deacon McMaster in his business reverse" and declared publicly "their entire confidence in his integrity as a businessman."[32]

In this case, there is cause to question the church's support. According to James Short McMaster's grandson, Wardley McMaster, mismanagement and greed accounted for the failure of the family business: "Grandfather refused to return to look after matters [in Canada] liking the life in England."[33] In addition, in the late 1880s, he bought "heavily," collected commissions on his purchases and then left England.[34] By the time James Short McMaster arrived in Toronto in 1889, the business was in trouble. "The business did not survive," recalled Wardley McMaster, "since the purchase costs and commissions could not be recovered in the panic. Grandfather escaped with the Lorne Park Estate and $125,000."[35] If Wardley McMaster's account is accurate, the church's confidence in

---

31. *Minute Book, 1892–1910*, January 22, 1896. JSBCA.

32. *Minute Book, 1892–1910*, January 22, 1896. JSBCA.

33. Wardley McMaster to G. P. Gilmour, June 16, 1962, G. P. Gilmour Papers, "Correspondence File re. William McMaster 1957–1962," CBA.

34. Wardley McMaster to G. P. Gilmour, June 16, 1962, G. P. Gilmour Papers, "Correspondence File re. William McMaster 1957–1962," CBA.

35. Wardley McMaster to G. P. Gilmour, June 16, 1962, G. P. Gilmour Papers, "Correspondence File re. William McMaster 1957–1962," CBA.

James Short McMaster's business integrity was misplaced. He was guilty of greed, carelessness, and neglect, but, instead of investigating the matter thoroughly and disciplining one of its most prominent businessmen, the church opted to blame circumstances.

The Lugsdin and McMaster cases showed how dramatically the treatment of bankruptcy had changed. In a generation, Jarvis Street had moved from an automatic presumption of guilt to expressing support for businessmen who experienced (often through no fault of their own) severe financial difficulties. "Circumstances" gradually replaced sin as the accepted explanation for bankruptcy. At the same time, the strict discipline for bankruptcy that had once marked Baptist separation from the secular world was relaxed as church practice was brought into conformity with the cultural reality of sociocultural integration. This change allowed Baptist businessmen to feel more secure and comfortable as they took their place within the Canadian cultural mainstream.

Music in the Church: Making Jarvis Street Culturally Respectable

Music was a thorny issue for Baptists. Debates over whether music compromised or complemented worship were common in Canada. Conservative views ranged from favoring unaccompanied Psalms in services to limited tolerance of instrumentation and contemporary hymns. Cultural liberals, including many businessmen, not only encouraged music in services but also sought to alter its status to that of worldly performance. Under the guiding hands of its leading businessmen, Jarvis Street had, by the early twentieth century, become a center for musical performances; the quality of its choral and instrumental music rivalled that heard in Massey Hall.

Disagreements among English Baptists over the purpose and power of music had a long history. In the late seventeenth century, both General and Particular Baptists engaged in these disputes. In the 1690s, an eight-year pamphlet war between Benjamin Keach and Isaac Marlow brought the issue to a head among Particular Baptists. In 1691, in a pamphlet entitled, *The Breach Repaired in God's Worship*. Keach argued that congregational singing was "a holy ordinance of Jesus Christ" carried on for the edification of God's people and the shame of the Devil. "The Devil" Keach noted, "is a great enemy to singing; he does not love Such Hosannas and Praises should be sung to Jesus Christ."[36] In 1692, Marlow countered with *The Truth Soberly Defended*, in which he contended that congregational singing was "dangerous and destructive to the peace and well-being of our churches, and to the pure worship of God therein."[37] Baptists like Marlow believed that innovations, such as the congregational singing of original hymns introduced by Keach, destroyed the solemnity of the service and sanctioned a "false worship" that could lead to impropriety and formalism.[38]

The belief that music promoted worldliness was also a staple in Baptist criticism. In 1678, in a tract entitled *Primitive Christianity*, the General Baptist Thomas Grantham condemned "plain song, prick-song, descant, or other poetical strains," as "men's devices," that are "very much unlike the gravity of Christian worship."[39] Such arguments laid the foundation for a continuing controversy.

In the eighteenth century, complaints about the use of music persisted even after the acceptance of congregational singing. In 1733, for example, the General Assembly of the General Baptists received word from Northamptonshire, "that some churches had fallen into the way of singing the Psalms of David, or other men's composures, with tunable notes, and a mixed multitude; which way of singing, appears to us wholly unwarranted from the Word of God."[40] Despite such objections, General and Particular Baptists gradually made music an integral part of the worship service.

For nineteenth century Canadian Baptists, church music continued to be a divisive issue. Fiddling at one of the tea meetings held on January 1, 1851, at First Baptist Church, Brantford, for example, brought the swift censure of deacon William Moyle. T. S. Shenston recalled the event:

> Notwithstanding the great height of the pulpit, a temporary gallery had been erected above it for the accommodation of the choir. This gallery as well filled with singers, led by Mr. John W-, who entertained the waiting congregation by fiddling some popular songs and dancing tunes. This 'vexed the righteous soul' of the late deacon Wm. Moyle, and he rose to

---

36. Keach, *Breach Repaired in God's Worship*, 25.
37. Marlow, *Truth Soberly Defended*, 140–41.
38. Marlow, *Truth Soberly Defended*, viii.
39. Grantham, *Christianismus Primitivus*, 112.
40. This report is quoted in Goadby, *Bye-Paths in Baptist History*, 348.

his feet, and, in a mild and dignified manner, objected to such fiddling in the house of God.

This stopped the fiddling with 'awful' suddenness, but it did not stop the fiddler, and 'you had better believe it' the fiddle box came down with a *whop!*; the fiddle was placed therein with a *whack!*; the lid brought down with a *bang!*, and the fiddler solemnly declared his intention *to* do a lot of naughty things and to leave undone some very amiable ones.

Elder D. took in 'the situation' in a moment, and saw that 'the fat was in the fire.' Oh, how he did plead! but all in vain. The fiddle was boxed, the cloak was on the enraged fiddler's back, and he partly down the steps, when he was taken in hand by that champion peace-maker, Wm. Buck. His oil was superior to that of Elder D. He used it lavishly on the troubled waters, and there was a calm, and the fiddling and singing went off 'O. K.' for the remainder of the evening, to the relief of all.[41]

This incident is but one of many. Similar objections persisted among Canadian Baptists well into the late nineteenth century.

The September 2, 1897, issue of *The Canadian Baptist* carried an ultra-conservative article by Joshua Denovan entitled "Christian Work and Worship." In the article, Denovan offered the strict Baptist definition of church music. "Praise," argued Denovan, "ought to be the united and audible adoration and thanksgiving of all the children of God present, without any pretence whatever to musical performance."[42] He then went on to condemn the many abuses present in Canadian Baptist worship services:

> Such a thing as musical vibrations, ground out of an unconscious machine, are mere atmospheric mockery. Such a thing as a soloist (whether voluntary or hired) is a gross outrage. Such a thing as a soloist or a choir, singing to please or attract the public singing to the people assembled or *for* the people, is a monstrous perversion of Church praise for which primitive Christianity furnishes no precedent or sanction. Instrumental music belonged to the Hebrew temple, and so did animal sacrifices, and so did holy water and holy lamp-light; but they never had a place in the spiritual worship of the Christian Church as it was constituted by Christ and his apostles.[43]

---

41. Shenston, *Jubilee Review*, 25.
42. "Christian Work and Worship," *CB*, September 2, 1897.
43. "Christian Work and Worship," *CB*, September 2, 1897.

This stern rebuke brought an equally sharp response from one that favored musical innovation. In a letter to *The Canadian Baptist*, G. B. Davis suggested, "Father Denovan struck a discordant note in his communication against instrumental music and choir-anthems in Christian worship, in last week's Baptist."[44] Davis contended, "The opinion of Father Denovan is certainly out of harmony with the inspired conviction of such men as Fathers Elisha, David and Samuel."[45] Sacred music, "both instrumental and vocal," were clearly sanctioned in the Scriptures.[46] To Denovan's argument that instrumental and choral music belonged exclusively to the Old Testament economy, Davis retorted, "As in our schools, some things are taught in God's First Books that do not require teaching in His Fifth."[47] For Davis, it was ludicrous for Denovan to suggest that because the "brief history of the planting and progress of New Testament churches" given in Scripture, "has in it no record of instrumental music and church choirs, therefore, there is to be none for all time."[48]

Despite pockets of strong opposition to certain musical forms new resources for worship emerged to satisfy the craving for musical innovation within individual churches. In Ontario, a number of significant initiatives were undertaken. Although not "officially" sponsored by the entire denomination, *The Canadian Baptist Church Hymn Book*, first published in 1873 by Copp, Clark & Co., provided a basic source for musical worship. The increasing interest and acceptance of music prompted H. E. Buchan, a medical doctor from Jarvis Street, to publish *Our Service of Song* in 1877.[49] In 1900, the publication of a denominational hymnal further promoted music by raising its visibility and providing a standard repertoire for Canadian Baptist churches.[50] The inclusion of a "Canadian Supplement" in editions of *The Canadian Baptist Church Hymnal* after 1902 added a nationalist dimension to its contents and brought about a "very satisfactory"

---

44. "Instrumental Worship in Christian Worship," *CB*, September 2, 1897.
45. "Instrumental Worship in Christian Worship," *CB*, September 2, 1897.
46. "Instrumental Worship in Christian Worship," *CB*, September 2, 1897.
47. "Instrumental Worship in Christian Worship," *CB*, September 2, 1897.
48. "Instrumental Worship in Christian Worship," *CB*, September 2, 1897.
49. A full-page advertisement for Buchan's hymn book is found in *Baptist Year Book for Ontario and Quebec, 1877*, 151.
50. A brief history and superficial analysis of the development of this hymnal is provided in Renfree, *Heritage and Horizon*, 241, 251–52, 293.

number of sales.⁵¹ The resources needed to support a growing acceptance of musical innovation were clearly present.

Debate over church music brought the issue of worldliness to the surface. The spirituality of those Baptists who accepted musical innovation was questioned by other countercultural Baptists who condemned new forms of musical expression as worldly "attractions."⁵² Still, cultural liberals, who desired sociocultural integration and respectability, remained convinced that musical innovation brought spiritual and temporal rewards that Canadian Baptists could ill-afford to miss.

Within Jarvis Street, musical innovation brought both criticism and praise. In 1857, the introduction of an organ to Bond Street Baptist Church offended certain members. Recalling the events in a letter to his brother, William Davies noted,

> I think that matters are mending some in our church. We have weeded out several disaffected ones. I don't know if I told you a few months ago some of the folks wanted an organ & it was carried. 5 or 6 of the minority were so incensed about it that they left and enlisted under the Banner of the City Missionary, one of their number, & met in a bdg for worship every Sunday & wrote to the Bond Street Baptist Church for letters of dismission. This of course could not be granted & as they still kept away & when visited by a committee declared themselves well satisfied with the position & said they would on no account return, their names by a unanimous vote were dropped from the Church Books. Be it understood there was a Melodeon before (a kind of halfbred thing between an organ and piano), but when an organ was substituted they could not conscientiously remain.⁵³

---

51. This assessment of sales was offered by Edwardo Freeland, Secretary of the Hymnal Committee, in "New Hymn Book," May 19, 1904.

52. In his letter of resignation from the pastorate of Alexander Street Baptist Church, A. H. Munro argued, "The attractions of a large and elegant place of worship of the same denomination in our immediate vicinity, have had the effect of diminishing in a very observable degree our Sunday evening congregation." Jarvis Street's "attractions" included an organ and a paid soloist. Munro's letter is found at The Canadian Baptist Archives, Alexander St./Immanuel St. Records, A. H. Munro to the congregation, January 29, 1877, Box 1 1866–1904, "General Correspondence Pile, 1867–1904." For a late nineteenth century condemnation of the worldliness associated with such musical innovations see the article by Joshua Denovan in "Churchianity versus Genuine Christianity," *CB*, October 12, 1899.

53. William Davies to James Davies, May 31, 1857. WOP, Box 4044, File 2, UWORC.

Here the attempt to introduce modern music to the church provoked a strong negative reaction. For the offended Baptists such change was indicative of worldliness.

While the motives behind the introduction of an organ to Bond Street remain obscure, later musical innovations at Jarvis Street were heavily criticized for their ostentation. Commenting on the changes that accompanied the move to Jarvis Street in 1875, William Davies, now a member of Alexander Street Baptist Church, complained: "This congregation were in a part of the city which was thickly populated but they had an old fashioned building. One of the members, an MLC [Member of the Legislative Council], say a Senator, very wealthy, married an American, natural result they soon had an American minister, then this new building also American, then the lady & the minister lay their heads together & get a professional singer a sort of *prima dona* & she is paid $300.00 per year and many are very much hurt about it."[54] Davies objected to the Americanization and professionalization of music in the church attributing the innovations to dry goods merchant turned financier, William McMaster (a Senator), and his second wife, Susan Moulton McMaster. Davies blamed their "hateful" spirit of "aggrandizement" for the move to a more respectable secular music ministry.[55] He also criticized the new building and Susan McMaster's gift of an organ as self-serving, charging that they had been "built regardless of the needs of the city."[56] Here then was a case of a wealthy Jarvis Street businessman and his wife displaying their commitment to effect change that would make their church socially respectable.

The new more secular values pursued by William and Susan McMaster were quickly adopted by others at Jarvis Street. In 1888, the church hired Augustus Stephen Vogt to be its first paid organist and choirmaster. Vogt, a native of Washington, Ontario, had previously served as organist of the St. James Lutheran Church of Elmira and the First Methodist Church in St. Thomas, Ontario. He received his musical training at the New England Conservatory of Music in Boston and the Royal Conservatory of Music in Leipzig, Germany. Vogt specialized in *a cappella* performances of the classics. Under his leadership, the Jarvis Street Baptist Church Choir gained the reputation as the finest church choir in Toronto. In 1894, Vogt selected the best choristers from Jarvis Street to form the

54. William Davies to a Friend, June 15, 1876. WOP, Box 4044, File 3, UWORC.
55. William Davies to a Friend, June 15, 1876. WOP, Box 4044, File 3, UWORC.
56. William Davies to a Friend, June 15, 1876. WOP, Box 4044, File 3, UWORC.

Mendelssohn Choir, enhancing the reputation of Jarvis Street as a thriving musical center (see Figure 20).[57]

When Vogt retired from Jarvis Street in 1906, Dr. Edward Broome was hired to replace him. With the encouragement of pastor H. Francis Perry and prominent businessmen like jeweller James Ryrie and investment broker Albert Matthews on the church Music Committee, Broome made music the focal point of the Sunday worship services.[58] By 1910, when T. T. Shields became pastor, music dominated the services. Shields later complained, "What was designed to be an 'opening sentence' sometimes turned out to be an anthem that required ten minutes to complete. The result was, that do as one would, the Jarvis Street preacher would begin to preach about the time other congregations were hearing the Benediction."[59]

In 1920, Shields took action and asked the deacons to restrict music in the services. The deacons passed a resolution calling for "the anthem to be sung in the morning service while the offering is being taken, and to not have more than two anthems at the evening service, one of which shall be sung while the offering is being taken."[60] When informed of the deacons' decision, Dr. Broome objected to the changes, and when he next met with the choir he stated, "Wait till our friend Mr. Ryrie comes home and we will fight this out."[61] According to Shields, "from that moment the choir became a hostile organization."[62] Upon his return, James Ryrie sided with Dr. Broome, and no action was taken on the resolution passed by the deacons. In *The Plot That Failed*, Shields offers his analysis of the controversy:

---

57. The facts in this paragraph are taken from Charles G. D. Roberts and Arthur L. Tunnell, *Standard Dictionary of Canadian Biography*, 2:981–82.

58. On the occasion of Broome's hiring as choir director, an editorial note in the May 10, 1906, issue of *Canadian Baptist* noted, "Jarvis St. is fortunate in having in Dr. Perry a pastor who is keenly in sympathy with this department of the church's work." Unfortunately, the minutes of the music committee are not extant. James Ryrie, who served as chairman of the committee, and Albert Matthews who was a long-time committee member steadfastly supported Broome and came to his aid when Shields sought reforms that would severely limit the amount of music in the worship services.

59. Shields, *Plot That Failed*, 186.

60. Shields, *Plot That Failed*, 187. For reference to the resolution in the church minutes see, *Jarvis Street Baptist Church Minute Book*, 1918–1928, May 5, 1920. (MS), JSBCA.

61. Shields, *Inside of the Cup*, 22.

62. Shields, *Inside of the Cup*, 22.

> The gentleman [James Ryrie] who had moved the amendment to my resolution at the Ottawa Convention [of 1919] was Chairman of the Music Committee. He was a very excellent man, but was not biblically informed. I never observed any evidence that he was a student of the Bible. From the kind of book he occasionally quoted in prayer-meeting, and what I learned from himself of his religious views, I know that he had never been 'rooted and grounded' in the principles of Evangelical Christianity as historically held by Baptists. His idea of a religious service, it seemed to me, was that the sermon should occupy a subordinate place, and that the music, as represented by the choir, was the most important element in the service.[63]

For Shields, the distinctive Baptist service in which preaching predominated had been compromised by the efforts of James Ryrie. On March 14, 1918, Ryrie had written a letter to Shields expressing dismay that his children took visitors to other churches because "'they feel uncomfortable lest you will be hitting people.'"[64] The abandonment, by James Ryrie, of a form of worship that separated Baptists from other denominations could not, in Shields's view, be tolerated. Ryrie's desire that Jarvis Street maintain its respectability impinged on Shields's definition of proper worship.

Convinced that both his personal credibility and the righteousness of the church were at stake, Shields called a meeting of the deacons after the Sunday morning service on May 2, 1920. He informed them of his intent to bring the matter of lengthy choir anthems before the entire church for a vote. Ryrie objected, noting that while the pastor might well be supported on the question of the amount of time taken by the choir, there were "other issues involved in the present situation."[65] Shields responded by saying that at the church meeting to be held on Wednesday, May 5, he would submit his resignation and allow the congregation to render its verdict on his future as pastor of Jarvis Street. If the congregation voted that he resign, he would do so; if they supported him, he would remain pastor. At the congregational meeting, Shields was reaffirmed as the pastor by an almost unanimous standing vote.

---

63. Shields, *Plot That Failed*, 187–88.

64. The original letter does not appear to be in the T. T. Shields Papers housed in the church archives. It is reprinted in Shields, *Inside of the Cup*, 9.

65. These words attributed to James Ryrie are quoted in Shields, *Plot That Failed*, 188.

A second resolution, presented and moved by Shields, passed "almost unanimously" at the meeting.[66] It stated,

> That the church hereby resolves that in the services for public worship, Sunday mornings and evenings, precedence shall be given to the ministry of the Word; and that each service shall be so ordered that all of the elements of the service may be of such character and in such proportion as to contribute to the exaltation of Christ through the exposition of the Word of God.
> And in order that these principles may be given effect, the church hereby places the conduct of the public services of the Lord's Day entirely in the hands of the pastor of the church ... it being understood, as a matter of course, that the deacons are the pastor's proper advisers in all matters relating to the conduct of the public worship of the church; and that, therefore, henceforth the Music Committee shall be considered a sub-committee of the deacons' Board, of which the pastor shall be, ex-officio, a member.[67]

Thus, control over music was taken from the Music Committee and given to the pastor. This action put businessmen like James Ryrie on notice that the respectable church they had worked so hard to create and maintain was threatened.

The skirmish over music at Jarvis Street was a test case for separation. While Baptist businessmen continued to profess their belief in separation from the world, they transformed their church music ministry so that it might better reflect the values and beliefs of the secular world. The installation of an organ, the hiring of a paid soloist, organist and choirmaster, the establishment of a link between the Mendelssohn and Jarvis Street choirs, and the dominance of music in public worship services were all efforts designed and promoted by businessmen to make Jarvis Street socially respectable. The professionalization of music at Jarvis Street was one avenue by which prominent businessmen introduced secular cultural values to the church.

---

66. These words and the account in the paragraph preceding it are taken from Shields, *Plot That Failed*, 188–91.

67. Shields, *Plot That Failed*, 191.

The Acceptance of Amusements

For Canadian Baptists, the avoidance of worldly activities constituted a hallmark of spiritual separation. As moral values were secularized, many Baptist businessmen grew more tolerant. Their willingness to participate openly in "popular amusements" represented a departure from strict Baptist morality that more conservative Baptists felt compelled to preserve. By the early twentieth century, many of Jarvis Street's most prominent and wealthy businessmen had rejected legalistic biblical interpretations that emphasized moral conformity to a single strict moral code. Fundamentalists, like T. T. Shields, believed that such rejection flowed from the moral laxity associated with modernism. Specifically, fundamentalists charged that those Baptists who accepted amusements were worldly, unspiritual, and wayward.

Like bankruptcy and music, amusements were a longstanding issue among Baptists. In the seventeenth century, English Baptists demanded adherence to a strict moral code that prohibited improper dress, card-playing, dancing, and participation in sports if it conflicted with church meetings. In 1645, the Broadmead Baptist Church, Bristol, disciplined its pastor, Nathanael Ingello, who "troubled and offended" many members "with his flaunting apparel together with his being given so much to music, not only at his own house, but at houses of entertainment out of town."[68] Similarly, the records of the Fenstanton Baptist Church show that George Michell of Eltisley, a parish in Cambridgeshire, was reproved and then "excommunicated" for "Running frequently upon the first day of the week, as well as at other times, to the vicious assemblies of the world, joining with them in their sports, and pastimes, and excess of riot."[69]

The tradition of keeping a close watch over behavior continued among English Baptists in the eighteenth century. In 1711, the General Assembly of the General Baptists declared that card-playing was "unlawful for such as profess the Gospel of Christ, and unfits for communion."[70] In addition, the Assembly confronted the question of "whether a pastor who contends for dancing and cockfighting, with many other vices, although being moderately used, be a sufficient cause for the church to deprive him of communion?"[71] The answer was decisive: "That for

---

68. Underhill, *Records of a Church of Christ*, 36.
69. Underhill, *Records of a Church of Christ*, 159–60.
70. Goadby, *Bye-Paths in Baptist History*, 260.
71. Goadby, *Bye-Paths in Baptist History*, 260.

a minister of Christ to countenance, encourage, or contend for such vices, do disqualify him for the ministerial office and church communion, until he shall appear of another mind, and give satisfaction to the church of which he is pastor."[72] In January 1745, the Broadmead church declared "playing at cards to be sinful, and not allowed in any member of this church without censure."[73] Thus, by the end of the eighteenth century, English Baptists had a long history of regulating the behavior of their members with regard to amusements.

Throughout the nineteenth and early twentieth centuries, Canadian Baptists were also exercised about popular amusements. Disturbed by the growing popularity of amusements and their debilitating moral impact, E. W. Dadson called in 1888, for a return to living circumspectly:

> No Christian wisely circumspect would dream of giving his countenance to worldly amusements, or his presence to questionable places. He would not frequent taverns, patronize horse-racing or theatricals, simply because he would not see anything in these amusements profitable to the carrying out of his purpose, and the fact that they are questionable, so advertised, would be sufficient reason against them in any case.
>
> But do not Christians countenance the theatre? Do they not dance? and play cards? and occasionally are they not seen in bar-rooms and on the race-course? Oh, yes! but foolishly circumspect are such Christians. They look around them, it is true, but not for the purpose of hastening the kingdom, or of warding off that which may make toward poverty of soul. Purpose for God is their great lack.
>
> We unhesitatingly advocate a return to the Puritanical idea of circumspection. Dancing, betting, drinking, and theatre going Christians are a sad damage to the cause whose name they bear.[74]

Dadson's call for a return to puritanical asceticism that characterized early English Baptist practice represented a conservative legalistic response to amusements. Other Baptists contended that the responsibility for decisions concerning amusements rested with the individual. In a classic application of the Baptist belief in liberty of conscience, these more moderate and liberal Baptists rejected legalistic arguments. The

---

72. Goadby, *Bye-Paths in Baptist History*, 260.
73. Goadby, *Bye-Paths in Baptist History*, 260.
74. "Circumspectly," *CB*, February 2, 1888.

response of *The Canadian Baptist* editor, James Edward Wells, in an 1892 article on "The Question of Amusements," typified the view of those who favored liberty:

> We are often asked for an editorial opinion as to whether this, or that, or the other amusement, recreation, or practice is consistent with a Christian profession. It is, of course, out of the question that a Baptist Editor, or any other Baptist or body of Baptists, should be able to draw up a Baptist Index Expurgatorious of books which may not be read, or a catalogue of amusements which may or may not be indulged in. Even were we wise enough, as we are sure we are not, to do so with an approximation of infallibility, we are quite sure that the possession of such a set of arbitrary rules would be highly injurious, rather than beneficial, to the individual Christian, young or old, who should make it his guide. The effect would be, so far as it went, to lift from his or her shoulders a responsibility which they alone should bear, and in doing so to take away a most valuable means of Christian exercise and growth. There is no moral and certainly no spiritual development in following fixed rules of conduct, prescribed by any external authority. The mind which is truly spiritual judgeth all things and becomes, under the guidance of the Divine Word and Spirit, a law unto itself. It is endowed with a spiritual instinct which, if conscientiously followed, becomes a safer guide than any hard and fast lines which could be laid down, since the latter can but guide the outward act and are devoid of spirit and life.[75]

For Wells, a return to legalistic puritanical asceticism violated the principle of liberty of conscience and robbed the individual of an important opportunity for spiritual growth. The conflicting messages concerning amusements articulated in *The Canadian Baptist* in the late nineteenth century undoubtedly created confusion. The lack of consensus on amusements left the door open for Baptists to adjust their practice to suit themselves. The potential for licentiousness that such freedom created loomed large in the minds of many Baptists by the end of the nineteenth century.

Within Jarvis Street, disagreements over amusements took on new significance after the fundamentalist-modernist controversy at the October 1919 Ottawa convention.[76] In the months before the convention, the

---

75. "Question of Amusements," *CB*, March 17, 1892.

76. For details of the events at the 1919 convention from a pro-Shields perspective, see Tarr, *Shields of Canada*, 63–71. For Shields's account, see Shields, *Plot That Failed*, 121–47.

pages of *The Canadian Baptist* carried the opening salvos in a debate over the inspiration and authority of Scripture that would eventually make their way to the Convention floor. Participants in the debate included T. T. Shields and C. J. Holman, a lawyer from Jarvis Street who upheld the traditional Baptist position, and D. E. Thomson, a prominent lawyer from Jarvis Street who defended the liberal position but above all desired compromise and peace.[77] By the time of the Convention, the stage was set for confrontation. Shields put forward a resolution which called for the Convention to declare its "disapproval" of a liberal editorial entitled "The Inspiration and Authority of Scripture" the first part of which had appeared in *The Canadian Baptist* of October 2, 1919.[78] He also called for a return to the orthodox view of the Scriptures "to which the Convention [had] declared its adherence in 1910."[79] In response, James Ryrie, a wealthy jeweller from Jarvis Street and one of its most well-known deacons, put forward an amendment to the Shields resolution which declared that "the Bible is the inspired word of God" but also called for peace when it declared, "the Convention strongly deprecates controversy at this time as to the interpretation in detail of our distinctive beliefs . . . when we ought to be presenting a united front in grasping the opportunity of the hour."[80] After a lengthy and heated debate, the amendment was defeated while the original motion was sustained.

This public confrontation between James Ryrie, his ally, Daniel Edmund Thomson, and T. T. Shields over the infallibility of Scripture deepened suspicion and distrust of both sides upon their return home. At a subsequent meeting of the Toronto Baptist Ministerial Association, Shields was informed, ironically by prominent businessman Samuel J. Moore (see Figure 21), that amusements were undermining separation.[81] Shields later summarized Moore's address:

> I recall how clearly Mr. Moore stated his own attitude, that it [amusements] had never presented to him a personal problem,

---

77. For the contributions of these participants in the debate, see "Inspiration and Authority of Scripture: A Protest," *CB*, October 16, 1919; "Destructive Critics," *CB*, October 16, 1919; "Those 'Settled Questions' in the Old Land," *CB*, October 16, 1919.

78. For Shields's resolution, see *Baptist Year Book, 1919*, 24–26. For the entire article entitled "Inspiration and Authority of Scripture," see *CB*, October 2, 1919; *CB*, October 9, 1919; *CB*, October 16, 1919.

79. *Baptist Year Book, 1919*, 26.

80. *Baptist Year Book, 1919*, 26.

81. For a biography of Moore, see Moore and Gaunce, *Printer's Devil*.

because he had long seen the necessity for being entirely separated from these things; and as I now recall the address, he urged the ministers to seek to lead their people to a similar separation. It was a fine presentation of the subject; and in moving a vote of thanks to Mr. Moore, I personally expressed a wish that it might be possible for Mr. Moore to give the same address to a company of laymen.

In replying to the vote of thanks, Mr. Moore said that while we had been discussing the matter, he had been going over in his mind the names of those who were sometimes described as the "leading laymen" of the Denomination; and he said he could not think of as many as twenty who would stand with him in this matter.[82]

Moore's alarming analysis prompted Shields to act. He became convinced that it was his "duty to preach on the subject of worldly amusements."[83] According to Shields's own account, "I had not the slightest idea that what I should have to say would have special application to members of Jarvis Street. So far as I was aware, the church was entirely free from any connection with such matters."[84] In hindsight, this statement is surprising. Shields had already been put on notice by a visiting deacon from another Ontario Baptist congregation and S. J. Moore that many members of Baptist churches had become "content with a respectable worldliness."[85] The visiting deacon informed Shields that many of his fellow Baptists "were fond of card-playing, and had their little dancing parties, and saw no inconsistency in being found frequently at the theatre."[86] That Shields saw no possibility of wrongdoing at Jarvis Street is shocking. His naivety in assuming that none of the prominent and successful businessmen that occupied key positions of leadership in his church could succumb to the temptation to alter their stand on amusements shows how out of touch he had become and how little he understood the sociocultural pressures that the Baptist businessman faced. On February 13, 1921, Shields preached his now-famous (or, perhaps, infamous) sermon entitled "The

---

82. Shields, *Plot That Failed*, 210–11. For Moore's own statement concerning amusements and what transpired at the meeting, see "Take Heed Lest by Any Means This Liberty of Yours Become a Stumbling Block to Them That Are Weak," *CB*, March 3, 1921.

83. Shields, *Plot That Failed*, 212.

84. Shields, *Plot That Failed*, 213.

85. Shields, *Plot That Failed*, 204.

86. Shields, *Plot That Failed*, 204.

Christian Attitude Toward Amusements." Arguing that "vast numbers of professed Christians are now being carried away by an ever-growing love of pleasure, which, like a mighty tide is sweeping over the world,"[87] Shields underscored the inconsistencies and immorality which, in his view, characterized current Christian practice:

> It cannot be denied that many church members go oftener to the theatre than to church, and pay more for their amusements than for their religion; that there is reason to fear that many such are better versed in rules "according to Hoyle," than in the principles of the gospel according to Matthew, and Mark, and Luke, and John; and are bolder and more expert in dealing cards than in disseminating the Word of God. Some, too, there are who are most punctilious in their observance of religious decorum; who would be offended by a colloquialism from the pulpit, or an inartistic performance from the choir; but who see no impropriety in the presence of professing Christians at the dance. ... It is a matter of general observation that vast multitudes of the professed disciples of Christ, by their addiction to these and other forms of amusement, openly advertise themselves to be "lovers of pleasure more than lovers of God."[88]

Following this stinging analysis, Shields exhorted his congregation not to allow their liberty to cause a weaker brother or sister to stumble. "The principles of the gospel applied to life and conduct," he noted, "will relate the believer in self-denying service to both God and his neighbour."[89] In a concluding "word of exhortation and application," Shields challenged his listeners to renounce worldly pleasures and "put Christ first."[90] In particular, he focused on himself and the deacons:

> I say frankly, that if there be any pleasure upon which my heart is so set that it is more to me than the interests of a soul for whom Christ died, I am unworthy of my office, and I ought immediately either to resign that pleasure or to resign my office. And I say the same to the office-bearers in this church. I say it to the deacons: If there be a deacon of this church who thinks more of an evening at the theatre, of the diversion of a game of cards, of or the pleasures of the dance, than of the interests of a soul for whom Christ

---

87. The entire text of the sermon is printed in Shields, *Plot That Failed*, 216–29; Tarr, *Shields of Canada*, 208–18. The quotation used here appears on page 208 of Tarr's book.

88. Tarr, *Shields of Canada*, 208.

89. Tarr, *Shields of Canada*, 212.

90. Tarr, *Shields of Canada*, 216, 218.

died, he is unworthy of his office; and he ought immediately to resign either his pleasure or his office.[91]

After issuing this challenge, Shields called for commitment: "What if some young man should rise in his pew before all the congregation and say, 'I have here and now resolved that henceforth at all costs, I will in all things put Christ first'—if such a thing should occur, who knows how many would follow his example, and perhaps the revival we have longed and prayed for would come today."[92] This invitation brought a swift response. A young man stood and said, "Pastor I have resolved to put Christ first!"[93] Shields invited others to respond, and many did.

However, not all of the responses to Shields's message were positive. Some businessmen on the deacon's board were embarrassed and offended. A certain deacon's wife rose in response to Shields's invitation while her husband remained seated. When she later asked her husband why he did not rise, he replied, "How could I when I had tickets for tomorrow night at the theatre in my pocket at the time?"[94] Another deacon told Shields that his sermon might have been "appropriate enough" for other Toronto congregations, "but I am sure that our dear people in Jarvis Street did not need it."[95]

Even more revealing was the response of deacon Quartus B. Henderson, president of the Davis & Henderson printing firm. While reading the *Globe* on Monday, February 14, 1921, Shields was doubtless shocked and dismayed to find the names of Henderson and his wife printed in the social column headed, "What Women Are Doing."[96] The column noted that, "The Toronto Dancing Club had another enjoyable dinner at the King Edward on Saturday evening, among those present being . . . Mr. and Mrs. Quartus B. Henderson."[97] The next day, Shields received a letter of resignation from Henderson dated February 14, 1921. "Yesterday the pastor asked for the resignation of every deacon who did certain things

91. Shields, *Plot That Failed*, 228.
92. Shields, *Plot That Failed*, 229.
93. Shields, *Plot That Failed*, 231.
94. Shields, *Plot That Failed*, 233.
95. Shields, *Plot That Failed*, 233.
96. Shields does not directly identify Henderson in his account. The characterization of Shields's emotions is mine based on his impressions expressed in Shields, *Plot That Failed*, 233.
97. "What Women Are Doing," *Globe*, February 14, 1921.

which he considered should not be done," Henderson stated, "and I hereby tender my resignation, to take effect immediately."[98]

Beyond his contribution to the emerging schism between pastor and deacons, Henderson's acceptance of amusements and his subsequent resignation from the deacons' board indicated his rejection of the traditional Baptist definition of separation. As a cultural liberal, Henderson, and many of his fellow businessmen at Jarvis Street, felt free to participate in activities that fundamentalists like Shields considered worldly. For Baptist businessmen like Henderson, separation from the world became an antiquated practice which called for a countercultural asceticism that they no longer believed necessary or relevant. Privately, many businessmen from Jarvis Street became more tolerant in attitude and accepted more liberal moral values that allowed them to fit more comfortably into the sociocultural mold set by the secular business world (see Appendix 2).

By the early twentieth century, the doctrine of separation had become, for many Baptist businessmen, an outdated nineteenth century religious relic. While many retained their commitment to the essential doctrines of their Baptist faith, doctrines like separation that required conformity to a strict countercultural morality were modified to facilitate sociocultural integration. As long as the theory and practice of separation remained a collective, unified, and strict moral code, the social and material aspirations of many Baptist businessmen could not be realized. Thus, they gradually modified their beliefs, attitudes, and actions to allow them the freedom to pursue their individual goals. When fundamentalists pushed for a return to the beliefs and behavioral norms of the past, many businessmen resisted.

By 1920, the Jarvis Street platform was set for a clash between conflicting sociocultural perspectives. The Baptist concern about moral compromise and worldliness had become a crisis for fundamentalists, and it would soon be the source of church conflict. Neither side could anticipate the ferocity of the battle to come.

---

98. Shields, *Plot That Failed*, 234.

Figure 19. McMaster, Darling & Company, ca. 1886. A splendid example of the second empire architectural style, this dry goods warehouse was erected in 1871 (MTRL, T2326).

Figure 20. Jarvis Street Baptist Church Choir, ca. 1920. The music performed by this choir figured prominently in the troubles of 1920-1921 (JSBCA).

Figure 21. Samuel John Moore, founded the Moore Corporation that produced business forms. For many years he was Sunday School Superintendent at Dovercourt Road Baptist Church. He told T. T. Shields that Baptist businessmen no longer avoided popular amusements (Greene, *Who's Who and Why 1919–20*).

Chapter 6

Secularization and Schism
The Fight for Control of Jarvis Street

FOLLOWING THE DEBATE OVER biblical infallibility at the 1919 Ottawa Convention, the battle lines between pastor T. T. Shields (see Figure 22) and some of his congregation's leading businessmen were fully drawn. Convinced that Shields's fundamentalism would destroy the church that they had worked so hard to create, these businessmen waged public and private campaigns to remove him. In his characteristic confrontational style, Shields fought back. The battle for the hearts and minds of the people in Jarvis Street's pews lasted two years.

Although both sides blamed the church's troubles on theological differences and opponents' character deficiencies, it is clear with hindsight that differing cultural perspectives precipitated the crisis that ultimately split the congregation. For fundamentalists like Shields, the tolerant attitude and accommodating spirit of businessmen like James Ryrie and Albert Matthews (see Figure 23) threatened the very essence of the Baptist church. Cultural liberals like Ryrie and Matthews found Shields's reactionary response to their acceptance of secular norms and values offensive. Ryrie, Matthews, and like-minded peers became convinced that, left unchecked, Shields's narrowmindedness would destroy their church.

This chapter examines the fight for control of Jarvis Street, the schism of 1921, and its aftermath. Essentially, it argues that the schism of 1921 resulted as much from the collision of contrasting sociocultural views as from any other factor.

"Children of Disobedience," "Ecclesiastical Mosquitoes," "Jungle Beasts," and the "Self-Appointed Bishop of the Baptist Church in Ontario and Quebec": The Struggle for Control of Jarvis Street

The year 1920 marked a turning point in the history of Jarvis Street Baptist Church. Skirmishes over doctrine and practice engaged Shields and the businessmen who opposed him. Which view of the church would prevail? On the one hand, leading businessmen maintained that by curtailing certain established practices, such as long classical Choral selections in services, the single communion cup, and managing church affairs with antiquated nineteenth century business methods, Shields was destroying "dear old Jarvis Street." On the other, Shields and his supporters argued that these same marks of respectability and tradition were "worldly" or outdated and should be eliminated.

After their defeat on the music question in the spring of 1920, certain liberal businessmen became convinced of the necessity to get rid of Shields. Tension turned to outright hostility. Shields later accused his opponents of plotting to gain control of church finances:

> Throughout the year 1920 I lived as a man in normal health suffering from a toothache which made existence little less than a prolonged torture. The bad tooth was the McMaster representative who had wormed his way into the Finance Committee, and whose operations were designed to keep the financial nerve of the church open and under constant irritation, with the evident intention of giving as much pain as possible.
>
> Jarvis Street had no financial problem. Its financial resources were adequate to meet every need of the church. The B. D. Thomas Hall, a name which, without suggestion, I had given it, had remained unfinished for nearly seven years. Nearly thirty thousand dollars of unpaid subscriptions were on the books of the Building Fund Secretary. These young men who, judged by any standard of Christian usefulness, could be likened to nothing better than ecclesiastical mosquitoes, suddenly developed a concern for the completion of this building, for the sake of the memory of the man whose name it bore.
>
> We find minutes too, proposing the increase of the Office Secretary's salary, a woman who later proved herself to be a not very distant relative of Iscariot. These young men became suddenly concerned over the salary of the caretaker of that time, and proposed an increase; and an increase for the caretaker of

> the Parliament Street Branch. While publically [sic] complaining of financial straitness, [sic] in committee they were constantly maneuvering to create a deficit and precipitate a financial crisis.[1]

This summary of events is accurate but incomplete; it overlooks the issue of Shields's own salary. A careful reading of the church minutes and Shields's statements in *The Plot That Failed* suggest that he bore a longstanding grudge against those businessmen who refused to recommend a raise in his yearly salary from its initial level in 1910 of $4,000.[2] Particularly irksome to him were the actions taken by a group of young men from establishment families. In describing the "humiliating stings" they inflicted on him in 1920, Shields noted, "I would not liken those responsible to jungle beasts—that would necessitate an apology to the whole animal kingdom."[3] Clearly, Shields's animosity ran deep.

For their part, most of the prominent businessmen at Jarvis Street campaigned to preserve their church. After the row over church music had begun, First Baptist Church in Brantford offered Choir Director Edward Broome a good position "at a considerable increase in salary," but he was asked by Jarvis Street's Music Committee to meet with them first.[4] According to Broome, he "was then asked to give up the idea of leaving" and "remain loyal" to Jarvis Street.[5] He agreed "on condition that a fixed understanding could be reached with the pastor regarding the time and place of the anthems."[6] Although Shields readily "consented to an arrangement," he, according to Broome's account, "promptly broke it the next Sunday."[7] Broome "struggled prayerfully to show as little resentment as possible" towards Shields, but he felt betrayed by

---

1. Shields, *Plot That Failed*, 202.

2. This amount was eventually raised to $6,000 at the stormy meeting of April 6, 1921. For details of the debate over the salary increase, see *Minute Book, 1918–1928*, April 6, 1921, JSBCA. See also the "First Increase in 20 Years," *Evening Telegram*, April 7, 1921.

3. Shields, *Plot That Failed*, 203.

4. Edward Broome to T. T. Shields, September 22, 1921, Shields Papers, "Correspondence," File 11B, (MS), JSBCA.

5. Edward Broome to T. T. Shields, September 22, 1921, Shields Papers, "Correspondence," File 11B, (MS), JSBCA.

6. Edward Broome to T. T. Shields, September 22, 1921, Shields Papers, "Correspondence," File 11B, (MS), JSBCA.

7. Edward Broome to T. T. Shields, September 22, 1921, Shields Papers, "Correspondence," File 11B, (MS), JSBCA.

the pastor's "utter loathing" of him and his work.[8] The issue of salary was clearly secondary for Broome. There is no written record that he was offered an increase at Jarvis Street. Broome's primary hope was that "by some concession on both sides we could arrive at some peaceful conclusion."[9] In the continuing turmoil, the Music Committee, consisting of deacon James Ryrie, deacon Gideon Grant, and deacon Albert Matthews, held the music program together.

On the issue of the pastor's salary, many of the leading businessmen in the church opposed any increase. G. D. Martin, a clerk at Lowndes Company Limited, a wholesale clothing company, L. H. Whittemore of Thomas S. Minton and Company, Insurance Agents, and J. B. McArthur, an officer of the securities firm of D. J. McDougald Company, articulated the problem at a church meeting held on May 26, 1920. According to the church minutes, Whittemore favored finishing B. D. Thomas Hall "before any other heavy expenditure [meaning the salary increase) was undertaken."[10] McArthur "emphasized the necessity for watching expenses" and noted that "Unforseen expenses were constantly occurring."[11] G. D. Martin underscored the "inadequacy of the Associate pastor's salary, and thought it should have first consideration." "If we knew where the money was coming from," he noted, "it would be all right to increase the pastor's salary too, but in the meantime, $4,000 a year was a comfortable salary, even though it had depreciated in value from ten years ago."[12] After a protracted debate, the issue of the pastors' salaries was referred back to the Finance Committee "with instructions to secure permanent written pledges to cover the total amount of the proposed extra expenditures."[13] Before the meeting adjourned, the church passed motions put forward by leading businessmen to pay C. M. Carew, the former assistant pastor, his full salary for December 1919, to increase the church secretary's salary by $1,200 per year, and to

---

8. Edward Broome to T. T. Shields, September 22, 1921, Shields Papers, "Correspondence," File 11B, (MS), JSBCA.

9. Edward Broome to T. T. Shields, September 22, 1921, Shields Papers, "Correspondence," File 11B, (MS), JSBCA.

10. *Minute Book, 1918–1928*, May 26, 1920. JSBCA.

11. *Minute Book, 1918–1928*, May 26, 1920. JSBCA.

12. *Minute Book, 1918–1928*, May 26, 1920. JSBCA.

13. *Minute Book, 1918–1928*, May 26, 1920. JSBCA.

have the Finance Committee "consider the matter of an increase in the caretaker's salary."[14] Each of these actions infuriated Shields.[15]

The growing tension at Jarvis Street increased with B. W. Merrill's decision to resign as associate pastor and Director of Religious Education effective November 30, 1920. According to Shields, Merrill had failed to stand with him "in the crisis" over music.[16] Shields promptly had informed Merrill "that a dissolution of [their] partnership was inevitable."[17] The falling-out between these two pastors exacerbated the dissatisfaction growing among Jarvis Street's most distinguished families. Merrill's supporters, including members of prominent business families, wrote letters asking the deacons "to do all in their power to retain Mr. Merrill in Jarvis Street."[18] Convinced that he no longer had Shields's confidence, Merrill resigned.

Throughout the winter of 1921, an intense, often volatile, atmosphere persisted at Jarvis Street. At a church meeting held April 6, for example, a stormy debate broke out over whether the time was right to raise the pastor's salary. Deacon Albert Matthews, senior partner in the investment firm of Matthews and Company and later Ontario's Lieutenant Governor, put forward a motion calling for a 50 percent increase in the pastor's salary "to date from April 1st, 1921."[19]

In many ways, Matthews typified the new breed of "money men" that Jarvis Street had begun to attract in the late nineteenth century.[20] Following William McMaster's change of business focus from merchandising to banking in 1866, the next generation of Baptist businessmen often made the shift to specialized financial services like life insurance, securities, or brokerage firms. For these businessmen, paper related to monetary speculation replaced, dominated or was partnered with their interest in manufacturing and merchandising. The ability to manage a diverse portfolio of business interests replaced an earlier emphasis on entrepreneurship.

14. *Minute Book, 1918–1928*, May 26, 1920. JSBCA.
15. For Shields's feelings, see *Plot That Failed*, 202–3.
16. Shields, *Plot That Failed*, 195.
17. Shields, *Plot That Failed*, 195.
18. *Minute Book, 1918–1928*, October 20, 1920. JSBCA.
19. *Minute Book, 1918–1928*, April 6, 1921. JSBCA.
20. This is Michael Bliss's term. For his analysis of the growth of financial services in Canada, see Bliss, *Northern Enterprise*, 255–82. For the Ontario context, see Drummond, *Progress Without Planning*, 309–39.

Matthews was the quintessential expression of what had become a well-established pattern for Jarvis Street's businessmen. Born in Lindsay, Ontario, on May 17, 1873, Matthews was raised in a Baptist family. His father, George Matthews, founded and built up a large pork-packing business, the George Matthews Company, with establishments in Ottawa, Hull, Peterborough, and Brantford. In 1892, after graduating from Lindsay Collegiate Institute, Albert Matthews became a representative of his father's company first in London, England and later in Ottawa, Montreal, and Toronto. Desirous of moving into financial services, Matthews founded a brokerage firm in Toronto in 1909. After the affairs of the pork-packing business, Matthews Blackwell were wound up in 1919, Matthews devoted his entire energies to his career in finance. At the time of his death on August 13, 1949, he was a senior partner in the investment house of Matthews and Company, President of the Excelsior Life Insurance Company, and a Director of Toronto General Trusts Corporation.[21]

At Jarvis Street, some middle-aged businessmen like Matthews, along with younger businessmen like J. B. McArthur, F. G. Lawson, and R. S. Stockwell, desired to maintain Jarvis Street's social respectability by keeping those programs and activities that former businessmen had considered essential for developing a congregation that would attract those of superior social standing. At the same time, these businessmen wanted to expand Jarvis Street's reputation through the expansion of its facilities and programs. The actions taken by businessmen in this period reflected their desire to maintain the church's respectability and enhance its reputation. Matthews's motion to raise the pastor's salary had these goals in mind. It was intended to preserve peace within the congregation and protect Jarvis Street's reputation in the community.

Events in the congregational meeting, however, took an unexpected turn. In response to Matthews's motion, J. B. Lawrason, a partner of

21. The information in this paragraph is taken from "Albert Matthews, 76 Former Lt.-Governor," *Telegram*, August 15, 1949; "Hon. Albert Matthews Dies Once Lieutenant-Governor," *Toronto Daily Star*, August 15, 1949; "Late Albert Matthews," *Toronto Daily Star*, August 15, 1949; "Albert E. Matthews," *Globe*, August 16, 1949; Greene, *Who's Who in Canada, 1923–1924*, 1505; *Who's Who in Canada, 1934–1935*, 768; *Who's Who and Why, 1919–1920*, 1069. For George Matthews, see Morgan, *Canadian Men and Women of the Time*, 742. I have not discussed Matthews's involvement in Baptist affairs or politics. He was, among other things, Chairman of the Board of Governors of McMaster University, President of the Baptist Convention of Ontario and Quebec, and Vice-President for Canada of the Baptist World Alliance. In politics he was an ardent Liberal. He co-founded the National Liberal Association and served as Ontario's Lieutenant-Governor from 1937 to 1946.

Lawrason-Doughty carton manufacturers, moved an amendment that "a vote by ballot now be taken to ascertain as to whether the pastor enjoys the confidence of the Church, and that the result be announced."[22] This motion was seconded by L. H. Whittemore. This amendment prompted supporters of Shields to put forward an amendment to the amendment "that this Church would take the opportunity of expressing its high appreciation of his remarkably strong power in the pulpit, his clear, fearless exposition of the great Christian verities and of his unfaltering faith in the Bible ... and the Church rejoices in the outstanding position on Biblical questions which our pastor, Dr. T. T. Shields, occupies in the denomination at large."[23] Citing "the lateness of the hour," J. B. McArthur requested that the amendment, along with the amendment to the amendment be withdrawn.[24] Lawrason and Whittemore consented to withdraw their amendment provided that a vote by ballot be taken on the original motion. This condition was voted on by the congregation and accepted. A subsequent vote on the original motion carried by a slim majority of five votes.[25]

The next day, the *Evening Telegram* carried news of the church meeting. Shields declared that "it was a case of the spiritually-minded and worldly-minded people taking side[s]."[26] When he was asked, "Who favoured the salary increase?" Shields responded, "The spiritually-minded people who have more interest in their church than in worldly things."[27] Chairman Gideon Grant was quick to point out that "only a small fraction of the 1,200 members" had voted.[28] The actual number was 221.

Both the length and tenor of the debate over Shields's salary revealed an acrimonious atmosphere. Clearly, the salary debates exposed feelings of anger and resentment against Shields and a deep-seated division in the congregation that had its roots in the Ottawa Convention of 1919 and the fight over music in 1920. The vote in favor of the pay raise amounted to a vote of confidence. With the pastor's opponents growing more restive, and Shields becoming increasingly defensive, the

22. *Minute Book, 1918–1928*, April 6, 1921. JSBCA.
23. *Minute Book, 1918–1928*, April 6, 1921. JSBCA.
24. *Minute Book, 1918–1928*, April 6, 1921. JSBCA.
25. *Minute Book, 1918–1928*, April 6, 1921. JSBCA.
26. "First Increase in 20 Years," *Evening Telegram*, April 7, 1921.
27. "First Increase in 20 Years," *Evening Telegram*, April 7, 1921.
28. "First Increase in 20 Years," *Evening Telegram*, April 7, 1921.

prospect of more open hostility between the two sides loomed large in the early days of April 1921.

By mid-April, dissatisfaction with Shields's ministry had become open revolt. A Young Men's Committee held a meeting on April 14 at which they chose a few delegates to forward a request to the deacons' board "with a view to obtaining the pastor's resignation."[29] Composed primarily of disgruntled and disaffected younger members of business families, this committee represented only the most vocal of Shields's opponents.

Faced with this direct challenge to his leadership, Shields called a meeting of the deacons on April 21. At this meeting, it was decided that Shields should send a letter to every member of the congregation informing them of a church meeting to be held on April 29 for the purpose of considering the question: "Do you desire the present pastor to continue in the pastorate of this church?"[30] Deacon James Ryrie, a Shields opponent, insisted that the letter also state that "The pastor hereby informs every member of the church, that unless he is supported by two thirds of the votes cast, he will tender his resignation."[31] Although Shields and his supporters on the deacons' board disliked this clause, they consented to its inclusion. Shields's allies insisted that two other caveats be added to the letter. These conditions were that "in the event that the pastor being supported by two thirds vote (1) every deacon who shall then feel that he cannot accept the church's decision shall immediately resign . . . and (2) . . . that a resolution be passed requesting all to accept the decision of the church, and enter heartily into the church's activities."[32]

Following the circulation of the letter, an article under the headline "Jarvis Street Committee Knock Rev. Shields" appeared in the April 27 issue of the *Toronto Daily Star*. It carried a statement by the Men's Committee in which its objections to Shields's leadership and its desire to remove him were clearly set out. The statement claimed that "For years there has been a growing feeling of dissatisfaction with Dr. Shields. Many members have taken their letters[33] to other churches, dozens of families have

29. These are the words used by Shields to describe their objective. See Shields, *Plot That Failed*, 239.

30. *Minute Book, 1918–1928*, April 23, 1921. JSBCA.

31. Shields attributes the inclusion of this clause to James Ryrie. For Shields's account of the April 21, deacon's meeting and another copy of his letter of April 22, 1921, see Shields, *Plot That Failed*, 240–42.

32. *Minute Book, 1918–1928*, April 23, 1921. JSBCA.

33. It was customary for Jarvis Street to grant a member in good standing a "letter of dismission." This letter testified to the member's status and served as one's introduction

retained their membership, but will not come to the church as long as Dr. Shields is pastor."³⁴ The dissidents also accused Shields of "trying to make a religious controversy out of what concerns principally the 1,100 members of Jarvis St. church."³⁵ From a cultural standpoint, the concluding statement in the article was particularly revealing: "If Dr. Shields wants to carry on a religious controversy we insist that he must do it in some other capacity than as pastor of Jarvis Street Baptist church. The men's committee trust there will be no more newspaper publicity to what is largely a local affair."³⁶ Here Shields's dogmatic fundamentalism, with its emphasis on separation from the world, was severely criticized. Because of their commitment to cultural integration, the young businessmen on the Men's Committee found Shields's crusades against amusements, music, and theological liberalism offensive. For them, tolerance had replaced separation as the hallmark of genuine Christianity.

For example, Shields's practice of constantly "knocking" his adversaries had already been a source of discomfort for James Ryrie, who in his letter to the pastor in March 1918, noted that many Jarvis Street young people felt "uncomfortable lest you will be hitting people" and thus, were "disposed to take visitors elsewhere."³⁷ Despite this criticism, Shields had persisted in his attacks on liberal lifestyle, Roman Catholicism, and modernism.

At the crucial church meeting held on April 29, 1921, the question of Shields continuing as pastor was considered. After non-members and the press were dismissed, a motion by James Ryrie that the vote concerning the pastor be taken by ballot was carried.³⁸ Deacon S. T. Hall moved that clause three of the pastor's letter of April 22 be withdrawn. The clause stated "it is proposed that a fraction over one third may deprive a majority of the ministry in which they have found profit, and which would thereby establish the precedent, that a condition already existing,

---

and transfer document. The letter would be given to the Church Clerk of the congregation that the former member of Jarvis Street desired to join.

34. "Jarvis Street Committee 'Knock' Rev. Shields," *Toronto Daily Star*, April 27, 1921.

35. "Jarvis Street Committee 'Knock' Rev. Shields," *Toronto Daily Star*, April 27, 1921.

36. "Jarvis Street Committee 'Knock' Rev. Shields," *Toronto Daily Star*, April 27, 1921.

37. The original of this letter is not in the Shields Papers. For the entire text of the letter, see Shields, *Inside of the Cup*, 9.

38. *Minute Book, 1918–1928*, April 29, 1921. JSBCA.

and approved by the majority of the members of the church, may, at any time, be overturned by a minority, which principle would give no reasonable security of tenure to any officer of the church." A heated discussion ensued. Shields stated that the clause "had been inserted ... because the deacons insisted on it." Deacon J. G. Scott, a longtime member of Jarvis Street and a distinguished lawyer and provincial civil servant who had retired in 1920, said that he "had understood that the pastor concurred with the opinion of the deacons in their meeting [of April 21] that no pastor could lead a church successfully unless he were supported by a large majority of the members." Deacons Albert W. Record, Reverend E. A. Brownlee, and George Greenway "separately disclaimed approval ... of the clause" and claimed that "It had been inserted because the majority of the deacons would not approve the sending out of the letter without it." T. B. Hughes asked "why it was that objection should be raised now to insisting on a 2/3 vote when, less than a year before, the pastor had resigned and had emphatically declared that he could not reconsider his resignation unless he were supported by an 'overwhelming majority.'" When put to a vote, the motion carried. Shields withdrew clause three and added that he could not continue in the pastorate unless he was supported by "a substantial majority."[39]

Shields was then given the opportunity to address the congregation for twenty minutes. In his address, he claimed that in 1910 some members were "strongly opposed" to his coming to Jarvis Street "because of the truths he preached." Furthermore, Shields claimed that "The leader of that opposition had criticised his preaching from the first." Although this man had moved on to another church, opposition continued through "lieutenants" left behind to carry on the criticism. Shields also stated that "he was sure that of those opposed to him now not all were opposed on theological grounds, but the opposition that had begun in a small circle had spread." Beginning with the 1919 Ottawa Convention, Shields recounted the history of events leading to the unrest. Although he was criticized within Jarvis Street for "failing to entertain young people in his sermons, and for lack of pastoral visiting," Shields contended that "underneath it all there was a movement in the Convention to destroy the man upon whom Higher Criticism had spit."[40]

---

39. *Minute Book, 1918-1928*, April 29, 1921. JSBCA.
40. *Minute Book, 1918-1928*, April 29, 1921. JSBCA.

Recent events within the church only served to confirm Shields's fears of a wider conspiracy against him. As proof, he cited the response of certain members to his sermon on amusements. Shields noted that this attempt to "apply the principles of His Master" (meaning Christ) had taught him a painful but valuable lesson that "if he must preach the principles of His Master, there were some members on whom he could not count."[41]

In his closing remarks, Shields attempted to win back his opponents. He expressed the desire to "love the members all back to Jesus Christ" and stated that there was not one member whom he did not "love in the Lord." Shields ended with a charge: "Consciously or unconsciously," he declared, "you vote tonight for or against the great body of evangelical truth for which this denomination stands. In due course it will be proved to you." Following Shields's statement, the resignation of deacons Q. B. Henderson, W. J. Lugsdin, H. R. Wellington, and Ephriam Sale, were read. Although a motion was put forward to accept the resignations, Shields suggested, in an amendment, that consideration of the resignations be delayed until after the results of the vote were known. This amendment was adopted.[42]

The congregation then proceeded to cast their votes. After counting, the scrutineers reported: Yes, 284; No, 199; Blank, 6.[43] Shields had obtained a majority of 85 votes. Following the announcement, the leader of the Shields supporters, Dr. C. J. Holman, put forward a motion intended to lay the matter of the pastorate to rest:

> That the members of Jarvis St. Baptist Church in annual meeting assembled desire to voice their love and attachment for their pastor, Dr. T. T. Shields, and their gratitude for the ministry of one who speaks not merely in the words of man's wisdom but in the power of the Holy Spirit and would take this opportunity of expressing their high appreciation of his remarkably strong power as a preacher and our admiration of his fearless exposition of the great Christian verities with his unfaltering faith in the Bible, in its inspiration, its integrity, and its Divine authority and the Church rejoices in the outstanding position on Biblical questions which Dr. Shields occupies in the denomination on this continent and this Church hopes that

---

41. *Minute Book, 1918–1928*, April 29, 1921. JSBCA.
42. *Minute Book, 1918–1928*, April 29, 1921. JSBCA.
43. *Minute Book, 1918–1928*, April 29, 1921. JSBCA.

it may long have the privilege of his faithful ministry, and that the Baptist Convention of Ontario and Quebec may long reap the benefit of his leadership.[44]

Seconded by Reverend E. A. Brownlee, the motion carried.

As Charles Johnston has noted, Dr. Charles J. Holman, K. C. was certainly not one of the "'sub-normal and untaught folk,'" as a later Shields critic characterized those who supported Jarvis Street's pastor.[45] Holman was a close friend of William McMaster, the author of the McMaster University charter, and a longtime member of the McMaster board of governors. He had steadfastly supported Elmore Harris and T. T. Shields in their opposition to liberal theology at McMaster. Holman was well educated. In 1872, he received a Bachelor of Arts degree from Victoria College, then located in Cobourg, Ontario. After studying law at Osgoode Hall, he was granted an LLB in 1876. He was called to the bar in the same year. In 1878, he received a Master of Arts degree from Victoria College, and in 1909, he was given an honorary LLD by McMaster University. Holman also enjoyed a long and distinguished law career. He began his career under Edward Blake in the legal firm of Blake, Lash & Cassels. In 1899, he was made a Queen's Counsel. He began his own law firm known as Holman, Elliot & Patullo. Later, he entered into a partnership with Sir Henry Drayton, and, in 1910, when Sir Henry became Corporation Counsel for the City of Toronto, Holman became the senior partner in the firm of Holman, Bisset & Peine. In 1913, Holman retired from active practice but continued to act as a legal consultant for friends and longtime clients. Holman died on December 23, 1928.[46]

Holman provided strong lay leadership for the fundamentalist element at Jarvis Street in 1921. Without his outspoken support, one wonders if Shields would have won on April 29. Long after the events of this important congregational meeting, Shields acknowledged his debt to Holman: "In all this battle, I had no truer friends, and no more faithful

---

44. *Minute Book, 1918–1928*, April 29, 1921, JSBCA.

45. Johnston, *Toronto Years*, 234.

46. For the biographical information in this paragraph, see "C. J. Holman, K. C., is Dead," *Evening Telegram*, December 24, 1928; "C. J. Holman, K. C., Buried," *Evening Telegram*, December 27, 1928; "Dr. C. J. Holman Called Home," *Evening Telegram*, December 27, 1928; "Dr. Chas. J. Holman Passed Away," *Evening Telegram*, January 3, 1929; "Zealous and Able Lawyer Borne to His Rest," *Globe*, December 27, 1928; Morgan, *Canadian Men and Women of the Time*, 542–43; C. J. Holman, "Correspondence File," Shields Papers, (MS), JSBCA.

and ardent supporters than Dr. and Mrs. C. J. Holman."[47] Indeed, a good case can be made for the argument that the support and leadership of the Holmans proved decisive.

Soon after the April 29 vote was taken, critics charged that the result was indecisive; a majority of 85 was less than the "substantial majority" Shields had said he needed. An undated, unsigned statement in the Jarvis Street Baptist Church Archives responded to this criticism:

> On Friday April 29, the church by a large majority expressed its desire for the pastor to continue in this church. This is really the third time that the church has expressed its unwillingness to allow the present pastor to retire its pastorate. It is now a matter of public knowledge that there has arisen a serious difference of view in the church, so that the pastor now feels free to openly refer to it. The vote at the last meeting must surely be regarded, by all fair minded persons, as decisive. The opponents of the pastor's ministry pressed into their service every agency which could possibly serve their purpose. Some openly set their names to announcements in the press which dragged the affairs of the church into public view. A canvass of a part of the church was made, personally, or by telephone, wherever it was thought votes adverse to the pastor could be obtained; and a fleet of motor cars was employed as in election days, to bring out the vote. On the other hand, prayer meetings were held, and the issue was committed to the hand of God. The result is now known to all. In view of these considerations the pastor feels there is but one thing for him to do, and that is to accept the decision of the church as an expression of the will of God. More and more clearly it will be seen that the difference has arisen over the pastor's message. He has only affection in his heart for every member of the church, and hopes that many who have hitherto been opposed will accept the decision of the church, and heartily cooperate in its activity. But the church has the right to expect that the opposition will now cease; and if there are those who feel that they cannot be comfortable in Jarvis St. Church, they will surely be able to find some way of finding spiritual help for themselves if they prayerfully seek it. Our main task at the moment is, that we should prayerfully set ourselves to seek the Lord. We have proved that prayer is no vain thing. We may make more real progress on our knees than on our feet. Let us seek to make Jarvis Street a church whose affairs shall be administered by

---

47. Shields, *Plot That Failed*, 249.

the Holy Spirit. Wherefore, let us pray more earnestly than ever. The revival we have sought is surely coming.[48]

Instead of ending criticism and controversy, statements of this kind stiffened the resolve of Shields's opposition. Shields later argued in hindsight, that the vote represented far more than a personal victory. In his mind, the decision of the church was a rejection of "minority rule."[49] For Shields, the vote served to strike at the heart of the notion held by a "few families" who were "under the delusion that they were Jarvis Street."[50] Although "hundreds of others might come to the church, find a place in its membership, attend its services, and even contribute to its support; . . . so far as these few families were concerned . . . they quietly assumed that . . . [they] were *the church*, to which others were permitted to belong by their sufferance."[51] Although Shields admitted that these "few families" had not "clearly defined their attitude even to themselves," he remained convinced that they operated on the assumption that it was their right to control church affairs.[52]

The response of James Ryrie and many other businessmen bears out Shields's analysis. Throughout the spring and summer of 1921, the war for the hearts and minds of the membership continued. In early May, Shields contracted scarlet fever. Forced to spend six weeks in quarantine, the pastor did his best to manage the church from his sickbed.[53]

Meanwhile, fallout from the April 29 meeting continued. Some prominent members withdrew their membership. On May 25, for example, Daniel Edmund Thomson, his wife and son, received letters of dismission so that they might unite with Walmer Road Baptist Church.[54] Thomson was the senior partner in the law firm of Thomson, Tilley, and Johnson. He had been a member of Jarvis Street since 1876, a trustee since 1882 and had served as deacon from 1896 to 1920.[55] Ironically,

---

48. This type written letter may have been prepared by C. J. Holman. It is undated, unsigned, and kept in JSBCA.
49. Shields, *Plot That Failed*, 251.
50. Shields, *Plot That Failed*, 253.
51. Shields, *Plot That Failed*, 253.
52. Shields, *Plot That Failed*, 253.
53. For Shields's account of this period, see Shields, *Plot That Failed*, 254–64.
54. *Minute Book, 1918–1928*, May 25, 1921. JSBCA.
55. For biographical information on Thomson, see Morgan, *Canadian Man and Women of the Time*, 1099; Johnston, *Toronto Years*, 46, 48, 53, 56, 151–58, 162–68; MTRL, *Biographical Scrapbooks*, 5:228–29. A few of Thomson's legal papers are housed

he was instrumental in the effort to secure Shields as pastor in 1910.[56] Now, he was the first major church figure to leave. Even some of Shields's recent supporters were altering their view and taking their membership elsewhere. At the same church meeting Violet Elliot, the matriarch of Elliot and Company Chemical Manufacturers, registered her protest as part of her request for a letter of dismissal:

> On account of Mr. Shields' orthodox preaching and his wonderful knowledge of the Bible, I was one of many who voted last year to ask him to withdraw his resignation tendered for the expressed purpose of finding out the wishes of the special meeting.
>
> Since then by his own actions and disregard of his spoken and written promises he has made it impossible to remain in Jarvis St. Church without a protest, and thus become a party to the destructive policy now in force.
>
> If the increase to the pastor's salary were granted on a business basis no doubt a majority of the members would be glad to show appreciation in this way, but the vote of the special meeting held April 6th made it practically certain that missionary contributions would be depleted to meet the call for [a] $2,000 increase. A suggestion to that effect was made in open meeting last year without any word of disapproval by the pastor. If missionary gifts are not transferred and no steps are taken to increase the revenue for general expenses it is evident that debt will result.
>
> It is regrettable that Mr. Shields' serious illness makes delay seem expedient but the only way in which I can record my disagreement with the action of the recent business meetings is to request that *a Letter of Dismissal from Jarvis St. Church* be granted, *or a Certificate* that I have been a member up to May 25th. If the meeting will not grant this I hereby ask that my name be erased from the Jarvis St. Church roll. I do not wish to use another Church as a convenience, and still hope that a spirit may in accord with our Lord's Missionary commission prevail in the Church which has been an inspiration to so many in times past.
>
> Violet Elliot.
> May 21, 1921,
> The Alexandra, 184 University Avenue.[57]

---

in AO, Thomson, Henderson, and Bell Papers, MU 7453-7464.
  56. For an account of this effort, see Shields, *Plot That Failed*, 15–20.
  57. *Minute Book, 1918–1928*, May 25, 1921. JSBCA.

Although such defections amounted to a trickle in May 1921, the fact that they included longtime church members who agreed with Shields's doctrinal views was cause for concern. Elliot's objection to the way in which the pastor's salary was granted was indicative of the worldview held by Shields's opponents. For them, it was essential that proper and current business methods be utilized in every church decision. Doing things on a "business basis" was not simply, as Shields claimed, a euphemism for "the principle of minority rule," but an expression of a deep-seated commitment to secular business values.[58] In the case of Violet Elliot, a Certificate of Membership was granted "with the expression of the hope that the certificate would soon come back to the Church."[59]

Other signs of continuing unrest at Jarvis Street included the withdrawal of financial support. Some businessmen cut back considerably in their giving. One millionaire, who unfortunately cannot be identified, reduced his weekly offering to the general expense fund from $6.00 to 0.25. He also stopped giving $24.00 a week to missions. By the time he left the church, his weekly pledge to the missions' fund was over $1600 in arrears.[60] Others followed a similar course.

According to Shields in *The Plot That Failed*, his opponents were involved in "a concerted effort to paralyse the general fund."[61] For evidence, Shields cited the actions of the Finance Committee. It printed a letter in the church calendar that appealed to "supporters of the church to increase their gifts for current expenses."[62] The letter claimed that "The plate and weekly offering collections show a sharp falling off when compared with the previous year."[63] If the present trend continued, there would be by the end of June "a shortage on current account of $2,085.44."[64] Consequently, "nothing will be available for the purchase of coal, or for July expenses."[65] Coinciding with the announcement of a potential financial crisis the

---

58. For this quotation, see Shields, *Plot That Failed*, 253.

59. *Minute Book, 1918-1928*, May 25, 1921. JSBCA.

60. Unfortunately, the records of offerings for this period do not exist. The information here is taken from Shields, *Plot That Failed*, 266. For an earlier record of offerings given by Jarvis Street's businessmen see the *Tithing Ledger, 1906-1911*.

61. Shields, *Plot That Failed*, 266.

62. This letter appears in Shields, *Plot That Failed*, 266-67. For the discussions of the Finance Committee, see *Jarvis Street Baptist Church Finance Committee Minute Book, 1907-1921* (MS), JSBCA.

63. Shields, *Plot That Failed*, 266.

64. Shields, *Plot That Failed*, 267.

65. Shields, *Plot That Failed*, 267.

Finance Committee, at a meeting hosted by Albert Matthews at the National Club, passed a motion "that the treasurer be instructed not to pay general expenses of any kind from the funds donated to missions, forward movement, war memorial, women's auxiliary or building fund."[66]

To Shields, these actions constituted "open warfare."[67] He charged that every "effort was being made to paint the picture as black as possible."[68] The supposed need for money for coal in May or June when "it was never put into the bins until October" was ludicrous.[69] The "utter hypocrisy" of an appeal by members of the Finance Committee for an increase in subscriptions while they had stopped their givings to the church "and were doing their utmost to persuade others to do so" also outraged Shields.[70]

While the hyperbole and hypocrisy of the Finance Committee were undeniable, Shields's confrontational response only further antagonized his opponents. When confronted with specific actions or attacks, Shields consistently failed to act on his belief in "majority rule." Knowing that the letter of the Finance Committee was merely one manifestation of the larger desire of the business element to protect and preserve "dear old Jarvis Street," Shields could have sought a church vote on its actions. Instead, after reading the letter, Shields called its chairman, Albert Matthews, "and reminded him that even in open warfare honourable combatants show respect for the Red Cross, but that the Finance Committee's letter was an example of the deliberate bombing of a hospital."[71] This response prolonged the conflict and hardened attitudes that might have been open to reconciliation had the situation been handled more delicately.

There is a strong case for the argument that the efforts of the Finance Committee were based more on consensus than conspiracy. In his anger, Shields sometimes lost sight of the larger sociocultural questions involved in the turmoil of 1921. While many businessmen, by May 1921, had openly declared their opposition to the pastor, that opposition was based primarily on the shared belief that their culturally respectable view of the church must be preserved. Their opposition was not, as Shields claimed, "a

66. *Jarvis Street Baptist Church Finance Committee Minute Book, 1907–1921* (MS), May 31, 1921. JSBCA.
67. Shields, *Plot That Failed*, 268.
68. Shields, *Plot That Failed*, 267.
69. Shields, *Plot That Failed*, 267.
70. Shields, *Plot That Failed*, 267–68.
71. Shields, *Plot That Failed*, 268.

concerted effort to paralyse the general fund."[72] The motion of the Finance Committee directing the treasurer not to pay general expenses from funds that the business element had largely established and now cherished must be seen within the wider context of the general desire to ensure that the agenda and interests of the church's businessmen would continue to receive financial support. Shields's tendency to lash out at specific people and actions alienated undecided members, angered his opponents, and obscured the debate on the central practical and theological questions of what constituted proper Baptist faith and practice.

By late June, many of the church's prominent deacons and leaders had joined the Men's Committee in open revolt. On June 23, they mailed a circular letter to church members. The letter noted that since voting "No" in April, these dissidents had "been asked to state their reasons."[73] They noted that on April 29, "the opportunity to state their case was not given" because "no further discussion" following Shields's statement "was allowed." Put on the defensive and faced with the destruction of their church, the rebels blamed Jarvis Street's troubles on the attitudes and actions of T. T. Shields: "We believe that the inharmonious, unsatisfactory and deplorable condition that exists in Jarvis Street Church today," they declared, "is not to be accounted for from any lack of spirituality, as the pastor has publicly stated. We are firmly convinced that this condition is the inevitable result of the pastor's administration of the church affairs." Near the end of their letter, the dissidents listed specific "conditions" that had prompted their public break with Shields:

> Briefly stated, these are some of the conditions existing in Jarvis Street today which we believe are due to Dr. Shields [sic] administration: Rev. Mr. Merrill, our beloved associate pastor, was driven from us; at least thirteen of our eighteen deacons are out of sympathy with the pastor, two of them, our revered deacons D. E. Thomson and J. G. Scott, have already transferred their membership; the Finance Committee is at variance with him; our organist, Dr. Broome, and his faithful choir have been disrupted; a great many of the Sunday School workers and young people have been estranged from him; the House Committee are opposed to him; our Church Treasurer and our

---

72. Shields, *Plot That Failed*, 266.

73. The letter is in *Minute Book, 1918-1928*, June 23, 1921. JSBCA. It is also reprinted in Shields, *Plot That Failed*, 280-83. There are minor differences in the two letters. I have used the *Minute Book* version.

Church Clerk, who have rendered faithful service, have already tendered their resignations.

Even more disturbing was Shields's attack on the faith and character of his opponents. This merited capital letters:

THE PASTOR HAS MADE THE STATEMENT THAT THOSE WHO ONCE SUPPORTED HIM AND WHO ARE NOW AT VARIANCE WITH HIM HAVE NO DESIRE FOR A NEW TESTAMENT MINISTRY. WE TAKE CLEAR AND DEFINITE ISSUE WITH HIM ON THIS POINT AND DECLARE THAT JARVIS STREET ALWAYS HAS AND DOES NOW STAND FOR A CHRISTLIKE PRESENTATION OF THE VERITIES OF THE CHRISTIAN FAITH.

Clearly, many church leaders were deeply offended: "Some of those who stand highest in the esteem and love of the Church members are forced to resign owing to the uncongenial spirit and unchristianlike attitude of the pastor." The letter concluded with a challenge: "it is essential that there should be a full expression of the opinion of the entire membership . . . on Wednesday, the 29th instant, at 8 PM." Forty-one signatures, including those of Albert Matthews and James Ryrie, were attached to this letter.[74]

Meanwhile, also on June 23, Shields sent his own letter to the congregation, imploring them to attend the June 29 meeting. In his letter, Shields noted that "It is known to all members of the church that several of the deacons have resigned. I am sure everyone will appreciate the necessity of electing officers and committees who are in agreement with the expressed will of the church, that the pastor continue his work in Jarvis St."[75] Shields pleaded: "I therefore appeal to every 'Yes' voter to be present at all costs, and to be sure to be on time, eight o'clock."[76] The urgent tone suggests that Shields was far from certain the outcome of the vote to be taken on June 29 would be favorable.

On June 29, the members gathered once again to consider their future. The meeting was bitter from the outset. Instead of proceeding with the first order of business, the election of officers, chairman deacon Grant allowed a resolution to be read, reviving the debate over whether Shields

---

74. *Minute Book, 1918–1928*, June 23, 1921. JSBCA. All of the quotations in this paragraph are taken from the same source.

75. This letter appears in Shields, *Plot That Failed*, 277–78. A copy is also found in *Minute Book, 1918–1928*, June 23 1921. JSBCA. I have used the copy in *Plot That Failed*.

76. Shields, *Plot That Failed*, 278.

needed to obtain a two-thirds vote to remain as pastor.[77] After a lengthy and acrimonious exchange of charges and counter-charges, it was decided to put the original motion concerning Shields's tenure to another vote. This time Shields was defeated. Of the 385 ballots cast, 204 supported the motion while 176 opposed it, and 5 ballots were blank.[78] Shields declared that "he had yet to choose whether he should yield to the majority of 28 when he had been supported in the former larger meeting by a majority of 85, and announced that he had no intention of resigning."[79] Shields accepted the majority decision on April 29; he disregarded it on June 29! Majority rule, it seemed, was involved only when the vote suited T. T. Shields. The meeting was adjourned until September 21.

A lull occurred over the summer of 1921. Many of Shields's opponents protested by staying away from church services, and others ceased to give their time and talent. When Shields arrived for the July 4 service, he found the entire choir absent.[80] Shields took advantage of the summer season and his opponents' withdrawal to re-assert his authority. At a church meeting on July 27, at which only a few of his adversaries were present, Shields chaired the proceedings and allowed two new members to be admitted to membership without consideration by the deacons.[81] F. G. Lawson "asked whether these applications for membership had come before the deacons and whether it was not the practice of the Church that all such applications should first be considered by the deacons before coming before the Church. The chairman replied emphatically that the Church is not managed by the deacons and that the motion just passed [to receive the two new members] was quite in order."[82]

Shields also announced his invitation to a leading American fundamentalist, John Roach Straton, pastor of Calvary Baptist Church, New York City, to hold an evangelistic crusade on the second, third, and fourth Sundays in August and asked the church to approve this plan. The church minutes record that when "J. B. Lawrason [a partner in

77. *Minute Book, 1918–1928*, June 29, 1921. JSBCA.
78. *Minute Book, 1918–1928*, June 29, 1921. JSBCA.
79. *Minute Book, 1918–1928*, June 29, 1921. JSBCA.
80. Shields, *Plot That Failed*, 292.
81. Press coverage of Jarvis Street's affairs diminished in the summer of 1921. Occasionally, however, the Toronto papers kept their readers informed of the latest developments. When the tent evangel of New York City passed a resolution of support for Shields the *Telegram* reported the event. "Resolution of Support," *Evening Telegram*, July 27, 1921.
82. *Minute Book, 1918–1928*, June 21, 1921. JSBCA.

the carton manufacturing firm of Lawrason-Doughty Company and a member of the men's committee opposed to Shields] asked whether the deacons had been consulted and whether the expense involved would be handled through the regular channels," Shields responded sternly: "The pastor declared that this meeting was quite in order in deciding this question without consulting the deacons." Shields explained that the "usual remuneration for summer pulpit supply would be paid" to Straton and "there would be an offering taken at each of the special services" which the pastor assumed would "be sufficient to meet all expenses involved in the meetings."[83]

Finally, Shields turned his attention to the issue of finances, challenging the practice of the Weekly Offering Treasurers, all of whom opposed him. The treasurers locked the plate collections in the safe after the services on Sunday, counting and recording the offerings on Monday night. Shields then said that "it had been suggested that someone be appointed to count plate collections after the morning and evening services until the adjourned Annual Meeting in September." Mrs. C. J. Holman moved "that two brethren be appointed to count the collections after every service and to enter the amounts in a book, the entries to be initialed [sic] by both of them, and suggested the names of Mr. E. Bonesteel and Mr. D. M. Young. Mr. [E. C.] Green seconded the motion."[84]

F. W. Merrill, owner of the drug manufacturing firm of F. W. Merrill Company, Limited, member of the men's committee and a staunch opponent of the pastor, "asked what the idea was in suggesting this plan and pointed out that it looked like a reflection on someone." Merrill's comments prompted Mrs. C. J. Holman to respond immediately to the insinuation that her motion was a personal attack, retorting "that the money was perfectly safe and that there was no reflection on anyone, but objection was taken to the undignified way in which the collection was handled." F. G. Lawson, a manager with W. L. Mckinnon, a firm specializing in the sale of government and municipal debentures, countered that "the Church had six Weekly Offering Treasurers holding office until the adjourned Annual Meeting in September and no one could be legally appointed to superced [sic] them." J. B. Lawrason then moved an amendment "that the Weekly offering Treasurers be asked to count the collections after each service." Immediately, "Mrs. Holman objected that

---

83. *Minute Book, 1918–1928*, June 21, 1921. JSBCA.
84. *Minute Book, 1918–1928*, June 21, 1921. JSBCA.

the Treasurer, Weekly Offering Treasurers, and members of the Finance Committee were absenting themselves from services, but finally agreed to Mr. Lawrason's alteration of the motion."[85]

Finally, a motion to have the Weekly Offering Treasurers count the collection after each service was passed.[86] Despite their small number, Shields's opponents succeeded in maintaining direct control over the church's finances. The battle for control was not over.

The meeting concluded with the passage of a resolution in support of T. T. Shields. Moved by Mrs. C. J. Holman and seconded by Mr. E. C. Green, the resolution reflected its sponsors' strong loyalty to the pastor:

> That this Monthly Meeting of the Jarvis Street Baptist Church desire to place on record its great gratitude to its pastor, Dr. T. T. Shields, and its appreciation of his giving up his vacation to remain at home and to conduct evangelistic services; and it would declare itself in hearty accord with the action of the Church on the 29th of April, 1921, when at a meeting specially called to consider the matter, the membership by a large majority voiced its wish that Dr. Shields should continue as pastor of this church; and this meeting again express their deep desire that we may long enjoy the blessing of his ministry, and we pray God's abundant blessings on his labors and messages among us.[87]

Despite this affirmation and the successes of the July 27 meeting, Shields still faced powerful and determined opposition.

By the fall of 1921, the stage was set for a definitive schism. Deeply divided over questions of church polity and lifestyle, the two sides dug in for a final confrontation. Both had used tactics unbecoming of their Christian faith. Shields's tendency to attack his enemies publicly instead of privately confronting them increased feelings of distrust. His abandonment of the principle of majority rule at the June 29 meeting hurt his credibility. The dissidents were also guilty of wrongdoing. The publicity-seeking of the Men's Committee violated the longstanding practice of handling congregational matters internally. The hypocrisy of the Finance Committee members who withdrew their financial support and then pleaded for an increase in subscriptions was reprehensible.

Although theological, personal, and institutional issues played important roles in the struggle for control of Jarvis Street, the battle between

85. *Minute Book, 1918–1928*, June 21, 1921. JSBCA.
86. *Minute Book, 1918–1928*, June 21, 1921. JSBCA.
87. *Minute Book, 1918–1928*, June 21, 1921. JSBCA.

divergent sociocultural perspectives was at the center of the controversy. Each fight over church polity and practice, whether Jarvis Street would be ruled by the pastor, the deacons or the people, whether it would have paid soloists and a choir of professional rank leading the worship services, or whether it would allow its members to engage in amusements, provided new evidence of a split over the doctrine and practice of separation from the world. Ultimately, this issue would tear the church apart.

By 1919, the leading businessmen at Jarvis Street, who with family members who held church membership numbered some 350 persons out of a congregation of 1200 members, had largely abandoned their belief in separation and embraced sociocultural integration. Their more tolerant approach to religious practice allowed for more latitude when it came to questions of individual behavior. This accommodationist spirit was challenged by fundamentalists like Shields, who crusaded for the purification of Baptist theology and practice and went on the offensive against all forms of compromise with the world. In their study of worldwide fundamentalism, Martin Marty and Scott Appleby have observed that, "*fundamentalists seek to replace existing structures with a comprehensive system* emanating from religious principles and embracing law, polity, society, economy, and culture."[88] Furthermore, they "do not simply reaffirm the old doctrines; they subtly lift them from their original context, embellish and institutionalize them, and employ them as *ideological weapons against a hostile world.*"[89] Both of these strategies were used effectively by Shields. Although he sometimes lost sight of the larger agenda, his personal attacks were motivated by a desire to see spiritual "revival" through the implementation of a puritanical fundamentalist ideology. In contrast to his opponents, Shields remained committed, at least in principle, to separation from the world.

Schism Accomplished: "Waterloo!" The Final Showdown Between Fundamentalists and Secularists

The period of open warfare at Jarvis Street had lasted five months. Everyone was eager to see the struggle ended decisively. Both sides came to the Annual Meeting on September 21, determined to achieve victory. Early in September, some of the disaffected deacons asked Shields to meet

---

88. Marty and Appleby, "Conclusion," 824 (emphasis added).
89. Marty and Appleby, "Conclusion," 826 (emphasis added).

with them privately in order to seek an amicable arrangement.[90] Shields refused. Anticipating that his opponents would question the legitimacy of those fifty to sixty members who had recently joined the church as a result of the August evangelistic crusade, Shields and his personal secretary, William Fraser, went on a covert mission to secure from the church minute books material to fend off any challenge.[91]

Furthermore, in advance of the church meeting, other Shields supporters conducted a letter-writing campaign to rally support. C. J. Holman, an avid supporter of Shields, circulated a four-page letter to the congregation in which he defended Shields and castigated his opponents. Holman argued that while "mistakes have been made," the "original and underlying ground of opposition is the pastor's position as to Higher Criticism." To prove this point, Holman cited the attempt by James Ryrie "to side track the motion of the Pastor" at the 1919 Ottawa Convention, that "stood for the Bible" in opposition to the "teaching of Prof. Matthews at McMaster."[92] At the end of his letter, Holman made a fervent plea:

> Do not permit yourself to be side-tracked by small issues. Take the high ground. This is a great issue . . . The message of Jarvis St. pulpit has been Evangelical and Evangelistic, and pronouncedly in defense of the Word of God. If you are in agreement with that message do not fail to be at the meeting of the Church on Wednesday, the 21st of September, and be prepared to see it through, and see that the message is not only supported, but that the Pastor is supplied with officers who are loyal.[93]

A similar letter was sent by the deacons, deaconesses, and trustees on September 15, 1921. This letter noted that "It is out task to preserve, not a delightful social institution, but the purity and effectiveness in service of a New Testament Church, that Christ may be honoured thereby." After arguing that the "best friends of Jarvis Street today are those who put Christ first in everything" these church leaders called on "all such" members to "attend the business meeting to be held on the 21st inst[ant] and vote in support of the Pastor." The stage was now set for a decisive showdown.

---

90. For Shields's account of this encounter, see *Plot That Failed*, 307–8.
91. Shields, *Plot That Failed*, 308–10.
92. Holman, Letter to Members, n.d., 2. JSBCA.
93. Holman, Letter to Members, n.d., 4. JSBCA.

The meeting of September 21 followed a predictable pattern. As the opening Scripture reading concluded, the acrimony began. The first squabble was over who should chair the meeting. Dr. C. J. Holman, a Shields supporter, moved that deacon Brownlee, another Shields ally, be appointed chairman. J. B. McArthur, a staunch Shields opponent, objected, noting that deacon Grant, also a member of the dissenting group, had been previously appointed chairman of the 93rd Annual Meeting. L. H. Whittemore then nominated deacon Grant as chairman. After some debate, Shields called for a vote of the members present. At the request of J. B. McArthur, all non-members were dismissed. Next, by a slim margin of six votes, ten scrutineers were elected and deacon Grant was confirmed as meeting chairman. The scrutineers chosen included five Shields supporters and five opponents.[94]

With the first two items of business completed, the meeting moved on to consider the central question of the evening, namely the pastorate. J. Francis Brown presented and moved a resolution, the preface of which stated, in part, that "Jarvis Street Baptist Church, notwithstanding the insinuations to the contrary, stands squarely today, as it has always stood, for the distinctive principles of Baptists including ... the inspiration of the Scriptures and the supreme authority thereof in all matters of faith and practice." The resolution went on to propose that three actions be taken: first, that the pulpit be "declared vacant as from this date, September 21st, 1921"; secondly, that the pastorate of T. T. Shields cease immediately but that his salary be paid for six months; and finally, that the deacons, trustees, Finance Committee and House Committee be given the authority to "take any and all such steps as shall be necessary to see that the above expressed will of the Church is carried out and the regular services of the Church maintained." H. R. Wellington, a member of the Men's Committee and vice president of ladies' wear manufacturer K. C. Boulter Company Limited, seconded the motion and moved that "the *question be now put and that the vote be by ballot.*" Wellington's probable intent was to prohibit any amendments to Brown's motion and force an immediate vote on the main question. After a standing vote on Wellington's motion, chairman Grant declared the motion carried. Those opposed to the motion protested loudly. Shields then suggested that those opposed to Brown's motion

---

94. The information in this paragraph is taken from *Minute Book, 1918–1928*, September 21, 1921. JSBCA.

should "consent to the vote being taken by ballot and without debate." Wellington's motion was again declared carried.[95]

Grant now launched an assault on the new members that had been approved for membership without the deacons' consent. Shields, of course, had anticipated this action. Grant "read the names of ten persons who had been received in an irregular way, and whose vote should not be counted." Shields responded that "in the reception of these members the same rule had been followed as throughout his pastorate." Grant then asked "whether their names had come before the deacons." Shields answered that "in the past six years 36 members had been received on experience without being previously reported to the deacons." Grant ruled that "they, too, were irregularly received, but agreed to allow the new members to vote."[96]

Following the debate over new members, Grant tried to move the meeting forward to consideration of the main issue. Again, he was interrupted. This time church member and usher A. F. Gay brought a request from the press for access to the meeting. Access was denied, but the meeting agreed to furnish a statement to the press at its conclusion. The vote on Brown's motion was finally taken. Of the 666 ballots cast, five were spoiled, and one no vote was rejected. Of the remaining 661 votes, 351 were no, while 310 were yes. On hearing the result, Shields's supporters spontaneously rose and sang "Praise God From Whom All Blessings Flow."[97]

Confident that they now had complete victory within their grasp, Shields's supporters moved to seize complete control over the church. Dr. C. J. Holman moved a resolution, seconded by R. S. Hudson, Joint General Manager, Vice-President and Director of the Canada Permanent Mortgage Corporation, affirming the resolution passed on April 29. As well as declaring support for Shields, this resolution struck a series of blows at the pastor's opponents. It stated the church stood for "the inspiration, integrity and Divine authority of the Bible . . . a pure and separated Church lite . . . an active continuing evangelism" and for "the time honoured spiritual principles, held by the Baptist body of our Convention." The resolution further noted that "this Church should be preserved in its purity and effectiveness as a New Testament Church, and that its officers and deacons should take office on the understanding that they are the

95. *Minute Book, 1918-1928*, September 21, 1921. JSBCA.
96. *Minute Book, 1918-1928*, September 21, 1921. JSBCA.
97. *Minute Book, 1918-1928*, September 21, 1921. JSBCA.

servants, not the masters of the Church." The final statement in the resolution declared "this Church desires to see in the department of music a spiritual choir, spiritually conducted." These attacks on Shields's opponents precipitated yet another heated exchange. Ralph Paget, a manager at the wool manufacturing firm of Crimmins & Pierce Company, asked C. J. Holman "whether the last clause of the resolution was an insinuation that the choir was not spiritual?" He went on to note that "75 per cent of the choir held church membership." Holman responded by repeating what he knew of a conversation had with one of the soloists. "When put to a standing vote the resolution passed."[98]

Next, Shields's supporters addressed the issues of loyalty to the pastor and who should rule the church. Deacon George Greenway, a staunch Shields supporter and superintendent of the Fegan Boys Home, read and moved a resolution that dealt with both issues:

> That inasmuch as it is necessary in the interests of the work in this Church that those holding office should be in entire sympathy with the pastor, giving him their loyal support, it is resolved that the offices of those deacons, deaconesses, and officers of the Church and Auxiliary societies and committees who signed the statement dated June 23rd, 1921, opposing the continuance of Dr. Shields as pastor be hereby declared vacant.

This attempt to oust the dissidents provoked an instant counter-attack. L. H. Whittemore moved that "all after the word 'that' be struck out and the words substituted to make the resolution read, 'Resolved that this Church regrets exceedingly the spirit shown by Dr. Holman and deacon Greenway.'" Shields stated that he expected those deacons who opposed him "to vacate their office anyway, but to avoid further delay" the Holman motion was presented. He further indicated that "he would regret very much any manifestation of an unkindly spirit."[99]

After a motion to adjourn was defeated, C. J. Holman protested the amendment. In his opinion, "it had no relevancy to the motion and was, therefore, out of order." Chairman Grant ruled in favor of the amendment. Again, Holman protested. The chair called for a standing vote on

---

98. *Minute Book, 1918–1928*, September 21, 1921. JSBCA.

99. *Minute Book, 1918–1928*, September 21, 1921. JSBCA. The underlining in the above quotations is in the original document.

whether his ruling should stand. The vote sustained the chair's ruling, but L. H. Whittemore then withdrew his amendment.[100]

Grant declared his doubts as to whether the meeting could elect new deacons by the required two-thirds majority. Shields replied that if the Greenway resolution passed, another would be presented to deal with the vacancies. The Greenway motion was put to a standing vote and carried.[101]

Shields then put forward a motion, surprisingly seconded by L. H. Whittemore, that effectively reconstituted the entire structure of church government.[102] Under the terms of the motion, all of the duties previously performed by the deacons' board and Finance Committee passed into the hands of a new body called the Prudential and Finance Committee. In his resolution, Shields named ten of his supporters as members and himself as chairman. The resolution was carried by a standing vote.[103]

After L. H. Whittemore failed to get a seconder to his motion to adjourn, Shields moved that the Prudential and Finance Committee be given the power to appoint standing committees as they saw fit for the rest of the church year. This was followed closely by another Shields motion that deacon A. W. Record be made General Treasurer of the Church. Both motions were carried. C. J. Holman then moved that deacon Greenway be re-elected as Treasurer of the Communion Fund. This motion carried. Again, a motion to adjourn was not seconded.[104]

With his opponents clearly on the defensive, Shields and his supporters sought retribution. Shields read a resolution that he had not written but wished to move. The resolution demanded that the "fifteen young men who had organized themselves in opposition to the pastor, be suspended until they apologise, and if their apology was not forthcoming within six months, their names should be dropped from the church roll."[105] Chaos ensued. The *Toronto Daily Star* later reported that complete "pandemonium broke loose."[106] The chair and many oth-

---

100. *Minute Book, 1918–1928*, September 21, 1921. JSBCA.

101. *Minute Book, 1918–1928*, September 21, 1921. JSBCA.

102. *Minute Book, 1918–1928*, September 21, 1921. JSBCA. Whittemore's support for this motion may have been motivated by a desire to end the proceedings quickly. Following the acceptance of this motion he moved that the meeting be adjourned.

103. *Minute Book, 1918–1928*, September 21, 1921. JSBCA.

104. *Minute Book, 1918–1928*, September 21, 1921. JSBCA.

105. *Minute Book, 1918–1928*, September 21, 1921. JSBCA.

106. "Shields Sustained, Opponents Ousted," *Toronto Daily Star*, September 22,

ers yelled, "Shame!" and called on Shields to name the author of the resolution.[107] Shields refused. When the howls of protest had subsided, Shields put forward a motion calling for "members who have hitherto opposed the ministry of the pastor ... to accept the Church's decision and cease from further opposition."[108] Instead of quieting the meeting, Shields's resolution added fuel to the fire.

J. B. Lawrason stated "that there had always been liberty of the pulpit in Jarvis St. Church and that the need was for liberty of the pew." J. B. McArthur accused Shields of trying to secure "his choice of a chairman" for the Finance Committee. Shields countered that some members of the Finance Committee had tried to do the same and noted that Albert Matthews had spoken of those opposed to the pastor at that time as "the wreckers." Shields claimed that Matthews referred directly to J. B. McArthur. Albert Matthews asked "to go on record as having no recollection of mentioning any name in the conversation recalled by the pastor." Q. B. Henderson then accused Shields of lying about a deacon who resigned over a political manipulation of the Finance Committee at the June 29 meeting. G. W. Holmes objected to the anonymous resolution read by Shields, "the aim of which seemed to be to silence the opposition." James Ryrie stated, "that if he had previously had any doubts, the fact that the pastor could get up and read such a resolution as he had with reference to the fifteen young men, was sufficient to convince him that he had taken the right course in opposing the pastor." Shields responded by reading the resolution without reference to the fifteen young men. There were howls of protest that this was not the original resolution.[109]

In another attempt to quiet the meeting, deacon E. A. Brownlee stated that the intent of the resolution was not "to deprive members of their right to a voice in the affairs of the Church, but to constrain all members to work together in harmony."[110] The meeting finally passed an abbreviated version of the resolution:

> That the members who have hitherto opposed the ministry of the pastor of this Church, in view of the Church's decision recorded at this meeting, be requested to accept the Church's

---

1921.
 107. *Minute Book, 1918–1928*, September 21, 1921. JSBCA.
 108. *Minute Book, 1918–1928*, September 21, 1921. JSBCA.
 109. *Minute Book, 1918–1928*, September 21, 1921. JSBCA.
 110. *Minute Book, 1918–1928*, September 21, 1921. JSBCA.

decision, and cease from further opposition, that an end may be put to contention in the church.[111]

With this statement, the meeting that the *Toronto Daily Star* was to call "the stormiest ever," was brought to an end.[112] Schism, a permanent division of the congregation, with all of its attendant ugliness, had arrived at Jarvis Street.

The question of what caused the schism at Jarvis Street in 1921 has received scant attention from historians. Those who have examined it have argued that doctrinal differences, such as evolutionary theory and biblical inerrancy, or class antagonism, between the working class and the business/professional classes, split the congregation.[113] Although it is clear that some businessmen at Jarvis Street, like John Northway, had embraced liberal theology, they were comparatively few. Throughout the controversy, many businessmen who opposed Shields made motions reiterating their belief in the inspiration of Scripture and their devotion to "Baptist distinctives." A more credible case exists for the argument that class played an important role in the schism. Yet, the presence of Dr. C. J. Holman and Rufus S. Hudson among Shields's supporters suggests that the congregation did not divide uniformly along class lines. Where Shields's opponents *were* liberal was on the question of their relation to the general secular culture of Toronto. Historian J. M. S. Careless has described the assumptions, values and social evolution of Toronto's elite in the years preceding the First World War:

> By now the prestigious families that dated back to Compact days at Little York had largely departed social leadership. Aside from surviving Jarvises, Ridouts and Denisons, such lineages as Gooderhams, Cawthras and Howlands had grown sufficiently wellaged to fill their place. But newer wealth was fully reputable when held by financial masters such as Osler, Walker or Pellatt, especially if knighthood gave a confirming accolade. Masseys and Eatons yet faced some doubts, being closer to shirt-sleeved shop work, but were plainly beyond rejection. Generally speaking, however, the Toronto elite was becoming still more North American-plutocratic in nature, in spite of its

111. *Minute Book, 1918–1928*, September 21, 1921. JSBCA.

112. "Shields Sustained, Opponents Ousted," *Toronto Daily Star*, September 22, 1921.

113. For a source that argues that both class antagonism and doctrinal issues contributed, see Ellis, "Social and Religious Factors." For an examination of class conflict, see Hill, "From Sect to Denomination."

imperialist devotions and infusions of counting-house knights. Against this should nevertheless be put traits inherited from earlier times. Colonial gentry survivals (though the reign of The Grange ended when Goldwin Smith [who attended Beverley Street Baptist Church] died in 1910), concern for obligations of rank, and enduring British customs or assumptions, continued to mark this urban upper crust. It did not cease to disdain brash dollar vulgarity, preferring more dignified display. Its considerably materialist members duly sought approved culture, at least in music, suitable art and "good" theatre-the last still not accepted by firm Methodists [or Baptists]. The rich also made substantial contributions to major public philanthropies as well as to churches. But equally they purchased expensive motor cars in the opening automobile age, kept elegant sailing craft at the Royal Canadian Yacht Club, supported golf and tennis clubs or thoroughbred stables, toured abroad, and held shining formal balls and dinners. In short, they had a high time, breathlessly reported in the social columns of the city press.[114]

It was to these assumptions and values that the businessmen of Jarvis Street had come to subscribe.

Like the Masseys and Batons, the prominent merchants and manufacturers at Jarvis Street had, in part, realized their goal of social acceptance and respectability among the city's elite. Like Henry Pellatt, Jarvis Street's financiers were on their way to reaping fortunes from the stock market and experiencing high life within high society. The willingness of these businessmen to compromise the separated lifestyle traditionally advocated by Canadian Baptists left them open to the charges of spiritual complacency and moral laxity. While they attempted to deny any wrongdoing, the dissidents failed to convince a majority of their fellow church members that they were *free of worldliness*. In addition, their lengthy tenures in key leadership positions gave credibility to the charge of minority rule that Shields and his supporters consistently made. Even the most substantive complaints against Shields, that he was constantly "hitting people" in his sermons and that he attacked his church enemies publicly, were motivated by the belief that the church practiced its Christianity best by adopting a more conciliatory tone towards those with whom it

---

114. Careless, *Toronto to 1918*, 163. For further evidence that Baptists shared in these activities, see, for example, the list of those involved in a tea for Mrs. John McLaren in "What Women Are Doing," *Globe*, February 23, 1920. For a listing of the clubs to which Baptist businessmen belonged, see *Torontonian Society Blue Book and Club List 1921*.

disagreed. This stance allowed liberal Baptist businessmen to become part of the sociocultural mainstream.

Shields and his supporters valued righteousness not respectability. Their goals were to make pure doctrine and pure living Baptist hallmarks. These ideals could only be realized through separation from a secular culture. Thus, they developed tests whereby the purity of faith and practice of any individual could be measured. When the tests for purity were applied to the dissidents at Jarvis Street they failed. Both their doctrine and practice were found to have been contaminated by the secular world.

In the final analysis, the schism of 1921 at Jarvis Street had its roots more in divergent sociocultural perspectives than in disagreements over doctrine, personality, or polity. Fundamentalists who saw the world as their foe could, by 1919, no longer tolerate the growing band of culturally liberal businessmen who had come to call the world their friend. Businessmen, who had grown accustomed to accommodating their religion to the sociocultural mainstream, refused to give up the respectability for which they, and a generation of their predecessors, had labored so diligently.

The Aftermath of Schism

CROSSING AT THE FLOOD
I am not climbing hills today,
I'm making brain and brawn;
In every obstacle I see
A challenge to go on!
A host of foes encamp around;
And clouds return again-
It is not raining rain to me:
It's raining mighty men.
I am not bearing burdens now,
But multiplying wealth;
Investing treasure for the Lord
To keep my soul in health.
Though compromise is everywhere
Nor principles bestir,-
It isn't raining rain to me:
It's raining character.

> I am not fighting hard today
> The foe's God's errand boy
> To bring me packages of peace
> And packages of joy!
> Though circumstances press and cramp,
> And winds are contrary,
> His clouds are full of blessing yet,
> It's raining victory.
> The river swollen to a flood,
> The rushing, raging tide,
> Conquered by simple faith in God,
> I cross it at His side!
> The blood He shed,
> His Spirit's power,
> His promise of a crown,-
> All tell me that His every cloud
> Is raining glory down.[115]

This poem by T. T. Shields reveals his view of the schism. A sovereign God was in control. No challenge would alter God's plans for Jarvis Street. The day after the church meeting, an elated Shields declared, "I believe that the result of the meeting is a direct answer to much prayer on the part of a host of people in this city and on the entire continent."[116] Frank Merrill, Secretary of the Finance Committee and one of the dissidents, stated in an interview with a *Globe* reporter that "the finances of the church are in very bad shape, notwithstanding how Dr. Shields may seek to hide the truth from his poor deluded followers."[117] Merrill also predicted that without the support of the dissidents, the road ahead would be difficult: "Dr Shields has a proposition on his hands, and it remains to be seen what he will make of it."[118]

Undeterred by such dire predictions, Shields moved to consolidate his victory. On September 23, the first meeting of the Prudential and Finance Committee was held. At that meeting, a new church organist and

---

115. Shields, *Plot That Failed*, 324.
116. "Shields Sustained, Opponents Ousted," *Toronto Daily Star*, September 22, 1921.
117. "Many Will Quit Jarvis Church," *Globe*, September 23, 1921.
118. "Many Will Quit Jarvis Church," *Globe*, September 23, 1921.

music director were appointed.[119] In the same week, Shields had the church books audited and "all the business affairs of the retiring regime were concluded by Saturday noon."[120] Despite the predictions of financial collapse, the amount of total receipts reported at the Annual Meeting of April 28, 1922, was $35,361.97.[121] The church had a credit balance of $1,831.33.[122] The financial report lamented, "We regret that through the withdrawals previously mentioned our offering for Missions this year is considerably less than last; but as our brethren who have withdrawn have been making their own collections for missions, we trust the mission treasuries have not suffered."[123] Still, the church was far from collapse.

In every department, the withdrawal of the dissidents created a sense of urgency and expectation that spurred pastor and people on to new heights. The list of Shields's accomplishments both inside Jarvis Street and outside in the wider Baptist context are too lengthy to list. It is, however, noteworthy that he founded the *Gospel Witness* in 1922, reorganized the Sunday School in 1923, making it the largest in the country for many years, established Toronto Baptist Seminary in 1927, led the fight against modernism in the Convention (a fight that led to his expulsion in 1927), commenced a weekly Sunday evening radio broadcast on CKGW on 25 May 1930, and became President of the Bible Baptist Union.[124]

Meanwhile, the Jarvis Street dissidents pursued a different course. It had become obvious that neither side understood the other. Differing views of what constituted a Baptist church and lifestyle had created a seemingly insurmountable obstacle to reconciliation. On Sunday, September 25, 1921, the defectors met in the Central YMCA for worship.[125] The early trickle of defections became a flood after September 21.[126] A steady flow of resignation letters from Sunday School workers and officers, for example, came to the church office. One letter dated September

---

119. Shields, *Plot That Failed*, 332–33.

120. Shields, *Plot That Failed*, 331.

121. *Minute Book, 1918–1928*, April 28, 1922. JSBCA.

122. *Minute Book, 1918–1928*, April 28, 1922. JSBCA.

123. *Minute Book, 1918–1928*, April 28, 1922. JSBCA.

124. For biographical information on Shields, I have relied primarily on Tarr, *Shields of Canada*, esp. 91–122. For an article on Shields's contribution to Protestant radio, see Johnston, "Early Trails of Protestant Radio, 1922–38," 376–402.

125. Shields, *Plot That Failed*, 332.

126. My discovery of the actual letters of dismission in the Jarvis Street Baptist Church Archives supports this assertion. For a list of those who left, see *Minute Book, 1918–1928*, June 7, 1922. JSBCA.

24, 1921, and addressed to W. J. Hutchinson, Assistant Superintendent, stated:

> In accordance with the request of Dr. Shields that all those not in favor with him resign, I would ask the teachers to accept my resignation as "Girls work Superintendent" + also as teacher of the "Win One" Bible Class.[127]

This letter expresses the sentiments of one who was adamantly opposed to Shields. Others found the decision to resign their positions extremely difficult:

> 13 Rathnally Ave.,
> Toronto, Sept. 28th 1921
>
> Dear Mr. Venn,
>
> The following teachers are in the primary—[four names given] and I—felt after the Church Meeting of last Wednesday that our services in the Sunday School would no longer be expected or desired and that consequently our written resignations would be superfluous.
>
> Our hearts are very sore at leaving the children but no other course seems possible. I am sorry, indeed, to have missed Lily and her small sister last Sunday. Please give my love to them and to John.
>
> If anything more official than this card is necessary kindly let me know. Thanking you for your kind words on your card. I am
>
> Yours Sincerely
> [signed][128]

Some of these women were relatives of protagonists in the controversy. Torn between family loyalty and their love for the children they served in the Sunday School, these young women faced a dreadful dilemma.

Many who had led the opposition to Shields took positions of leadership in the formation of a new church, initially called Central Baptist Church, which met originally in the auditorium of the YMCA on College Street. It was officially organized on June 28, 1922, after 340 former

---

127. Sensibilities concerning these events remain high. Therefore, I have not revealed the identity of the author. For the actual letter see [Redacted] to W. J. Hutchinson, *Jarvis Street Baptist Church Sunday School Minute Book, 1917–1922* (MS), JSBCA.

128. [Redacted] to J. Venn, September 28, 1921. *Jarvis Street Baptist Church Sunday School Minute Book, 1917–1922* (MS), JSBCA.

members of Jarvis Street had received letters of dismission.[129] The new church began with 350 members.[130] The first deacons board included some of the most prominent members and former leaders at Jarvis Street: J. Francis Brown (chair), J. E. Clark, Gideon Grant, Q. B. Henderson, W. J. Lugsdin, James Ryrie, Ephriam Sale, Rev. H. B. Stillwell,[131] H. R. Wellington and Thomas Wilkins.[132]

By the fall of 1922, the church had made considerable progress. In addition to acquiring the use of Castle Memorial Hall at McMaster University on Bloor Street for its Sunday and mid-week services, the church had hired Reverend Ira Smith as interim pastor. A year later, in November 1923, Reverend Harold W. Lang was ordained and served as pastor of the church until 1938. In 1925, the decision was made to secure property for the construction of a permanent church home. A lot situated at the corner of Park Road and Asquith Avenue was procured. Deacon J. Francis Brown was appointed architect, and plans were drawn. The first worship services held in the Gothic building took place on Easter. Sunday, April 17, 1927. The church also acquired a new name, "Park Road Baptist Church"[133] (see Figure 24).

It is clear as one reads K. E. Martin's brief history of Park Road that the former members of Jarvis Street made every effort to build a church that reflected their vision of what a respectable Baptist church should be. Among many notable gifts intended to make that vision a reality was the gift of a Casavant-Freres organ by Christine Ryrie in memory of her late husband, Harry Ryrie. James Ryrie and family donated the furnishings for the pastor's office. Perhaps the most outstanding feature of the new church building, however, was the double rows of stained-glass windows along both aisles. It was decided that these should be

129. *Minute Book, 1918–1928*, June 7, June 21, 1921. JSBCA.

130. Martin, "History of Park Road Baptist Church," 1. MTRL. The discrepancy in numbers is explained by the failure of some to request a letter of dismission.

131. Reverend H. B. Stillwell was a retired Baptist minister and missionary. He was a McMaster graduate who was ordained in 1895 and served at the Baptist church in Grimsby, Ontario. He subsequently became a missionary to India. Ill health forced him to retire from foreign missionary service in 1913. Stillwell became General Treasurer of the denomination's Foreign Mission Board in 1915 and General Secretary of the same board in 1919. For information on Stillwell, see *Baptist Year Book 1895–96*, 169; *Baptist Year Book 1912*, 109; *Baptist Year Book 1913*, 108; *Baptist Year Book 1915*, 92; *Baptist Year Book 1919*, 111.

132. "Central Baptist Church, Toronto," *CB*, July 13, 1922.

133. The information in this paragraph is found in Martin, "History of Park Road Baptist Church," 2.

given as memorials to deceased church members. It was also stipulated that the windows would represent only two themes. The upper row of windows along the south aisle depicted events in the life of Christ while those above the north aisle displayed his teachings. The lower windows along both aisles portrayed famous characters in the Old Testament. Each window contained the inscription "To the Glory of God" and the name of the person commemorated. All of these architectural features were in keeping with the desire of the members to build a church that reflected their commitment to respectable religion.[134]

This commitment was also apparent in the church program. The choir and an emphasis on music became hallmarks of the church's weekly ministry. Religious education, the women's missionary circle and the Dorcas Society each in their own way also became integral parts of church life.[135]

On March 8, 1961, disaster struck when, in the midst of a terrible winter storm, fire gutted the educational wing and vestry of Park Road Baptist Church.[136] Eventually, the decision was made to amalgamate with Yorkminster Baptist Church to form Yorkminster Park Baptist Church on September 10, 1961.[137]

For the dissidents, the days of confrontation with T. T. Shields did not end with their departure from Jarvis Street and their creation of a new Baptist church. In the Senate meetings of McMaster University, on the Convention floor, and in public discourse, they continued to enrage their former pastor. For example, shortly after the schism on October 7, 1921, ten "retired deacons" published a pamphlet that contained "a full and frank statement" of their side of the story. In this pamphlet entitled, *The True Story of the Jarvis Street Baptist Church Trouble: By Its Retired Deacons*, sought to set the record straight and present their case to a Convention audience. The "real issue" and "cause" for the schism at Jarvis Street was "Dr Shields' own personal conduct which has alienated him from half his church members." "A small difference with him," the

---

134. Martin, "History of Park Road Baptist Church," 2. The interpretation concerning respectability is mine.

135. Martin, "History of Park Road Baptist Church," 6–7.

136. Estimates of the damage to the building ranged from $60,000 to $200,000. "$60,000 Pire at Park Rd. Baptist," *Toronto Daily Star*, March 9, 1961; "Flames Sweep Park Road Baptist Church," *Globe and Mail*, March 9, 1961; "$200,000 Church Blaze," *Telegram*, March 9, 1961.

137. For information on this decision, see "New Church for Toronto," *CB*, October 1, 1961.

retired deacons claimed, "is never healed as he seems entirely devoid of any capacity for reconciliation." The root cause of this incapacity was Shields's "inordinate egotism and vanity."[138]

Furthermore, these former deacons claimed that Shields's charge that "we do not want truth preached to us" was unfounded. "Jarvis Street Church," they noted, "stands today, as it has always stood, for sound doctrine and we challenge Dr. Shields to give one single instance even remotely hinting at anything to the contrary." Furthermore, these deacons took Shields to task for making false charges against his congregants: "For years he has been fighting in his church a straw man of Higher Criticism. There is not and has not been any such man or woman there." They concluded that "We have no quarrel with his doctrine: it is the man in whom the fault lies."[139] While there was certainly cause to take issue with Shields's behavior, his claim of the presence and acceptance of "Modernism" was certainly evident in the changing beliefs of John Northway. Evidently, these deacons were either ignorant of Northway's modernist views or they chose to ignore them.

In response to Shields's claim of increasing "worldliness" and the charge that "the Deacons and members of Jarvis Street find their chief joy in life in worldly pleasures" such as, "dancing" the deacons claimed that they never engaged in such behavior, and when the one deacon (Quartus B, Henderson, a signatory to this pamphlet), who did engage in dancing, resigned, Shields "begged him to withdraw his resignation as Deacon, which had been sent to the Pastor. Consistency! Thou art a Jewel!"[140] On this matter, there is no clear evidence, beyond that about Henderson's actions, to support or challenge the claim of the deacons with regard to their participation in dancing or other amusements that Baptists condemned.

To the charge that there were "too many rich men" in Jarvis Street, these former deacons claimed that "no Church in the City or in the denomination is more misunderstood regarding the wealth of its members." Moreover, "Of the few who can even be suspected of having a moderate amount this world's goods most have been standing with the Pastor until the end of June."[141] To claim that men like James Ryrie, Albert Matthews, and Q. B. Henderson, all signatories of this pamphlet,

138. All quotations in this paragraph are taken from Ryrie et al., *True Story*, 2. CBA.
139. Ryrie et al., *True Story*, 2. CBA.
140. Ryrie et al., *True Story*, 3–4. CBA.
141. Ryrie et al., *True Story*, 4. CBA.

possessed a "moderate amount" of wealth was disingenuous at best and was, in fact, a denial of reality. By any reasonable measure, these men were wealthy Baptists.

The pamphlet went on to claim that Shields had "preached the choir empty," had said "that he would empty Jarvis Street Church and then fill it" in part through the "summer campaign" of 1921, and that "his last victory (?)" (in September 1921) "was by a campaign by himself and his followers of intimidation."[142] As we have already seen, to some extent these claims and charges had some merit.

Another attempt to press the case of disaffected and dismissed Jarvis Street members and set the record straight on what happened was put forward in a pamphlet published on October 14, 1922, by former deacon and still prominent lawyer and businessman, D. E. Thomson.[143] Thomson added additional charges against Shields to the earlier account published by the deacons, deaconesses, and trustees. In particular, Thomson claimed that Shields "forced" associate pastor B. W. Merrill to resign and then "Members of the congregation were led to believe that it was voluntary."[144] Similarly, Thomson noted "the resignation of Rev. Mr. Wilks, the Church Clerk, who claimed such resignation had been forced by unfair treatment on the pastor's part."[145] Furthermore, once Merrill had resigned, Thomson claimed that Shields "threatened resignation" on the matter of a salary increase and his voicing of the "danger of the triumph of heresy and worldliness" only occurred "after the $6,000 stipend had been assured."[146] Thomson also highlighted Shields's refusal to resign after he promised to resign if he did not achieve a two-thirds majority who voted in favor of retaining the pastor. The vote was 284 for Shields and 199 against him, which meant the vote "for" total was short of two-thirds. Having not met his own standard to remain as pastor, Shields reneged on his promise and refused to resign.[147] Finally, "Shields' methods" were destructive.[148] "In the gentle art of making the worse seem the better cause," Thomson concluded, "Dr. Shields has

---

142. Ryrie et al., *True Story*, 4. CBA.
143. Thomson, *Dr. Shields*, 1. CBA.
144. Thomson, *Dr. Shields*, 1. CBA.
145. Thomson, *Dr. Shields*, 1. CBA.
146. Thomson, *Dr. Shields*, 1. CBA.
147. Thomson, *Dr. Shields*, 1–2. CBA.
148. Thomson, *Dr. Shields*, 2. CBA.

few peers and no superiors."[149] Thomson further mused that "Having demonstrated his ability as an efficient and ruthless wrecker he should remain in the background until he has made abundantly good his boast of constructing something better."[150] If Thomson hoped his pamphlet would lay the 1921 schism to quiet Shields or put him on the sidelines, he was soon to be disappointed.

Shields responded in a four-page diatribe of his own. He cast Thomson's pamphlet as "a last-hour bitter, personal, attack on the Pastor of Jarvis St. Church and is manifestly an attempt to discredit him in the eyes of the delegates to the Convention as to lessen the force of anything he may have to say about McMaster University."[151] No doubt Thomson, a Trustee of William McMaster's will and a member and chair of the McMaster Board of Governors, was concerned that Shields would deploy tactics similar to those he used at Jarvis Street to "wreck" McMaster. Thomson's fears were validated by the ongoing and seemingly never-ending battle between Shields and McMaster that would reach its ultimate conclusion in the schism of 1927.[152]

In the meantime, in a letter dated January 18, 1924, to his friend and fellow businessman John Northway, James Ryrie rejoiced in a vote by McMaster University's Senate, of which he was a member, to censure Shields for "his conduct and methods":

> I suppose you have seen and read the doings of our friend, T. T. Shields. They certainly gave him the best dressing down he ever received with between 25 or 30 members of the Senate to meet him. He had only one who had a word to say for him. It wasn't for him either, but really for peace. When he said we were to forgive till 70 times 7, someone remarked that we had done better—we had made it 80 times 8. John MacNeill didn't spare him I can tell you. Of course it will be more fight but it had to come the more's the pity.[153]

Ryrie's letter reveals how deeply the animosity towards Shields went. Former members of Jarvis Street felt betrayed and cheated out of their heritage. Grudges were clearly sustained for years. As Victor Fry, a

149. Thomson, *Dr. Shields*, 4. CBA.
150. Thomson, *Dr. Shields*, 4. CBA.
151. Shields, *Dr. Shields' Reply*, 1. JSBCA, CBA.
152. For detailed analysis of the McMaster controversy, see Adams, "Great Contention," 119–56.
153. As cited in Wilson, *John Northway*, 204.

longtime member of Jarvis Street, recalled in a 1992 interview, "people from the two churches had nothing to do with each other."[154] Not even Shields's expulsion from the Convention in 1927 put an end to the feelings of anger and bitterness.

To those unacquainted with Baptist theology and practice, the schism of 1921 at Jarvis Street may, at first glance, appear petty, maybe even ludicrous. In fact, it was the logical outcome of a slow but steady process of secularization. As the church's businessmen abandoned their belief and practice of separation for greater sociocultural integration, they became targets for fundamentalists like T. T. Shields, who had as their mission the preservation of a countercultural Christianity. Having transformed their church into a respectable institution that reflected their accommodation to the secular business world, the leading businessmen from Jarvis Street fought to maintain the changes that they and their predecessors had instituted.

Clearly, a number of factors thwarted the business element's attempts to maintain their hold over "dear old Jarvis Street." First, and most importantly, the dissidents failed to shake the "wealthy, worldly, and wise" image used so skillfully by their fundamentalist opponents to discredit them. Although they retained their allegiance to the Baptist church, they failed to recognize that their beliefs and values had been secularized. To many of their fellow church members, they appeared too at home with "the world." Their tolerance of behavior that Baptists had traditionally abhorred left them vulnerable to the charge of moral laxity. Their drive for business success and their conspicuous displays of wealth made them susceptible to the charge of materialism. Their longstanding control over the affairs of the church led to accusations of elitism. Lastly, their commitment to social respectability undermined their attempts to fend off the charge that they had become spiritually complacent. In addition, Jarvis Street's businessmen underestimated their adversary. Shields proved himself a formidable opponent. His skill as an orator and his charismatic personality provided him with advantages that he used effectively to rally support for his cause. The church's businessmen did not possess great oratorical skills. They also had no single charismatic leader who could rival Shields in the battle for people's affections. Their devotion to respectability initially made them shy away from confrontation

---

154. Personal Interview with Victor Fry, Toronto, March 31, 1992. Victor Fry sat under Shields's ministry for 31 years.

with their pastor. This, combined with the lack of strong leadership, put the dissidents on the defensive.

The schism of 1921 was a result of the secularization process, and it clearly revealed the presence of divergent views of Canadian culture and Baptist belief and practice. Fundamentalism and modernism would both continue. As Shields made Jarvis Street a leading Canadian Baptist bastion against modernism, the secessionists eventually moved but a few miles north to become the guardians of more modern versions of the respectable Baptist cathedral.

Figure 22. T. T. Shields, ca. 1920, as he appeared about the time the troubles began at Jarvis Street (JSBCA).

Figure 23. Albert Matthews, began as a Shields supporter but became one of the pastor's strongest opponents in 1921 (Greene, *Who's Who and Why 1917-18*).

Figure 24. An etching by Owen Staples of the interior of Park Road Baptist Church (MTRL, T 34482).

Chapter 7

Conclusion

> For me to live is—WEALTH? Know thou,
> Who thinkest tis in paltry gold
> All things consist, that thou hast sold
> Thy soul, and naught of worth remaineth now.
> For me to live is—FAME? Ah then
> May all applaud with loud acclaim,
> And add their honours to thy name,
> If thou but seekest praise of mortal men.
> For me to live is—PLEASURE? Yes,
> But in thy quest, pray, be not blind
> To values, but the essence find
> Of sweetest pleasure without bitterness.
> For me to live is—CHRIST! Ah, soul,
> Thou knowest life's secret, for, with him
> Thy life shall ever to the brim
> Be filled, while on eternal ages roll.[1]

THE PRIORITY GIVEN TO the spiritual life in this poem by L. C. Kitchen, a member of McMaster's graduating class of 1920, might lead one to conclude that all was well with the central Canadian Baptist soul. In fact, the schism at Jarvis Street in 1921 was indicative of a secularization process that engendered a deep-seated fragmentation over social and cultural

---

1. "Life's Motive," *CB*, September 9, 1920.

issues which would eventually play an important role in destroying the unity of the Baptist denomination. Chief among the "disturbing elements" that Reverend H. McDiarmid of Walkerville noted in his 1919 report on the state of the denomination's religion in Ontario and Quebec, was "the spirit of worldliness."[2] "There is no question as to its presence in our midst," wrote McDiarmid, "and certainly it is exercising a devitalizing and paralyzing influence upon our life which constitutes a mighty challenge to the effectiveness of our message."[3] While the dissidents from Jarvis Street continued to deny that they were guilty of finding "their chief joy in worldly pleasures" and that among their number there were "few" who could "even be suspected of having a moderate amount of this world's goods," their lavish city mansions and stately summer homes, their trips overseas and south for the winter, and their participation in amusements and desire for respectability serve as evidence of their acceptance of worldliness and hedonism.[4]

The secularization of the businessman at Jarvis Street Baptist Church, between 1848 and 1921, suggests that the social and cultural changes that recast Canadian society in this period had a profoundly negative impact on traditional religion. But important questions remain unanswered. Was the experience of Jarvis Street's businessmen an anomaly or the norm among Canadian Baptists? One might argue that the Baptist belief in the independence of the local church could act as a barrier to secularization. Indeed, Donald Goertz has shown that when it came to music, for example, Walmer Road Baptist Church in Toronto, which included in its membership the wealthy and socially respectable Harris and Shenstone families, "rejected the professional model [adopted by Jarvis Street], realizing that the participation of everyone in church music would be necessary to bridge the gap between rich and poor."[5] Here a conscious countercultural decision was taken. It discouraged segregation based on social class and secularization that used professionalization as the means to turn church music into respectable entertainment. Yet, Goertz admits that "paid organists and singers were standard"

---

2. Rev. H. McDiarmid, "Report of Committee on the State of Religion," *Baptist Yearbook for Ontario and Quebec 1919*, 58.

3. Rev. H. McDiarmid, "Report of Committee on the State of Religion," *Baptist Yearbook for Ontario and Quebec 1919*, 58.

4. "Retired Deacons Tell of Jarvis Church Case," *Toronto Daily Star*, October 12, 1921.

5. Goertz, *Century for the City*, 21.

for Baptist churches when Walmer Road began in 1889.⁶ Thus, it would seem that culturally conservative churches, like Walmer Road and Immanuel (previously Alexander Street), were increasingly the anomalies. However, the differences in attitudes and actions between Walmer Road and Jarvis Street deserve further study. Certainly, both the depth and scope of secularization within Toronto's Baptist churches and beyond, in the wider Canadian context, requires further investigation.

Academics who have examined the troubles concerning biblical inerrancy in the Southern Baptist Convention (SBC) have concluded that the response of fundamentalists, moderates, and liberals to modernity today is less shaped by social class, social status, and regional identity than it was a generation ago. Sociologist Nancy Tatom Ammerman, for example, has argued that even though "there were social sources" in the battle for control of the denomination, "the denomination's loss of its exclusively regional identity" and "differences in the status of the parties contending for domination of the SBC's future" only partially explained the conflict of the late 1980s.⁷ Ammerman found that issues of "private morality" played a key role in the tensions within the denomination.⁸ In his critical analysis of the so-called "Southern Baptist Holy War" between those who support biblical inerrancy and those who doubt or oppose it, Joe Edward Barnhart charges that many Southern Baptists have become "Christian hedonists" and "Christian materialists" who have adopted a "this-worldly outlook."⁹ According to Barnhart, one does not have to look far to see these views in action: "There is no question that the First Baptist Church of Dallas, with its 26,000 members and annual budget of $12 million dollars, has wittingly or unwittingly spearheaded the Christian hedonism movement among Southern Baptists."¹⁰ Based on the evidence offered by Barnhart, there is a strong case for the argument that the Southern Baptist experience has also been transformed by the process of secularization. The mega-church model, as exemplified by First Baptist, Dallas, with its combination of business methodology, respectability, and spectacle, has won the admiration and become the envy of Southern Baptist pastors throughout the United States.

6. Goertz, *Century for the City*, 20.
7. Ammerman, *Baptist Battles*, 164.
8. Ammerman, *Baptist Battles*, 106–10.
9. For Barnhart's discussion of these topics, see Barnhart, *Southern Baptist Holy War*, 209–28.
10. Barnhart, *Southern Baptist Holy War*, 217.

In a study of the American Bible Society (ABS), Peter J. Wosh has argued that the evangelical merchants who founded the society in 1816 found it impossible to resist the success and influence of British commerce. Through an analysis of changes in thought and methodology, Wosh documents how ABS managers moved from an emphasis on "spreading the word" to a concentration on selling the word. According to Wosh, profits replaced evangelism as the primary goal of the ABS as its managers accepted the highly rationalized methods of organization, production, and distribution utilized by British commerce. The trends apparent in Wosh's microcosmic study run parallel to those found at Jarvis Street. The shift in priority from spiritual to material through the adoption of business ideology and methodology are evident in both cases. The commercialization of such a large and powerful evangelical organization as the ABS provides another outstanding example of the secularizing effects of business.[11]

In a similar vein, Kathryn Long's analysis of the application of business marketing methods to the businessman's revival of 1858 in the US, reveals both the growing influence of business on religion and its corrosive effects. Long argues that American protestants, including the well-known Baptist pastor of First Baptist Church in Newark, New Jersey, Henry Clay Fish, believed that "piety could invade and sacralize commercial space and its inhabitants."[12] However, Long notes that "in most instances, influence seemed to move in the opposite direction as business methods were put to use for stimulating religious fervor."[13] Consequently, Long concludes that "The revival celebrated not so much the religious transformation of business or the businessman as the affinity between urban revivals and a nascent corporate culture."[14] Long's findings are yet another example of how business methods and culture began to reshape and secularize the nineteenth century Protestant experience.

Closer to home, the Coxes, Flavelles, and Fudgers of Sherbourne Street Methodist Church shared common values with the McMasters, McNaughts, and Ryries of Jarvis Street. Their desire to make their churches culturally and socially respectable through the construction of lavish church buildings, the introduction of business methods and more

---

11. Wosh, *Spreading the Word*.
12. Long, "Turning . . . Piety Into Hard Cash," 246.
13. Long, "Turning . . . Piety Into Hard Cash," 246.
14. Long, "Turning . . . Piety Into Hard Cash," 246.

sophisticated and professional musical programs all contributed to the secularization of their churches.

They also believed that material wealth and spiritual health were inextricably linked together. This belief opened the door for acceptance of the "gospel of wealth," the idea that the rich had an obligation to accumulate wealth for the benefit of the general populace, most notably advanced by American steel baron Andrew Carnegie in 1889.[15] As Ramsay Cook has pointed out, social critics like J. W. Bengough "heaped scorn on the idea of the 'gospel of wealth' and took particular pleasure in attacking the Massey family's ostentatious acts of public charity."[16] Many of Jarvis Street's businessmen took Carnegie's idea to its logical conclusion and rationalized not only their pursuit of riches but also their abandonment of stewardship. While outstanding examples of philanthropic acts, such as those by John Northway, still existed among Jarvis Street's business circle in the early twentieth century, they were gradually being replaced by a more self-serving perspective that sought to satisfy personal wants and business needs before any consideration was given to the needs of the church.

We have also seen that at Jarvis Street, the tensions between Baptist faith and a business-dominated culture led many of Jarvis Street's businessmen to abandon the doctrine of separation for sociocultural integration. This meant compromise, accommodation, and toleration of different lifestyles. Conspicuous consumption replaced modesty as the primary lifestyle characteristic for many businessmen. Service to God and mammon or even mammon *over* God also followed the rise of a business-dominated culture.

While religion continued to play an important role in the lives of businessmen, it lost its central place. Giving patterns changed as stewardship of time, money, and energy declined in the face of the increasing demands of business life. In addition, the pursuit of sociocultural integration led some businessmen to reject traditional Baptist teaching concerning "the world." Specifically, the move from suspicion to acceptance of worldly beliefs and values resulted in significant lifestyle changes. The willingness of Baptist businessmen to engage in questionable business practices and in amusements traditionally condemned as evil created a sense of moral decay and decline.

15. For a discussion of Carnegie's concept, see Livesay, *Andrew Carnegie*, 127–28.
16. Cook, *Regenerators*, 130.

Juxtaposed to Shields's fundamentalism with its reactionary countercultural perspective was the cultural liberalism of Jarvis Street's businessmen. Faced with the difficulty of living as cultural liberals in an increasingly hostile puritanical religious setting, the business element fought to preserve their view of the church and its more integrated relationship with Canadian culture. Although they failed to retain control over Jarvis Street, their commitment to a more secularized religious vision enabled them to establish their own Baptist church. Eventually, these businessmen found that many in the Baptist Convention of Ontario and Quebec shared their more tolerant view of Baptist faith and practice.

This book has argued that business helped to secularize religion. Implicitly, doubt has been cast on whether, as Canadian intellectual historians like David Marshall and Michael Gauvreau have claimed, theological debate was the major change agent in the church. While theology at a theoretical level was important to the clergy and intellectuals, this study has argued that questions of faith were experienced most profoundly at the practical level for businessmen in the pews. For many businessmen, the ethical and moral questions related to their everyday business and personal lives mattered far more than theological constructs or debates. This is not to suggest, as Michael Bliss seems to imply, that businessmen were so pragmatic that they seldom, if ever, engaged in reading theology or thinking about its implications. The fact that book merchant James Lesslie analyzed sermons for their Calvinistic content in the 1830s, chemical manufacturer and wholesaler William Elliot wrote about his eschatological views in *The Canadian Baptist* in the early 1880s, and clothing manufacturer, wholesaler and retailer John Northway read the latest liberal theological scholarship in the early twentieth century, suggests that some Baptist businessmen maintained a keen interest in the finer points of theology.[17] Nevertheless, Bliss is correct in his assertion that there is no evidence to suggest that such behavior was the norm among businessmen.

There is also no doubt that business acted in conjunction with urbanization and intellectual change to secularize religion. Business helped to shift the focus from the spiritual world to the material world, and—in the case of the Baptist businessmen studied here—this shift had profound effects on the conduct and content of their religion. While it

---

17. James Lesslie, *Diary*, March 25, 1832; "Some Remarks on Prophecy in General and on Some of the Prophecies of Our Lord Jesus Christ," *CB*, October 5, 1882. For a discussion of Northway's theological reading, see Wilson, *John Northway*, 193–202.

would be a mistake to argue that the secularization process began with the rise of a business-dominated culture, business became a key factor in secularization. The evidence presented in this book suggests that business accelerated the process by encouraging accommodation between itself and religion. Businessmen offered the church wealth, new management techniques, and an avenue to sociocultural integration. In return, the culturally liberal version of Baptist religion offered businessmen personal respectability and the moral sanctification of capitalism. Business benefitted far more than religion from this exchange. As Baptist businessmen acquired wealth, they increasingly put their trust in it to realize their dreams of success in this world. Religion's promise of future reward could not compete with the possibility of present financial and material gain that business offered.

Critics of this study will undoubtedly argue that it is elitist and too narrowly focused. It fails to compare Jarvis Street's businessmen with other Baptist businessmen or those in other denominations. The aspect of education, admittedly a key element in any social group's realization of respectability, is ignored in this study. Critics will also point out that marriage patterns, family life, and political involvement have not been explored. In addition, this study says little, if anything, about the role of women in business and the church. Finally, with its consistent focus on one social group, it ignores the perceptions and actions of professionals, clerical workers, and labor, who together constituted the vast majority of those occupying church pews. Each of these criticisms has its merits. There is no question that each of these issues is not fully examined here. Some topics—most notably the involvement of the central Canadian Baptist business elite's involvement in education—have been covered by other historians.[18] Admittedly, these other issues deserve further study. Space limitations and organizational considerations rendered them secondary in importance to those examined. Nevertheless, a beginning has been made here to understand the struggles of an influential social group. The businessmen from Jarvis Street in the selected sample were models for the entire denomination, and as such, their response to social and cultural change was closely scrutinized and often emulated by other Baptists. This reason alone provides justification for the present study.

18. See, for example, Wilson, *John Northway*, 191–92, 203–6. For William McMaster's contributions to higher education, see Johnston, *Toronto Years*, 21, 26, 44–57. Johnston also covers the contributions of other Jarvis Street businessmen and professionals, such as Albert Matthews, D. E. Thomson, John Firstbrook, and James Ryrie.

Despite recent interest in religious history, our knowledge of local and individual responses to intellectual, social, economic, and cultural change remains in its infancy. Although the major contours and patterns have been well documented and defined, the number of specific studies on social groups, parishes, and individuals remains paltry. Without more studies that examine beliefs, attitudes, and actions at these levels, it will remain impossible to assess accurately the impact of larger social and cultural changes on religion.

Allen Robertson's study of Methodist merchants in Halifax, Peter J. Wash's examination of the American Bible Society and Kathryn Long's study of the 1858 businessman's revival have illustrated the usefulness of the microcosmic approach. This book has followed the cue of these historians. It makes no pretense about its shortcomings. Its focus has been narrowed to serve the interest of close investigation and the belief that such studies are needed in themselves and to provide substance for a more complete historical analysis that appreciates the nuances of local and individual religious belief and practice.

In part, this book has also examined the general Baptist response to progress. There is no question that the businessmen from Jarvis Street gradually forged an alliance between religious and material progress. They became convinced that one could not succeed without the other. Thus, they devoted their lives to advancing the causes of Christ and capitalism.

Implicitly, this study has also extended the task of testing the Weber-Tawney thesis. On the surface, it would appear that Weber was correct in his assertion that Calvinism promotes capitalism. Yet, the Calvinism held by many Canadian Baptists in the late nineteenth century was markedly different from that of two centuries earlier. The shift of priorities from the spiritual to the material coincided with the modification and muting of Calvinism. Many conservative Baptists would have empathized with Joshua Denovan when he lamented to his friend James Hogg in 1872 that "the world, the flesh and Arminianism are right across my path once more."[19] It appears that for central Canadian Baptists in urban centers, by the end of the nineteenth century, the rise of capitalism had resulted in a corresponding decline of Calvinism. In a study of the linkage between Baptist religion and social science in the life of historian Harold Innis, Michael Gauvreau has argued that Innis's rural upbringing with its "reformist

---

19. Joshua Denovan to James Hogg, January 25, 1872, in *Joshua Denovan*, 176.

temper, which emphasized the traditional Calvinist doctrines" provided the young student with the convictions "to overcome his initial astonishment of encountering McMaster students 'who tend towards materialism or who believe there is no God.'"[20] Yet Innis was the product of a version of the Baptist faith that was on the wane. Many of his urbanized and secularized classmates from wealthy business families were the inheritors of a more hedonistic and liberal religion that de-emphasized belief in God's sovereignty and encouraged belief in humanity's ability.

By 1921, Jarvis Street's businessmen could claim to have gained "the whole world." They were respectable and respected members of Toronto's business community. They enjoyed wealth and the power that flowed from this new reality. Over the past three-quarters of a century, they had gradually exchanged separation for integration and the ethical restrictions of their faith for personal freedom and tolerance. Material consumption had replaced spiritual commitment as the priority of their lives. In short, by the world's standards, they were a modern Canadian success story. Nevertheless, from their fundamentalist brethren came condemnation and scorn. Even the words of Jesus raised doubts about the course they had taken: "For what is a man profited, if he shall gain the whole world and lose his own soul?" (Matt 16:26).

---

20. Gauvreau, "Baptist Religion and the Social Science of Harold Innis," 167.

Appendix 1

Selected Sample of Businessmen from Jarvis Street Baptist Church, 1818–1921

KEY:

NR   NO RECORD   B   BAPTISM

E   EXPERIENCE   L   LETTER OF TRANSFER

Name and Date of Death	Church Membership	Occupation-Business
Alexander Stewart d. June 21, 1840	NR	Land Agent, Alexander Stewart, Land Agency
John B. Maxwell	NR	Landlord
James Lesslie d. April 19, 1885	NR	Partner, Lesslie and Sons, Booksellers, Stationers & Druggists Proprietor, Lesslie Brothers, *Examiner* (1842–1855)
Robert Cathcart	(B) December 6, 1840	Wholesaler and Retailer, Robert Cathcart General Dry Goods
Thomas Lailey d. June 3, 1897	(B) June 2, 1843	Clothing Retailer, Wholesaler, Manufacturer Thomas Lailey & Company
William Davies d. March 21, 1921	Applies April 6, 1851 NR of membership	Pork Packer, William Davies Company

APPENDIX 1: BUSINESSMEN FROM JARVIS STREET BAPTIST CHURCH

Name and Date of Death	Church Membership	Occupation-Business
Francis T. Parson	NR	Partner, Parson Bros., Provision and coal oil Merchants
William McMaster d. September 22, 1887	(L) May 23, 1843	Founder, William McMaster & Company, Dry Goods; Canadian Bank of Commerce
Arthur R. McMaster d. July 8, 1881	(B) September 4, 1870	Merchant, Partner, William McMaster and Nephews, A. R. McMaster and Brother
James S. McMaster d. May 11, 1920	(B) October 5, 1843 (L) October 7, 1890	Merchant, Partner, William McMaster and Nephews, A. R. McMaster and Brother, McMaster and Company, McMaster, Darling and Company
William Elliott d. June 3, 1893	(B) June 28, 1865	Chemical Manufacturer and Wholesaler, Elliot and Company
John Firstbrook d. March 22, 1942	(L) March 30, 1892	Box Manufacturer, Firstbrook Brothers
William Firstbrook d. December 30, 1924	(L) June 27, 1906	Box Manufacturer, Firstbrook Brothers
William K. McNaught d. February 2, 1919	(B) February 2, 1868	Jewellery Manufacturer and Wholesaler, American Watch Case Company
William Hewitt, Sr. d. April 9, 1905	(B) May 7, 1843	Hardware Retailer and Wholesaler, Wm. Hewitt & Company
Daniel E. Thomson d. December 13, 1923	(E) April 26, 1876	Lawyer and Businessman, Senior Partner, Thomson, Henderson, & Bell; Thomson, Tilley, & Johnston
James Ryrie Jr. d. June 7, 1933	(L) June 27, 1884	Jewellery Retailer and Manufacturer, Ryrie Brothers, Limited

APPENDIX 1: BUSINESSMEN FROM JARVIS STREET BAPTIST CHURCH

Name and Date of Death	Church Membership	Occupation-Business
Harry Ryrie d. September 16, 1917	(L) September 23, 1885	Jewellery Retailer and Manufacturer, Ryrie Brothers, Limited
Albert Matthews d. August 13, 1949	(L) November 20, 1912	Bond Dealer, Partner, Matthews-Blackwell Company, R. C. Matthews Company, Limited
Edmund Burke d. January 2, 1919	(B) December 29, 1867	Architect for numerous firms, including Langley & Burke, Burke, Horwood & White
Quartus B. Henderson d. January 21, 1961	(B) February 24, 1901	Partner, Davis & Henderson, Limited, Printers
George Lugsdin d. December 3, 1915	(B) April 26, 1863	Partner, Lugsdin & Barnett, Saddle, Harness and Trunk Manufacturers
John Lugsdin d. October 13, 1894	(B) December 30, 1866	Partner, J&J Lugsdin, Hatters and Furriers
Joseph Lugsdin d. May 22, 1919	(B) December 30, 1866	Partner, J&J Lugsdin, Hatters and Furriers
John Northway d. November 6, 1926	NR	Clothing Manufacturer, Wholesaler, Retailer, John Northway & Son, Limited

Appendix 2

Examples of Religious and Social Interconnections

Name	Church Office(s)	Clubs
Alexander Stewart	Pastor of Baptist Church at York, 1818–1820 Pastor at Market Lane Hall and March Street, 1829–1836 Upper Canada Bible Society [UCBS] Vice President, 1840	
John B. Maxwell	Preacher at March Street, 1834–1836	
James Lesslie	Church Trustee, 1832– UCBS Member, 1841– Committee Member, 1848–1850	
Robert Cathcart	Deacon, 1846–1853 UCBS Member, 1841– Committee Member, 1841	
Thomas Lailey	UCBS Member, 1853– Director, 1857	National Club, York Pioneers
William Davies	UCBS Member, 1868–	
Francis T. Parson	UCBS Member, 1869–	
William McMaster	Deacon, 1851–1855 UCBS Member, 1841– Secretary, Treasurer, Vice President	National Club

APPENDIX 2: EXAMPLES OF RELIGIOUS AND SOCIAL INTERCONNECTIONS

Name	Church Office(s)	Clubs
Arthur R. McMaster	UCBS Member, 1841–	National Club
James S. McMaster	Deacon, 1891–1920	National Club
William Elliott	Deacon, 1869–1893 UCBS Member, 1855– Director, 1869	
John Firstbrook	Deacon, 1896–1913	National Club, Rosedale Golf Club, Lambton Golf and Country Club
William Firstbrook		National Club, Rosedale Golf Club, Lambton Golf and Country Club
William K. McNaught		National Club, Royal Canadian Yacht Club
William Hewitt Sr.	Deacon, 1869–1876 UCBS Member, 1868–	National Club, York Pioneers
Daniel E. Thomson	Deacon, 1896–1920	National Club, Royal Canadian Yacht Club
James Ryrie Jr.	Deacon, 1889–1920	National Club, York Pioneers
Harry Ryrie	Deacon, 1911–1912	National Club, York Pioneers, Lambton Golf and Country Club, Royal Canadian Yacht Club
Albert Matthews	Deacon, 1913–1920	National Club, Rosedale Golf Club
Edmund Burke	Deacon, 1885–1918	National Club, Rosedale Golf Club
Quartus B. Henderson	Deacon, 1919–1920	National Club, Lambton Golf and Country Club
George Lugsdin	Deacon, 1882–1915 UCBS Member Director, 1880	York Pioneers
John Lugsdin		
Joseph Lugsdin	Deacon, 1880–1895 UCBS Member Director 1885	
John Northway		National Club, Lambton Golf and Country Club

Bibliography

Primary Sources

Business and Private Manuscripts

Archives of Ontario

Canada Packers Collection
Crooks-Wood Papers
Dun and Bradstreet Reference Books, 1864–1921
Eaton's Company Records
George Brown Papers (Microfilm Copy)
J. C. B. and B. C. Horwood Collection
Lesslie Family Papers
Lindsey-Mackenzie Papers
Michell F. Hepburn Papers
Thomson, Henderson & Bell Papers

Canadian Baptist Archives

Biographical Files
T. F. Caldicott Papers
G. P. Gilmour Papers
McMaster Estate Minute Books, 1891–1920

Dundas Historical Society Museum

Lesslie Diaries

Jarvis Street Baptist Church Archives

T. T. Shields Papers
R. A. Fyfe. *Theological Lectures, 1867–1911*

McGill University Archives

Lyman Pharmaceutical Company Records

Metropolitan Toronto Reference Library

Alexander Stewart Papers, E. W. Banting Collection
Thomas S. Shenston Papers
John E. Maxwell Papers

National Archives of Canada

Henry Birks & Sons Company Records
R. G. Dun and Company Records—The Original R. G. Dun & Co. Credit Report volumes are held at Baker Library, Harvard Business School. Used by permission.
Toronto Board of Trade Records
Upper Canada Bible Society Records

Trent University Archives

Northway Company Ltd. Fonds

University of Toronto: Thomas Fisher Rare Book Library

Alexander Stewart Papers, Louis Melzack Collection

University of Western Ontario: Regional Collection

Papers of William Davies

Church Records

Canadian Baptist Archives

Alexander/Immanuel Baptist Church Records
Bond/Jarvis Street Baptist Church Records

Jarvis Street Baptist Church Archives

Bond Street Baptist Church Minute Book, 1845–1855
Finances in Sterling of the March Street Baptist Church, 1840–1846
Jarvis Street Baptist Church Deacons Minute Book, 1900–1903
Jarvis Street Baptist Church Finance Committee Minute Book, 1901–1921
Jarvis Street Baptist Church Minute Book, 1866–1881
Jarvis Street Baptist Church Minute Book, 1892–1910
Jarvis Street Baptist Church Minute Book, 1918–1928
Jarvis Street Baptist Church Sunday School Minute Book, 1917–1922

Jarvis Street Baptist Church Tithing Ledger, 1906–1911
Jarvis Street Baptist Church Treasurers Book, 1887–1914
Minutes of the Baptist Church at York, 1829–1832
Unprocessed Correspondence and Files

Government Records and Documents

Archives of Ontario

County of York. Surrogate Court Records [RG 22].
County of York. Unprocessed Chancery Court Records, Civil Suits and Country Causes, 1868–1921 [RG 22]
Department of the Provincial Secretary and Citizenship. General Correspondence [RG 8, Series I-1-D]
Ministry of Consumer and Commercial Relations. Corporate Files [RG 53 and RG 55]

City of Toronto Archives

Assessment Rolls for the City of Toronto, 1850–1921

Metropolitan Toronto Reference Library

City of Toronto, Directories 1836–

University of Western Ontario

Province of Canada. *Statutes: 1842*. Kingston: Queen's Printer, 1842.
———. *Statutes: 1858*. Ottawa: Queen's Printer, 1858.
Canada. *Statutes: 1869*. Ottawa: Queen's Printer, 1869.
———. *Statutes: 1875*. Ottawa: Queen's Printer, 1875.
———. *Statutes: 1880*. Ottawa: Queen's Printer, 1880.
———. *Statutes: 1919*. Ottawa: Queen's Printer, 1919.
———. *Statutes: 1920*. Ottawa: Queen's Printer, 1920.
———. *Report of the Royal Commission on the Relations of Labour and Capital in Canada Evidence–Ontario*. Ottawa: Queen's Printer, 1889.
Ontario. *Revised Statutes: 1887*. Toronto: Queen's Printer, 1887.
———. *Revised Statutes: 1897*. Toronto: Queen's Printer, 1897.
———. *Statutes: 1889*. Toronto: Queen's Printer, 1889.
———. *Statutes: 1892*. Toronto: Queen's Printer, 1892.

Newspapers, Religious Papers, and Trade Journals

Baptist Magazine (London, England)
Canadian Baptist (Toronto)
Canadian Manufacturer (Toronto)
Christian Guardian (Toronto)
Christian Messenger (Brantford)

Christian Observer (Toronto)
Colonial Advocate (Toronto)
Daily Star (Toronto)
Evangelical Pioneer (London, Ontario)
Examiner (Toronto)
Forward Movement News (Toronto)
Globe and Mail (Toronto)
McMaster University Monthly (Toronto)
Monetary Times (Toronto)
Montreal Register
Rosedale-Hill Topics (Toronto)
Star Weekly (Toronto)
Telegram (Toronto)
Toiler (Toronto)
Trader and Canadian Jeweller (Toronto)

Interviews

Bob Shaker (with author)
Victor Fry (with author)

Printed Sources

The Baptist Forward Movement. *The Financial Objective, $300.000*. Folder 2. Toronto: Forward Movement Executive, n.d.
———. *General Scheme*. Folder 1. Toronto: Forward Movement Executive, n.d.
———. *The Spiritual Aims of the Baptist Forward Movement*. Form 11. Toronto: Baptist Forward Movement, n.d.
Baptist Year Books, 1857–1962.
Barclay, John. *Preface to the Psalms*. Chesley: A. S. Elliot, 1880.
Bunyan, John. *The Life and Death of Mr. Badman, Presented to the World in a Familiar Dialogue Between Mr. Wiseman and Mr. Attentive*. Edited by James F. Forrest and Roger Sharrock. Oxford: Clarendon, 1988.
Caldicott, T. F. *Systematic Beneficence*. Toronto: Canadian Baptist Office, 1863.
The Canadian Bank of Commerce. *Charter and Annual Reports 1867–1907*. Vol. 1. Toronto: Canadian Bank of Commerce, 1907.
The Canadian Baptist Pulpit. Toronto: E. O. White, 1902.
Catalogue for the Ryrie Brothers Limited, Toronto, 1913. Toronto: Southam, 1913.
Catalogue of the Trustees, Officers, and Students of the Canadian Literary Institute for the Year 1861. Woodstock, CW: n.p., 1861.
Crossley, H. T. *Practical Talks on Important Themes*. Toronto: William Briggs, Wesley Buildings, 1895.
Declaration of Faith, Covenant and Rules of Order of the College Street Baptist Church, Toronto. Toronto: Dudley and Burns, 1890.
Directory of the Jarvis Street Baptist Church, Toronto, 1876–1877. Toronto: Dudley and Burns, 1877.
Directory of the Jarvis Street Baptist Church, August, 1897. Toronto: Dudley and Burns, 1897.

BIBLIOGRAPHY

Directory of the Studies, Terms, &c. of the Canadian Literary Institute for the Year 1875-76. Woodstock: Woodstock Sentinel, 1875.

The Doctrines and Discipline of the Wesleyan Methodist Church in Canada. Toronto: Samuel Rose, 1873.

Dyke, S. A. *Systematic Beneficence.* Toronto: Dudley and Burns, 1879.

Farmer, Jones H., ed. *E. W. Dadson, BA, DD, The Man and His Message.* Toronto: William Briggs, 1902.

Firth, Edith G., ed. *The Town of York, 1815-1834: A Further Collection of Documents.* Toronto: Champlain Society, 1966.

Fox, William Sherwood, ed. *The Letters of William Davies 1854-1861.* Toronto: University of Toronto Press, 1945.

Fyfe, R. A. *A Forty Years Survey From Bond Street Pulpit.* Toronto: Dudley and Burns, 1876.

———. *Suggestions to Canadian Baptist Churches, Pastors and Deacons.* Toronto: Canadian Baptist Office, 1866.

Grantham, Thomas. *Christianismus Primitivus.* London: Francis Smith, 1678.

Henderson, Quartus B. *The Dollar in Business and Religion.* n.p., 1919.

Joshua Denovan. Toronto: Standard, 1901.

A Jubilee Commemoration: Being Exercises at the Fiftieth Anniversary of the Ordination of Rev. William Stewart, DD, Principal and Secretary of The Toronto Bible Training School to the Work of the Christian Ministry. Toronto: L. S. Haynes, 1909.

Keach, Benjamin. *The Breach Repaired in God's Worship; or Singing of Psalms, Hymns, and Spiritual Songs, Proved to be an Holy Ordinance.* London: n.p., 1691.

Langley, William. *A Correct Statement of the Proceedings in Bond Street Baptist Church, Whereby A Member was Tyrannically Expelled for Telling the Truth!* Toronto: n.p., 1858.

Limscott, T. S. *The Path of Wealth or Light from my Forge.* Saint John, NB: Bradley, Garretson, 1888.

Marlow, Isaac. *The Truth Soberly Defended.* London: n.p., 1692.

McNaught, W. K. *Lacrosse and How to Play It.* Toronto: Rose-Belford, 1880.

Memoir of Daniel Arthur McGregor. Toronto: Dudley and Burns, 1891.

Metropolitan Toronto Reference Library. *Biographical Scrapbooks.* n.p.

Minutes of the Haldimand Association, 1861. Toronto: Canadian Baptist Office, 1861.

Mullins, E. Y. *Baptist Beliefs.* Louisville, KY: Baptist World, 1912.

Now Concerning the Collection. Form No. 6. Toronto: Baptist Forward Movement, n.d.

Robinson, Christopher. *Reports of Cases Decided in the Court of Queen's Bench.* Vol. 21. Toronto: Henry Rowsell, 1862.

Scadding, Henry. *Toronto of Old.* Edited by Frederick H. Armstrong. Toronto: Dundurn, 1987.

Shenston, T. S. *Jubilee Review of the First Baptist Church, Brantford 1833-1884.* Toronto: Bingham and Webber, 1890.

Shields, T. T. *The Inside of the Cup: An Address by T. T. Shields Delivered October 14, 1921.* Toronto: Jarvis Street Baptist Church, 1921.

———. *The Plot That Failed.* Toronto: Gospel Witness, 1937.

Sissons, C. B., ed. *My Dearest Sophie: Letters from Egerton Ryerson to His Daughter.* Toronto: Ryerson, 1955.

Smith, James F., KC, ed. *The Ontario Law Reports, 1904.* Vol. 8. Toronto: Canadian Law, 1904.

———. *The Ontario Law Reports, 1905*. Vol. 10. Toronto: Canadian Law, 1905.

Strachan, John. "Sermon on the Death of the Lord Bishop of Quebec." In *Claims of the Churchmen & Dissenters*, 5–24. Kingston: Herald Office, 1828.

Tibbutt, H. G., ed. *The Minutes of The First Independent Church [Now Bunyan Meeting] at Bedford 1656–1766*. Vol. 55. Luton: Bedfordshire Historical Record Society, 1976.

The Toronto Board of Trade. "A Souvenir." Toronto: Sabiston Lithographic, 1893.

The Torontonian Society Blue Book and Club List, 1921. Toronto: William Cobington, 1920.

A Treatise of Faith of the Freewill Baptists with an Appendix Containing a Summary of Their Usages in Church Government. Dover, NH: David Marks for the Freewill Baptist Connexion, 1834.

Underhill, Edward Bean, ed. *The Records of a Church of Christ, Meeting in Broadmead, Bristol, 1640–1687*. London: J. Haddon, 1847.

———. *Records of the Churches of Christ, Gathered at Fenstanton, Warboys, and Hexham*. London: Haddon Brothers, 1854.

Upham, Albert G. *The Baptist Position*. Montreal: D. Bentley, 1887.

Wayland, Francis. *The Elements of Moral Science*. Cambridge, MA: Harvard University Press, 1963.

Wells, J. B. *Life and Labors of Rev. R. A. Fyfe*. Toronto: W. J. Gage, 1885.

Wesley, John. *A Plain Account of Christian Perfection*. Toronto: William Briggs, n.d.

White, E. O. *A Perpetual Baptist Calendar and Remembrancer for the Twentieth Century Commencing 1901*. Toronto: Henderson, 1901.

Secondary Sources

Adams, Doug A. "Fighting Fire with Fire: T. T. Shields and His Confrontation with Premier Mitchell Hepburn and Prime Minister Mackenzie King, 1934–1948." In *Baptists and Public Life in Canada*, edited by Gordon L. Heath and Paul R. Wilson, 53–106. Eugene, OR: Pickwick, 2012.

———. "'The Great Contention': Ontario Baptists and the Fundamentalist-Modernist Struggle for McMaster University, 1919–1927." In *Canadian Baptist Fundamentalism, 1878–1978*, edited by Taylor Murray and Paul R. Wilson, 119–56. Eugene, OR: Pickwick, 2022.

———. "The War of the Worlds: The Militant Fundamentalism of Dr. Thomas Todhunter Shields and the Paradox of Modernity." PhD diss., University of Western Ontario, 2015.

Airhart, Phyllis D. "Ordering a New Nation and Reordering Protestantism 1867–1914." In *Canadian Protestant Experience, 1760–1990*, edited by George A. Rawlyk, 98–138. Burlington, ON: Welch, 1991.

———. *Serving the Present Age: Revivalism, Progressivism, and the Methodist Tradition in Canada*. Montreal and Kingston: McGill-Queen's University Press, 1992.

Allen, Glynford P., and Dale R. Calder, eds. *Trials and Triumphs: The 150-Year History of Ebenezer/Renforth Church*. Toronto: Renforth Historical Committee, 1990.

Allen, Richard. *The Social Passion: Religion and Social Reform in Canada, 1914–1928*. Toronto: University of Toronto Press, 1990.

Bibliography

Ammerman, Nancy Tatom. *Baptist Battles: Social Change and Religious Conflict in the Southern Baptist Convention*. New Brunswick: Rutgers University Press, 1990.
Armour, Leslie, and Elizabeth Trott. *The Faces of Reason: An Essay on Philosophy and Culture in English Canada, 1850–1950*. Waterloo: Wilfrid Laurier University Press, 1981.
Armstrong, Frederick H. "The Carfrae Family of Toronto and London, Ontario." *The York Pioneer* (1985) 45–54.
———. *A City in the Making: Progress, People and Perils in Victorian Toronto*. Toronto: Dundurn, 1988.
Bangs, Carl. *Arminius: A Study in the Dutch Reformation*. Grand Rapids: Zondervan, 1985.
Barnhart, Joe Edward. *The Southern Baptist Holy War*. Austin: Texas Monthly, 1986.
Belisle, Donica. *Purchasing Power: Women and the Rise of Canadian Consumer Culture*. Toronto: University of Toronto Press, 2020.
Berger, Carl. *The Sense of Power: Studies in the Ideas of Canadian Imperialism, 1867–1914*. Toronto: University of Toronto Press, 1970.
Bliss, Michael. *A Canadian Millionaire: The Life and Business Times of Sir Joseph Flavelle Bart, 1859–1939*. Toronto: University of Toronto Press, 1992.
———. *A Living Profit: Studies in the Social History of Canadian Business, 1883–1911*. Toronto: McClelland and Stewart, 1974.
———. *Northern Enterprise: Five Centuries of Canadian Business*. Toronto: McClelland and Stewart, 1990.
Bruce, Steve. *A House Divided: Protestantism, Schism and Secularization*. London: Routledge, 1990.
Brown, Raymond. *The English Baptists of the Eighteenth Century*. London: Baptist Historical Society, 1986.
Bullock, James, and Andrew L. Drummond. *The Church in Victorian Scotland, 1843–1874*. Edinburgh: Saint Andrew, 1975.
The Canadian Biographical Dictionary and Portrait Gallery of Eminent and Self-Made Men. Ontario vol. Toronto: American Biographical, 1880.
Careless, J. M. S. *Toronto to 1918: An Illustrated History*. Toronto: James Lorimer; National Museum of Man, 1984.
Carr, Angela. *Toronto Architect Edmund Burke: Redefining Canadian Architecture*. Montreal and Kingston: McGill-Queen's University Press, 1995.
Cathcart, William, ed. *The Baptist Encyclopedia*. Philadelphia: Louis H. Everts, 1881.
Chadwick, Owen. *The Secularization of the European Mind in the Nineteenth Century*. Cambridge: Cambridge University Press, 1975.
Clark, S. D. *The Canadian Manufacturers Association: A Study in Collective Bargaining and Political Pressure*. Toronto: University of Toronto Press, 1939.
———. *Church and Sect in Canada*. Toronto: University of Toronto Press, 1948.
———. *The Developing Canadian Community*. Toronto: University of Toronto Press, 1968.
Cook, Ramsay. *The Regenerators: Social Criticism in Late Victorian English Canada*. Toronto: University of Toronto Press, 1985.
Cox, Jeffery. *The English Churches in a Secular Society*. Oxford: Oxford University Press, 1982.
Creighton, Donald. *The Story of Canada*. Toronto: University of Toronto Press, 1971.

Bibliography

Crocker, Chris W. "A Worthy Cause: The Lord's Day in the Baptist Press Amongst Nineteenth Century Upper Canadian Regular Baptists." MA thesis, McMaster Divinity College, 2013.

Curnow, Tim, et al. *A Marvelous Ministry: How the All-Round Ministry of Charles Haddon Spurgeon Speaks to Us Today*. Ligonier, PA: Soli Deo Gloria, 1993.

Dent, John Charles. *The Canadian Portrait Gallery*. Vol. 3. Toronto: John B. Magurn, 1881.

Dickens, A. G. *Lollards and Protestants in the Diocese of York*. Oxford: Oxford University Press, 1959.

Dictionary of Canadian Biography. Vols. 1–12. Toronto: University of Toronto Press, 1966.

The Dictionary of National Biography. Oxford: Oxford University Press, 1917–.

Dictionary of Scottish Church History and Theology. Downers Grove: IVP, 1993.

Dozois, John D. E. "Dr. Thomas Todhunter Shields (1873–1955) in the Stream of Fundamentalism." BD thesis, McMaster University, 1963.

Drummond, Ian M. *Progress without Planning: The Economic History of Ontario from Confederation to the Second World War*. Toronto: University of Toronto Press, 1987.

Elgee, William H. *The Social Teachings of the Canadian Churches: Protestant, The Early Period, Before 1850*. Toronto: Ryerson, 1964.

Ellis, Walter W. E. "Gilboa to Ichabod: Social and Religious Factors in the Fundamentalist-Modernist Schisms Among Canadian Baptists, 1895–1934." *Foundations* 20 (1977) 109–26.

———. "Social and Religious Factors in the Fundamentalism-Modernist Schisms Among Baptists in North America, 1895–1934." PhD diss., University of Pittsburg, 1974.

Escott, Harry. *A History of Scottish Congregationalism*. Glasgow: Congregational Union of Scotland, 1959.

Ewen, Stuart. *Captains of Consciousness: Advertising and the Social Roots of the Consumer Culture*. New York: McGraw-Hill, 1977.

Ford, Murray J. S., ed. *Canadian Baptist History and Polity: Papers from the McMaster Divinity College Baptist History Conference, October 1982*. Hamilton: McMaster University Divinity College, 1982.

Forster, Ben. *A Conjunction of Interests: Business, Politics and Tariffs, 1825–1879*. Toronto: University of Toronto Press, 1986.

Fountain, Andrew M., and Glenn Tomlinson, eds. *"From Strength to Strength": A Pictorial History of Jarvis Street Baptist Church 1818–1993*. Toronto: Gospel Witness, 1993.

Fox, William Sherwood. *A Century of Service: A History of Talbot Street Baptist Church. London, Ontario, 1845–1945*. London, ON: Hunter, 1945.

Fraser, Alexander. *A History of Ontario: Its Resources and Development*. Toronto: Canadian History Company, 1907.

Gauvreau, Michael. "Baptist Religion and the Social Science of Harold Innis." *The Canadian Historical Review* 76 (1995) 161–204.

———. "Protestantism Transformed: Personal Piety and the Evangelical Social Vision, 1818–1867." In *Canadian Protestant Experience, 1760–1990*, edited by George A. Rawlyk, 48–97. Burlington, ON: Welch, 1991.

Gauvreau, Michael, and Ollivier Hubert. *The Churches and the Social Order in Nineteenth- and Twentieth-Century Canada*. Montreal and Kingston: McGill-Queen's University Press, 2006.

———. *The Evangelical Century: College and Creed in English Canada from the Great Revival to the Great Depression*. Montreal and Kingston: McGill-Queen's University Press, 1991.

George, A. Robert. *The House of Birks*. N.p., 1946.

Gibson, Theo T. *Robert Alexander Fyfe: His Contemporaries and His Influence*. Burlington, ON: Welch, 1988.

Gidney, R. D., and W. P. J. Millar. *Professional Gentlemen: The Professions in Nineteenth Century Ontario*. Toronto: University of Toronto Press, 1994.

Goadby, J. J. *Bye-Paths in Baptist History*. Watertown, WI: Baptist Heritage Publications, 1987.

Goertz, Donald. *A Century for the City: Walmer Road Baptist Church, 1889-1989*. Toronto: Walmer Road Baptist Church, 1989.

Goodwin, Daniel C. "'The Footprints of Zion's King': Baptist in Canada to 1880." In *Aspects of the Canadian Evangelical Experience*, edited by George A. Rawlyk, 191-207. Montreal and Kingston: McGillQueen's University Press, 1997.

Grant, John Webster. *A Profusion of Spires: Religion in Nineteenth Century Ontario*. Toronto: University of Toronto Press, 1988.

Green, Robert, ed. *Protestantism, Capitalism, and Social Science: The Weber Thesis Controversy*. Lexington, MA: D. C. Heath, 1973.

Greene, B. M., ed. *Who's Who and Why, 1919-1920*. Toronto: International, 1920.

———. *Who's Who in Canada, 1923-1924*. Toronto: Hodder and Stoughton, 1924.

———. *Who's Who in Canada, 1934-1935*. Toronto: International, 1935.

Hall, Alfreda. *Per Ardua: The Story of Moulton College, Toronto, 1888-1954*. Oshawa: Tern Graphics, 1987.

Haykin, Michael A. G. *Jesus, Wondrous Saviour: The Roots and Legacy of Some Ontario Baptists, 1810s-1920s*. Ancaster, Ontario: ALEV, 2023.

Haykin, Michael A. G., and Roy M. Paul, eds. *Set for the Defense of the Gospel: A Bicentennial History of Jarvis Street Baptists Church, 1818-2018*. Toronto: Jarvis Street Baptist Church, 2018.

Heath, Gordon L., et al. *Baptists in Canada: Their History and Polity*. Eugene, OR: Pickwick, 2020.

Hewitt, W. E., and James J. Teevan, eds. *Basic Sociology: A Canadian Introduction*. Scarborough, ON: Prentice-Hall, 1995.

Hill, Christopher. *A Tinker and a Poor Man: John Bunyan and his Church, 1628-1688*. New York: Knopf, 1988.

Hill, Douglas. *The Opening of the Canadian West*. New York: John Day, 1967.

Hill, Mary Bulmer. "From Sect to Denomination in the Baptist Church in Canada." PhD diss., State University of New York, Buffalo, 1971.

Hotson, Zella M. *Pioneer Baptist Work in Oxford County*. Woodstock: Commercial PrintCraft, n.d.

Ivimey, Joseph. *A History of the English Baptists*. London: I. T. Hinton, 1827.

Ivison, Stuart, and Fred Rosser. *The Baptists in Upper Canada Before 1820*. Toronto: University of Toronto Press, 1956.

Jackson-Lears, T. J. "From Salvation to Self-Realization: Advertising and the Therapeutic Roots of the Consumer Culture, 1880-1930." In *The Culture of Consumption: Critical Essays in American History, 1880-1980*, edited by Richard Wightman Fox and T. J. Jackson-Lears, 1-38. New York: Pantheon, 1983.

Jeremy, David J. *Capitalists and Christians: Business Leaders and the Churches in Britain 1900-1960*. Oxford: Clarendon, 1990.

Johnson, Curtis D. *The Power of Mammon: The Market, Secularization, and New York Baptists, 1790-1922*. Knoxville: University of Tennessee Press, 2021.

Johnson, Ronald A. "The Peculiar Ventures of Particular Baptist Pastor William Kiffin and King Charles II of England." *Baptist History and Heritage Society* 30 (2009) 61–70.

Johnston, Charles M. *The Toronto Years*. Vol. 1 of *McMaster University*. Toronto: University of Toronto Press, 1976.

Kallman, Helmut, et al., eds. *Encyclopedia of Music in Canada*. Toronto: University of Toronto Press, 1981.

Kealey, Gregory S. *Toronto Workers Respond to Industrial Capitalism*. Toronto: University of Toronto Press, 1980.

Kruppa, Patricia Stallings. *Charles Haddon Spurgeon: A Preacher's Progress*. New York: Garland, 1982.

Landon, Fred. *Western Ontario and the American Frontier*. Toronto: Ryerson, 1941.

Liverant, Bettina. *Buying Happiness: The Emergence of Consumer Consciousness in English Canada*. Vancouver: University of British Columbia Press, 2018.

Livesay, Harold C. *Andrew Carnegie and the Rise of Big Business*. Glenview, IL: Scott, Foresman, 1975.

Long, Kathryn T. "'Turning . . . Piety Into Hard Cash': The Marketing of Nineteenth Century Revivalism." In *God and Mammon: Protestants, Money, and the Market, 1760-1860*, edited by Mark A. Noll, 236–61. New York: Oxford University Press, 2000.

Lower, Arthur R. M. *Colony to Nation*. Toronto: McClelland and Stewart, 1977.

Marsden, George M. *Fundamentalism and American Culture: The Shaping of Twentieth Century Evangelicalism, 1870-1925*. Oxford: Oxford University Press, 1982.

———. *Understanding Fundamentalism and Evangelicalism*. Grand Rapids: Eerdmans, 1991.

Marshall, David B. *Secularizing the Faith: Canadian Protestant Clergy and the Crisis of Belief, 1850-1940*. Toronto: University of Toronto Press, 1992.

Marshall, Gordon. *Presbyteries and Profits: Calvinism and the Development of Capitalism in Scotland, 1560-1707*. Oxford: Clarendon, 1980.

Masters, D. C. "The Canadian Bankers of the Last Century: William McMaster." *Canadian Banker* (1942) 389–96.

———. *The Rise of Toronto, 1850-1890*. Toronto: University of Toronto Press, 1947.

McCalla, Douglas. *The Upper Canada Trade, 1834-1872: A Study of the Buchanans' Business*. Toronto: University of Toronto Press, 1979.

Middleton, J. E. *The Municipality of Toronto; A History*. Toronto: Dominion, 1923.

Mikolaski, Samuel J. "Canadian Baptist Ordination Standards and Procedures." In *Canadian Baptist History and Polity; Papers from the McMaster Divinity College Baptist History Conference, October 1982*, edited by Murray J. S. Ford, 10–22. Hamilton: McMaster University Divinity College, 1982.

Moir, John S. *Church and State in Canada West, 1841-1867*. Toronto: University of Toronto Press, 1959.

Monod, David. *Store Wars: Shopkeepers and the Culture of Mass Marketing, 1890-1939*. Toronto: University of Toronto Press, 1996.

Moore, Brian, and Bradford Gaunce. *The Printer's Devil: The Life of Samuel J. Moore*. Saint John, NB: Windsway Ventures, 2017.

Morgan, Henry James, ed. *The Canadian Men and Women of the Time: A Handbook of Canadian Biography of Living Characters*. Toronto: William Briggs, 1912.
Parent, Mark. "T. T. Shields and the First World War." *McMaster Journal of Theology* 2 (1991) 42–57.
———. "The Christology of T. T. Shields: The Irony of Fundamentalism." PhD diss., McGill University, 1991.
Pinnock, Clark H. "The Modernist Impulse at McMaster University, 1887–1927." In *Baptists in Canada: Search for Identity Amidst Diversity*, edited by Jarold K. Zeman, 193–208. Burlington, ON: Welch, 1980.
Pitman, Walter G. *The Baptists and Public Affairs in the Province of Canada*. New York: Arno, 1980.
Pomfret, Richard. *The Economic Development of Canada*. Toronto: Methuen, 1981.
Porter, John. *The Vertical Mosaic: An Analysis of Social Class and Power in Canada*. Toronto: University of Toronto Press, 1992.
Porter, Roy. *English Society in the Eighteenth Century*. Harmondsworth, UK: Penguin, 1982.
Prentice, Alison. *The School Promoters: Education and Social Class in Mid-Nineteenth Century Upper Canada*. Toronto: McClelland and Stewart, 1988.
Quebedeaux, Richard. *The Worldly Evangelicals*. San Francisco: Harper and Row, 1978.
Rack, Henry D. *Reasonable Enthusiast: John Wesley and the Rise of Methodism*. Philadelphia: Trinity International, 1989.
Rawlyk, George A. "A. L. McCrimmon, H. P. Whidden, T. T. Shields, Christian Education, and McMaster University." In *Canadian Baptists and Christian Higher Education*, edited by George A. Rawlyk, 31–62. Kingston and Montreal: McGill-Queens University Press, 1988.
———, ed. *Aspects of the Canadian Evangelical Experience*. Montreal and Kingston: McGill-Queen's University Press, 1997.
———, ed. *The Canadian Protestant Experience 1760–1990*. Burlington, ON: Welch, 1991.
———. "The Champions of the Oppressed? Canadian Baptists and Social, Political and Economic Realities," In *Church and Canadian Culture*, edited by Robert B. Vandervennen, 105–23. Lanham, MD: University Press of America, 1991.
———. *Champions of the Truth: Fundamentalism, Modernism. and the Maritime Baptists*. Montreal and Kingston: McGill-Queen's University Press, 1990.
———. *Ravished by the Spirit: Religious Revivals, Baptists, and Henry Alline*. Montreal and Kingston: McGill-Queen's University Press, 1984.
Renfree, Harry A. *Heritage and Horizon: The Baptist Story in Canada*. Mississauga, ON: Canadian Baptist Federation, 1988.
Roberts, Charles G. D., and Arthur L. Tunnel. *A Standard Dictionary of Canadian Biography*. Vol. 2. Toronto: Trans-Canada, 1938.
Robertson, Allan Barry. *John Wesley's Nova Scotia Businessmen: Halifax Methodist Merchants, 1815–1855*. New York: Peter Lang, 2000.
Rose, George M. *A Cyclopedia of Canadian Biography*. Toronto: Rose, 1886.
Russell, C. Allyn. "T. T. Shields, Canadian Fundamentalist." *Ontario History* 70 (1978) 263–80.
Santink, Joy. *Timothy Eaton and the Rise of His Department Store*. Toronto: University of Toronto Press, 1990.

Schama, Simon. *The Embarrassment of Riches: An Interpretation of Dutch Culture in the Golden Age.* London: Fontana, 1991.
Semple, Neil. "The Impact of Urbanization on the Methodist Church in Central Canada, 1854–1884." PhD diss., University of Toronto, 1979.
———. "The Quest for the Kingdom: Aspects of Protestant Revivalism in Nineteenth Century Ontario." In *Old Ontario: Essays in Honour of J. M. S. Careless,* edited by David Keane and Colin Read, 95–117. Toronto: Dundurn, 1990.
Smith, Gary Scott. *The Seeds of Secularization: Calvinism, Culture, and Pluralism in America 1870–1915.* Grand Rapids: Eerdmans, 1985.
Stanford, G. H. *To Serve the Community: The Story of Toronto's Board of Trade.* Toronto: University of Toronto Press, 1974.
Tarr, Leslie K. "Another Perspective on T. T. Shields and Fundamentalism." In *Baptists in Canada: Search for Identity Amidst Diversity,* edited by Jarold K. Zeman, 209–24. Burlington, ON: Welch, 1980.
———. *Shields of Canada.* Grand Rapids: Baker, 1967.
Tawney, R. H. *Religion and the Rise of Capitalism.* London: Peregrine, 1987.
Thompson, Austin Seton. *Jarvis Street: A Story of Triumph and Tragedy.* Toronto: Personal Library, 1980.
Thompson, F. M. L. *The Rise of Respectable Society.* London: Fontana, 1988.
Thomson, Dale C. *Alexander Mackenzie: Clear Grit.* Toronto: Macmillan, 1960.
Tomlinson, Glenn. *From Scotland to Canada: The Life of Pioneer Missionary Alexander Stewart.* Guelph, ON: Joshua, 2008.
Van Die, Marguerite. *An Evangelical Mind: Nathanael Burwash and the Methodist Tradition in Canada, 1839–1918.* Montreal and Kingston: McGill-Queen's University Press, 1989.
Veblen, Thorstein. *The Theory of the Leisure Class: An Economic Study of Institutions.* Toronto: Penguin, 1979.
Wallace, W. Stewart. *The Macmillan Dictionary of Canadian Biography.* Toronto: Macmillan, 1963.
Walvin, James. *Victorian Values.* London: Sphere, 1988.
Watts, Michael. *The Dissenters.* Oxford: Clarendon, 1978.
Weber, Max. *The Protestant Ethic and the Spirit of Capitalism.* London: Unwin Hyman, 1985.
Westfall, William. *Two Worlds: The Protestant Culture of Nineteenth Century Ontario.* Montreal and Kingston: McGill-Queen's University Press, 1989.
White, B. R. *The English Baptists of the Seventeenth Century.* London: Baptist Historical Society, 1983.
Williams, Rosalind H. *Dream Worlds: Mass Consumption in Late Nineteenth Century France.* Berkeley: University of California Press, 1982.
Wilson, Alan. *John Northway: A Blue Serge Canadian.* Toronto: Burns and MacEachern, 1965.
Wilson, Bryan R. *Religion in Secular Society: A Sociological Comment.* London: C. A. Watts, 1966.
Wilson, Paul R. "Caring for Their Community: The Philanthropic and Moral Reform Efforts of Toronto's Baptists, 1834–1918." In *Baptists and Public Life in Canada,* edited by Gordon L. Heath and Paul R. Wilson, 219–62. Eugene, OR: Pickwick, 2012.

———. "Central Canadian Baptists and the Role of Cultural Factors in the Fundamentalist-Modernists Schism of 1927." *Baptist History and Heritage* 36 (2001) 61–81.

———. "Joshua Denovan: A Prototypical Militant Fundamentalist." In *Canadian Baptist Fundamentalism, 1878–1978*, edited by Taylor Murray and Paul R. Wilson, 49–92. Eugene, OR: Pickwick, 2022.

———. "Torn Asunder: T. T. Shields, W. Gordon Brown, and the Schisms at Toronto Baptist Seminary and within the Union of Regular Baptist Churches of Ontario and Quebec, 1948–1949." *McMaster Journal of Theology and Ministry* 19 (2017–2018) 34–80.

———. "William Kiffin (1616–1701)" In *The British Particular Baptists 1638–1910*, edited by Michael A. G. Haykin, 1:65–78. Springfield: Particular Baptist, 1998.

Wosh, Peter J. *Spreading the Word: The Bible Business in Nineteenth Century America*. Ithaca: Cornell University Press, 1995.

Yuille, J. Stephen. "Robert A. Fyfe (1816–1878)." In *A Noble Company: Biographical Essays on Notable Particular Regular Baptists in America: The Canadians*, edited by Michael A. G. Haykin and Terry Wolever, 12:243–87. Springfield: Particular Baptist, 2019.

Zeman, Jerold K. "The Changing Baptist Identity in Canada Since World War II." In *Celebrating the Canadian Baptist Heritage: Three Hundred Years of God's Providence*, edited by Paul R. Dekar and Murray J. S. Ford, 1–19. Hamilton: McMaster Divinity College, 1985.

Index

Note: Page numbers in **bold** format indicate a photograph.

"An Act for Abolishing Arrest in Civil Actions in Certain Cases and for the Better Prevention and More Effectual Punishment of Fraud" (1858), 104n93, 109, 177
   See also preferential assignments (debt settlements)
advertising, 162
Airhart, Phyllis D., 8, 16, 18
Albert Street Baptist Tabernacle, 70, 110
Alexander Street Baptist Church (later Immanuel Baptist Church)
   on Americanization of church music, 188
   Bond Street Baptist Church and, 110–12
   Munro, letter of resignation, 187n52
Allen, Richard, 11, 16, 18, 137, 138
American Bible Society (ABS), 248, 252
American consumerism, 19
American Watch Case Co, 162
"The American Watch Case Company," **74**
Ammerman, Nancy Tatom, 247
amusements, acceptance of, 192–99
Anderson, M. B., 29n40
Anglican Thirty-Nine Articles, 32
Anglin, A. W., 142–44
Appleby, Scott, 224
Arminianism, 252

Arminius, Jacobus, 91n34
authority and decision-making power, 24–25
avarice, 124, 150
Ayer, Albert Azro, 10–12, **180**

bankruptcy, 44–45, 45n104, 70, 104, 108, 175–83
   See also credit, use of
Baptist Church at York, 88–89
Baptist Convention of Ontario and Quebec (1913), 4
Baptist Magazine, 176
Baptists in Canada
   beliefs of, 21–26, 85–86
   businessman's perspective, 66–81
   business-religion relationship, 8–12
   centralization and aggrandizement, 115–16
   contextual background, 53–58
   Maritimes presence, 3–4, 10
   marks of Baptist Church, 115
   materialistic culture and, 12–14
   new world experience, 58
   present study (1848–1921), 3–4
   sanctification, 31–36, 50
   separation, 36–48, 50
   split into cultural camps, 51
   statistical survey (1851–1921), 2–3
   stewardship, 48–50

275

Baptists in Canada *(continued)*
    view of "the World," 26–31
    wealth and worldliness, 61–66
    See also specific churches by name
Barclay, John, 89n25
Barnhart, Joe Edward, 247
"Becoming Prosperous" (editorial), 63
Belisle, Donica, 14
Bell, Thomas, 69
Bengough, J. W., 249
Benny, James, 149
Bereans (Barclayites), 89n25
Bible Baptist Union, 235
biblical inerrancy, 194–95, 247
birthright membership, 22
Black Baptist, 98n63
Blake, Edward, 73, 73n69, 213
Bliss, Michael, 5, 8, 11, 38, 250
Boland, W. J., 145–46
Bond Street Baptist Church, Toronto
    on bankruptcy, 181
    Caldicott, as pastor, 93
    Fyfe, as pastor, 85, 99, **119**
    homogeneity of members, 58
    organ, introduction of, 187
    on preferential payments, 69
    schism (1858), 36
Bonesteel, E., 222
Bosworth, Newton, 95
The Breach Repaired in God's Worship
    (pamphlet), 183
breaking, term usage, 54n5
Brink, Nancy, 86
Broome, Edward, 189, 204–5
Brown, George, 154–55
Brown, Graham, 144–47
Brown, J. Francis, 226, 237
Brown, Raymond, 55
Brownlee, E. A., 210, 213, 226, 230
Buchan, H. E., 186
Bunyan, John, 53–54
Burke, Edmund, 41–42, 157
Burns, Robert, 68
Burrows, J. L., 10
Burwash, Nathanael, 15, 38
business ethics decline, 136–50
business methods in the church, 115–20
businessman/businessmen, term usage,
    2n3
businessman's perspective, 66–81
business-religion relationship, 8–12,
    19–20, 52–53, 111–12, 116–17,
    121n1, 122–25

Caldicott, Thomas Ford, 49n113, 90n32,
    93–94, 99–100, 113, 117, 129
Calvary Baptist Church, New York City,
    78
Calvinism
    "Articles of Faith," 26n23
    capitalism and, 9, 252
    disagreements about, 91–93
    principles, 2, 25–26
    total depravity and, 33
Campbell, Alexander, 98
Campbell, James, 95
Campbellites (Disciples of Christ), 88,
    98
Canada Baptist Union, 23
Canadian Bank of Commerce, 153
The Canadian Baptist
    "Becoming Prosperous," 63
    business-religion relationship, 122,
    125
    centralization and aggrandizement,
    115–16
    "Concerning Criminally Careless
    Christians," 134
    Dadson, E. W., as editor, 23
    "The Danger of the Age," 150
    "Dangers of Baptists," 38–39
    "Division in Churches," 84
    "The Dominance of the Spiritual,"
    47
    eschatological views of Elliot, 250
    inspiration and authority of
    Scripture, 194–95
    "Let George Do It," 134
    materialism, 63–64
    Methodists, position of, 33–34
    moral decline, 180
    music in church, 185–86, 189n58
    new Gothic church, 102
    "Our New Minister, 60
    progress in Ontario and Quebec, 38

INDEX

"The Question of Amusements," 194–95
questions on religion, 1–2
social integration, 66
Spurgeon's message, 93
Standard Publishing Company and, 78
state of Canadian Christianity, 46
steward, defined, 48
stewardship, 117, 133
strict morality, defined, 40–41
system of government, 116
"the World," 37
world mission trips, 159
worldliness, 65
"worldly prosperity and soul prosperity, 30
Young Men's Union Concert Committee, 41–42
The Canadian Baptist Church Hymn Book, 186–87
Canadian Jeweller Convention (1919), 161–62
Canadian Manufacturers Association, 75
capitalism
    Calvinistic principles, 2, 252–53
    evangelical businessmen and, 12, 15–17, 30–31
    Protestantism and, 9
Capitalists and Christians (Jeremy), 12n35
card-playing, 192–93
Careless, J. M. S., 231
Carew, C. M., 205
Carfrae, Johanna, 94
Carfrae, Thomas, Jr., 94
Carnegie, Andrew, 249
Carter, John, 90n32, 93, 105
Cassels, Robert, 145
Castle, J. H., 100
Cathcart, Robert, 68, 96, 154
Caughley, James, 33
Central Baptist Church (later Park Road Baptist Church), 236–37
Chadwick, Owen, 6
child labor, 140–41

"The Christian Attitude Toward Amusements" (Shields), 197–98
Christian Guardian (publication), 98, 102
Christian hedonism movement, 247
Christian Helper (publication), 115
Christian Messenger (publication), 91, 106
Christian Observer (publication), 44
"Christian Work and Worship" (Denovan), 185
Church and Sect in Canada (Clark), 16
circumcision, 112n135
Clark, Benjamin, 108
Clark, J. E., 237
Clark, S. D., 16
Clergy Reserves, 24, 24n13
Cohoe, William P., 29
Coleman, Richard, 113
Colonial Advocate (publication), 90
Colony to Nation (Lower), 9
communion stance, 25
Confederation Life Association (later Insurance), 153
congregational autonomy, 85n8, 115, 115n142
Congregational Magazine, 150
"The Consecration of Business Talent" (Smith), 59–60
conservative evangelicals, 27–29, 79
Consolidated Acts of Upper Canada, 103
conspicuous consumption, 12–13, 150–71, 249
Constitutional Act (1791), 24n13
consumer culture, 13–14, 160
contextual background, 53–58
Cook, Ramsay, 16, 18–19, 249
Coombs, W. H., 95
Cooper, James, 61–62
court disputes, 86–87
Court or Assizes for the Counties of York and Peel (1858), 104
Cox, Jeffery, 6
Craigie, John Burnett, 149
Craigie v. Firstbrook (1888), 149n115
credit, use of, 72–73
    See also bankruptcy

Creighton, Donald, 24
Cross, Darius, 84
Crossing at the Flood (poem), 233–34
Crossley, Hugh T., 37
"cultural integration," term usage, 6n14
Curnow, Tim, 92
cutters' strike, 139–40

Dadson, E. W., 22–23, 40, 65–66, 105, 137, 193
Dadson, Stephen, 108
Dakin, Alderman, 155
Dakin, Sir Thomas, 155
"The Danger of Riches" (Cooper), 62
"The Danger of the Age" (article), 150
"Dangers of Baptists," 39
Darling & Company (1886), **200**
Darwinian, 26
Davies, James, 147, 187
Davies, William
  on bankruptcy, 176, 181
  as Bond Street deacon, 106–8
  business-labor relations and, 139
  on construction of new church, 100–101
  on court action with Parson, 147
  on discipline of Parson, 108, 110
  letter to James Davies, 187
  member of Alexander Street Baptist Church, 188
  on method of church business, 116
  on organ, introduction of, 187
  on preferential assignments, 107–8
  on preferential payments, 69–70
Davis, G. B., 186
Deane, Richard, 54
debt, instruction on, 44–45
Declaration of Faith for the First Baptist Church, Brantford, 22, 25
Denovan, Joshua, 28, 32, 179–80, 185–86, 187n52, 252
diaconate, term usage, 105
Disciples of Christ (Campbellites), 88, 98
"Division in Churches" (article), 84
Doble, A. R., 151
Doctrinal Truth, compendium, 32

Doctrines and Discipline of the Wesleyan Methodist Church in Canada, 37
The Dollar in Business and Religion (pamphlet), 134
"The Dominance of the Spiritual," 47
Dovercourt Road Baptist Church, Toronto, 77, **201**
Drayton, Sir Henry, 213

Eaton, Timothy, 14, 160, 161
Edward Lesslie and Sons (store), 90
Edwards, Matilda C., 174
The Elements of Moral Science (Wayland), 40
Elliot, Violet, 216–17
Elliot, William, 153, 178, 250
Ellis, Walter W. E., 9, 10, 102, 137
employer-employee relationships, 137–39
"entire separation" doctrine of, 7, 7n17
The Evangelical Pioneer (weekly publication), 59
evangelicals/evangelicalism, 10–12, 78–79, 174, 174n4
Evening Telegram (newspaper), 208
Everitt, Alan, 55
Ewen, Stuart, 160
Examiner (publication), 84, 115, 116
exclusion, term usage, 85n8

Factories' Act (1889), 140–41
faith alone, 32n49
First Baptist Church in Newark, New Jersey, 248
First Baptist Church of Dallas, 247
Firstbrook, John, 139, 142–47, 159
Firstbrook, Joseph, 139, 147
Firstbrook, William, 139, 147, 149
Firstbrook Brothers Box Factory, 139–42, **165**
Firth, Edith, 90
Fish, Henry Clay, 248
Flavelle, Joseph, 11, 38
Flint, Richard, 57
Forster, Ben, 127
Forward Movement, 49, 133–34n53, 133–35
Foster, W. A., 2n4

Fox, William Sherwood, 86
Fraser, William, 225
fraud cases, 104n93, 109, 109n116, 148
Free Communion Baptist church, 84
Freeland, Edwardo, 187n51
Fry, Victor, 241–42
fundamentalist-modernist schisms, 10, 137
fundamentalists belief, 27, 78, 80, 224
Fyfe, Robert Alexander
    on Alexander Street Baptist Church, 110–12
    on Baptist theology, 40
    biographical information, 95–97
    on business disputes, 103, 108–9
    on Clergy Reserves, 24
    homogeneity, among church members, 58
    as pastor. *see* Bond Street Baptist Church, Toronto; March Street Baptist Church
    photo of, **119**
    on stewardship, 49, 126

Garrow, J. A., 141
Gauvreau, Michael, 8, 16, 17–18, 250, 252–53
Gay, A. F., 227
George, Robert, 161n164
Gibson, Theo, 97
Gidney, R. D., 60, 60n32
"Gilboa to Ichabod" (Ellis), 10
Gilmour, J. L., 136–37
Gilmour, John, 95
Girvin, James, 108
Globe (newspaper), 97, 102, 159, 161, 234
Goertz, Donald, 246–47
Goodwin, Daniel, 111
"gospel of wealth," 249
Gospel Witness, 234–35
Grant, Gideon, 205, 208, 237
Grant, John Webster, 7, 19, 28n32, 86, 87, 174, 226–29
Grantham, Thomas, 184
Green, E. C., 222–23
Greenway, George, 210, 228–29

Hagarty, J. H., 109
Haldimand Association, 30
Halifax Methodist Merchants, 11–12, 252
Hall, S. T., 210
Harris, Elmore, 213
Harris, James, 84
Henderson, Quartus B., 134–36, 198–99, 212, 230, 237, 239–40
Herbert, Ollivier, 16
Hewitt, William, 181
Hewitt, William, Sr., 74, 126–28, 149
Hill, Christopher, 53, 54
Hill, Mary Bulmer, 137
Hogg, James, 252
holiness revival, 33–35
Holman, Charles J., 195, 212–14, 225–29, 231
Holman, Mrs. C. J., 222–23
Holmes, G. W., 230
Hudson, R. S., 227, 231
Hughes, T. B., 210
Hurd, Albert, 138
Hutchinson, W. J., 236
Hyper-Calvinist, 91–92

Immanuel Baptist Church, Toronto (previously Alexander Street), 28, 32, 247
Ingello, Nathanael, 192
Innis, Harold, 252–53
Insolvency Act (1869), 177–78
Insolvency Act (1875), 177–78
insolvency legislation, 75–76, 177, 179n22
    See also bankruptcy
"The Inspiration and Authority of Scripture" (Shields), 195
intellectual camps, 27–31, 78–80

Jackson-Lears, T. J., 13
Jarvis, Aemillus, 145–46
Jarvis Street Baptist Church, Toronto
    on amusements, 78
    brief history, 87–102
    business-religion relationship, 19–20, 76–77
    choir, **200**

Jarvis Street Baptist Church *(continued)*
  church finances, control of, 203–6, 217–20, 234–35
  former deacons response, 238–43
  music in the church, 183–91, 204
  photo of, **120**
  Prudential and Finance Committee, 229, 234–35
  relocation (1875), 5
  schism (1921), 10
  selected businessmen for study, 3
  on sociocultural integration, 224
  struggle for control, 203–4
  study methodology, 4–8
  Weekly Offering Treasurers, 222–23
Jemmett, F. G., 145–46
Jeremy, David J., 12n35
Jerusalem Council, 112, 112n135
John Northway & Son Limited, 138
John Northway (Wilson), 11
"John Wesley's Nova Scotia Businessmen" (Robertson), 11–12
Johnston, Charles M., 153, 213
Jolly Beggars (Burn), 68

Keach, Benjamin, 183–84
Kiffin, William, 54–55, 57
King's College, Toronto, 24n13
Kitchen, L. C., 245
Knights of Labour, 140

labor relations, with business, 136–39
Lacrosse And How To Play It (McNaught), 159
Lailey, Thomas, 70, 105, 108, 148n111, 153
Lailey, Watson & Bond, 138–39
Lang, Harold W., 237
Langley, William, Jr., 70, 108–9, 110
Lawrason, J. B., 221–23, 230
Lawson, F. G., 207–8, 221, 222
Lawson, Robert, 114, 117–18
Laymen's Missionary Movement, 50, 76–77, 133–36, 134n54
"Leading Men in the Churches," 59
leisure activities, 159
Lesslie, James, 90, 91, 250

"Let the Redeemed of the Lord Say So" (Thomas), 123–24
liberal evangelicals, 27, 29–31, 79–80
liberal's belief, 27
The Life and Death of Mr. Badman (Bunyan), 53–54
Limscott, T. S., 153
Liverant, Bettina, 13–14
"A Living Profit" (Bliss), 11
Long, Kathryn T., 12n35, 248, 252
Lorne Park Estate, 182
Lower, Arthur, 9
Lugsdin, Joseph, 181–83
Lugsdin, W. J., 212, 237
Lyon, James F., 105, 108

Mackenzie, Alexander, 73, 73n69
Mackenzie, William Lyon, 89
March Street Baptist Church
  Caldicott, Ford, as pastor of, 93
  Campbell, James, as pastor of, 95
  Fyfe, Robert Alexander, 24, 96, **119**
  political and religious arenas, 97
  Pyper, James, as pastor, 97
  tensions at, 95
Marlow, Isaac, 183–84
Marsden, George, 174n3
Marshall, David, 6, 8, 16–18, 28, 250
Marshall, Gordon, 9, 56
Martin, G. D., 205
Martin, K. E., 237
Marty, Martin, 18, 224
Marx, Karl, 30
Massey, Eliza, 156
Massey, Hart, 156
Massey-Harris Manufacturing Company, 77
Masters, D. C., 9, 102
materialism/materialistic culture, 12–14, 63–64, 124, 150, 156
Matthews, Albert
  biographical information, 27n21, 206
  cultural perspectives and church, 202
  on finance committee, 218, 230
  on Music Committee, 189, 205
  on pastor's salary, 206–7

photo of, **244**
on Shield's attack, 220
wealthy Baptists and, 239–40
Matthews, George, 207
Matthews, Herbert, 67
Maxwell, John Eglinton, 68–69, 94–95
McArthur, J. B., 205, 207, 208, 226, 230
McCalla, Douglas, 8, 70
McCord, A. T., 97, 105
McDiarmid, H., 246
McDonald, J. F., 142
McGregor, Daniel A., 22, 25–26, 115
McIntosh, John, 181
McIntosh v. Firstbrook Box Company (1904), 140–41
Mckinnon, W. L., 222
McLaughlin, A. J., 24
McMaster, Arthur Robinson, 129, 156, **167**, 178–79
McMaster, James Short, 45n104, 151, 179, 182–83
McMaster, Susan Moulton, 101, 188
McMaster, Wardley, 182–83
McMaster, William
    Bloor Street Mansion, **166**
    on building of new church, 96, 101, 102
    on business disputes, 107–10
    Canadian Bank of Commerce, 153
    on church music, 188
    Confederation Life Association (later Insurance), 153
    conspicuous consumption, 154–56
    country estate, **166**
    Darling & Company building, **200**
    emulated by businessmen, 153
    on labor relations, 136–37
    photo of, **165**
    on preferential assignments, 69–70, 181
    published first catalogue, 161n164
    religion//business relationship, 29
    schism (1927), 241
    on stewardship, 129
    value of his business, 151–52
McMaster and Company, 45n104, 151, 182
McNaught, William Kirkpatrick
    "fraudulent misrepresentation, charges of, 147–49
    Lacrosse And How To Play It, 159
    lawsuit brought by Stavert, 142–46
    photo of, **164**
    sports enthusiast, 159
    on stewardship, 129
    The Trader and Canadian Jeweller, 74–76, 128, 160, 162
    wealth of, 129n32
    will of, 129n30, 129n33
Menzies, John, 88–89, 89n25
Merrill, B. W., 206, 240
Merrill, F. W., 222
Merrill, Frank, 234
Methodist tradition, 11, 32–33, 36, 84, 102
Michell, George, 192
microcosmic approach, 3
Millar, W.P.J., 60, 60n32
"money men," 5
Monod, David, 14
Montgomery, Robert J., 146, 146n101
Montreal Register (newspaper), 23, 24, 97
Moore, Samuel John, 77, 159, 195–96, **201**
moral code, 192
Morgan, J. P., 143
Moyle, William, 184
Mullins, E. Y., 115n142
Munro, A. H., 187n52
music in the church, 183–91, 246–47

Negus, Joseph, 57
Nesbitt, W. H., 41–42
New Brunswick, Baptist presence in, 3–4
new world experience, 58
non-sacramental belief, 25
Northway, John
    on censure of Shields, 241
    clothing manufacturer, 5
    employer-employee relationships, 138
    lack of membership, 5n10
    on liberal theological scholarship, 250

Northway, John *(continued)*
  on liberal theology, 231
  on materialism, 157
  on modernism, 239
  philanthropic of, 249
  photo of, **164**
  on social and economic justice, 80
Nova Scotia
  Baptist presence in, 3–4
  Methodist tradition, 11–12

Ochse, Orpha, 157–58
Ontario, Baptist growth in, 3–4
Ontario Factories' Act (1884), 140
ordination, process of, 90, 90n29
Osborne, William, 69
Osler, Featherstone, 141–42
Ottawa convention (1919), 194–95
"Our New Minister" (article), 60
Our Service of Song (hymn), 186

Paget, Ralph, 228
Palmer, Phoebe, 33
Panic of 1873 (economic), 75–76
Parent, Mark, 174n3
Park Road Baptist Church (formerly Central Baptist Church), 237–38, 238n136, **244**
Parson, Francis T., 69–70, 107–10, 181
pastor, term usage, 93n45
pastoral ministry, 60–61, 60n33
Paterson, David, 104, 105–6
The Path of Wealth or Light From My Forge (Limscott), 153
Peck, James H., 149
Peck, Thomas, 149
Pellatt, Henry, 232
pension plans, 138
Perry, H. Francis, 189
pew rents, 91, 117, 117n153
  See also stewardship
Pinnock, Clark, 26–27
Pitman, Walter G., 24
The Plot That Failed, 189–90, 204, 217
Porter, John, 9
Porter, Roy, 56
poverty, instruction on, 44

preferential assignments (debt settlements), 103–5, 104n93, 107–9
Presbyterian Church (USA), 84
Primitive Christianity (tract), 184
"A Psalm for the Trade" (poem), 74–75
Pyper, James, 97–98, 106–7

"The Question of Amusements" article, 194
Quigley, R. J., 74

R. G. Dun & Company, 127
Rawlyk, George, 10, 19, 26–27, 30, 79–80, 136, 138
Record, Albert W., 210, 229
regenerate church requirement, 22
The Regenerators (Cook), 18
Reid, W. Stanford, 58
religion and business. *See* business-religion relationship
Religious Herald, 38
Renfree, Harry, 25
repentance, 86
respectability, term usage, 7
revivalism, 32–33
Riddell, Jane, 148–49
Roberts, E. H., 42–43
Robertson, Allen, 11–12, 252
Robinson, Arthur, 151
Ross, John, 105
Ryerson, Egerton, 155
Ryrie, Christine, 237
Ryrie, Harry, 129–30, 157, 158, 237
Ryrie, James
  censure of Shields, 241
  Central Baptist Church deacon, 237
  Chestnut Park Mansion, **169–71**
  cultural perspectives and church, 202
  on inspiration and authority of Scripture, 195
  on Laymen's Missionary Movement, 50, 76–77, 134–36, 134n54
  Music Committee, 189–91, 205
  on opposing Shields, 230
  organ pipes drawing, **168–71**
  Park Road Baptist Church, 237
  photo of, **167**

Ryrie Bros. building, 171
schism (1921), **167**
   on Shields resignation debate, 209, 210, 215, 220
   on stewardship, 50, 134–36
   summer home, **168**
   theological dispute, 225
   wealth of, 239–40
Ryrie, James, Sr., 106
Ryrie brothers, 157–59, 160–61, 161n164, **171**

sacramental beliefs, 25
Sale, Ephriam, 212, 237
salvation, 91n34
sanctification, 31–36, 50
Santink, Joy, 14
Scadding, Henry, 90n32
Schama, Simon, 9
schisms
   Bond Street Baptist Church, Toronto, 36
   fundamentalist-modernist, 10, 137
   fundamentalists and secularists, 224–43
   Jarvis Street Baptist Church, 10, **167**
   North America (1974), 10
   Regular Baptist church, Oxford Township (1822), 84–85
   Shields/McMaster conflict (1927), 241–42
Schomberg, H. A., 114
Scott, J. G., 131, 211, 219
Scriptural Confession of Faith, 32
secularization
   argument, 3–4
   beginning of (1848–1880), 82–83
   business-dominated culture and, 251
   corruption within, 103–14
   division, discipline, disputes, 83–87
   effects of worldliness. *see* worldliness
   historical literature on, 16–19
   Jarvis Street 1921 schism, 245
   Jarvis Street Baptist Church, 87–102, 175
   term usage, 6
   through sociocultural integration. *see* sociocultural integration

Semple, Neil, 15, 32, 37–38
separation
   Baptist theology, 36–48, 50
   of church and state, 23–24
   "entire separation" doctrine of, 7, 7n17
   term usage, 7, 89n24
separation, maintaining
   amusements, acceptance of, 192–99
   bankruptcy, 175–83
   music in the church, 183–91
   poem, 172–74
Serving the Present Age (Airhart), 18
Shackell, Robert, 103
Shenston, Thomas S., 28, 44–45, 71–73, 76, 77, 184
Shenstone, J. N., 77
Sherbourne Street Methodist Church, 248–49
Shields, T. T.
   accomplishments of, 235
   on amusements, 192–99
   attacks on worldliness, 4, 175
   "The Christian Attitude Toward Amusements," 197–98
   on church music, 189–91
   Crossing at the Flood (poem), 233–34
   cultural perspectives and church, 202
   "The Inspiration and Authority of Scripture," 195
   on Jarvis Street financial situation, 132–33
   on moral laxity and modernism, 43
   Ottawa convention (1919), 195–96
   The Plot That Failed, 189–90, 204, 217–20
   on resignation debate, 209–13, 240
   on salary debate, 204, 204n2, 208–9
   scarlet fever, 215
   on secularization, 175
   on separation from the world, 76
   summer evangelistic crusade, 221–22
   on Thomson's pamphlet, 241
   Weekly Offering Treasurers, 222–23
   on worldly amusements, 77–78

Shorter Catechism of the Church of
    Scotland, 32
Sinclair, John, 67
slavery, 98n63
Smith, Goldwin, 232
Smith, Ira, 28, 29, 47, 237
Smith, W. W., 59–61
social and economic justice, 80
social ethic, 28–29
social integration, 66
The Social Passion (Allen), 18
sociocultural change on religion, 19
sociocultural integration
    business ethics, decline of, 136–50
    businessman's impact, 121–22, 162, 249
    business-religion relationship, 122–25, 175
    conspicuous consumption, 150–71
    at Jarvis Street Church, 224
    monetary stewardship, 125–35
    term usage, 6–7, 6n14
Southern Baptist Convention (SBC), 247
Spurgeon, Charles Haddon, 92–93
Standard Publishing Company, 78
Star Weekly, 158
statistical survey, Baptist in Canada
    businessmen (1848–1921), 2–3
    business-religion relationship, 8–12
    methodology, 4–8
Stavert, W. E., 142
stewardship, 48–50, 77, 91, 117–18, 125–35, 162, 249
Stewart, Alexander, 67–68, 88–90, 95
Stewart, D. M., 145
Stewart, William Boyd, 2n4, 100
Stillwell, H. B., 237, 237n131
Stockwell, R. S., 207
Stovel, Joseph, 104n94
Strachan, John, 23
Straton, John Roach, 78, 221
systematic beneficence, 99, 129

Talbot Street Baptist Church, London, 36, 85
Tapscott, Samuel, 95
Taylor, William, 67

Temperance Colonization Society, 148
Thomas, B. D., 45, 62, 123–25, 152
Thomas, Micah, 176
Thompson, Austin Seton, 5
Thomson, Daniel Edmund, 131, 195, 215–16, 219, 240–41
Toronto
    Bond Street. *see* Bond Street Baptist Church, Toronto
    Dovercourt Road Baptist Church, 77, **201**
    Immanuel Baptist Church, 28, 32, 247
    Jarvis Street. *see* Jarvis Street Baptist Church, Toronto
    King's College, 24n13
    University of Toronto, 24
    Walmer Road Baptist Church, 77, 246–47
Toronto Baptist Ministerial Association, 77
Toronto Baptist Seminary, 235
Toronto Board of Trade, 178
Toronto Christian Observer (journal), 64, 98
Toronto Daily Star (newspaper), 209, 229, 231
Tovell, John, 45n104, 104–6, 104n94, 181
The Trader and Canadian Jeweller (trade paper), 74–75, 128, 160
The True Story of the Jarvis Street Baptist Church Trouble (pamphlet), 238–43
The Truth Soberly Defended (pamphlet), 184
Tucker Stephen, 96
"Turning . . . Piety into Hard Cash" (Long), 12n35

United States, emerging cultural crisis, 174, 174n3
University of Toronto, 24

Van Die, Marguerite, 15, 33, 38
Veblen, Thorstein, 12–13, 153–54, 155
The Vertical Mosaic (Porter), 9
Vogt, Augustus Stephen, 188–89

INDEX

Walmer Road Baptist Church, Toronto, 77, 246–47
Warren, R. D., 78–79
Wash, Peter J., 252
Watkins, Sarah, 54
Watts, Charles, 103
Watts, Michael, 55, 56, 57, 175
Watts *v.* Howell (1860), 103
Wayland, Francis, 40, 40n80
wealth and worldliness, 61–66
Weber, Max, 56–57
Weber-Tawney model, 9
Weber-Tawney thesis, 252
welfare plans, 138
Wellington, H. R., 212, 226–27, 237
Wells, James Edward, 97, 194
Wenham, Joseph, 91
Wesley, John, 33
Westfall, William, 14–15, 16, 28
Wetherbe, C. H., 38–39
White, E. O., 87

Whittemore, L. H., 205, 208, 226, 228–29
"Why Merchants Fail" (McNaught), 128
Wilkes, Robert, 74
Wilkins, Thomas, 237
Wilks (Church Clerk), 240
William Massey Birks, 157
Williams, Rosalind, 13
Wilson, Alan, 11, 138
Wilson, Bryan, 6
"World," separation from, 36–48, 172–75
worldliness, 4, 64–65, 77, 124, 180, 249
Wosh, Peter J., 248

Yorkminster Baptist Church, 238
Young, D. M., 222
Yule, Pamela Vining, 48n109

Zeman, Jarold, 22

www.ingramcontent.com/pod-product-compliance
Lightning Source LLC
Chambersburg PA
CBHW061433300426
44114CB00014B/1660